KU-278-689

A Social History of
Modern Spain

A Social History of
Modern Spain

Adrian Shubert

London and New York

First published 1990 by Unwin Hyman Ltd

Reprinted 1992, 1996 by
Routledge
11 New Fetter Lane, London EC4P 4EE
29 West 35th Street, New York, NY 10001

Printed in Great Britain by The University Press, Cambridge

British Library Cataloguing in Publication Data

Shubert, Adrian
  A history of modern Spain.
  1. Spain. Social life, history
  946

Library of Congress Cataloguing in Publication Data
A catalogue record for this book is available from the Library of Congress

ISBN 0–415–09083–0

Contents

Acknowledgements

I began working on this book as a Mellon Fellow at Stanford University and I completed it as a SSHRC Canada Research Fellow. In between I had a research grant from the Faculty of Arts at York University. I thank them all.

I also want to thank the many colleagues and friends who shared their thoughts on modern Spanish history or who took the time to read and comment on parts of this book. Dr Mary Vincent of the University of Sheffield and Professor Richard J. Evans, the editor of the *Social History of Europe* series, provided useful commentaries on the manuscript. I am especially grateful to my colleagues in the Department of History at York University who have, over the past four years, heard more about Spain than they had ever expected, or probably wanted to. I want to single out Russ Chace, for offering valuable advice and administering a well-placed kick in the shins when both were badly needed.

For Agueda

Introduction

Spain and Europe: the Peculiarities of the Historians

Although this book is a social history, politics is at its heart. Political events set the chronology, from 1808 and the Napoleonic invasion which began the final disintegration of the Old Regime, to 1982 and the overwhelming electoral victory of the Socialist Party which confirmed the triumph of democracy following the death of Francisco Franco in 1975. Politics also determines the internal organization, with the Spanish Civil War as the dividing line between a long section on Spain from 1800 to 1936 and a shorter one on the period since 1939.

The book offers the social background to the two central events of modern Spanish history: the Civil War of 1936–39 and the democratic transition of 1975–82. Or to put it another way, it helps explain why democracy did not survive in the 1930s as it has done since 1975. I do not want to propose a social determinism whereby political forms are bound by levels of socioeconomic development. Politics has its own dynamic but questions of power, especially power in the state, cannot be autonomous of social relations and the conflicts they engender. Neither the Spanish Civil War nor the contemporary constitutional regime was inevitable but the differing social contexts of the democratic experiments of the 1930s and the 1970s and 1980s contributed mightily to the short life of the first and the longevity of the second.

This study has a second, but not secondary, major theme: in the nineteenth and twentieth centuries Spain has been in the European mainstream. For most historians of modern Europe Spain barely exists in its own right; it comes into view only on those occasions when it served as the stage for broader European events, as a major theatre for the Napoleonic Wars and as the battleground for hostile ideologies in the 1930s. And too many people, Spaniards included, are willing to accept the description of Spain given by W.H. Auden in his poem *Spain 1937* as 'that arid square, that fragment nipped off from hot/ Africa, soldered so crudely to inventive Europe'.

There are a number of reasons for this but the most important has to do with the nature of historical concern itself. When history was limited to high politics, diplomacy and war, second and third rate powers could be of no more than passing interest. There was a clear hierarchy. The more powerful the nation the more attention it deserved. Washed–up great powers got no credit for their former greatness. As the scope of historical interest broadened and as social history became ever more important, the hierarchy of concern for various national histories lost whatever rationale it had had and a country such as Spain could be returned to the first division. Economically, socially and even politically Spain has been fully a part of the European mainstream over the last two centuries. The Spanish experience has been as different from those of Britain, France, Germany and Italy as they have been from each other but the family resemblance is undeniable. Put another way, when everyone is 'peculiar' peculiarity itself becomes a common ground. We already have the 'peculiarities of the English' and the 'peculiarities of German history'.[1] Perhaps this book should be called the 'peculiarities of the Spaniards'?

At best, Spain is seen as the black sheep of the European family because, it is said, it did not have that obligatory rite of passage, a bourgeois revolution. Little wonder, then, that things went wrong in the nineteenth and twentieth centuries: repeated coups, civil wars, military dictatorship. . . Because the dismantling of the Old Regime and the disentailments left the nobility relatively unscathed, left the structure of landholding unchanged and produced a new landed elite which appeared to have neglected agricultural improvements there has been much debate as to whether those changes constituted a bourgeois revolution.

In his highly influential text, *Spain: A Brief History*, Pierre Vilar argued that 'nineteenth century efforts on behalf of agrarian free enterprise brought no great success', that the disentailments failed to produce 'the highly exploited estates of the English or the Prussian type. . . [and that] the agrarian structure did not change'. Overall, 'agrarian Spain placed material, legal and psychological obstacles in the way of capitalism'.[2]

This position has been stated even more strongly by the doyen of Spanish labor and social historians, Manuel Tuñón de Lara. There was a bourgeois revolution of a sort, but a failed one. The elimination of the 'shackles of the feudal or seigneurial regime' are necessary but not sufficient components of a real bourgeois revolution. This took place in Spain but it did not lead to 'an authentic capitalist society'. There was constitutional government and economic development but there was not a real bourgeoisie. 'The idea that the Duke of Medinaceli', he writes, 'went to bed one night the heart and soul of the feudal nobility and woke up the next day a bourgeois because his seigneuries had been turned into disentailed property is a matter for serious thought. A strange bourgeoisie, this! Or should we believe that from one day to the next Medinaceli, Alba, etc. changed their ideology, their values, their outlook?' Even worse, the business elite was incorporated into the nobility and, he says, took on its mentality and ideology, which were anything but democratic and based on 'the wholehearted defence of the existing structural order, a very "old regime" scale of values, a concept of legitimacy in which the historical and traditional aspects of the dynasty and the Crown have priority over the legitimacy of circumstances or a patchwork in which the representatives of the people are at least theoretically allowed to *collaborate* in the exercise of power'.[3]

By favoring the landowning oligarchy the Spanish model of bourgeois revolution cut itself off at the knees. A new 'power bloc' emerged in which 'the noble ideology of the Old Regime dominated, in which the bourgeoisie which did exist was co-opted by the aristocracy and in which there was no agricultural modernization and little industrial investment'. The *sexenio*, the six year period of extreme political instability, opened by the Revolution of 1868 was a key moment: a new power bloc led by the Catalan industrial bourgeoisie might have appeared but did not. In Catalonia, where the Capitalist Mode of Production – in capitals – was already in place, class conflict so frightened the bourgeoisie that 'it became clear that the bourgeoisie would never lead the democratic revolution and would prefer to ally with the agrarian and financial bourgeoisies'. And fifty years later, when the First World War had put the political system on the ropes, yet another class, or part of one, did not know how to act properly. 'Claiming that the historical protagonism, the direction of events "was the task of the bourgeoisie" and that "our time will come later", the leadership of the most important working class party [the Socialist Party] did not respond to the demands of the economic situation.'[4] The end result was the Civil War and the establishment of Franco's (fascist) regime.

Richard Herr has also argued that the landed elite which emerged was not a bourgeoisie. The method of selling land at auction necessarily meant that the purchasers were people with cash to spend – or government bonds to redeem – and that in a predominantly agrarian economy that meant those people who already owned or leased land. The result was a 'lay landed elite. . .[that] was an amalgam of old and new elements, and not properly speaking bourgeois, either culturally or economically'; an elite which 'included many more large landowners, aristocrats, clergymen, farmers and even tenant farmers than merchants, civil servants and professionals'.[5]

David Ringrose examined the bourgeoisie of the capital and found it wanting in revolutionary impulses. As late as 1850 there was not, he says, 'a cohesive bourgeois class' in the capital. The impetus for change came from lawyers and bureaucrats who had moved to the city and whose social background lay in the more dynamic elements of the southern landed elite. If the bourgeois revolution 'ended as it did' – but not, presumably, as it should – it was precisely because 'the landowning class sponsored it'.[6]

Such interpretations are based on Spain's failure to hold to an already scripted scenario which, it is believed, was successfully acted out elsewhere. Because there was no fully developed industrial society, because large estates remained in place, because the agrarian elite was dominated by the nobility and, allegedly, lacked a certain outlook and because the bourgeoisie made peace with it, Spain did not have a bourgeois revolution. Or, at best, it had a truncated, distorted one. This view amounts to an argument for the peculiarities of the Spaniards: that Spain was exceptional in western Europe and that the blame lies with a bourgeoisie which was incapable of performing the role for which it was destined.

An almost identical analysis, that the political failure of the bourgeoisie in 1848 prevented Germany from enjoying democracy and ultimately led to Nazism, has long been made about Germany. Geoff Eley and David Blackbourn have taken this approach to task in a book whose main lines are highly relevant to the Spanish case.[7] Bourgeois revolution, Eley writes, appears to mean 'a set of changes forced through by the bourgeoisie itself, acting in its own interests, in direct confrontation with a feudal or "pre-industrial" ruling class'. The bourgeoisie is assumed to be necessarily liberal in politics and if a liberal order is not created then the bourgeoisie has somehow been co-opted or 're- feudalized'. It has failed to follow in the heroic footsteps of its British and French peers. For Eley, measuring bourgeois revolutions by their political outcome and assuming a 'causal chain "bourgeoisie = liberalism = democracy" rests on a fundamental misconception of the nature of bourgeois revolutions'. These are defined not by their political outcomes but by 'the conditions of bourgeois predominance in society' which themselves rest on property relations and forms of control over the means of production. The bourgeois revolution becomes, then, a 'longer process of structural change' and can be found within 'a considerable diversity of political regimes'. There is no single script but various national versions.[8]

Moreover, according to Blackbourn, the bourgeoisie as a ruling class is hard to find anywhere. 'If one looks at nineteenth century Europe it is difficult to identify an unambiguous instance where the bourgeoisie ruled as a class, without the help of an old elite or oligarchy, without strongmen or allies from some other class or classes.' It was not unusual for European bourgeoisies to take on some of the symbols or trappings of their partners from an older ruling class, nor when they did was this a sign of their feudalization. 'It signalled, rather, the formation of a newly extended dominant class, with a symbiotic relationship between the old and new parts of this class.'[9] This was quite normal in Europe.

Even in France, the site of the classic bourgeois revolution, historians have found the bourgeoisie hard to identify. As William Reddy says in his analysis of the recent historiography of the French Revolution:

> it has become clear that such a class not only had no representatives in the revolutionary assemblies but in effect did not exist. There was no revolutionary bourgeoisie. Members of the upper strata of eighteenth century French society were more or less homogeneous in their values and based their status on 'proprietary' rather than profit-maximizing investments . . . Proprietary wealth was the support both of those who made the Revolution and those who resisted it.

It is no longer viable to identify political groups with social ones they are supposed to represent.[10]

A number of Spanish historians who have addressed this question, such as Bartolomé Clavero, Angel García Sanz and Josep Fontana, have taken an approach congruent with that suggested by Blackbourn and Eley and by Reddy. While accepting for the most part Herr's argument that the disentailments did not lead to substantial changes in the structure of land ownership or the identity of the landowners, they have argued that this is less important than the changes in the legal nature of property and property ownership. It is a mistake to make bourgeois revolution synonymous with expropriation. As García Sanz argues, 'revolution implies changes more sweeping than limited changes in the ownership of property'; 'transfers of property are not essential to it, although they may be imposed by the political situation if the revolution is to triumph'.[11] Respect for the property of the existing elite, or part of it, may also be encouraged by the existence of significant popular opposition to the political and legal changes taking place. In Spain, as we shall see, this was certainly the case. From this perspective then, the bourgeois revolution is what Clavero has called 'a radical change in the way society is constituted' and one which 'does not imply any change in the groups which dominate'. It is fundamentally a legal, and not an economic, revolution.[12]

This is, I think, correct. There certainly cannot be any doubt that in the thirty years following the Napoleonic invasion the legal superstructure of the Old Regime was dismantled and a new type of society was created. Privilege as an integral part of the organization of society was destroyed and although the nobility emerged in a strong position and the structure of landholding was little modified this did not mean that important changes had not taken place. The Church was stripped of its lands, the municipalities would lose theirs before the century was out and in many places the peasantry found its position on the land less favorable than before. Vast amounts of land changed hands and a new class of landowners was created. Many, although not all, already had contact with the land, often as tenants or agents of the institutions they were now supplanting. In addition, after 1834 Spain was definitely committed to some form of political liberalism, even if it was far from democracy. By my calculation, between 1812 and 1914 Spain had more years of constitutional, representative government than any other continental country, including France.[13] The new class of landowners would form the bulwark of the liberal polity which emerged so haltingly during the nineteenth century and which found its most lasting expression in the Restoration monarchy (1875–1923). They would also form the bulwark of the opposition to the agrarian reform efforts of the Second Republic and be the most fervent supporters of the military reaction to it.

For the time being the most convenient solution is to replace the term bourgeois revolution with one less freighted with implications, such as liberal revolution. Such a term is applicable to Spain in the first forty years of the nineteenth century and allows us to resolve the apparent contradiction that revolutionary change was overseen by the 'wrong' social group. It also allows us to locate Spain in the mainstream of nineteenth-century European history and not excommunicate it for failing to live up to standards which other nations supposedly met.

Little real harm is done if historians err on a question such as this, but if political leaders base their strategy on such faulty historical analyses the result can be disastrous. Some of the problems which beset Spain's Socialist Party (Partido Socialista Obrero Espãnol [PSOE]) during the Second Republic (1931–9) stemmed from the mistaken belief that the Republic heralded the long delayed bourgeois revolution. Taking republican politicians such as Manuel Azaña for the political wing of the bourgeoisie and not for what they really were, more or less free-floating intellectuals without any particular social base, Spanish Socialists grossly over-estimated their influence and the prospects for realizing a programme of wide-ranging social reform by parliamentary means. They also failed to recognize that the symbiosis of bourgeois and former seigneurial lords which had been produced in the nineteenth century was the bourgeoisie and would see the Socialists' reforms as revolution and do whatever they had to in order to forestall it. When reality did not live up to the formula the divisions within the party reappeared and became much more bitter than they had been:

> To a large extent the development of the Socialist movement during the 1930s was influenced by the importance of an essentially incorrect historical analysis of what was happening in Spain. The calculations of all three sectors of the PSOE were based on the certainty that a bourgeois directed progressive revolution was about to take place. When it became apparent, by 1933, that this was not happening, each sector reacted according to the norms of behaviour it had established during the pre-Republican period. [14]

When, in the spring of 1936, the political situation demanded a strong and unified response from what was the most important political party in the country, and when such a response *might* have forestalled the military revolt which began the Spanish Civil War, Socialist leaders were unable to provide one.

The Book

From its geography to its economic and social formations and even to its politics Spain is, more than most, a country of regions. In the post-Franco period this has even been recognized and embodied in the structure of the state. I have tried to be faithful to this regional diversity, and to do so looking beyond Catalonia and the Basque Provinces, whose regionalist movements have, since the late nineteenth century, made them a political problem, to regions which have received much less consideration, such as Galicia and Old Castile.

Finally a *caveat*. The modern history of Spain, and especially its modern social history, is much less developed than that of France or Germany. We know much more about populations than families, about relations between social classes than between men and women, about labor than leisure. This poses problems for a book such as this which, necessarily, relies heavily on the work of others. The effect is akin to putting up road signs for a highway which has yet to be built. The ride – and the read – will be bumpy. Still, such a situation has its brighter side. There is nothing like being jarred by a pothole to call attention to a job that needs doing. It is too much to hope that the potholes in Spanish social history will soon all be filled in but perhaps there will soon be a few more signs at the roadside saying 'Historians at work'.

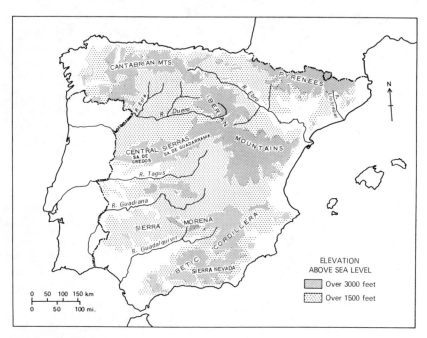

Figure 1.1 *Spain: Physical Features*

1
A Century of Dynamism

Spain stands at the western extreme of the European continent. It is a large country, some 500,000 square kilometers, with a large variety of physical environments. The most striking feature, as Figure 1.1 shows, is the prevalence of mountains. Spain is, after Switzerland, the most mountainous country in Europe. The Pyrenees, at a constant height of at least 5,000 feet which exceeds 11,000 in places, block the entrance to the Iberian pensinsula. The Cantabrian range, which averages between 5,000 and 6,000 feet, cuts the northern tier, Galicia, Asturias, Santander and the Basque Country, from the rest of the country. After a narrow gap, the Iberian Mountains begin, running roughly parallel to the Pyrenees. The vast central meseta is broken into two by the central sierras, the Guadalupe and the Guadarrama. In the south the Betic Cordillera, an irregular series of mountain ridges broken by north–south rifts, contains the country's tallest peak, at 11,420 feet.

Beyond the mountains, the country is dominated by the vast central tableland. The northern meseta has an area of some 15,000 square miles and an average altitude of 2,700 feet. The southern meseta is three times as large but, at less than 2,000 feet, has a lower average elevation. The coastal lowlands are very small. Catalonia, for example, has a very narrow coastal strip which is brought to an abrupt end by mountains only twelve miles inland. The only large lowland area is the Andalucian plain.

The mountains make movement from one region to another difficult and even obstruct movement within some others, such as the Ebro basin and the Cantabrian strip. The principal rivers, the Tagus (600 miles), the Ebro (540 miles), the Duero (525 miles), the Guadiana (465 miles) and the Guadalquivir (395 miles), are too fast flowing or suffer too much silting at their mouths to compensate much as aids to communication and transportation.

Spain also has a tremendously wide range of climates, from temperate in the north-west to semi-arid in the south. Some areas in the north-west get between 60 and 70 inches of rain per year but some two thirds of the country is deficient in rainfall, that is, does not get enough rain to sustain normal plant growth for four months out of twelve.

There are three main climatic zones. The maritime zone, from the north coast to the Cantabrian mountains which includes Galicia, Asturias, Santander, and the Basque Provinces, has mild winters, abundant precipitation spread throughout the year and warm, but not hot, summers. (Few Britons take vacations here. The weather would remind them too much of home.) The inland areas, the mesetas, the Ebro basin and adjoining mountains, have a continental climate. Temperatures fluctuate greatly, both from winter to summer and from day to night. The summers are very hot and the winters very cold. In January the average temperature in many parts of the northern meseta is only a couple of degrees above freezing. Rainfall is low and irregular throughout the year. The south frequently experiences alternating drought and flood. The final climate is the Mediterranean zone, which takes in the Andalucian plain and the southern and eastern coastal strips. There is little variation in temperature from winter to summer and in both seasons temperatures are higher than in the interior. The hottest area is between Seville and Córdoba, where the mean temperature in July and August is between 85 and 88 degrees Fahrenheit and readings of more than 100 are common. Rainfall is unreliable. This is what package tour operators mean by 'Spain'.

A country's basic geographic and climatic facts of life do change, albeit very slowly. Landscapes, however, are shorter lived. By the economic activities they choose to undertake men and women can change the face of a country very quickly: woodlands disappear, the frontiers of cultivation expand – or recede – rivers are polluted, wildlife is killed off. While very often ecologically harmful, such changes are also indicators of economic dynamism and demographic expansion. In the nineteenth and early twentieth centuries the face of Spain changed markedly, as industrial development scarred the beauty of many rural landscapes and an expanding agriculture reclaimed land long given over as privileged pasture to the sheep. When he travelled through Spain in 1796 Róbert Southey noted that 'rich tracks of land are uncultivated . . . we have often travelled five or six hours without seeing any trace of man except the agreeable memento of a few monumental crosses'.[1] Had he been able to return five or six decades later he would have had to look much harder to find such a scene.

An Evolving Economy

The Spanish economy in the nineteenth century and the first decades of the twentieth presents something of a paradox. Industrialization began early, in the latter decades of the eighteenth century and even though Spain experienced continual economic growth over the nineteenth century it fell further and further behind other European countries such as Britain and France and, after 1870, even Italy. As Leandro Prados has put it 'growth and backwardness are two sides of the same coin . . . long term sustained growth was accompanied by backwardness in relative terms'.[1] The Spanish pattern of economic development was not identical to that of north-western Europe, but it was even less like that of the contemporary Third World. Spain was not, as

Nicholás Sánchez Albornoz has claimed, 'an underdeveloped economy *avant la lettre*.[2] It was fully a part of European economic development although *sui generis*, with a 'sustained increase in per capita income after 1830'. From 1780 to 1930 'Spain experienced a moderate but constant transformation which followed its particular route to modernization'.[3] Spain was not an economic failure, as Jordi Nadal has called it,[4] nor was it trapped in stagnation. Its economy was growing and changing, but more slowly than those of other countries. It was a laggard.

Agriculture

In 1914 agriculture was still the core of the economy: it produced almost 40 per cent of the national income and employed over 60 per cent of the labor force, compared to 18.5 per cent in manufacturing and mining. Even in 1930 it remained the dominant sector, employing almost half of all working Spaniards, while wines, fresh fruit and other agricultural products accounted for 35 per cent of total exports, down only 10 per cent from 1850.

There are few reliable statistics for Spanish agriculture in the first half of the nineteenth century but contemporaries believed, and historians generally agree, that production increased substantially, keeping pace, at least, with the increase in population. Certainly throughout the first half of the century, Spain was able to feed itself, and in a number of years export surplus grain. This increase culminated in the 1870s and was followed by decades of crisis at the end of the century and then by a strong recovery in the twentieth century.

There were a number of reasons for this expansion of production. Josep Fontana has argued that the loss of the American colonies and the wealth derived from them forced Spain to cut back on its imports from Europe, basic foodstuffs among them.[5] The decree of August 5, 1820, issued by a liberal government, banning imports of wheat and other key cereals so long as the price in Spain remained below stated levels was a major stimulus to domestic production. This policy of rigid protectionism was retained until 1869 and over the course of the half century in which it was in effect grain was imported during only four subsistence crises.

This expansion in production was due almost entirely to the extension of cultivation. The only estimate of the actual amount of land brought into cultivation is 4 million hectares between 1818 and 1860, although the reliability of the sources on which it is based has been questioned.[6] There was not much in the way of technical improvements before 1850 and yields of wheat and other grains actually declined between 1800 and 1860. There is evidence that by the 1860s grain cultivation was becoming more sophisticated, at least in Andalucia, as some leading landowners invested in modern agricultural machinery. François Heron has gone so far as to claim that there was 'a vast movement of mechanization in the Andalucian countryside in the second half of the nineteenth century'.[7]

Wheat producers benefited from a growing domestic market as well as from exports to Cuba and, until 1881, regular exports to other countries. After that date, however, Spain imported much more wheat than it exported and failed to generate a trade surplus in grains before the First World War. Improvements in transportation and the opening of the American west brought grain from the Ukraine and the United States into Spanish ports at prices below those for Castilian grains. Castilian landowners responded, as did their German and Italian counterparts, by lobbying for increased protection, which they got in 1892. They also took land out of production, almost 3 million hectares between 1888 and 1893.

Castile was the region most affected by the expansion of cereal cultivation. For most of the region the nineteenth century brought what Sánchez Albornoz has called an 'economic involution'.[8] The economy became less complex and diverse than it had been under the Old Regime and more dependent on a single agricultural product, grain. Wool production did not expand and small-scale textile manufactures were killed off by Catalan products. The agricultural sector was oriented to the market, as it had long been, but the changes stemming from the liberal revolution did not lead to the investments required to improve efficiency and increase output.

The economy of the interior had long been dominated by the needs of the capital. This did not change in the nineteenth century, when Madrid continued to shape the economy of its vast hinterland, which covered

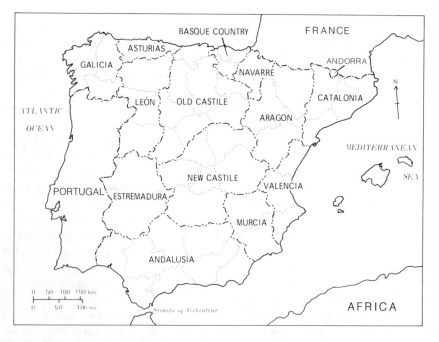

Figure 1.2 *Spain: Historical Regions*

virtually the entire central meseta. David Ringrose has summarized this relationship:

> Because of its dependence on primitive overland transport, the size of Madrid was a factor of extreme importance in the economy of Castile, if only because the city constituted a market for agricultural products with few alternative sources of supply. The structure of that market was such as to provide its hinterland with only a limited range of incentives, and the city could not provide the variety and depth of demand needed to draw the Castilian economy out of subsistence agriculture embedded in a self-contained regional economy. Madrid could mobilize surpluses that traditional systems of rural control accumulated, but had little effect on productivity.[9]

The changes in land ownership prompted by the liberal revolution allowed for 'agricultural commodities [to be] more uniformly accumulated as rents rather than tithes, or through direct management . . . before they moved into supply systems focused on Madrid' but did not produce any more basic changes.[10]

Orientation to the market and new opportunities did produce important changes in some branches of agriculture. Perhaps the most sweeping took place in the sherry producing region of Jerez de la Frontera. Export markets for sherry began to expand in the 1840s, prompting the merchants who controlled the trade 'to consolidate sherry production from vine to wine'.[11] They sought to purchase existing vineyards, which were in the hands of peasant owners, or expand cultivation into new, less suitable lands. The area in vineyards increased by 50 per cent between 1817 and 1851 and by another 50 per cent in the next twenty years. This option was highly capital intensive: in addition to the purchase price of the land, owners had to buy the vines, put up buildings and fences and buy wine presses – and then wait four years for the first crop of grapes. However, the cheaper sherry which was produced from these new vineyards found expanding markets in Britain in the 1860s and, as a result of the phylloxera epidemic, in France after 1875. The peasants from whose grapes the traditional, expensive sherries were produced were faced with rapidly declining prices, from about 110 pesetas per butt in 1865 to 40 in 1880, and many were forced to sell their land. By the end of the century the owners of the large sherry firms, many of them such as Duff, Garvey and Byass originally British, controlled most of the vineyards and had assumed positions of local social and political influence.

Jerez was not the only place in Spain for which wine production was important. Vineyards were crucial to the Spanish economy in the nineteenth century. The area under cultivation grew four times over the course of the century, much of this in Catalonia, and production increased six times between 1860 and 1890 alone. The importance of wines lay in the fact that they were a bulwark of Spanish exports: they accounted for one-third the value of all exports in 1857 and their weight increased until 1890. And even though phylloxera hit the country hard in the 1880s, Spain remained

Figure 1.3   *Spain: Provinces*

the leading wine exporting country in Europe from 1880 to 1914. On the eve of the First World War wines were the country's second most important export, accounting for only slightly less value than did minerals.

Two other crops, oranges and olives, both of them exported in large quantities, also advanced during the nineteenth century. Oranges were grown in Valencia using both irrigation and fertilizers. The area dedicated to orange trees increased from 2,675 hectares in 1872 to 37,500 in 1915 and the value of exports rose from 2.7 million pesetas in 1855–9 to 57.7 million in 1905-9. Olive cultivation underwent a tremendous expansion, especially in the first three decades of the twentieth century, when the area under cultivation increased by 50 per cent. Traditionally grown in Seville and Córdoba and the lower Ebro, olive trees expanded into eastern Andalucia. The early twentieth century also saw an improvement of the quality of the oil produced, at least in western Andalucia, due both to better care of the trees and to more advanced processing techniques. In 1914 olive oil was Spain's tenth most valuable export.

Livestock production also recovered from its nineteenth-century decline, especially in regions like Asturias where a burgeoning urban population provoked what is known as a 'dairy revolution'. Overall, the live weight of livestock increased by 63 per cent between 1900 and 1930 and the value of livestock production more than doubled, from 589 million pesetas in 1900 to 1.3 billion pesetas in 1930.

In sum, Spanish agriculture was more dynamic and varied than has often been pictured. Production of basic foodstuffs was more than able to keep pace with population growth, especially after 1895. Grain production increased slightly more than population between 1795 and 1895 but between 1895 and 1925 output per head increased 0.72 per cent per year. Spanish agriculture became increasingly export oriented, but it was not dependent on a single crop and was able to respond reasonably quickly to changes in demand and market conditions. As Garrabou and Sanz have observed, 'the fact that Spanish farmers could feed a growing population better and better and meet the needs of the industrial nations with the rapidity, variety and quantity that they did allows us to maintain that we are far from a static and backward agricultural sector'.[12]

Even so, in comparative terms the performance of Spanish agriculture was lacklustre. During the nineteenth century production increased more in Spain than in Britain or France but productivity grew more slowly. By the First World War the gross value per hectare was less than half the French and less than one-third the British. This was largely due to the composition of the crops: cereals were much more important to Spanish production, 41 per cent compared to 20 per cent in France and 11 per cent in Britain, and livestock much less, 18 per cent in Spain compared to 30 per cent in France and 68 per cent in Britain.[13]

The Textile Industry

As elsewhere in Europe, the lead sector of industrialization in Spain was the manufacture of cotton textiles, which was located in Catalonia. Production experienced rapid expansion in the 1780s and 1790s as rising wages stimulated the adoption of new techniques. The spinning jenny was introduced in 1784 and the mule jenny in 1803, but further mechanization was interrupted by the Napoleonic Wars and the subsequent political instability. Although 14 water-powered mills had been set up by 1808 there were only 36 in 1836. After 1814 the main problem facing the industry was the contraction of the market caused by the loss of the bulk of the American empire but the prohibition on imports of cotton goods declared in 1832 provided a safe, if limited, market and set the stage for significant growth and rapid mechanization. The industry became more concentrated, both geographically and in the number and size of firms. A small number of cities, Reus, Mataró, Manresa and especially Barcelona, became the undisputed centers of the industry. At the same time, the number of textile manufacturing firms was reduced and the average size grew larger: between 1841 and 1861 the average number of workers per firm increased from 18 to 71.

The 1860s were a period of stagnation, mostly due to the cotton famine caused by the US Civil War. In 1874, following the re-establishment of political stability and legislation which made the colonies captive markets for Spanish products, the industry experienced a new boom. As a result exports of Catalan textiles jumped from 458 tons per year between 1876 and 1880 to 7,859 tons per year between 1891 and 1895. The loss of Cuba and Puerto Rico in the Spanish–American War threw the industry back into dependence on the home market, for unlike their Italian counterparts, Catalan textile manufacturers had never been able to develop export markets outside the empire. As a result, after 1904 the industry 'sank into stagnation and atrophy' although it did enjoy a temporary boom during the First World War.[14]

The small size of the domestic market has frequently been blamed for the weakness of the textile industry but Leandro Prados has recently argued that lack of exports was the reason, since by measuring just internal markets 'the gap which separates Spain from the more advanced countries of Europe is narrowed'. Much of the blame lies with industrialists who sought a safe haven behind high tariff walls rather than fighting for a share of the international market.[15] This is borne out by the export figures. Manufactured goods accounted for 6 per cent of exports in 1830 and only 12 per cent in 1910, much lower shares than for any other industrial country in Europe.

While the Catalan textile industry made, in a limited way, a successful transition into the industrial world the traditionally strong silk industry, centered in Valencia, did not. Following a boom in the second half of the eighteenth century, the silk industry was almost killed off by warfare and instability between 1793 and 1830. Control of the industry passed from independent artisans to merchants, as it did in Lyons, but each individual controlled fewer looms than had been the case in the middle of the previous century. In addition, the quality of spinning and weaving, which remained in the hands of peasant families, was poor. The industry did begin something of a comeback between 1830 and 1850. Steam-powered machinery was introduced and some woven silk was exported. However, crops of raw silk were much smaller than in France and after an epidemic hit the silkworms in 1854 the industry had to deal with increasing prices and an unreliable supply of raw material. The importation of Japanese silk into Europe applied the *coup de grâce*.

Transportation

The transportation network contributed significantly to Spain's economic problems, especially in the central regions of the country. In the first half of the nineteenth century there were 'no fundamental changes in the basic mechanism of transportation', which depended on pack animals and carts. Many people engaged in transportation were peasants who did it on a part-time basis, while most of the professional carters were tied up by the government to supply the capital. The government was too poor to build new roads or canals and the privileges which it had given carters in the eighteenth century – access to common grazing lands and guaranteed winter pasture – were done away with during the liberal revolution. All this had had direct and severe economic consequences, contributing to

Figure 1.4   *The Railway Network*

'an absolute ceiling for the level of development' while at the same time effectively isolating the interior from Catalonia, restricting the accessibility of much of the domestic market and forcing it to rely on the colonies.[16]

The railroads broke this transportation bottleneck, but their contribution to Spain's economic development was much more limited than it might have been. The first line was built in 1848, between Barcelona and Mataró, but before 1855 the pace of construction was slow and only 456 kilometers had been put down. The system really began to take shape following the Railway Law of June 1855, and by 1868 almost 5,000 kilometers of track had been built. The law provided numerous benefits to railway companies, such as government subsidies and the use of public land. Most important for the national economy was the provision which allowed companies to import all construction materials and fuels duty free for ten years. The result was that the railway system was built and controlled by foreign companies. The two biggest companies, the Madrid, Zaragoza and Alicante and the Caminos de Hierro del Norte were both owned by French capitalists, the former by the Rothschilds, the latter by the Pereires. By the end of the nineteenth century they controlled some 80 per cent of all the railways in the country.

The manner in which the railway system was built undermined its economic value in a number of ways. First of all, the ability of the companies to import components duty free meant that railway construction did not provide any of the backward linkages which could have stimulated Spanish industry, especially iron. Jordi Nadal has calculated that between 1861 and 1865 imports of iron for railway construction amounted to more than twice the output of the national iron industry, while according to one British historian 'in the 1850s Spain was the leading country in Europe in the absorption of machinery and railway iron'.[17]

Second, lines were built according to the interests of the foreign capitalists who controlled the companies, not according to the needs of the Spanish economy. Madrid was the hub of the network, with lines radiating outwards. This pattern 'did not correspond to the traditional channels of commerce', nor did it facilitate the economic integration of the various regions of the country so they could feed off each other's growth.[18] Nowhere was this truer than in Asturias. Although it was only 200 kilometres from the principal market, the foundries of Vizcaya, the province's coal was consistently undersold by imports from Wales, in large part because of the unreliability and high costs of rail transport. The radial pattern did facilitate the export of raw materials, especially minerals, and the import of foreign manufactures, especially to Madrid. Even so, the domestic demand for rail transport when the lines were built was very limited. As George Stephenson remarked after visiting the country in 1845 in order to investigate the potential for building a railway there, 'I have been a whole month in the country, but I have not seen during the whole of that time enough people of the right sort to fill a single train'.[19]

Finally, although the railway companies were controlled by foreigners, much of the capital used to build the rail system was Spanish. By 1890 the state had provided some 766 million pesetas in subsidies, which amounted to about 30 per cent of the total construction costs. Another source of financing was the issue of vast amounts of bonds, most of which were purchased on the Paris Bourse by Spaniards. The railways absorbed large amounts of capital which could have been invested in other sectors of the economy. According to Gabriel Tortella, Spaniards invested almost seven times as much in railways as they did in industry. In Britain, with a much denser railway system, industry drew more capital than did railways.[20]

On top of everything else, the railways continually lost money and represented an ongoing drain on an already overtaxed Treasury, so that they were unable to expand or improve their service to meet new needs. The inadequacies of the system were all too apparent during the First World War, when the wartime boom had stretched the rail system to breaking point, and in some places beyond. Between 1920 and 1922 the government provided 420 million pesetas in subsidies and the Primo de Rivera regime also invested heavily in the rail network.

In spite of all this the railways did contribute to Spanish economic development in one very significant way, by lowering the price of Castilian grain in markets on the periphery of the country, especially Barcelona. Ramón Garrabou and Jesús Sanz Fernández have calculated that 'transport costs were reduced at least 25 per cent right away and by the beginning of the twentieth century [they] had been reduced by 65 per cent'.[21] The difference in grain prices between cities in the interior and on the coast was cut substantially and areas such as Extremadura, which had not exported grain to other regions, were incorporated into an increasingly more articulated national market.

Mining

Railways were not the only part of the Spanish economy in which there was a large foreign presence. In the nineteenth century Spain was one of the world's most important mining centers and, except for the coal mines of Asturias, most mining activities were controlled by foreign interests. Laws passed in 1859 and 1869 opened mineral deposits to all investors and as a result foreign capital, mostly British but also Belgian and French, flooded into the country. Deposits of copper in Huelva, lead in Jaén and Almería, mercury in Almadén, as well as manganese, cobalt, silver and tin were exploited by non-Spanish firms. Spanish governments, facing suffocatingly large deficits which in the late 1860s ate up over 40 per cent of revenues, tried to deal with the situation by giving the Rothschilds monopoly rights to sell the products of the famous Almadén mercury mines in 1870 and selling off such important resources as the copper mines of Río Tinto to the British Río Tinto company in 1873.

To what extent did foreign control benefit the Spanish economy? Most Spanish economic historians argue that the contribution was not significant. Manuel González Portilla, for example, states that outside of iron mining little benefit accrued to the national economy, while in his study of the Río Tinto Company, which was the most profitable company in Spain until the 1920s, Charles Harvey calculates that the company's direct contribution to the Spanish economy was less than one million pounds per year. He also concludes that it had little positive effect on the Spanish economy and through its social and political power it actively sought to ensure that this was the case.[22] Leandro Prados dissentss. He argues that foreign capital 'financed the economic infrastructure, brought mineral resources into exploitation and increased exports' as well as mobilizing unemployed workers.[23]

In one sector, the Basque iron mining industry, the benefits were clear. The invention of the Bessemer process in 1856 brought Basque high grade iron ore into demand in other European countries, especially Britain, and in the 1870s foreigners began to take an increasing interest in the Basque iron mines. Iron mining took off following the end of the Carlist War in 1876; by 1901 some 98.6 million tons had been extracted, of which 90 per cent was exported, with 60 per cent of the exports going to Britain. (In the 1880s and 1890s between 60 and 75 per cent of all British iron imports came from the Basque Provinces.) Some of the most important mining companies were subsidiaries of foreign iron manufacturers, such as the Orconera Iron Ore Company, which was founded by two British iron makers and the Krupps, but foreign interests were not nearly so dominant as they were in the mining zones of the south.

Most of the land on which the Basque iron mines were situated had come into the hands of the local bourgeoisie through the disentailments which took place after 1841. By the 1870s it was controlled by 'a small clan of Basque families, such as the Ibarra and the Chávarri' who were able to engage in their development. In 1890 these two families owned almost half of the producing mines and the Ibarras were also heavily involved in the two largest foreign companies, the Orconera and the Franco–Belge.[24] Basque interests also controlled some 60 per cent of the substantial profits of the region's iron mines, which jumped from 82 million pesetas in 1891/5 to 273 million in 1896/1900. They also did well out of shipping, since most of the iron exported was carried in Spanish ships.

The profits from mining were the basis for the iron and steel industry which was created in Vizcaya in the 1880s. Iron production had initially been centered in Málaga, where charcoal-fired blast furnaces had been set up. Aided by the upheaval in the north produced by the Carlist War the south retained its dominance until 1860. Then it was overtaken by Asturias, where the presence of coal mines provided a significant saving in fuel costs. Asturian predominance was brief and by 1879 it had been surpassed by Vizcaya.

The development of such an industry was further favored by the importation of inexpensive Welsh coal on the ships which had carried local iron ore to Britain. The existence of this Bilbao–Cardiff axis meant that Asturian coal was consistently undersold in the principal Spanish market. In 1882 the Altos Hornos de Bilbao was founded by a group of local businessmen led by the Ibarras while at almost the same time the Chávarris were creating La Vizcaya. Using the latest technology from Britain and Belgium these large new companies quickly dominated the national iron industry: between 1890 and 1910 these two companies alone produced over 60 per cent of all the cast iron in Spain. In the process they forced many small Basque iron producers to shut down, so that the number of active foundries fell from 97 in 1868 to 15 in 1896. In 1902 La Vizcaya and Altos Hornos de Bilbao merged with the third large firm, La Iberia, to create Altos Hornos de Vizcaya, the largest and most profitable Spanish-owned industrial enterprise. The Altos Hornos complex covered 70 hectares, had a mile of dock space, 7 blast furnaces, 7 Siemens–Martin furnaces and 17 rolling mills. and employed 6,000 workers.

The only significant branch of Spanish mining in which foreign capital was not heavily involved was coal mining, which was centered in Asturias. But then Asturian coal was not too attractive to foreign investors: it was not competitive on foreign markets and there were few profits to be made. Large-scale mining in the region began in the 1860s, under the stimulus generated by the railways and the local iron industry, which displaced the charcoal-fired Andalucian foundries. It was only in the 1880s that large producers came to dominate the industry, but there was always a large number of small producers in operation. Atomization was one of the enduring characteristics of the industry. Of the four most important companies, Fábrica de Mieres, Duro–Felguera, Hulleras del Turón and Hullera Española, only the first was foreign owned, but the owners soon became nationalized Spaniards. Duro–Felguera was an integrated mining–metallurgical firm started by Pedro Duro, Hulleras del Turón was started by Victor Chávarri to supply coal to Altos Hornos de Vizcaya, and Hullera Española was part of the industrial and shipping empire of the Marquis of Comillas.

The industry achieved long term growth; production increased almost ten times between 1887 and 1929, but its economic health was never secure. The Asturian mines suffered from the high cost and unreliability of rail transport to their principal markets in Vizcaya. Mine owners constantly complained about inadequate tariffs, which allowed British coal to undersell their product in Bilbao, even though the tariff on coal increased by 650 per cent between 1906 and 1922. Only during the First World War, when British coal imports were temporarily cut off, did the industry thrive. Production rose a modest 20 per cent during the war but prices rose by over 500 per cent, providing the mining companies with an unprecedented bonanza. However, they did not grasp the opportunity to modernize the industry and the end of the war brought an immediate crisis which lasted virtually unabated until the Spanish Civil War.

From Boom to Crisis, 1914–36

Neutrality during the First World War left Spain in a position to realize substantial economic benefits. The disappearance of imports such as coal and chemicals provided the opportunity for import substitution while demand for textiles and metals from the combatants gave Spanish industrial products unprecedented access to export markets. Foreign sales of cotton goods increased two and a half times during the war and the value of woollen exports increased twenty times. Imports fell in both volume and value while the value, if not the volume, of exports increased. Spanish shipping carried a smaller volume of cargo during the war than before but even so registered vast profits. Banks also did extremely well, with profits quadrupling between 1915 and 1920.

As with coal mining in Asturias, wartime profitability was totally artificial and the end of the war brought with it a widespread crisis. Inefficient producers which had sprung up to take advantage of the situation went to the wall in large numbers. In Catalonia 140 factories closed by April 1921. Nor had the benefits of the war years touched all sectors of the population. Even where nominal wages did increase they could not keep pace with the spiralling inflation. The growing impoverishment of the working classes, side by side with the ostentatious affluence of the wealthy, triggered both a newly intense labor militancy during the war and ongoing class conflict during the conversion back to a peacetime economy.

The liberal governments of the mid-nineteenth century have been strongly criticized by Spanish economic historians for so heavily favoring inappropriate investments, such as the railways, and for selling the country out to foreign capital, in effect turning Spain into a European version of the economically colonized nations of Latin America. Before the Restoration development policies were limited to the prohibition of cotton imports but after 1875 governments became more aggressive in promoting industrialization: tariffs were raised substantially beginning in 1891 and programs of naval construction introduced in 1887 and 1908 included provisions to favor domestic shipbuilders. Even so, this was much less than countries such as Germany and Italy were doing.

The new economic nationalism reached its peak before the Civil War with the Primo de Rivera dictatorship (1923–30). The regime has been characterized by Shlomo Ben–Ami as 'a fairly measured, even incipient, essay in development [which] . . . rested on, and was instrumental in, formulating a fairly coherent economic ideology for the Spanish Right that was based on a "productive" and nationalist approach', and as such was a forerunner of the autarky of the Franco regime. An enemy of economic liberalism, Primo's governments were unprecedentedly 'interventionist and . . . zealously nationalist'.[25] The regime favored Spanish-owned firms for defense contracts, subsidized big business and favoured monopolies. While some multinationals, especially International Telephone and Telegraph (ITT), did find lucrative opportunities others were attacked if their presence was felt to be inimical to national interests. This was what happened to the American, British and French petroleum companies which were nationalized in 1927 so that a national petroleum monopoly, Compañía Arrendataria de Monopolio de Petróleos Sociedad Anónima (CAMPSA), could be set up.[26] The government also created a plethora of regulatory agencies which affected, in theory at least, all aspects of the economy. The regime was probably most active in public works, a policy which was popular with both business and the Socialist unions. Over 9,000 kilometers of roads were built. The rail network was expanded slightly, by 800 kilometers, but the government provided subsidies and issued bonds to finance a modernization of the system. There were impressive plans to build irrigation systems but only one, along the Ebro, was actually built, with the state contributing 52 million pesetas. The government also took some interest in promoting tourism and built the first of what would become under Franco a considerable chain of government-owned hotels in historic buildings, the *paradores*.

The regime raised Spain's already high tariff walls even higher, making it the most protectionist country in Europe after the Soviet Union. It attempted to promote exports by providing export subsidies for Catalan textiles and in 1928 it created the Banco Exterior de España to stimulate exports, especially to South America, through credits and commercial facilities. These policies did have some success in reducing the chronic trade deficit as exports rose by a third between 1923 and 1929. However, primary products, and especially foodstuffs, continued to dominate exports – more so in 1929 than in 1914 –

and there was little reduction in imports, which fell by only 4 per cent over the same period.

Primo's economic policies were favored by the general economic buoyancy of the 1920s, but they ran into trouble with the onset of the Depression. The regime quickly came to be recalled as a kind of golden age of prosperity but there has been some disagreement among historians over its real economic achievements. Jordi Nadal and Josep Fontana have described these as a 'debased capitalism, on the defensive' which produced 'no signs of genuine economic growth'.[27] On the other hand, Ben–Ami has pointed to a significant 'modernization' of the social structure which took place with an intensity which 'almost matched, and in some aspects surpassed, that which took place during the Francoist boom'.[28] The workforce in agriculture fell from 57 to 45.5 per cent while that in industry and services rose from 21.9 and 20.8 to 26.5 and 27.9 per cent, respectively, while a massive flow of migrants swelled the major cities. Ben-Ami is on shakier ground when he claims that the regime's economic policies were 'not extravagant' and did not exceed the country's financial capacities.[29] Primo de Rivera left a legacy of even further inflated government indebtedness and a falling currency, problems which would obsess the political leaders of the Second Republic and obstruct their ability to deal with the pressing social demands of the working class.

Of course the Republic was not helped by the fact that it coincided with the Depression. In this case, however, the relatively self-enclosed nature of the Spanish economy was something of a perverse advantage. Less integrated into the world economy than other European states, Spain was less seriously hurt by the Depression. The relatively small external sector – minerals, citrus fruits, olive oil and wine – declined, due to both decreasing international demand and the government's strong peseta policy. On the other hand, cereals and consumer goods did well, an indication that the Republic's reformist labor and social policies were having some effect in increasing domestic demand. However, Spanish elites were not prepared to accept the costs, economic, social and political, that this development entailed. Increasing domestic demand, and much else, was cut short by the Civil War and would not be resumed until the 'economic miracle' of the 1960s.

Men, Women and Children

By the time of the Second Republic there were more Spaniards than there had ever been before. More of them were getting married and having children, although each couple had fewer than had been the case in the past, and men, women and children alike were living longer. They were also more mobile, moving around the country and abroad in greater numbers. Spaniards shared these changes with most other Europeans. The course of Spanish population growth followed the European model of the demographic transition, but with a different chronology. Spain made the transition later, tentatively, almost hesitantly. The destination was the same, but the route and itinerary were different.

The usual European pattern was for population growth to begin in the eighteenth century, as catastrophic mortality relented, and continue into the nineteenth as ordinary mortality rates also began to decline. The fall in birth rates in the second half of the century then led to a much slower rate of growth which continued into the twentieth century. Spain followed this broad pattern of reduced mortality, both catastrophic and structural, a lower birth rate and a deceleration of population growth, although with a delay of almost a century. Spanish population increased at a rate slightly above the European average between 1800 and 1950, but followed a different rhythm. From 1800 to 1850 it equalled the European rate, from 1850 to 1900 it was below and from 1900 to 1950 it was above it.

Basically this was due to persistently high death rates, so that even while Spain retained a high birth rate throughout the nineteenth century its rate of population growth was slower after 1850. Epidemics stayed with Spain longer than with the more economically advanced states of western Europe and were eliminated only in the twentieth century, while ordinary rates did not begin to drop substantially until around 1914. Infant mortality remained high until well into the second half of the century. The birth rate began to fall in the twentieth century but the major drop did not come until the 1960s and 1970s. The period of most rapid growth before the Civil War came in the period 1910–30 and after the interruption caused by the war itself rapid growth continued into the 1960s. It was only then, very recently indeed, that Spain's demographic patterns came to closely approximate those of its more advanced neighbors.

What were the basic figures? At the end of the eighteenth century the total population was about 10.5 million; by 1857, the year of the first modern census, it was 15.5 million. The numbers for succeeding years are in Table 1.1.

Table 1.1 *Population growth, 1787–1930*

Year	Population	Year	Population
1787	10,393,000	1887	17,550,000
1797	10,536,000	1897	18,109,000
1821	11,662,000	1900	18,594,000
1857	15,455,000	1910	19,927,000
1860	15,645,000	1920	21,303,000
1877	16,622,000	1930	23,564,000

Source: V. Pérez Moreda, 'La modernización demográfica, 1800–1930'.

Death

The persistence into the twentieth century of a stubbornly high death rate was the most important cause of this 'important chronological lag'.[1] Only then did the death rate enter into a consistent decline.

Spain, and especially central Spain, remained subject to demographic crises longer than other important European countries. The frequency of such crises remained steady from the seventeenth century through the nineteenth, with an average of one every twelve years. Vicente Pérez Moreda has calculated that the crises of the nineteenth century were, on average, more intense than those of the two preceding centuries. The most intensive one of all was the last, in 1855.[2] On this score Spain clearly was different: 'The European trend was towards an almost continual decline in mortality crises. The interior of Spain . . . regressed sharply in the first quarter of the nineteenth century and only showed marked improvement in the following period.'[3]

Epidemics were frequent. Yellow fever hit Barcelona in 1821 and Andalucia throughout the 1820s and 1830s while cholera entered Spain through Galicia in 1833–4 and returned in 1855, 1865 and 1885. There was also a long series of subsistence crises: in 1817, 1823–5, 1837, 1847, 1868, 1879, 1887 and 1898. However, with the exception of the cholera epidemic of 1855–6 none contributed substantially to overall mortality rates, although the cholera outbreaks were all significant on a local level.

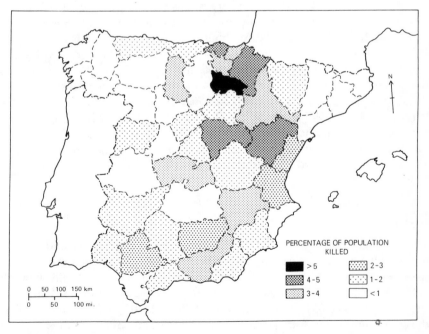

PERCENTAGE OF POPULATION
KILLED

■ >5   ▦ 2–3
▦ 4–5   ▦ 1–2
▦ 3–4   □ <1

0   50   100   150 km
0   50   100 mi.

Figure 1.5   *Impact of the Cholera Epidemic, 1854–1855*

Epidemics were vanquished only in the twentieth century. The last significant outbreak of cholera, in 1885, accounted for 120,000 deaths. An outbreak
which began in Catalonia in 1911 was quickly contained by measures taken
by the government. The only major epidemic of the century was the influenza
epidemic of 1918–19, and that was worldwide.

But catastrophic mortality was less important than the refusal of the rate
of ordinary, and especially infant, mortality to fall substantially until the
twentieth century (see Figure 1.6). In the second half of the nineteenth
century the death rate generally hovered around 30 per thousand before
beginning to drop slowly in the mid-1890s. Spain entered the twentieth
century with mortality rates much higher than were the norm elsewhere:
29 per thousand in 1900 compared to a European average of 18.

The gap began to close in the first thirty years of the twentieth century.
In 1911 the Spanish death rate was 3.3 per thousand higher than the French,
and 8.6 per thousand higher than that of England and Wales. By 1930 the
gap had been narrowed to 1.7 per thousand more than France and 5.8 per
thousand more than England and Wales. This convergence can be seen in
Figure 1.7.

Progress, both relative and absolute, was much slower in one important
area, the reduction of infant mortality. This is apparent in Figure 1.8.
According to Vicente Pérez Moreda infant mortality rates in the interior of the
country may actually have increased in the first half of the nineteenth century.
Among the reasons he cites are an increase in the number of children in
foundling hospitals, the *inclusas*, where deaths were very frequent. According
to one senator who was also a doctor, 580 of every thousand children in the
Inclusa of Madrid died before reaching the age of 5 and between 1884 and
1889 a total of 6,918 had died there.[4] A second reason was the widespread
failure after 1814 to take advantage of the availability of free vaccinations
for smallpox, one of the major killers of the nineteenth century, and the
failure of the government to make vaccination obligatory before 1902.[5] But
Pérez Moreda is talking about the interior. In parts of Catalonia this was
not the case. Nadal has found that 'in the coastal municipality of Palamos,
for example, vaccination meant that the number of children surviving to
14 years rose from 571 per thousand in 1790–9 to 729 per thousand in
1830–4.[6]

Birth

The persistence of high mortality rates through the entire nineteenth century
meant that Spain's population growth was relatively slow even though birth
rates remained high by European standards. Between 1858 and 1900 the
birth rate fluctuated between 33 and 40 per thousand and, as Figure 1.9
shows, Spain entered the twentieth century with the highest birth rate on
the continent outside Austria. In 1900 the Spanish rate of 35 per thousand was
substantially higher even than the Portuguese rate of 31. The birth rate finally

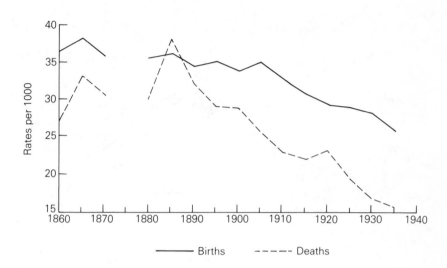

Figure 1.6 *Birth and Death Rates, 1860–1935*

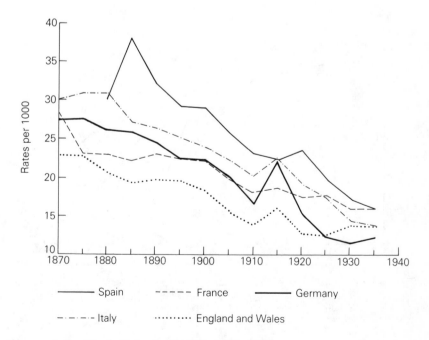

Figure 1.7 *Death Rates in Europe, 1870–1935*

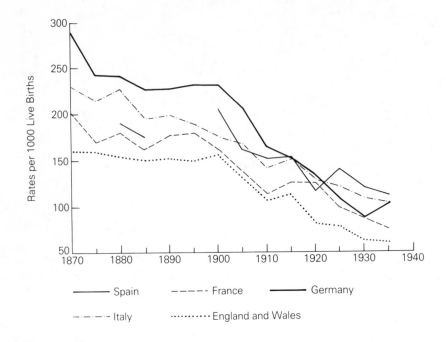

Figure 1.8   *Infant Mortality in Europe, 1870–1935*

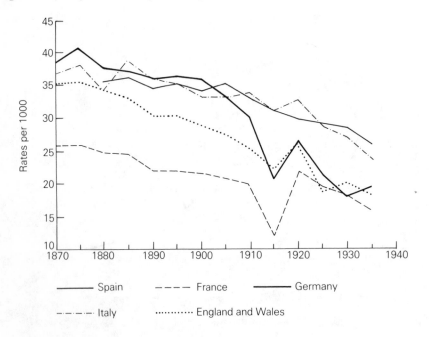

Figure 1.9   *Birth Rates in Europe, 1870–1935*

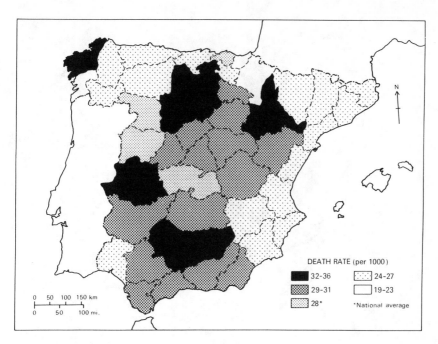

Figure 1.10   *Death Rate by Province, 1901*

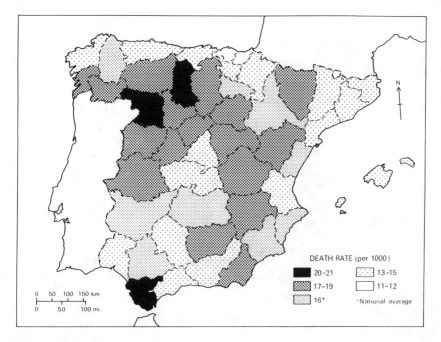

Figure 1.11   *Death Rate by Province, 1935*

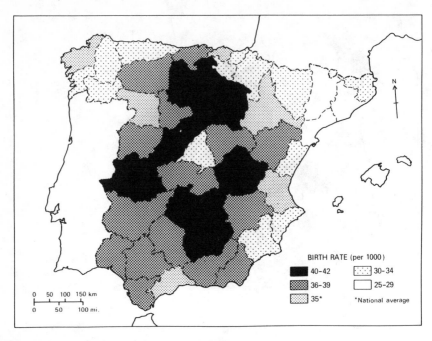

Figure 1.12 *Birth Rate by Province, 1901*

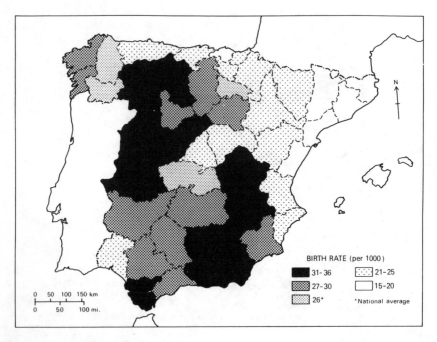

Figure 1.13 *Birth Rate by Province, 1935*

began a steady decline in 1905 and by the Civil War it had fallen to 25.7. This decline was especially pronounced during the first years of the Depression.

The decline in the birth rate was due in part to the spread of birth control practices. Nadal claims that this had begun in Catalonia in the first half of the nineteenth century, and the dramatic collapse in the region's birth rate after 1860 tends to bear this out.[7] In the rest of the country it came later. By the 1920s the clergy of Madrid were complaining about the spread of what they referred to as 'neomalthusianism'. All classes were affected, but the middle and upper classes to a much greater degree than the working class and much more frequently in the capital than in the surrounding villages. One parish priest wrote that 'One hears things in the confessional which create fears about a great plague this century.' For his part, the Archpriest of Buitrago expressed 'suspicion that even in these villages birth control is practised, in relation to the education of the residents'.[8] This is a very difficult question to assess, but one study done in the 1940s claimed that between 1920 and 1940 the practice of birth control in Madrid and Barcelona, denounced as 'the Malthusian leprosy', had spread to the working classes while the upper classes had begun to have more children.[9]

Another reason for the falling birth rate was an increase in age at marriage. The proportion of both men and women in the 16 to 25 age group who were single rose between 1787 and 1910. The increase among the women was slight but that for the men was dramatic, from 80.4 to 90.4 per cent. This increase continued in the twentieth century. The average age at first marriage rose from 27 for men and 24.2 for women in 1887 to 28.2 and 25.8 in 1930. In some places the change over the course of a century was remarkable. In the town of Bencarrón de los Condes (Seville), the age at first marriage jumped from 22.9 for men and 21.6 for women in 1840–5 to 32.3 and 29.3 in 1946–50.

The national aggregates, the figures for Spain as a whole, which we have discussed so far, hide important local and regional differences. These differences are shown in Figures 1.10 through 1.13. In 1901 the death rate was 28 per thousand but this included Jaén, with a rate of 36, and Córdoba, Ciudad Real and Palencia, with 34, as well as Santa Cruz de Tenerife, at 19, and the Balearics at 21. The gap had narrowed somewhat by 1935 but it remained large, ranging from 21 per thousand in Palencia and 20 in Cádiz and Zamora to 12 in Guipúzcoa and Santa Cruz de Tenerife and 11 in Vizcaya.

The situation was similar with birth rates. The national rate of 35 per thousand in 1901 hid the chasm between the six provinces with a rate of 41 (Cáceres, Ciudad Real, Jaén, Logroño, Segovia and Soria) and Barcelona with its rate of 27. By 1935 the difference was, if anything, even greater. The national average of 26 per thousand included Cáceres and Cádiz at 36 as well as Tarragona and Gerona at 18.

There were also differences within regions. While Catalonia and the Basque Provinces were expanding, not all the provinces in those regions did so. During the second half of the nineteenth century the Catalan provinces of Lérida and Gerona and the Basque province of Alava were three of the four provinces where total population declined. Provincial capitals often had death rates well above those for their province as a whole. In 1901 Zamora had an incredible death rate of 51.6 per thousand and Gerona, Jaén and Salamanca were all well over 40. The city of Bilbao had death rates double those of the province of Vizcaya in the 1890s and within the city the rates were highest in the working class districts.

Marriage

The demographic impact of these developments would have been offset to a certain extent by an increased propensity to marry, what demographers call nuptiality. The percentage of unmarried 50-year-old males fell from 12 to 6 per cent between 1787 and 1900; the percentage of unmarried women also fell but by a smaller amount. The change was least in those regions with large numbers of smallholders where marriage would be delayed until property was transferred. It was greatest in regions with large populations of agricultural labourers, for whom there was no economic disincentive to marriage. In Andalucia the change was dramatic: from 16 per cent of 50-year-olds of both sexes single at the end of the eighteenth century to about 6 per cent at the beginning of the twentieth.[10]

There were marked regional differences in nuptiality, throughout the nineteenth and into the twentieth century. In Galicia, Asturias and the Canary Islands the proportion of married women in the fertile age group was below 50 per cent, compared to national rates of almost 60 per cent. Emigration was the major cause: these three regions were traditional zones of emigration and, as a result, had a 'permanent deficiency of males' and the greatest number of unmarried women.[11]

What did marriage mean to Spanish men and women? How did they relate within it?

Throughout the nineteenth century Spanish women labored under major legal disabilities, as did women in all European and North American countries. These disabilities were much more severe for married than unmarried women. On reaching the age of majority, 23, the legal position of a single woman was 'analogous in a number of respects to that of a man', in that she could sign contracts and conduct business in her own right. Still, her position was not one of equality since she was barred from a number of roles, among them belonging to a Chamber of Commerce, voting, holding elected office and being a civil servant at any level.[12]

The situation of the married woman was much worse. Upon marriage she automatically lost most of her legal rights and became an appendage of her husband. She required his permission to be in business and he had the authority to administer her property: she could not sell or mortgage the property she brought to the marriage without his approval, nor could she accept or reject an inheritance by herself. The Civil Code told wives that they should obey their husbands and punished disobedience with jail terms of five to fifteen days. This legal subordination remained in effect until 1931. Wives had to live where their husbands did and could not leave without permission. Nor was this a dead letter. Leonor Campos, who successfully sued for *divorcio*, legal separation, from her husband in 1830 had previously left their village, San Martín de Trevejo (Cáceres), for Ciudad Rodrigo 'without her husband's permission [and] was fined by the Corregidor'.[13] The archives are no doubt full of such cases. Only with the death of her husband or through legal separation could a woman recover her legal rights.

The law treated married women harshly in other respects too. Any sexual infidelity committed by a wife was defined as adultery. A husband's affairs had to cause 'public scandal' before they constituted a legal offence. Women were also punished more severely for crimes of passion, receiving life imprisonment compared to the six months to six years of exile for their husbands.

Real divorce, with the right to remarry, was unavailable until March 1932. Legislation made divorce possible either by mutual agreement of the spouses or by the presentation of cause, among them adultery, bigamy, attempt to corrupt children, abandonment, attempt to kill the spouse, or contraction of venereal disease outside marriage. The law treated both spouses equally, a change from previous legislation. Few people actually took advantage of the law and most of the divorces which were granted, almost half, were in Madrid and Barcelona. The national rate of 1.65 divorces per thousand marriages was low, but in some provinces, such as Zamora, Teruel, Alava, León, Cáceres and Cuenca, all with rates below 0.40 per thousand, there were almost none at all. Most divorces affected couples who were already separated; in fact separation for at least three years was the most frequently stated cause, accounting for one fifth of all divorces.

Beyond the laws there was a set of expectations, a moral prescription, which women were supposed to respect and which coincided completely with the theory of the two spheres and the cult of domesticity so prominent in other countries. A woman's role was to get married and be a good wife and a good mother. Her realm was the home; beyond was the realm of men. These ideas were so deeply ingrained that even political progressives and early advocates for improving the position of women adhered to them into the last third of the nineteenth century. In 1871 *Rochefort*, the Federal Republican newspaper of Salamanca, could describe the three stages of a woman's life as passing from loving dolls in childhood, to youth, when all her energies were directed towards finding a man, to motherhood. Sofía Tartilán, a writer and the editor of *La Ilustración de la Mujer* and an advocate for better education for Spanish women, concluded her *Páginas para la educación popular* (1877) with a classic statement of the separation of the spheres: 'do not think that we advocate education to prepare our sex for public life. Our true emancipation lies within the home, in the bosom of the family.'[14] The one area of public activity considered acceptable for women was, as we will see, charity work, but then this was considered a logical extension of their nature.

Marriage was very much an economic arrangement, at least until the 1860s. Amongst the elite the accumulation, or acquisition, of titles and the preservation of family fortunes played prominent roles. In his study of the industrial elite of Barcelona Gary McDonogh found that the 'Good Families' increasingly used marriage as a form of 'strategic alliance' and that the available marriage pool was highly restricted, rarely including managerial or political groups or even elite families from outside the region. Moreover, as other social groups gave up their use of the marriage contract in the nineteenth century the elite expanded their use of this form which, as 'a cornerstone of the extended family', facilitated the cohesion of the family business.[15]

Outside the elite, marriage was also likely to have had an economic function. It certainly had for the men of very different social positions who took out the following classified ads. The first appeared in *El Clamor Público* (Madrid), early in 1848:

> Three young men with brilliant careers, respectively 35, 26 and 25 years old, good looking, the first with an income based on 100,000 pesetas, the other two with 80,000 each, wish to marry young ladies who have at least an equal amount of capital. **There are no other conditions**. Qualified young women from the capital may **enter into negotiations directly** or through a representative. (emphasis added)

The second appeared in the Madrid *Diario de Avisos* in June 1854:

> A thirty-year-old male store clerk wishes to find a young woman who wants to get married. **I earn enough only to support myself.** She should be well educated, with a good appearance and **have at least enough [money] on which to live**. I am well educated, of average height and do not have any physical defects'. (emphasis added)

If this lonely clerk found a wife we might guess that the economic equality within the marriage meant that the relations between husband and wife were not those of total submission prescribed by the Civil Code.

The memoirs of González Arranz, a royalist who served as mayor of his town of Roa (Burgos), illustrate how marriage also fulfilled an economic function for landowners. They also provide another example of couples in which the wife probably had something to say about the family finances. González Arranz married for the first time at the age of 30; his first wife was within the second degree of consanguinity. When she died four years later he decided to join up with his father-in-law: 'We all benefited. We joined our resources . . . my father-in-law looked after the house and the property while I oversaw the farm and the labourers.' Three years later he remarried, again within the degrees of consanguinity, because he needed someone to 'look after the house and family' and to prevent the 'decadence of my household and the dissipation of my wealth' since his father-in-law was now too old to do so properly. He gave his new wife his furniture, as well as 'real property such as vines and lands to look after. **The money from her dowry was invested in her mother's store.** We went to live with her mother as we had agreed on beforehand.' (emphasis added) This wife soon died but González Arranz continued to carry on his business affairs with his brother-in-law, with the profits to be shared equally. He soon married for a third time, but this time not a relative, 'after noting important losses at the store, chaos in my household and my children being ignored'.[16]

By the last few decades of the nineteenth century such hard-headedness may have begun to give ground to a more romantic vision of marriage. José Castro y Serrano denounced what he saw as this new trend in his *Cartas trascendentales*:

> if by disinterested marriages one means an unhappy young man without resources blindly marrying an unfortunate young woman without a fortune on the pretext that love is blind and that one should not consult the head in matters of the heart . . . I condemn, loathe and laugh at such spiritual marriages as much as at evidently materialistic ones.[17]

Farmsteads and Families

Peter Laslett, the British demographer, once guessed that the Mediterranean family pattern, characterized by large extended families, 'probably marked the whole of Spain'.[18] He was wrong. Family structure was far from uniform across the country and varied with patterns of landholding.

Laslett was close to the mark for the country's northern tier; Asturias, the Basque Provinces, León and Catalonia, where a system of small, often indivisible farmsteads, single heirs and the transfer of property from one generation to the other taking place while the parents were still alive made the stem family much more prominent. Even there, however, it was far from universal.

In the villages of León where smallholding predominated the peasants practised partible, in fact strictly equal, inheritance and there was a preponderance of simple families. Even so, more complex households were common and accounted for as much as 20 per cent at times. Indeed, most people passed through an extended family stage. As dowries were small and property was rarely passed on before the parents' death most newlyweds were not in a position to establish an independent household right away. Instead they began their married lives living and working in the houses of their respective parents until they could become independent. For as long as nine years they 'ate in their houses, were clothed and supported by their houses. Only at night were they reunited, when the husband went to his wife's house and they slept together in their matrimonial bed.'[19] The practice persisted until the middle of the twentieth century.

Rural society in the Basque Provinces was based on the *baserria*, an indivisible farmstead consisting of a large house surrounded by crop land, part of which was used for a garden, meadows, some of which were used for orchards, and mountain lands. The farm was passed on to a single heir at his marriage, usually while the parents were still alive. Male primogeniture existed in Vizcaya but not in Navarre where parents were free to choose the heir, regardless of age or gender. Stem families were a minority at any given moment but all but one of the twenty farmsteads in Echalar housed a stem family at one time or another between 1842 and 1960. The Basque stem ideal was a reality, but life expectancy and the extremely late age at marriage (31 for men and 27 for women) prescribed a 'lengthy simple phase' for most families and meant that many parents would not survive to live with their married heir.[20]

Rural society in Asturias was based on farmsteads known as *caserías* which were very similar to the Basque *baserria*. They too had a house and lands which were the basis of a subsistence polyculture. There was a single heir, usually the eldest male, and the transfer was made at his marriage through a written contract.

The stem family was also common in rural Catalonia but there too there was no single type of family structure. Household form varied greatly by social group. The stem family was most common among the peasantry who exploited their farms directly; small landowners, tenant farmers and sharecroppers, and whose practice was to pass the property to a single heir, the *hereu*. Frequently one of the remaining children would enter the Church and the rest would marry and leave. It was least common at the two extremes of rural society, among landless laborers and large landowners.

In the south and center of Spain, however, the nuclear family, neolocal residence and partible inheritance were close to universal. This, by far the largest part of the country, fell into Laslett's 'West or West/Central' typologies.

In the province of Cuenca from 1700 to 1970, 80 to 85 per cent of all families were nuclear, and extended and multiple families never accounted for more than 6 per cent of the total. These more complex families were somewhat more common among those groups with land or other property to protect – farmers and professionals and the 'privileged' – than among the landless, but even here they never represented as much as 7 per cent. Marriage and the creation of separate households were 'practically simultaneous phenomena'.[21] There was a similar pattern in the Segura valley, where more than eight of every ten families were nuclear in structure. This percentage rose in the late nineteenth century as the increasing commercialization of agriculture permitted greater fragmentation of landholdings and a decrease in the age at marriage, especially for women.[22]

The Home and Beyond

Since women were expected to marry and not carry on any public activity they were educated accordingly. The numerous guides for the education and comportment of respectable young women emphasized 'domestic competence [and] social savoir faire', especially modesty.[23] After 1868 there were some demands for better education for women, but these took the line that better education would contribute to bringing women closer to the ideal of domesticity. Sofía Tartilán's *Páginas para la educación popular* is a good example. If women were to educate their children, she argued, they had to be better educated themselves: 'The superficial and at times dangerous education which most women receive today does not allow them to educate their children properly . . . nor does it even prepare them to adequately fulfil their role as a wife.' Tartilán wanted to avoid the 'moral divorce' which was so common in married couples because 'the wife's ignorance separates her from her husband' by making women incapable of 'understanding their husbands [and] taking an active role in their work, helping with advice and reasoned discussion'. She did not want women to enter the professions since 'it is beyond doubt that it would lead to chaos'.[24] Tartilán's concerns were borne out by Prosper Mérimée, a lover of things Spanish, and above all of Spanish women. During one of his seven trips to Spain he wrote that: 'I think that it would be good to get married here . . . but it is a shame that the [women] do not know more about history, geography and other essential knowledge, the basis of all good education.'[25]

Educational opportunities were fewer for women than for men at all levels, but the disparity was greater the higher one went up the educational, and social, hierarchy. Illiteracy was higher among women but fell for women and men over time. By 1930 the figures were 38 and 23.6 per cent. The sharp regional differences in the female illiteracy rate changed very little however. Northern regions of smallholding peasants, such as Navarre, the Basque Provinces and Old Castile, tended to have little illiteracy. In southern latifundia regions the rate was generally twice that of the north.

The declining illiteracy rate reflected the greater availability of schools. In the middle of the nineteenth century there were almost four times as many boys as girls in primary schools but by 1930 the numbers were almost equal. At just over 50, the percentage of school age children of each gender attending school was almost the same as well. Beyond the primary level the differences were vast and declined much less. As access to education was more restricted in terms of social class it was also more restricted in terms of gender. In 1930 only one out of every eight students in the high school academic stream was a girl. They did dominate one branch of secondary education, training for *magisterio*, elementary school teaching. Throughout the first three decades of the twentieth century they were more than half of all students in the field and close to half of all girls enrolled in secondary schools did this course.

The disparities were greatest in the universities. In 1927–30 only 3.5 per cent of young men between 16 and 20 were at universities. The figure for young women was 0.1 per cent. The number of women did increase but in 1928 they still represented only 4.2 per cent of the student body. Within the universities the opportunities for women varied greatly from one faculty to another. By 1928 more than a third of all women were studying pharmacy, where they accounted for 18 per cent of all students. Just over a quarter were in Arts, a faculty which twenty years earlier had been the least popular. This change was probably due to new employment possibilities, especially in secondary schools, libraries and archives. Women were rare in Law School, only 4 per cent of the students in 1927–8, since there was very little they could do with their degree. Women were prohibited from taking the *oposiciones*, state examinations, for positions as notaries, registrars of property and judges. Before the Second Republic only two women lawyers, Victoria Kent and Clara Campoamor, had actually appeared in court and they both had other jobs.

These proscriptions limiting women to the home constituted a middle and upper class ideal. At lower levels of society women could expect to work for some, if not most of their lives. Overall, the number of women in the workforce declined continually between 1877 and 1930, from 1.5 million to 1.1 million, as did the percentage of women who worked, from 17 per cent in 1877 to 9 per cent in 1930.

Marriage, that central event in the female life cycle, took women out of the workforce in large numbers. In 1930, 20 per cent of women between 16 and 20 and 17 per cent of those between 21 and 25 worked. Thereafter the figures dropped markedly, to 12 per cent between 26 and 30 and to around 10 per cent between 31 and 60, only to rise to 13.4 per cent for those over 60, many of whom were widows. Marriage was a great impediment to work in the service sector. In 1900 the ratio of single to married women employed in the sector was nine to one; thirty years later it was eight to one. The situation for those involved in domestic service was even more dramatic. In 1900 there were fifteen single servants for every married one; thirty years later there were eleven.

Throughout the nineteenth century most women worked in agriculture – the primary sector. Many worked on family farms, providing unpaid labor for struggling smallholders. This was particularly true in Galicia, where massive emigration left women in charge of farms and where, in 1887, they made up 43 per cent of the workforce. Women also worked as wage laborers in the south, especially in the periods of peak labor needs when tasks such as harvesting olives were left to them. Their wages were much lower, from a half to two-thirds, than those of the men. After 1900, however, both the absolute and relative number of women involved in the primary sector declined. By 1930 fewer women worked in agriculture than in either industry or services. But agriculture remained the most hospitable economic activity for married women. Of the women employed in agriculture in 1900, 39 per cent were married; in 1930 the figure was 30 per cent.

Women were present in the industrial (secondary) sector in a wide variety of manufacturing occupations but the vast majority were concentrated in a handful of activities: textiles, the sweated trades and tobacco. This affected the geographical distribution of women in the sector. Over 40 per cent of all women workers were in Catalonia. The Basque Provinces and Asturias, the next most important industrial regions, were centres of heavy industry and mining which, in Spain as elsewhere, offered relatively few employment opportunities for women.

Textiles were, as everywhere, the most important industrial occupation for women: in 1930 a third of all women in the secondary sector worked in the textile industry. Women had been prominent in the textile industry from its beginnings but as the industry became more mechanized, employers were able to use more inexpensive workers, replacing 'adults with children and men with women'.[26] Women retained and expanded their place in the textiles workforce in the twentieth century, so that by 1930 they made up 52 per cent of the workers, and 57 per cent in the city of Barcelona itself. Women's wages were consistently well below those of men. In the 1850s they were about half and in the 1870s they ranged from 40 to 66 per cent of men's wages. By 1914 they were up to two-thirds but then fell to about 50 per cent by 1930.

A similar process took place in the province of Alicante in the 1920s when the mechanization of the textile and shoemaking industries made it possible for women to supplant men. Almost two-thirds of these women were under 25, and presumably single.

The sweated trades employed the largest number of women in manufacturing and in the twentieth century were the largest employer of women after agriculture and domestic service. These trades included a wide range of products such as fans, paper articles, leather goods, toys, jewelry, firearms, musical instruments and rabbit pelts, but clothing was by far the most important. In 1900 it employed 93,000 women, just over half of all women in manufacturing; in 1930 it employed 90,000, but by then they were less numerous than the textile workers.

Sweating took place in every province but its importance varied greatly. There were many provinces, such as Teruel, Cuenca, Soria, Avila and Segovia, in which it was merely an anecdotal activity, employing fewer than 200 women in 1925. There were other, in which it was a major industry: Málaga (3,432), Pontevedra (3,502), La Coruña (4,609), Madrid (9,327), Barcelona (16,269) and Valencia (18,973). Wages also varied from province to province but they were low everywhere. In 1914 the average hourly wage in clothing, 0.17 pesetas, was the lowest of any industry, but that national average hid the chasm between the 0.06 pesetas per hour in Salamanca, and the 0.29 in Barcelona. There was no legal regulation of sweating until the 1920s but there is no evidence that this legislation was at all effective. The low level of the wages in sweating contributed to driving many women into part-time or full-time prostitution.[27]

Textiles and the sweated trades were staples of manufacturing work for women everywhere. In Spain there was a third, and distinctive, female manufacturing occupation: cigarette making. The manufacture and sale of tobacco products was declared a state monopoly (the Tabacalera) in the late eighteenth century and was an immediate fiscal success. The first 'factory' was opened in Seville – that most famous of all fictional Spanish women, Bizet's Carmen, worked there – and new ones were quickly added. By 1914 there were ten. The tobacco factories, which were huge by Spanish standards, almost immediately became strongholds of women workers. In the 1840s, when Carmen would have been there, 4,046 of the 4,542 workers in the Seville factory were women. This did not change much. In 1925 the Tabacalera's factories employed 14,163 women and only 120 men.

The tobacco workers were paid on a piecework basis and despite having to pay for work materials (a chair, scissors and a special rolling stand) as well as to have workshops cleaned and to buy a midday meal, they were better paid than most women workers. In Gijón, where they earned a reputation for being stylish dressers, their wages were 50 to 100 per cent higher than the average for women workers in 1911.

They quickly developed a reputation for combativeness. Benito Pérez Galdós has one of the characters in his *Episodios Nacionales* describe them as 'the joy of the people and the nightmare of the authorities'. Pamela Ratcliffe suggests that their high level of solidarity was a product of their 'lifelong job commitment', rare among women workers, which made them similar to male artisans. In the mid-nineteenth century the women at the Gijón factory created a mutual aid society, the Hermandad, which offered burial costs and medical services. They also strove to pass on their jobs to relatives: 'daughters and nieces were given lottery numbers according to the seniority of their employee relative' and in 1921 the *cigarreras* staged a strike when one girl was hired out of turn.[28]

In 1830 the 3,000 women in the Madrid factory rioted for five days against a cut in wages and the condition of the tobacco with which they worked. On at least two occasions they attacked machines which were being introduced and a similar incident took place in Gijón. By the twentieth century their combativeness took other forms. Beginning in 1910 they created unions and in 1918 a National Federation. Unionization led to increased wages: they doubled between 1914 and 1920 and tripled by 1930. Unions also created mutual aid societies and consumer co-operatives and purchased 100,000 shares in the Tabacalera itself. The women were, however, unable to achieve one of their longest-held demands, the replacement of piecework with an annual salary.[29]

The vast majority of the women in the tertiary (service) sector worked as domestic servants. There were 313,000 female servants in 1877 and 322,000 in 1887. The number then dropped somewhat but by 1930 it had recovered to more than 338,000. Since marriage generally meant an end to employment servants were overwhelmingly young, between 15 and 25, and there was a constant turnover.

Young women of middle class families which had come down in the world also found work in the upper ranges of domestic service, as these two advertisements from the *Diario de Avisos* suggest: 'An unfortunate lady who has had a very good education is looking for a lady and gentleman for whom to work as a housekeeper' (January 3, 1854), and 'an orphaned young lady, 17 years old, who has received a polished education, wishes to find a position as a lady's maid with a family going to America or abroad'. (May 23, 1854). There was also a certain demand for foreign women: 'We are looking for a young French or English lady with good manners and a polished education to work as a nanny for a young girl. In addition to room and board we will pay from 200 to 600 reales per month, according to her qualifications' (June 26, 1854).

Another type of service work available to women, and most frequently widows, was to offer lodgings or run guest houses: 'A widow is looking for a gentleman or priest as lodger or for whom to serve as housekeeper' (January 3, 1854).

Towards the end of the nineteenth century women began to find opportunities in the modern service sector. The government first experimented with hiring women in 1880 when it allowed the wives or daughters of telegraph operators to work temporarily after passing a test of reading, writing, arithmetic and operation of a Morse machine. The experiment was a success – the Minister of the Interior stating that the women worked even better than their husbands – and in 1882 women became eligible for permanent employment. However it was only in 1918 that the civil service was opened to women. (When this was debated in the Senate in the 1880s it was rejected because of 'the threat to the decorum which should preside over a woman's life from dealing with the public.')[30] By 1930 there were 2,788 women in the civil service, 3.3 per cent of the total.

Women also found employment in private companies with large white-collar workforces such as the railroads, where they worked as ticket sellers or in the offices, and in the 1920s in the Madrid Metro, as ticket sellers and inspectors as well as office workers. They were also present in commerce, although in Madrid at least, their weight was greater as employers, 6 per cent in 1920, than as employees, 2.7 per cent. Between a third and half of these female employers were widows, most of whom would have taken over the business following the death of their husbands. (Indeed, even today one sees 'Viuda de. . .' on the signs of small businesses in Spain.)

The numbers, especially for the employees, are very small, mirroring the small scale of the retail business: in 1920 there were only three employees for every employer. Between 1920 and 1930 the number of people involved in commerce increased by over 50 per cent to 55,000 and the number of women by 350 per cent to 4,200, due at least in part to the appearance of the first large department stores with their demand for young female clerks. The Almacenes Madrid-Paris, which opened in 1920, was the capital's first imitation of the Bon Marché, over half a century after that legendary store had opened.[31]

The professions did not provide many opportunities for women. Law was the least welcoming but the universities were little better. The first woman to hold a university chair, Emilia Pardo Bazán, was not appointed until 1916 and then only because the Minister of Education forced her upon a resistant University of Madrid. Medicine was more open. The first woman doctor,

Martina Castells, graduated in 1882 and the less prestigious ancillary professions in the field, such as nursing, were considered appropriate. Pharmacy was the most open of all, having the advantage 'that it could be considered as a superior type of cooking'.[32] There were also women writers and journalists. At least fifty-six women, most of them now forgotten, published novels in the nineteenth century and some women even edited magazines, among them Sofía Tartilán's *La Ilustración de la Mujer* in the 1870s and Enriqueta Lozano de Vílchez's *La Madre de la Familia* in the 1870s and 1880s.

Only one profession, teaching, provided opportunities for large numbers of women. Even so, this was limited to a specific type of teaching, elementary education for girls, which was seen as an extension of natural maternal drives. The first teacher's college school for women opened in 1858 and by 1900 there were 12,000 women teaching in public primary schools. An 1847 law had set the women's incomes at a third that of the men, but equal pay was mandated in 1883. Outside the state school system there were thousands of women who set up their own village schools or who offered private classes in a small number of subjects through advertisements in papers such as the *Diario de Avisos*.[33]

Women monopolized two other activities within the service sector. The first was wetnursing. The large number of advertisements in the *Diario de Avisos* makes it clear that there were undoubtedly many of them. The advertisements are not very informative, but they tell us that both married and unmarried women were available, that they nursed both in their own homes or those of the parents and that they frequently mentioned their province of origin, often Santander or Asturias. The following advertisement, from May 23, 1854, is unusual only in its verbosity and its well-developed sense of public relations:

> At number 18 rivera de Curtidores [in the very heart of Madrid] there is a wetnurse who has just arrived from the mountains of Santander, an honest and trustworthy person, with abundant and healthy milk and who recently gave birth . . . the owners of the establishment will provide all the necessary information as I nursed their son who is now three years old and one of the most beautiful children of that age ever seen.

The prevalence of wetnursing at the end of the nineteenth century provoked a stern attack, 'A las Madres', in the newspaper in Vitigudino (Salamanca). The author admitted that wetnursing was less common that it had been in the recent past but that a 'multitude' of women did not nurse their own children.[34]

The second activity was prostitution. This was legal until 1935 although after 1850 it was increasingly regulated by local governments. In 1858 Madrid introduced municipal regulations, intended to control the spread of venereal diseases, calling for the voluntary registration of prostitutes, twice-weekly medical checks and prohibiting prostitutes from working in the streets 'during the hours when the streets are crowded', and these were quickly copied in a number of other cities. The first national regulation came in 1908.

There are no clear figures for the number of prostitutes since those who registered with the municipal health departments were a minority. According to the director of the special hygiene section in Barcelona, in 1881 that city had 1,022 registered prostitutes and over 5,000 illegal ones. In 1899 Madrid had 2,000 registered prostitutes and, by official estimates, some 7,000 who worked clandestinely. Among those who registered were some 400 who worked in the city's 150 legalized brothels. (These numbers suggest that the business was on a very small scale.) The brothels too were regulated: divided into three categories with a registration fee for each, subject to inspection by the health department and required to close, in Alcoy at least, at midnight, 11 pm in the winter. The conditions inside the brothels were harsh. The protagonist of Pío Baroja's novel, *El Arbol de la Ciencia*, a doctor who did the medical inspections of prostitutes, described the women who worked in the brothels as a 'sad proletariat of sex'. They were given new names, were dressed and fed – poorly – by the madame, who kept their earnings, kept them in a kind of debt servitude and enforced a rigid discipline, including the use of physical force. Baroja's hero mentioned one brothel 'where the pimp is an effeminate man . . . who dresses like a woman, even wearing earrings in his pierced ears . . . who treats the girls with terrible cruelty and has them terrorized'.[35]

How did women come to prostitution? According to Rafael Eslava, head of the special hygiene section in Madrid, 31 per cent of the city's prostitutes began their careers after having been seduced by their lovers and another 27 per cent had been domestic servants, many of whom were also likely to have been seduced. Six per cent were seamstresses and 25 per cent, among whom there would have been many women engaged in the sweated trades, were driven to it by poverty. According to Eslava, there were also a number of middle class women involved: the widows and daughters of civil servants whose miserable pensions, 10 pesetas per month in 1900, drove them to prostitution.[36]

Migration

Emigration was a fact of life throughout almost all our period, even though Spanish governments retained a 'populationist' philosophy into the 1850s and did not lift the last legal obstacle to emigration until 1903.

There were three principal flows of emigrants. The first and most important was transoceanic, above all to America. This was a European-wide phenomenon, into which Spaniards were fully integrated. From 1846 to 1932 almost 5 million people left Spain, putting it in fifth place behind Britain, Italy, Austria–Hungary and Germany. As one would guess, the vast majority went to Latin America, to the remaining colonies of Cuba and Puerto Rico and to the former colonies, especially Argentina. A third of the 4.5 million Europeans who went to Argentina between 1857 and 1915 came from Spain.

For Spaniards this was a movement with a long history, since they had had colonies in America since the end of the fifteenth century. The wars of independence and the subsequent Spanish refusal to recognize the newly independent states temporarily interrupted emigration, but this resumed when Spain finally did recognize the new republics in 1836. Since emigration was still restricted, these first emigrants had to leave clandestinely, which meant that they were easily exploited. Many went in conditions which effectively amounted to debt servitude, signing contracts like the following:

> upon arriving in Venezuela I will remain at the orders of the mentioned Nicolás Trujillo who will be able to place me with whatever corporation or private individual or individuals who pay the stated sum for me and my family . . . I renounce the help of whatever laws or rights which I might enjoy and I state that this private document be given the same force as if it were a public [notarized] document.[37]

The problem of clandestine emigration, and the abuses to which it gave rise, only worsened in the 1850s, when Argentina opened itself up to immigration. A number of particularly outrageous incidents in 1852 prodded the Spanish government to attempt to regulate an activity it could not prevent and in September 1853 it issued a decree, aimed specifically at the Canary Islands, permitting emigration to Spanish colonies or states with Spanish diplomatic representation. Males between 18 and 20 had to leave a deposit as a guarantee of returning to do their military service. Recruiters, among whom was a company owned by a president of the Argentine legislature, required government authorization to organize voyages, had to guarantee sanitary conditions on the ships, give the emigrants two years to pay their crossing and allow them to choose their employer freely.

Emigration was also increasing from the provinces of the Cantabrian tier, Galicia, Asturias and the Basque Provinces, where population growth outstripped the ability of a subsistence agriculture to support it. Many Galicians slipped into Portugal and left from there; Basques could do the same in France. In Galicia, and perhaps elsewhere, there was a virtual network of recruiting agents working for colonization companies in America. Some Spaniards also attempted to cash in on the New World's need for colonists and workers. Following the reduction of the slave trade Cuba had to find an alternative source of labor. In 1853 Urbano Feijoo Sotomayor, a merchant from Orense and a member of parliament, set up a Sociedad Patriótica–Mercantil to introduce Spanish workers into Cuba. The Captain General of the island rejected his request for a monopoly but did grant him more limited privileges. The first ship landed in March 1854 and by August some 1,700 men had arrived. However, the Cuban planters scuttled the project. They preferred Chinese coolies and refused to hire the Spaniards.[38]

Spaniards joined the transatlantic flow in a major way only in the 1880s. About 360,000 left between 1882 and 1896. From 1904 to 1915 the figure was 1.7 million, of whom 500,000 went to Argentina alone. Most of these emigrants came from a small group of provinces: the Canary Islands, Galicia, Asturias and Santander. These were all provinces with a poor and overpopulated countryside; however, Oviedo remained a major source of emigrants even after the mining industry had become well established and was able to provide employment.[39]

The second major flow, which took people from the Levante (Valencia, Murcia and Alicante) to Algeria, began virtually from the inception of French colonization there in 1830. Most of these emigrants were birds of passage who returned to Spain after a relatively short stay. The flow began to diminish in the 1880s, as natives replaced Spaniards in the labor force, and by the early 1890s more Spaniards were returning from Algeria than going there. Still there were years, such as 1914 when 30,000 Spaniards went, in which the flow of emigrants was substantial.[40]

The third movement was to continental Europe, which before the Civil War meant France. This flow was already underway early in the nineteenth century: in 1851 there were over 29,000 Spaniards and Portuguese in France. The Spanish population rose to 80,000 in 1900, 105,000 in 1911 and 351,000 in 1931. The peak came during the First World War, when French authorities actively recruited Spaniards to make up the labor shortage caused by the war. According to official French statistics 220,000 Spaniards entered the country between January 1, 1916 and March 31, 1918, and many others surely escaped the statistics. Spanish figures, which show only 126,000 emigrants, reveal once again the small number of provinces of origin with the Levante alone accounting for 40 per cent.[41]

Spain was, then, fully integrated into the massive flow of population from Europe to the Americas which marked the period 1840–1920. It was so much so that it became a field of activity for recruiters of immigrants from even such an out-of-the-way place as Hawaii. Faced with a chronic labor shortage after 1850, the Hawaii Sugar Planters Association invested heavily in the importation of workers. Most came from Japan but by the end of the century the planters were turning to Europe. In 1907 they had agents looking at Málaga, itself a sugar-producing area. Handbills went up announcing 'emigration with free passage to the State of Hawaii'. The offer was open to married agricultural workers under 45 years of age; those with sons over 17 were especially favoured. In addition to wages, emigrants were promised a house worth $500, a garden plot, free schooling and freedom from labor contracts. By 1914 a total of 7,735 Andalucians, apparently mostly landless labourers and dispossessed former smallholders, had gone to Hawaii. Just over 1,000 remained there, however. The rest had moved on to California, where the orchards of the Vaca and Santa Clara valleys offered a less bureaucratized, more personal set of work relations than did the Hawaiian plantations.[42]

Internal migration was also important, although not as important as it would be after 1950. Alfonso García Barbancho has calculated that there were some 3

Table 1.2   *Distribution of population by size of place of residence*

	1900	1910	1930
1,000 or fewer	14.8‰	13.5‰	10.6‰
1,001 to 5,000	36	34.5	29.8
5,000 to 10,000	16.9	17.2	17.1
10,000 to 30,000	15.5	16.8	16.8
30,000 to 100,000	7.6	7.6	10.8
More than 100,000	9	10.3	14.9

Source: J. Sánchez Jiménez, 'La población, el campo y las ciudades', *Historia de España*, vol. 37 (Madrid, 1984), p. 402.

million migrants between 1900 and 1930, with almost 40 per cent moving in the 1920s.[43] After 1950 the numbers engaged in this movement were greater, but the two periods shared a fundamental characteristic: movement away from the areas of monoculture, especially wheat, towards those with industry or export–oriented agriculture.

There were many more source than target provinces. The number of provinces which had a net inflow of migrants was 12 in the first decade of the century, 16 in the second and 10 in the third. Those with net losses numbered 38, 34 and 40 respectively. Galicia, for example, lost 327,000 people in those three decades. Between 1787 and 1910 four regions (Aragon, Old Castile, Galicia and León) saw their percentage of the national population fall. Figure 1.14 shows the differences in growth by region. A number of provinces actually lost population, in absolute terms, between censuses. From 1887 to 1900 there were 9, from 1910 to 1920, 13, and from 1920 to 1930, 7. A number of names appear repeatedly: Soria, Gerona, Huesca, Guadalajara, Pontevedra and Lérida. Figure 1.15 shows which provinces lost populations between 1910 and 1920.

Urbanization

As they moved from one region of the country to another, these migrants also moved from small centers of population to larger ones. Villages and towns housed a decreasing percentage of the population while cities – provincial capitals and especially the major economic and administrative centers – grew. In the nineteenth century provincial capitals generally grew at a rate well above the national average and between 1843 and 1877 seventeen of them actually doubled in size.

The greatest period of urban growth was the early twentieth century, especially the fifteen years between the First World War and the Depression. There was a shift in the centre of gravity to the largest cities and the decline of smaller centers, which was absolute for villages with fewer than one thousand. Table 1.2 shows these changes.

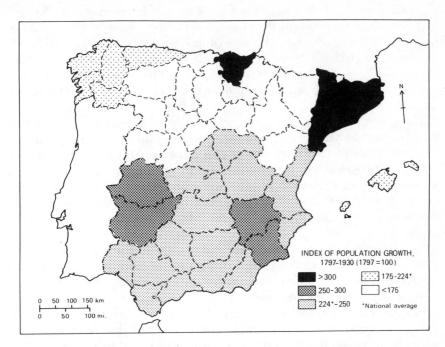

Figure 1.14 *Population Growth by Region, 1797–1930*

Figure 1.15 *Provinces Which Lost Population, 1910–1920*

As the capital, Madrid had long been a magnet for immigrants. As early as 1850 only 40 per cent of the population had been born in the city or the province. Although the largest group of immigrants came from Oviedo, the impact of Madrid was most dramatic on the adjacent provinces, Toledo, Guadalajara, Segovia, Ciudad Real and Cuenca. Men were much more likely than women to have come from more distant provinces, such as Oviedo and Lugo.[44]

The growth of other large cities was breathtaking, many of them almost doubling in size. Barcelona, which had more than doubled its population between 1877 and 1900 (due in large part to an exodus from rural Catalonia which had begun in the 1860s) nearly did so again between 1900 and 1930, when its population stood at just over one million. Bilbao, which had grown from 33,000 in 1877 to 83,000 in 1900, almost doubled its population again by 1930. Valencia, Seville, Málaga and Zaragoza had similar experiences.

Such growth was not limited to traditionally important urban centers. Towns which had previously been of little significance but which became centers of industry or mining experienced the most rapid growth of all in the three decades after 1900. Among them were Badalona, Manresa, Mataró and Sabadell in Catalonia, Mieres and Sama de Langreo in Asturias and Baracaldo and Sestao in Vizcaya. Again, the Basque towns had already experienced a bout of explosive growth: Sestao's population increased from 1,074 in 1877 to 10,833 in 1900 while that of San Salvador del Valle jumped from 901 to 6,836.

These vertiginous rhythms of growth had important, and generally unpleasant, consequences for Spanish cities. In the quieter days of the mid-nineteenth century a number of cities had undertaken planned expansions, or *ensanches*. Barcelona, for example, finally received permission to pull down its walls in 1856 and in 1860 the central government approved the rigid grid proposal designed by the noted planner Ildefons Cerdá. The Castro Plan for the expansion of Madrid was authorized that same year and in 1876 Bilbao began its *ensanche*, 'straight and wide paved streets and comfortable modern buildings to which the growing upper middle class quickly moved'.[45] The city spent 17 million pesetas on infrastructure and the provision of services.

These new additions differed from the socially heterogeneous cores of the cities in that they tended to segregate people by class. The *ensanche* of Madrid separated the well off, the more modest middle class and the artisanate into distinct neighbourhoods. The elegant and famous Salamanca district dates from this time. However, the periods of explosive growth meant that cities rapidly overflowed these nineteenth-century additions. Immigrants to Bilbao found themselves in improvised slums which sprouted up on the periphery of the cities without any regulation or planning. One result was a constant *increase* in the city's mortality rates, which by the 1890s were almost double those of the rest of the province of Vizcaya. Within the city mortality rates in the crowded and unhygienic worker districts were often double those in others.[46]

By the time of the Second Republic, Madrid, which was not an industrial city, was divided into three clear zones: the traditional core, the Ensanche developed following the approval of the Castro Plan in 1860, and the *extrarradio*, or outskirts, where building – development is hardly the word – went on free of any planning and without access to any services such as water or sewerage. Massive immigration hit the city after 1910 but by then the Ensanche was both too small and too expensive to house the new arrivals who were, for the most part, unskilled young men who found work in services and construction. They found housing in the areas beyond the Ensanche, which became heavily populated long before the city got around to planning for it. The result was 'the grid surrounded by chaos; the logic of urban planning surrounded by its total opposite: houses built here and there without any planning, following rural patterns in an urban setting, especially with the small pen for animals so that every family could have its own reserve supply of food'.[47]

A similar process was at work in the smaller but even more rapidly growing industrial centres. The major towns of the Asturian coalfield, Mieres, Sama de Langreo, Laviana and Pola de Lena, are good examples. The coalfield towns had not been particularly pleasant places to live before the tremendous expansion of the mining industry provoked by the First World War – the number of miners increased from 18,000 in 1914 to 39,000 in 1920 due to a flood of immigrants, primarily from Galicia, Old Castile and Portugal – but the completely unregulated urban growth of those years only made things much worse. Housing was desperately short and in Mieres and Sama de Langreo, Socialist city administrations tried to promote affordable housing. Pollution of the rivers, which had been home to an abundant salmon population well into the nineteenth century, had been an increasingly severe problem ever since mining had become a major activity. In 1918 a study claimed that pollution had made the Nalón river completely useless, the streets were filthy and the sewage system inadequate. Nothing had changed by 1923 when *El Socialista* complained that 'the [mining] companies have repeatedly been asked to supply water for public use and until now we have gotten only a little, and that of poor quality. At the moment [Sama] has water at certain hours only . . . and the situation is the same in other municipalities.'[48] Epidemic disease was a growing problem. Cholera hit the region for the first time in 1885 and there were typhus outbreaks in 1911, 1914, 1916 and 1927. The deleterious effects of such conditions were eloquently summed up in 1922 by one mining company doctor.

> Allowing boys of 11, 12 and 13 to work in the mines, the double shifts that wear workers out, the falling wages and the rising cost of living, the high rents

produced by excessive demand, and the consequent overcrowding . . . the poor
sanitary conditions . . . even in purpose built housing . . . the lack of drinking
water . . . and the faulty drainage systems all contribute to the evolution of a
new truly degenerate race of human beings.[49]

These developments did not fail to arouse the concern, sometimes provoked
by humanitarian impulses, sometimes by fear for the security of the social
order, of the middle and upper classes. The 'social question' was on the agenda
as early as the middle years of the nineteenth century and the provision of good
housing for workers was seen as a key to its solution. There were, however,
debates over just what was to be done: should workers become home owners
or not? Should they be housed in segregated districts or should they live in
mixed housing alongside members of the 'superior' social classes so as to
promote class harmony? The Castro Plan for Madrid opted for the former
on the grounds that

> this system is producing much good for society as a whole, for it sees the masses
> becoming more moral. Before, abject and abandoned by society, they were an
> unruly element always ready to go against those who were so little concerned
> for their welfare and saw in them their most powerful enemy.[50]

The case for integration was made by Aurelio de Llano in his 1906 pamphlet,
with the interesting title *Home and Fatherland. A Study on Workers' Housing*.
Isolating workers in a proletarian ghetto meant isolating them

> from the ideology of social peace, since the division of society into classes will
> be given physical form . . . The worker who lives in the attic of a gentleman's
> house unconsciously acquires a certain amount of education he would never get
> in an isolated district . . . Will this worker, his wife and children, be capable of
> committing any unjust act against the ruling classes? No![51]

The first project for workers' housing in Madrid was put forward in
1846 by the writer Antonio Mesonero Romanos, but little was actually
done until the last quarter of the century. The city government was too
indebted to act itself, even when it was controlled by radicals with the
political will to do so, but in the 1870s a number of private organizations,
profit-seeking companies, worker co-operatives and charitable associations,
were created to build workers' housing. Of these the most important
was La Constructora Benéfica. The idea for the Constructora, which was
started in 1875, came from Concepción Arenal, the leading advocate of
philanthropy in nineteenth-century Spain. For Arenal the 'social problem'
could be solved if the wealthy fully accepted their Christian obligation to
provide charity and built an 'International of Love' to fight the 'International of Hate', that is, the First International. The provision of adequate
housing was central to this, contributing to 'the education and moraliza-
tion' of the workers. Starting with a donation of 30,000 pesetas from the

Austrian Countess Krasinscky and subsequent contributions from, among others, King Alfonso XII, Queen María Cristina, the city government of Madrid, the Mediodía railroad company and the Casino of Madrid, the Constructora Benéfica built or acquired 102 homes by the end of the century.[52]

In the smaller centers of rapid industrialization another approach, the provision by companies of housing for their workers, was more common. In Asturias housing was the key component of the social services offered by the mining companies in order to attract and retain a stable and disciplined workforce. Employers operated in their own self-interest. As one leading manager put it, 'Philanthropy goes hand in hand with self interest.' But the provision of social services was generally explained in more attractive terms: the need to improve the morality of the miner, to shape him as both worker and citizen. Comfortable housing was seen as the best way of keeping miners out of the taverns where they imbibed large quantities of alcohol, which undermined their ability to work, and encouraged 'socialism'.[53] However, despite the rhetoric the actual performance of the mining companies was uneven at best and did not even come close to meeting the needs of the workforce or, for that matter, the goals of the employers. Only occasionally did company housing manage to accomodate even 10 per cent of the employees of any individual company.

There were some attempts, influenced by the garden city concept, to provide different and attractive urban environments, but these were not directed at the working class. The bourgeoisie of Bilbao flocked to the garden city of Neguri after 1901. In Barcelona, the attempt to build a similar development around Antonio Gaudí's Guell Park failed in the face of the preference of the local elite for living in the city center.

The most innovative and visionary attempt to create a new urban environment was the Ciudad Lineal, in Madrid, the idea of the noted planner Arturo Soria. His linear city, which emerged out of a 'geometric theory of evolution' drawing on Darwin and Spencer, was designed to serve the needs of a modern economy while reducing class conflict. Soria hoped to build what amounted to a new city housing some 30,000 people in individual houses surrounded by gardens and trees which shielded them from traffic and other unpleasantries of city living. But his city had a peculiar form,

> consisting of only one wide street extending over great distances. Through the centre and entire length of this extraordinary street railroad and trolley lines would be laid . . . Parallel to the main street houses would be constructed on individual plots of land . . . Stores, offices, factories and municipal structures were to be located close to and along the side of the transport corridor.

The residential districts were to be segregated by class, with the wealthy living near the main street and the poor furthest away. But workers would own their homes and the principle of private property would dissolve class conflict. Part of the city was built after 1894 but the project ran into trouble during the First World War and came to a halt when Soria died in 1920.[54]

The Fear of Mobility

Plans for building worker housing were directed at the working poor who were more or less already established in the cities. They did not deal with the marginal, the unemployed and the transient who flocked to the cities as population growth and changes in the countryside cut people loose from the moorings of a relatively stable society. Such people, moving between the rural and urban worlds but not solidly integrated into either, frightened the respectable, many of whom were not too comfortable with the idea of a more urban Spain anyway, and prompted an intensive and wide-ranging debate about the problem of the poor. Even an urban backwater untouched by urbanization, such as Burgos, did not escape the fear of mobility. Immigration from the countryside was, according to Pedro Caraso Soto, 'the source which fed the ranks of the labourers, the nursery of mendicity and a stimulus to the strong rejection within the city'.[55]

When Joseph Townsend visited Spain at the end of the eighteenth century he was impressed by the degree of tolerance with which beggars were treated and by what he called the 'excessively generous' manner in which charity was practised.[56] The poor did keep a special place in important public celebrations into the twentieth century. In 1820 the Oviedo Economic Society celebrated Ferdinand VII's taking the oath of loyalty to the Constitution of 1812 with a Mass in which thirty-six paupers chosen by lot from among the city's poor played a key role and were given a civic lunch at the end of the day. Over a century later, on the eve of the Second Republic, Alfonso XIII performed the traditional Easter ceremony of washing the feet of twelve paupers and serving them a meal.

These may have been highly visible relics of a past age but they were far from representative of attitudes to and ways of dealing with the poor in liberal Spain. The traditional way of giving charity came under increasing attack from government and from social commentators, even those who approached the matter from a self-consciously 'Catholic' position. Moreover, the image of the poor changed radically. Paupers lost their unfortunate, but God-given and morally useful place in society and became instead a nuisance and even a danger. They ceased to be a stimulus to good works and came to constitute a 'social question' which had to be solved.

Spaniards warmly embraced a vision of poverty which denied the existence of any obligation to assist the poor, claiming instead the right to choose the types of poor deserving of their help and, at the same time, asserting the right to do whatever they wanted with their property which, following the liberal revolution, was theirs absolutely and not held on sufferance from God. Their solutions: sweeping the poor from the streets, putting them in institutions and teaching them the virtue of labor, creating voluntary associations to offer them relief, invade their homes and restructure their private lives, and using women of the 'respectable' classes who were not allowed any other public role to do so, closely resembled the responses of contemporaries in Britain and the United States. When it came to producing visions of the poor and ideas of how to deal with them, Spaniards were neither laggard nor different.

The first point of their response was to attack begging and the giving of alms in the street. One line of argument was that this was an inefficient means of distributing poor relief. A second, more widespread argument was that it diverted resources from the truly needy to professional vagrants. Street beggars were denounced as 'thieves' and 'scum' comprising 'a huge industry', the product of an 'oriental concept of charity' which was 'always dangerous. . . and incompatible with order'.[57]

Much of this critique was justified on religious grounds, with long-standing concepts of 'Christian charity' taking a beating in the process. Concepción Arenal, the most prolific writer and most persistent activist in the field, was one of the few not repelled by the sight of beggars in the streets, so long as they had been provided with an official badge attesting to their worthiness, because 'they represent pain in society and pain is an indispensable element of morality and improvement'. At the same time, she felt that alms given in the street was 'unthinking charity . . . badly given'.[58] Some denounced such public alms-giving as a cheap way of displaying one's generosity. The most forthright, and meanest, attack came from the distinguished poet Ramón de Campoamor:

> Before Christianity . . . poverty could be a claim to virtue but today, when work is sanctified by religion and ennobled by the state, poverty is, with only rare exceptions, the product of laziness, vice and ineptitude . . . In individuals poverty is a sign of incompetence; in nations it is an indication of their degradation.[59]

No longer of Providential origin and therefore to be tolerated, Spaniards came to see poverty as a sign of moral failure which had to be treated by attending to the moral weaknesses of the poor, and they offered two approaches. The first was home relief, providing material assistance, but never money, and moral support to the poor in their homes. This was seen as having a number of advantages. It kept the poor out of institutions and with their families. It contributed to social harmony by casting social relations in terms of 'benefactors and the grateful'. Home relief also meant prying into every aspect of the lives of the poor: improving the sanitary conditions of their homes, encouraging them to wash their clothes, discouraging them from 'vices' such as taverns and 'non-rational entertainments' such as bullfights, getting the children to attend school, and having couples regularize their 'marriages' in Church. (One Madrid charity association claimed to have regularized the situation of one hundred such couples in 1864 alone.)[60]

The second approach was to subject the poor to discipline and work. This was not an invention of the nineteenth century but it became a more commonly held idea then. Work was, in Arenal's words, 'necessary to sustain the soul . . . the idle person attacks society directly'.[61] Labor and routine had a prominent place in the institutions to which the poor were sent. The regulations of Madrid's San Bernardino asylum would have done Jeremy Bentham proud The inmates were segregated by sex and then divided into groups of ten to fifteen called brigades and squadrons, each with a *cabo* (corporal) chosen by the administrator from among the best behaved. Inmates were given a uniform, a number which had to be visible at all times, a haircut and a bath. During the spring and summer they awoke at 4.30 am, had roll call at 5, worked from 5.30 until 12 and then from 3 until 7, read and attended religious services until supper and went to bed at 9.30 pm. They could be sent out to work as day laborers for private businesses in the city or as servants or nannies. Infractions of the rules earned a variety of punishments: loss of recreation time or permission to go out; a reduction in the amount of food; fines and loss of wages; or time in the correction room, an isolation cell or one of the 'punishment machines'. Children had a special discipline. They awoke and dressed to a drum roll, made their beds, had roll call, prayed and washed. They moved at all times in brigades and in absolute silence and were always to sit in the same place at meals and in school. Obedience was 'the first obligation which must be imposed on the children'.[62]

Traditional alms–giving was most frequently described as unthinking and indiscriminate. Thought and discrimination were necessary because the poor were not all alike or deserving of like treatment. The poor had to be classified and each category had to be dealt with in a different way: the sick, aged, insane and orphans were to be put into specialized institutions; those who were physically able should be given work whenever possible and aid in kind when it was not; the professional beggar had to be locked up and taught the virtues of labor. All this supposed a well–organized poor relief system. The organizational role was allotted to the state but no–one proposed that poor relief be a state monopoly. Private efforts were complementary to and, in the eyes of most commentators, superior to state action because they were more flexible and provided moral assistance as well as material relief, thereby contributing to the preservation of social order.

The emphasis on private charity did not imply a reliance on the isolated acts of individuals. For private charity to be effective it had to be channelled through voluntary associations. Such voluntary organizations were seen as a powerful social force. The case for these associations was put best by the charter of the Oviedo Charity Association, which was founded in 1904. Association was 'the only cure for all the problems of our time' and a way to 'do away with begging in the streets, that affront to the progress of a nation'. Only by creating charity associations would 'the conscience of the wealthy be able to rest easy'. Associations were, in sum, 'charity properly understood'.[63]

The reasons for dealing with the poor were now secular rather than religious in inspiration and lay people and the state were both claiming a more prominent role in poor relief than had been the case in the past. Yet this did not mean that the Church had been pushed out of the field. Quite the contrary, for religious personnel remained absolutely essential to the functioning of the poor relief network. Some female orders had been spared the disentailment of 1837 because the government knew their welfare role was essential. Many of the new female orders which were created in the second half of the nineteenth century engaged in charitable and educational work. Frances Lannon has suggested that the influx of women into such orders was one response to the limited opportunities for women in Spanish society, that the orders 'despite their discipline and sexual and social restrictions, could, paradoxically, offer liberating scope'.[64] In 1909 nuns were running more than 1,000 beneficent institutions and a few years later 90 per cent of the people who worked in the 546 municipal and provincial welfare establishments were religious.

Philanthropy was the only important public activity in which respectable Spanish women could legitimately take part since it was considered merely an extension of their nature. (There were some, very few, organizations of other types, such as the animal protection societies, which accepted women as equal members and even allowed them to serve as officers. Could it be that middle and upper class Spanish women were allowed a somewhat broader public role than their American and British counterparts?) Women were seen as better suited than men to charity work because they had moral qualities men lacked. They were often likened to the clergy in this regard. For one author 'the priest and women are the natural ministers of charity' because only religion could inspire in men the sentiments which were innate in women.[65] Concepción Arenal reversed this comparison, calling on the state to encourage the clergy to become more active in welfare work. Women did not need any encouragement, they only needed the opportunity.[66]

Women, and especially members of the nobility, did take an active interest in philanthropy. Some helped run charitable institutions, such as the Madrid Foundling Hospital, but most of their efforts went into charitable associations. There were even associations, such as the Royal Association for Home Relief, which were run entirely by women. Founded in 1845 by the Queen Mother, it was composed of 'the most distinguished ladies who are known for their piety and philanthropy'. Its officers, including the sixteen parish presidents, were all women.[67]

The state recognized, and even encouraged, these activities. When the Cruz de la Beneficencia, a civil decoration for philanthropy, was created in 1856 both men and women were eligible. In June 1875 the Minister of the Interior created a Women's Junta 'to assist the government in welfare matters', attempting to co-ordinate the activities of women's charity associations across the country, encouraging the creation of new ones, inspecting charitable associations and institutions and looking after the Foundling Hospital.

Behind most of this concern for the poor was the larger, and much more threatening, 'social question'. From the middle of the nineteenth century people who discussed the poor drew a thin line, at best, between them and the workers and more often than not they conflated the two groups. As early as 1850 Manuel Balbín de Unquera described the beggar as a morally degraded being, in contrast to the pauper, who was not. Paupers came from all social classes but beggars came only from the proletariat. He shared, along with Concepción Arenal and others, a view of the city and industry as poisonous for morality and social discipline, both of which flourished in the countryside.[68]

For Arenal, as for most people who wrote on the subject, philanthropy was to serve as a cure for social conflict. The problem was much more one of morality than economics and, in her view, even when workers earned enough money they remained 'a disruptive social element'. By 1880, when she wrote *Cartas a un señor* (Letters to a Gentleman), and by which time the organized labor movement had made its appearance, her tone took on a new urgency. The hour was late, but it was not yet too late to act. With a little moral leadership the ruling classes could save themselves from the coming storm, since the poor would tread the right road 'if only somebody would show it to them'. If this moral leadership did not appear, however, 'the threatening storm' could not be avoided: 'Poor Spaniards do not, in general, hate the gentlemen (*señores*), but they will come to hate them if the gentlemen do not make themselves loved. And after the day of hate will come the day of anger.'[69] Just over fifty years later, in the revolution within the Spanish Civil War, the 'day of anger' arrived.

2
The Land

The watchwords of nineteenth-century liberalism were freedom and liberty. These applied first of all to people – or at least to men – but not to them alone. Property, particularly landed property, also had to be freed from the constraints of the Old Regime. One of the tasks of the liberal revolution was the creation of private property. As it affected the land this protracted liberal revolution had three main points: the abolition of entail, the disentailment of all land held in mortmain and the abolition of the seigneuries. This was achieved by 1840 and for virtually a century the reign of private property was questioned only by those who wanted more. Only under the Second Republic would those in power try to mount a challenge to private property.

The Creation of Private Property

The cornerstone of wealth in Old Regime Spain was the land and this was dominated by three groups: the nobility, the Church and the municipalities. Between them, the first two may have owned as much as 60 per cent of the country's productive land. The landholdings of all the groups were privileged in that they could never be lost or sold, that is, they were entailed. In addition, the Church and nobility had also been granted judicial and administrative authority over the lands they owned and, in the seventeenth century, over areas of the country which they did not own. In these jurisdictional seigneuries the lord had the right to control local government, run the courts of first instance, receive payment of a number of dues and exercise a number of monopolies. In the País Valenciano (Valencia, Alicante and Castellón), where the feudal regime was most comprehensive, these included control of pastures, wood and water, collection of taxes on products entering cities, monopolies on such things as shops, bakeries, inns, mills and butchers and the right to keep one-third of the tithe.

This delegation of jurisdiction was very widespread by the end of the Old Regime. In 1811 only about a third of the country and half its population were under direct royal jurisdiction, although the Crown did control 126 of the 148 largest towns and cities. About half the country was under the jurisdiction of the nobility and a sixth under ecclesiastical jurisdiction. The extent of this authority varied from region to region. In some the Crown barely existed: it held jurisdiction over only 6 per cent of Galicia, less than 1 per cent of La Mancha, 14 per cent of Valencia, 17 per cent of Extremadura and Asturias and León and 10 per cent of Valladolid. It had a larger, but still minority, presence in Catalonia (28 per cent), Córdoba (23 per cent) and Seville (27 per cent).

The conversion of privileged property into private property is known as *desamortización*, disentailment. This was a long, complex and intermittent process which began during the reign of Charles III and only concluded a century later. The first, hesitant measures were taken between 1766 and 1770 as an attempt to help the landless in the south and extend cultivation. When disentailment was revived in the 1790s it was in response to pressing circumstances: the soaring government indebtedness created by Spain's participation in the wars triggered by the French Revolution. All future disentailment would be conditioned by this partnership of war and debt.

Until 1837 disentailment was directed principally at Church lands. Between 1798 and 1808 Charles IV's chief mininster, Manuel de Godoy, used disentailment as a means of staving off financial collapse and during the Napoleonic invasion both King Joseph Bonaparte and the Cortes of Cádiz used disentailment for the same purpose. The Cortes of Cádiz's disentailment laws were revived during the three-year liberal regime of 1820 to 1823 but definitive disentailment had to wait another fourteen years, for the victory of liberalism over absolutism in the First Carlist War (1833–40). Once again war exacerbated the financial distress of the government and once again the government turned to selling entailed land as a solution. However, the disentailments of 1834–7 focused solely on the lands of the Church and ignored those of the municipalities which, for the time being, were spared.

The disentailments of the 1830s bear the name of the great politician and financier Juan Alvarez Mendizábal. His two disentailment laws, February 19, 1836 and July 29, 1837, abolished the tithe and expropriated the property of the secular as well as the regular clergy. All properties were to be sold at public auction with payment in either cash or government debt. The law had little immediate effect, but it was applied in 1841 during the regency of General Espartero and sales continued until the accession of the moderates to power in 1844. Anxious to restore good relations with the Vatican the moderates returned to the secular clergy all the property which had not been sold and in the Concordat of 1851 committed Spanish governments to respecting ecclesiastical property in the future.

The disentailment of the Church lands diverted attention from the question of municipal lands. Even when the state had concerned itself with this issue it had never expropriated these lands, only encouraged local governments to lease them out. This changed on May 1, 1855 with Pascual Madoz's Law of General Disentailment. All land belonging to the state, the Church, charitable institutions and municipalities was to be sold at public auction. Only cash payments were accepted and the funds raised were to be used to reduce the debt and finance public works. Institutions which lost property were to be reimbursed with annual payments of 3 per cent of their value. The Madoz Law brought to an end the legislative activity surrounding disentailment of lands held in mortmain although the actual sale of land continued until the end of the nineteenth century.

The second aspect of the liberal revolution on the land was the abolition of entail. Such legislation was passed by both the Cortes of Cádiz and the liberal government of 1820 but without any lasting effect. Entail was abolished forever in 1836. This was a change in property law, as the special legal status of noble property was abolished, but not a change in the ownership of the previously entailed lands, which remained in the hands of their noble owners; although it did allow those with economic problems a chance of resolving them by selling land that had been inalienable.

The third, and most controversial, aspect of the liberal revolution was the abolition of the seigneurial regime and the restoration of all jurisdiction to the state. The importance of this development lay less in the actual loss of authority and income for the nobility – indeed one can argue that economically the nobility benefited from the way in which the abolition was carried out – than in the way the question of land ownership in the jurisdictional seigneuries was handled.

The original legislation, passed by the Cortes of Cádiz in 1811, gave rise to conflicting interpretations. The first interpretation was that 'only those *señoríos* which did not have jurisdictional rights would become private property; the rest, the vast majority, would be totally abolished, leaving their former owners with only the prescribed indemnity'.[1] This broad interpretation was adopted by towns which were concerned to throw off seigneurial authority. This was particularly the case in Valencia, where the seigneurial regime was most extensive.

This broad interpretation of the 1811 law was not accepted by the courts in Valencia or elsewhere, which upheld the territorial rights of the nobility. The real purpose of the law of 1811 was in line with this narrow interpretation. As Martínez de la Rosa stated in parliament in the 1820s, the purpose of the law was 'to totally uproot feudalism without causing the least damage to the trunk of property'.[2]

Again, the legislation of the Cortes of Cádiz was revived in the 1820s but the definitive abolition of the seigneuries came only in August 1837. The basic principle of the new law was to preserve property rights while eliminating all rights that did not spring from the ownership of property. All seigneuries without jurisdiction automatically became private property while the owners of those with jurisdiction were given two months to present their title to the land.

By 1840, then, the liberal revolution was more or less complete. The Old Regime had been dismantled and a new framework of property relations had been established. How did these changes affect the actual ownership of land? Did much land change hands? Who acquired land and who lost it? Did social relations in the countryside change? How did the peasantry and the rural poor fare in the new society?

Landowners

A New Agrarian Elite

Between 1836 and 1895 some 615,000 properties covering about 10 million hectares, between a quarter and a third of the total national land surface, changed hands. However, despite their massive scale, these land sales did not substantially alter the structure of land ownership nor the shape of the agrarian sector. In effect a deal was struck: the nobility did not oppose the institution of liberalism and agreed to accept the loss of its jurisdictional rights in return for the recognition of its property rights and the conversion of its important feudal dues into Treasury obligations. In addition the nobility would continue to play a political role, especially in the upper house of parliament, and a prominent social role.

The liberal revolution did not lead to significant changes in the structure of landholding but it radically changed the nature of ownership and caused vast amounts of land to change hands. The result was the creation of a new agrarian elite which brought together the many members of the Old Regime nobility who survived with their landholdings intact, and in some cases augmented, and men who took advantage of the disentailments to become landowners on a large scale. This agrarian elite was new, then, in that it was an amalgam – and eventually a fusion – of traditional and newly minted landowners and that both owned their property absolutely.

As a landowning elite the nobility came through the liberal revolution in good shape. They lost their jurisdictional rights and the income derived from them but were reimbursed for a number of feudal dues which were treated as property and therefore subject to compensation from the state. In most parts of the country, they retained their lands intact and in some cases were even able to expand their holdings. As late as 1933, when the Agrarian Reform Institute of the Second Republic was putting together its inventory of lands liable to expropriation, the nobility was still a key presence. In the six provinces studied by Edward Malefakis (Badajoz, Cáceres, Cádiz, Córdoba, Seville and Toledo), the nobility owned over half a million hectares, about 8 per cent of all cultivated land. He estimates that its holdings nationally represented about 6 per cent of all cultivated land. The largest holdings belonged to the older noble titles. The most important noble landowner was the Duke of Medinaceli, with 79,147 hectares. He was followed by the Duke of Peñaranda (51,016 hectares), the Duke of Villahermosa (47,204 hectares) and the Duke of Alba (34,455 hectares).[1]

The liberal revolution was kind to the nobility in another way as well. They were allowed to retain a number of seigneurial dues, which liberal legislatures recognized as property. Between 1836 and 1851 the nobility was reimbursed for its rights to the *alcabala* − a sales tax − the tithe and its ownership of royal annuities. The generosity of the settlement was magnified by the decline in noble income from feudal and jurisdictional dues in the first three decades of the nineteenth century, as legal challenges from towns and the middle class and resistance from the peasantry had brought the economic basis of the nobility into question.

The desperation of the Treasury meant that the *alcabala*, which had been the most important feudal due, was retained after the abolition of the seigneuries, and with it the collection by the nobility of its share. In his reform of the Treasury in 1845 Mon y Santillán abolished this tax and provided for the owners of the rights to it to be reimbursed by the state. The Duke of Alba, for one, received as much in Segovia from this source as from land rents.

The *juros*, the value of which had already been called into question in the eighteenth century, were recognized by law in December 1836, although they were still considered 'difficult to collect' and in 1840 the Duke of Alba did not assign his, some of which were 400 years old, any value. A law of August 1, 1851 ended the doubt, converting them into first-class amortizable debt and thereafter the *juros* represented an important part of the finances of many noble houses. The Marquis of Falces had 3.9 million reales from this source, the Duke of Frías 8.2 million and the Duke of Alba 7.4 million.

Finally, the nobility was reimbursed for its share of the tithe, which was abolished in 1841. These payments were crucial for some nobles: in 1859 they represented 2.1 of the 2.9 million reales liquid capital of the Duke of Gor, produced 6.3 million reales for the Duke of Abrantes and, along with the *juros*, accounted for all of his liquid capital. In 1870 the Duke of Alba listed 22.9 million reales in government bonds at 3 per cent as compensation for his share of the tithes.

There is no doubt that the way the liberal revolution dealt with the question of these feudal holdovers, treating them as property, contributed in a very real way to the survival and even economic vigor of the nobility in the rest of the nineteenth century. Many important noble houses were on the economic ropes by the 1830s. Even the powerful house of Alba was in trouble: its inventory for 1835–40 showed 23.4 million reales of expenses against only 11.6 million in income. By 1870, however, the situation was radically different, as the house had a patrimony of 100 million reales after expenses. The maintenance of the nobility was a major obligation of the Spanish Treasury even in the second half of the century. Moreover, the fact that the granting of compensation coincided with the sale of lands following from the Madoz disentailment allowed the nobility to reinforce its position as a landed elite.

Not all members of the nobility were able to adapt to the new circumstances and some soon found that their landholdings were reduced or lost altogether. This was especially the case for those nobles who held land in Valencia and

Alicante which was under emphyteutic leases. Most were unable to turn their seigneuries into private property and the leases generally wound up being redeemed by the tenants who thus became landowners.[2] Even property which had been recognized by the courts as fully private was far from secure: in 1873 the widow of the Count of Casal sold all her land in the *huerta* and between 1870 and 1872 the Duchess of Almodóvar sold her lands there to her former steward.

Elsewhere the position of the nobility declined, though not as dramatically as in Valencia. In Pilas, in the Aljarife region of Seville, the nobility actually increased the percentage of the land they owned between 1760 and 1860, from 33 to 43 per cent, only to have it decline to 23 per cent by 1925. Some individual noble families fared very badly. The Marquis of Motilla, who was the largest landowner in the town in 1760 had lost more than half of it by 1904 and the Marquisses of Dos Hermanas and of Castellón had disappeared from the roll of property owners by 1854. Even in Carmona (Seville), where the nobility as a group greatly strengthened its grasp on the land in the first half of the nineteenth century, there were some families who lost out. The Count of Fuente del Sauco was the seventh most important landowner in 1755, but a century later he did not even appear on the list of landowners. The Marquis of Astorga and the Count-Duke of Benavente had also lost all their substantial holdings in the municipality by 1850.

Not even all the traditional great noble houses were able to retain their position. The Dukes of Medinasidonia, owners of 'the strongest Andalucian seigneurie', are a striking example. The destruction of their landed wealth took place across the entire nineteenth century and by the time the holdings of the grandees were inventoried in 1933 for the agrarian reform of the Second Republic they had only 464 hectares of land in the six southern provinces of Badajoz, Cáceres, Cádiz, Córdoba, Seville and Toledo, and under 1,000 hectares in the whole country. This collapse was due to a combination of heavy spending and lack of interest in their lands, although this was exacerbated by the Duke's support for Carlism – a rarity among the aristocracy – which led to the sequestration of some property by the liberal state. The Dukes began to sell lands in 1858 and the sales became massive in 1869, culminating with the sale of the 15,000-hectare Coto Donana in 1900.[3]

But the greatest failure was surely that of the Dukes of Osuna, four times grandees of Spain and one of the most prestigious noble houses in the country. The Osunas, and their property, survived the liberal revolution in fine shape: in 1855 the Duke was the leading taxpayer in the country, paying taxes in twenty different provinces, and twenty years later he was second, behind the Duke of Medinaceli, but paid taxes in only seven provinces. (The twelfth Duke supported the liberals during the Carlist War and even served as aide-de-camp to Baldomero Espartero, a soldier of plebeian origin who had risen through the ranks during the Napoleonic and American wars to become a general and Commander in Chief of the liberal armies. This relationship, although brief, nicely illustrates the combination of continuity and change in nineteenth-century Spain.)

The liberal revolution did no direct harm to the Dukedom's finances but it did remove the guarantees, especially entail, which had permitted the nobility to survive incompetent financial management in the past. The Dukes of Osuna proved unable to adapt to the new conditions; by the end of the nineteenth century all their lands had been taken to pay off debts. Their fate was the result of 'bad management of the patrimony . . . the conclusion of a situation which had been chronic since the seventeenth century'. In the seventeenth and eighteenth centuries their properties were constantly protected by the Crown and in the eighteenth they were accused of illicitly selling entailed lands. By the 1750s 'the situation was unbearable. The annual accounts generally closed with such large deficits that they could not even pay the interest due on the bonds'.[4]

The Duke of Osuna began to sell off properties shortly after the abolition of entail in 1841 but he was unable to get out of debt. In 1861 he reorganized his fiscal administration but to little effect. The next year his accounts showed a deficit of 4.8 million reales against a total income of 12.6 million. They had some other interesting features: administration costs ate up 62 per cent of the Duke's income, of which 70 per cent came from rent on land and *nothing* from industrial or commercial investments.

This situation provoked a new loan, for 90 million reales, from a consortium headed by the prominent financier Estanislao de Urquijo and including 'the cream of the class of "merchant capitalists" which played so active a role in Madrid financial circles in the nineteenth century'. Further loans were made but now the urban properties, which had been exempted in 1863, were mortgaged. In 1869 the creditors allowed the Duke to sell lands, but only on condition that 90 per cent of the money realized was used to pay debts and the rest to pay interest. A number of these creditors also served as the Duke's agents, which left them in a perfect position to make some very good deals, buying lands for which they said there had been no bidders. One of them, Fernando Fernández Casariego, acquired over 9,000 hectares of land in Benavente in this way. By 1877, 47 sales, 'some of them worth millions', had taken place and the sales continued until 1881 when the Banco de Castilla agreed to issue 43 million pesetas worth of bonds at 5 per cent interest backed by the Duke's properties. Three years later the bank suspended payment of the interest and this began a series of lawsuits which lasted ten years and ended, in 1894, with the sequestration of all the remaining lands of the house of Osuna. According to Atienza Hernández, this land wound up either in the hands of speculators or, more frequently, in the hands of 'substantial farmers, many of whom had been tenants of the House, who added ownership to exploitation and came to reinforce the figure of the capitalist farmer'.[5]

Indebtedness was common among the nobility in the first three-quarters of the century. In his study of the private loans handled by one Madrid notary, José Alejandro Martínez found that noblemen borrowed 39 million of the

150 million reales loaned. They also had great difficulty in repaying what they owed: only 16 of 56 paid fully and on time. There were numerous examples of debts passed from one generation to another: the Counts of del Real, the Counts of Altamira and the Marquisses of Alcañíces, for example, and in some cases 'accumulated debts and the interest multiplied to reach fabulous amounts'.[6] Another sign of economic difficulties was the sale of palaces in Madrid to help pay off debts. There were at least 37 such sales, among them the palaces of the Count of Poltentinos, the Marquis of Alcañíces, the Duke of Hijar, the Marquis of Santa Cruz and the Duke of Medinasidonia. Fernández Casariego, who purchased so much of the Duke of Osuna's land, also acquired the palace of the Count of Saceda in Madrid. The lesser nobility frequently returned to provincial palaces and kept rented accommodation in Madrid. The rest sought new homes in the capital which were at once prestigious and more economical and found them in the new Salamanca district.[7]

Some nobles adapted very well to the new situation. Between 1840 and 1873 the house of Medinaceli was able to greatly reduce its vast debt, 126 million reales, by selling off almost a third of its property and the bonds received to compensate for the loss of tithes. At the same time, the Dukes were able to make some new purchases and invest heavily in improvements to their existing estates. The Dukes of Alba followed a similar pattern. In general, though, the old aristocracy had rather restricted economic interests. They did not often invest in stocks or bonds, and the larger the fortune the less important were these types of investment. Nor did they show much interest in urban property, at least in Madrid. By the beginning of the twentieth century this had changed as the nobility invested more actively in industrial and service enterprises. Forty-four of the 120 nobles who participated in the investment activities of Alfonso XIII had old titles, although they were a little slower to do so than the more recently-minted nobles, and for the most part did not get involved until the 1920s. These investments favoured innovative industrial and financial ventures over traditional and safe ones such as real estate. The stock portfolio of the Marquis of Argueso, whose title dated from 1475, included shares in railroads, sugar refineries, cork production, explosives and that eminently vanguard industry of the early twentieth century, electricity. Guillermo Cortázar concludes that the aristocracy not only 'adapted to the liberal economy but in large measure led private initiative and therefore the economic modernization' during the reign of Alfonso XIII.[8]

The new situation provided both opportunities and challenges for the nobility. On the one hand they enjoyed a new liquidity which, as in the case of the Dukes of Alba, could be used to rebuild economic solidity. On the other, the safety net of privilege had been withdrawn so that those who could not pay their bills would have to put their property on the line. The situation of the Duke of Osuna resembles that of the Aragonese nobleman described by Ramón de Mesonero y Romanos in one of the most famous of his *Escenas Matritenses*, 'Grandeza y Miseria', written in 1832. Shortly after the death of his father the young Marquis moved to Madrid, 'where his desires had been leading him for many years' but he soon found himself in deep financial trouble and in debt to his own employees:

> that steward who lends me the products of my own lands at enormous interest
> . . . those greedy administrators who make the poor farmers curse my name
> which is invoked to exploit them without pity . . . also force me to negotiate
> with them if I am to collect what they owe me.

The result was that he had already sold the lands which were not entailed and 'heavily mortgaged' those which were. This situation provided the author with a fine opportunity for some bourgeois moralizing, as he tells his young friend to return to his estates and live moderately, but the situation was real enough.[9]

The nobility survived the liberal revolution in economic terms, albeit with some casualties. Revitalized by new additions throughout the nineteenth century, it retained its social prestige and continued to play an important, if secondary, political role. These new additions came from various other elites, military, political and economic.

The Isabelline nobility drew heavily from the military, a reflection of its central political role during her reign. The queen ennobled 31 military men, among them the leading political figures of the period: Ramón María Narváez (Duke of Valencia), Espartero (Count of Luchana and Duke of Victory), Leopolodo O'Donnell (Duke of Tetuan), Juan Prim (Count of Reus) and Manuel Concha (Marquis of the Duero). Given their frequent military provenance, it is not surprising that by 1850 all the captains-general and almost 40 per cent of lieutenant generals were nobles. The world of business also produced a number of nobles during this period. Among the most famous were the financier and stock promoter José de Salamanca and the financier Estanislao de Urquijo, who played a central role in the dissolution of the House of Osuna. These new nobles were prominent in the Senate. Between 1845 and 1868, 272 of 637 senators were nobles. Of the 272 noble senators 76 had titles created since 1833, compared to 19 from earlier in the century, 85 from the eighteenth century, 57 from the seventeenth, 18 from the sixteenth, 9 from the fifteenth and one each from the fourteenth and thirteenth.

The real expansion of the nobility came during the Restoration (1875–1931) when 200 titles, including 20 Dukes and 30 grandees, were created and 300 were rehabilitated. The number of titles created in Spain was similar to the number created in Great Britain: between 1886 and 1914, 246 people entered the House of Lords; during the same period 210 Spaniards were ennobled. By 1930 there were some 1,900 titled people in the country.

The new Restoration nobles also came from the worlds of politics, business and the military, but the first two were relatively much more important and the last much less than during the reign of Isabella II. The decline of the military as a breeding ground for nobles reflects the success of Cánovas del Castillo in establishing a peaceful alternation in power of the two main political parties and consequently reduced the role of officers in effecting political change. Those generals who received titles did so for their services in wars, not politics; for example, Fernando Primo de Rivera in the Carlist War and Gómez Jordana, José Sanjurjo and Damaso Berenguer in the Moroccan war.

A number of leading industrialists and financiers received titles during the Restoration. Many were *indianos*, men who had made their fortunes in the colonies. In 1878 Antonio López y López, the founder of a large and varied industrial empire, was made Marquis of Comillas, and three years later he was made a grandee of Spain. Comillas was also a major landowner. His 23,720 hectares of arable land put him sixth on the list of noble landowners in 1932. Another group came from the industrialists and financiers of the Basque Country, among them Eduardo de Aznar y de la Sota, Evaristo de Churruca, Benigno Chávarri, Victor Chávarri and Luís de Urquijo. Among the Catalan business elite to receive titles were José de Caralt and three members of the Guell family.

Many Restoration political figures also received titles. This had happened under Isabella II, but then these politicians were also usually military men. After 1875 the political and military functions were largely separated and the newly ennobled politicians were civilians. The widows of a number of political figures, among them three Prime Ministers who had been assassinated, Cánovas, José Canalejas and Eduardo Dato, were also ennobled.

There was a convergence between the old and new nobilities. Manuel Tuñón de Lara has pointed to marriage as one mechanism. 'Generally the ties take place between newly minted nobility and bourgeoisie, or between politicians and the upper bourgeoisie. Ties with the old nobility are more common in the second generation.'[10] While he gives a number of examples of the first type of marriage, for example between the Marquis of Comillas and the Guell family, he does not give any examples of the second. He does provide evidence of another form of convergence, as leading members of the old nobility participated in other types of business activities with their newer colleagues. In the 1920s the Duke of Infantado, owner of 17,000 hectares of land, sat on the boards of two banks and was president of Ferrocarriles Andaluces. Along with his 34,000 hectares the Duke of Alba also sat on the board of the Bank of Spain and Compañía Hispana-Alemana de Electricidad (CHADE), the international hydroelectric conglomerate which also enjoyed the services of the leading political representative of the Catalan bourgeoisie, Francisco Cambó.

The formation of the new nobility and its fusion with the old is well illustrated in the saga of the Figueroa family.[11] Luís Figueroa, born in 1781, was the sixth child of a modest hidalgo family from Extremadura. At seventeen he entered the gards de corp in Madrid but during the Napoleonic occupation he supported the French regime and fled to France when it fell in

1814. He went to Marseilles, where a relative had a shipping business, and quickly became one of the most important businessmen in the city. In 1844 he was named Gentilhombre de la Cámara by Isabella II. His son, Ignacio, was born in 1808 and educated in Paris. He took over his father's business interests in Spain in 1833 and took up residence in Madrid in 1845 where his father's influence allowed him to move in court circles. In 1852 Ignacio Figueroa married Ana de Torres, Viscountess of Irueste.

His new wife brought a title, but little else. The Torres family had been ennobled during the War of the Spanish Succession by the Habsburg pretender to the throne and the title was later affirmed by Philip V. The Torres had limited economic means. By the beginning of the nineteenth century they were unable to pay the annual tax on their title and in 1813 they got royal permission to sell part of their entailed estates. This was not enough: in 1835 their back taxes amounted to 60,000 reales, compared to a total annual income of 15,000. José de Torres was planning to renounce his title in 1832, but changed his mind when his daughter Ana was born, so that he could leave her something of value. His widow later renounced the title Marquis of Villamejor but kept that of Viscount of Irueste for her daughter.

The marriage between Ignacio Figueroa and Ana de Torres brought together an immense bourgeois fortune and a penniless aristocrat, providing social cachet for the former and wealth for the latter. (The process is similar to that of English aristocrats who would find financial salvation at the hands of American heiresses.) It is also clear who had the upper hand. As Cortázar says, 'this is not the supposed co-optation, the incorporation by an aristocrat of a bourgeois'. Shortly after the marriage Ana de Torres successfully petitioned the queen to restore the title Marquis of Villamejor. Ignacio Figueroa was not much interested in politics but he realized that political connections were good for business and got himself elected to the Cortes in 1864, 1872 and 1876. He was a life senator from 1866 until his death in 1899.

The saga of the Figueroa culminated with the children of Ignacio and Ana. The eldest daughter married the Count of Almodóvar, a grandee of Spain, and the eldest son married a Loring, from the ennobled family of Málaga industrialists. The second son, a businessman, acquired the titles of Count of Majorada and Duke of las Torres, while the fourth was also ennobled and even became a grandee. But the most important of all was the third son, Alvaro, Count of Romanones, one of the most significant political figures of the early twentieth century, who became a minister in 1902 and prime minister in 1912.

For the most part, the nobility did not wield formal political power. The nobility had much more political clout in Britain than it did in Spain. Throughout the liberal period men who were both important political figures and nobles came to their titles by way of their political careers and not the other way around. As Becarud has noted:

> No political noble played a role comparable to that of . . . Lord Rosebery in Great Britain . . . We do not even find in Spain a person who played as

important a role as the Duke Albert de Broglie in the early days of the Third Republic in France. Apart from Romanones, Spanish nobles, and especially those with the longest pedigree . . . were, between 1875 and 1931, people who were more decorative than influential.[12]

Much the same could be said of the reign of Isabella II, although there were some exceptions, such as the Duke of Rivas and the Marquis of Miraflores.

What formal political strength the nobility did retain lay in the Senate. In the Isabelline period just over 40 per cent of all senators were nobles. Even so, there was never a hereditary Senate analogous to the House of Lords and two attempts to create one failed. Nobles were also prominent in each of the three categories of the Restoration Senate: grandees with a certain level of income 'in their own right', royal nominees, and through election. Late in the Restoration, in 1916, over a third of all senators (125 of 360) bore titles.

The noble presence was much smaller in the more important lower chamber. The percentage of titled deputies dropped from 14 per cent in 1877 to 10 per cent in 1920. Within the noble caucus the Old Regime titles were generally in a minority, although they did account for over half in 1899 and 1907. The nobility was even less frequently found in positions of political power. Only one of the 41 Prime Ministers in the years 1875–1923 was a noble. (Primo de Rivera, the dictator who ruled from 1923 to 1930, also had a title, Marquis of Estella, but the title had been awarded to his father for his role in the Carlist War and Primo's own influence came from his being a serving general.) Similarly, only one Minister of Finance had a title.

However, nobles were more common in some other portfolios: 10 served as Minister of Justice, 12 as Minister of Development and 13 as Minister of Foreign Affairs. They were also noticeable in some key administrative positions such as civil governor, 81 of 1,049 during the Restoration, and especially the diplomatic corps, where they filled some 30 per cent of ambassadorial posts. Surprisingly, they were scarce in the upper ranks of the army, especially in the infantry. By the time of the First World War not one of the 70 infantry regiments had a colonel with a title. By the late nineteenth century the Spanish officer corps had become the province of men of much humbler origin than was the case in France, Germany or Great Britain.[13]

Despite its lack of formal power the nobility was not powerless. It was able to retain its social prestige and influence, especially through the royal Court. During the regency of Espartero (1840–3) the nobility had withdrawn from the Court. Despite his achievements and his stature as a national hero the Regent lacked social grace and was not much to the nobility's liking. María Cristina, the Queen Mother who had been serving as regent since 1833 and who fled the country following a coup led by Espartero, is said to have told him that she had made him a duke but not a gentleman. It was a feeling apparently shared by many.

Court life and aristocratic predominance returned when Espartero fell. In his memoirs Fernando Fernández de Córdova, himself a leading political general on the moderate side, describes in some detail the social life of the capital which accompanied the dominance of the moderates after 1844. It was stimulated by 'the animation of the Court, which was the source of every impulse . . . Her Majesty began to receive in the Palace, inviting the flower of the nobility'.[14] The palaces of the Marquis of Miraflores and the Countess of Montijo, the mother of the future empress of France, were particular centers of social life. The Queen's wedding was celebrated with, among other things, a number of spectacular bullfights in the Plaza Mayor of Madrid sponsored by the Duke of Frías, the Duke of Abrantes, the Duke of Medinaceli and, now well on the way to ruin, the Duke of Osuna. The Queen's retinue was the province of the aristocracy:

> The leading senators and ladies filled the highest posts so that whatever time one went to the Palace one found a brilliant crowd. The Count of Santa Coloma and the Marquis of Malpica were *mayordomos mayores* at that time and the *sumiller* of the Guardia de Corps was the old and illustrious Duke of Hijar, who had held that position for thirty years without interruption . . . The Marquise of Santa Cruz . . . the Duchess of San Carlos, the Countess of Montijo and the Duchess of Gor were successively chief ladies in waiting from 1843 to 1854 . . . The Queen's ladies, who constantly shone at Court, included the Duchess of Villahermosa . . . the Marquise of Alcanices, the Marquise of Villadarias, who was the sister of the Duke of Medinaceli . . . and the noble Duchess of Berwick and Alba.[15]

Predominance at the Court gave political influence as well as social prestige for, as José María Jover tells us, 'in those "inner rooms" peopled with gentlemen and ladies was a seventeen-year-old queen who had two constitutional prerogatives which were central to her power: the right to name and dismiss ministers and the right to give a ministry a dissolution of parliament'.[16] Isabella II relied heavily on the court nobility for political advice throughout her reign and the influence of the *camarillas*, cliques, contributed to her growing unpopularity and to the alienation of important political forces in the 1860s and ultimately to her losing the throne. The nobility retained its social influence and its proximity to the Crown in the Restoration, but in the twentieth century the aristocratic salon gave way to a more open elite social life centered on institutions like the Palace Hotel. Even so, Alfonso XIII relied on his court nobility, but in his case they were frequently military men.

The New Landowners

The nobility remained an important part of the landowning elite in liberal Spain but it alone did not make up that elite. The nobles were joined by a new group of large landowners who emerged from the disentailment process and which by the early part of the twentieth century had surpassed them and come to form a distinctive agrarian elite. Even in the south, the bastion of both the nobility and the large estate, people without title came to own the bulk of the land and through marriage strategies control large areas. Both at the local level and across entire provinces there were what Malefakis calls 'interlocking family directorates' which dominated economic affairs. Among individual municipalities he cites Caanaveral (Cáceres), a town of 2,792 people where 'two sets of cousins owned at least 80 per cent of the . . . 5,548 hectares'. And after analyzing the situation in Badajoz he found that 'some 400 individuals organized into roughly one third as many sibling groups, most of which were in turn linked together into a handful of extended families' owned over half a million hectares, a quarter of the total area of the province.[17] In a province whose economy was overwhelmingly agrarian, this represented a remarkable concentration of power.

We can also see this development through the prism of a single family. Ignacio Vázquez, whom we will meet later at greater length, emerged from the disentailments as the largest non-noble landowner in Seville. Four of his five children who married found their spouse from the fifty leading agricultural families of the province. (The other one married the son of a prominent merchant from Cádiz who lived in Havana.) But these families had other strings to their economic bows. The fathers-in-law included a lawyer, a merchant, a deputy and a senator. This pattern of intermarriage continued in later generations:

> The eldest daughter of Ignacio Vázquez's eldest son married the eldest son of the Osborne [one of the leaders in the sherry industry] family in 1889 while the youngest daughter married the youngest son in 1895 . . . Two of Vázquez's grandsons married two sisters from the Torres Toreno family, who were landowners in Marchena in 1896 . . . [and] two daughters of Ignacio Vázquez's third son, Manuel, married two Benjumena brothers . . . All these alliances consolidated an extraordinary class endogamy while at the same time they added to the diversification of the initial economic base of the family.[18]

In addition, these families had high rates of celibacy which Heran attributes to a limited marriage market.

Who made up this new elite, this agrarian bourgeoisie? By origin they were a diverse lot. They came from both the cities and the countryside and from occupational backgrounds which would have provided them with the resources to acquire large amounts of land in the disentailment auctions: large landowners and tenants, financiers, merchants, professionals and officials. These 'privileged ones', to use Germán Rueda's word for the people who benefited most from the disentailments, were 'an internally heterogeneous "bloc" which only becomes a coherent group in contrast to the lower classes. The middle and upper classes are not "a" social class but an amalgam of classes'.[19] In the latifundia provinces they were mainly urban; elsewhere they were mainly rural people with direct ties to the land, especially the wealthier landowners and tenants.

Many of the largest holdings, and ones which have most frequently caught the eye of observers, both at the time and subsequently, were acquired by members of the financial and political elites based in Madrid. The elites of the capital were probably the biggest winners of all. In Valladolid they ended up with a sixth of the property sold whereas previously they had owned none. And Valladolid was not an exception. Most of the large purchases in the province of Madrid were made by residents of the capital, merchants, landowners and professionals for the most part, and many of the largest properties in Granada, Toledo and Guadalajara also wound up in the hands of people from Madrid. In Cáceres 73 people, 'among whom those from Madrid stood out for their importance', bought two-thirds of all the land sold.[20] Fifteen of the 25 people who spent more than 100,000 reales in Soria were from Madrid. Only 21 people from Madrid bought property in Logroño but they bought the largest properties and made a quarter of all investments in property in the province.

Among the leading financiers was José Safont Lluch, who bought land in Gerona, where he was the single largest buyer, as well as in ten other provinces: Barcelona, Tarragona, Lérida, Mallorca, Avila, Ciudad Real, Seville, Toledo, Valladolid and Madrid. Safont's father had made his fortune supplying the army and Safont himself was involved in a wide range of activities including running the stamped paper monopoly, founding two important banks, promoting railroads and serving as an agent for Manuel de Godoy, who had been the favorite of Charles IV. Politically he was a progressive, a supporter and close friend of Mendizábal. The most important purchase of lands sold by the aristocracy in Seville was made by the Count of Buena Esperanza, the son of a financier who had been ennobled for arranging an important government loan in 1836. In the early 1850s he spent five million reales in cash to buy 7,200 hectares from the financially strapped Duke of Alcalá.

Among the leading political figures who became property owners through the disentailments was Juan Alvarez Mendizábal himself. He bought 1,800 *fanegas* in Cáceres in 1842. Salustiano Olózaga, another leading progressive, spent over a million reales on two mills and a farm in Logroño in 1843. General Concha, who later became the Marquis of the Duero, acquired 1,200 hectares in Carmona (Seville).

Another principal component of the new elite were the well-off *labradores*, tenant farmers who worked the estates of the Church and nobility. They were, according to Miguel Artola, central and misunderstood figures in the rural world of the Old Regime:

> a social class composed of people who exploited the land, that is assumed control, invested the resources necessary to cultivation and collected the crop which they sold on the market . . . The tenant can also be a landowner,

with a small patrimony, but the more representative figure is the well off, and often very rich, tenant who had capital in the form of animals, tools, warehouses, seeds and money which they applied to the land they leased.[21]

In Valladolid some 350 of the 1,300 buyers were such farmers. They bought land generally in large amounts in or near their place of residence. They were, according to Rueda, 'members of the middle classes, many appear in the lists of electors in 1846 [under a constitution which gave less than 1 per cent of the population the right to vote] . . . they have servants and when they have enough land they farm part of it and rent the rest; they are, then, both farmers and rentiers'.[22] Who were they? Francisco Pescador, a tenant on 31 hectares of land, made twelve separate purchases totalling 145 hectares. Gregorio Fraile, the mayor of Bobadilla, bought 211 hectares, among them the 23 he had been renting. Finally, Toribio Canillas of Mayorga acquired 700 hectares in that town, including the land on which he had been a tenant. He too invested in the railroad.

Some 79 of the 400 people who purchased land in Granada were tenants or administrators, two of whom worked for religious orders. In the 1840s another 230 called themselves landowners but before 1836 many had been something else, usually landowners or merchants. In Carmona (Seville) tenants were central to the new group of landowners thrown up by the disentailments. A number had previously been involved in livestock on a large scale and they were often tenants. They were, according to Cruz Villalón, 'agricultural entrepreneurs' for whom 'access to property ownership through the leasing of large estates' was a frequent occurrence.[23]

Elsewhere in Seville, this incipient agrarian bourgeoisie, some of whom had been leasing the same large estates since the seventeenth century, began to acquire land in their own right in the late eighteenth century by taking control of village commons where these were available. This is what Bernal has called the 'predisentailment'. They were also prominent in the Mendizábal disentailments. Among them were Manuel Aunón, a tenant of the Duke of Osuna and brother of a future civil governor of the province, J.M. Arias de Saavedra, a large tenant of the Duke of Medinaceli; and Simón Candau, a tenant of the Duke's in El Coronil, one of a number of towns in which he bought land, and one of whose relatives became Minister of the Interior.

A prime candidate for the most oustanding example of the new landed elite was Ignacio Vázquez y Gutiérrez of Seville. During the reign of Isabella II he built a landed empire of some 6,000 hectares which made him the most important landowner in the province of Seville after the Duke of Osuna. The story of the Vázquez family illustrates how monied people, often with some prior connection to the land, took advantage of the opportunities provided by the disentailments to assemble large amounts of land. It also reveals the close interconnection between the new agrarian elite and the emerging liberal political order. Ignacio Vázquez was himself mayor of Seville and his brother-in-law, Manuel Cortina, a prominent liberal politician who became a cabinet minister.

Vázquez's father was a lawyer with no ties to the land but his maternal grandfather was a merchant, part owner of a ship and the tenant of a local monastery, who in turn sublet the land to peasants. Although a practising Catholic – he had 40 priests at his funeral and ordered 3,000 masses for his soul – he purchased Church lands during the Godoy disentailment of 1805–6. The family of Ignacio's wife had a similar background. Her grandfather, an olive merchant and owner of a brick factory, also bought Church land put on the market before 1808.

All the Vázquez lands were acquired in the disentailments but they were acquired by various means of which direct purchase was only one. Indeed, fewer than half the purchases, 50 of 111, were made directly by Vázquez or by members of his family. The rest were made at second, third or even fifth hand by professional buyers or speculators in Seville or by an agent in Madrid, where all properties valued above 10,000 reales could be purchased.

Agents were important figures in the land sales across the country. They were often businessmen themselves and a number were also involved with newspapers. Vázquez used a number of agents. The most important were Antonio María Otal, a Seville merchant who was also director of an insurance company and publisher and editor of a weekly paper, *La Agricultura Española*, and Ramón Piñal Martínez, a wood dealer who also edited *El Porvenir*, the most important liberal paper in Seville.

Agents made half of all the purchases in Gerona and almost 60 per cent in Asturias. For Extremadura J. Merino Navarro discovered 'a number of truly important agents; in some cases one can speak of authentic offices dedicated to buying for others'.[24] The most significant was Pedro de la Hera, who made 112 purchases in the province of Badajoz. The single largest property sold in the region, 10,582 *fanegas*, was bought for 8.4 million reales by one Bartolomé Santamarca to pass to another. Germán Rueda found 493 in Valladolid. The majority of these people were involved in only one, or at best, a handful of sales but there were also some who made a business of it. The most important was Blas López Morales, who was also a journalist and publicist. He personally represented 122 clients for whom he acquired 213 properties, but he in turn employed a number of agents who among them purchased 634 properties, a seventh of all those sold in the province. In the process López Morales also acquired over 1,600 hectares for himself.

Ignacio Vázquez's agents also bought government bonds at good prices on the Madrid exchange and this allowed him to pay for much of his land with bonds whose face value was much higher than the price he had paid for them. This was possible because a decree of February 19, 1836 allowed the buyer to pay either in cash in seventeen installments or in government bonds at their face value in nine installments. Francois Heran has calculated that, all told, Vázquez actually paid only 43 per cent of the auction price, which made the 3.5 per cent he paid as commission a bargain.

Practices such as this have led many people, both contemporaries and historians, to criticize the disentailments as a fraud on the Treasury. This view has recently been vigorously attacked by Josep Fontana. To begin with, Fontana points out that the lands sold during the Mendizábal disentailments were valued at 2.5 billion reales, only about a quarter to a fifth of the outstanding government debt. The lands which were actually sold were valued at 1.75 billion reales, for which the government received 500 million reales in cash and 5 billion in bonds at face value. The government saved 250 million per year in interest payments and retired almost half of the outstanding debt. This can be judged a success in terms of Mendizábal's goal of 'reducing the volume of debt to a level which could be serviced out of ordinary revenues while at the same time reviving payment of interest . . . it would allow Ministers of Finance to get loans on the international market at normal rates'.[25] That Mendizábal's successors oversaw a further expansion of the debt was not his fault.

Vázquez bought land from a number of different sources. Almost half, some 2,600 hectares, had belonged to the Church, monasteries and convents for the most part. Vázquez also acquired former municipal lands, but he always did so through intermediaries, often local office holders who were able to manipulate the sales. He bought forty-two lots in the town of Alacalá del Río, twenty-one of them from a family which held key posts in the town government. Vázquez also took advantage of numerous smallholders who went into debt and bought their land. For example, in 1813 part of the common land of Guillena was distributed in parcels of some 13 hectares to soldiers who had fought against the French, as rewards for patriotism. Vázquez was able to 'take advantage of inheritance crises . . . when division had broken the homogeneity of the farms . . . And if they survived once the problem of division resurfaced, more acutely, in the next generation'.[26] This instability of small farms was a recurring theme in the south.

About 14 per cent of Vázquez's lands had formed part of noble entails. His ability to raise large sums of cash allowed him to take advantage of those aristocratic families which found themselves in financial straits. Between 1822 and 1859 he bought 862 hectares of land from noblemen in eleven purchases. Vázquez came by another noble property at second hand. In 1822 the widow of the the Marquis of Alcañíces, a grandee, sold an estate to a Seville merchant who immediately resold it to the Marquis' administrator. However, when Ferdinand VII was restored in 1823 he forced the new Marquis to take back the land and return the money. The Marquis replied that his mother had been 'under severe pressure' and that he did not have the money to buy back the estate. In the end, the sale was allowed to stand. When the administrator died his sister contested the will and in an attempt to keep the property intact she borrowed 350,000 reales from Vázquez. When she was unable to meet the terms of the loan – to pay it off within a year – she gave up the property.[27]

This was a fairly common pattern, especially in the second half of the nineteenth century when more and more nobles began to sell off parts of their landholdings. When the Duke of Osuna sold his lands in Marchena after 1869 they were bought by large local and regional landowners, many of whom were already tenants. José Torres Diez de la Cortina, who leased 1,814 hectares, most of them from the Duke, was the largest buyer. Once they left the Duke's hands, however, over half of these lands were broken up either due to inheritance or for sale in smaller units. Likewise, lands sold by the Dukes of Medinasidonia wound up in the hands of people such as Martín de Larios, the industrialist from Málaga and later Marquis of Larios, and the Garveys, who were leaders in the sherry industry.

Local businessmen, whom Rueda calls the 'business bourgeoisie' of merchants, manufacturers, lawyers and other professionals, were present among the buyers in considerable numbers, although their acquisitions were necessarily on a smaller scale than those of Ignacio Vázquez and other members of the elite. In Valladolid, for example, 116 of them bought property, spending over a third of all the money invested there. They were particularly important in buying flour mills, a key institution in a rural economy dominated by cereals.

Let us look at some individuals.[28] Juan Manuel Fernández Vitor bought 359 hectares. He was the son of a farmer in Burgos. He went to Valladolid to run a store and chocolate factory for his brother and then set up on his own as a grain dealer. By 1841 he was the most important taxpayer in the city and employed four servants. He was a moderate liberal and served as mayor a number of times. José Garaizábal Arzubialde was a Basque who became a very successful merchant in Valladolid; by 1842 he was one of the richest people in the city. That same year he set up a paper factory which used both water and steam power and which employed forty-six people. He bought 58 hectares of land while he was still a merchant. Politically he was a liberal.

Outside the provincial capital there were similar figures. Dionisio Enríquez of Medina de Rioseco was a grain dealer who bought land during the liberal triennium and in both the Mendizábal and Madoz disentailments. Millán Alonso Tejada of Quintanilla de Abajo owned three paper factories. He was an active liberal, serving as a substitute deputy in 1821, for which he was arrested and heavily fined in 1823, deputy from 1837 to 1858, life senator from 1858 to 1868 and senator from 1869 to 1872. He was also president of the Crédito Castellano and a promoter of the Alar del Rey–Santander railroad. He bought land in the liberal triennium and acquired 645 hectares between 1839 and 1848.

About a fifth of the professionals (lawyers, notaries, architects and doctors) bought property. Mariano Barrasa Diez, a lawyer, was son of a grain speculator. He was an active progressive, captain in the National Militia (1835–44, 1854–6) and mayor during the First Republic, and was deported to Ciudad Real when the *moderados* returned to power in 1844. He bought 7 hectares. Eugenio Alau was a doctor from Oviedo who became professor of Medicine at the University of Valladolid. He too was active politically: he was civil governor of four different provinces and played a leading role in the city during the Revolution of 1868. He bought 6 hectares of good land near the capital. Finally, there was Victor Lázaro Barrasa, a priest, professor of theology at the university and director of the insane asylum, who bought 93 hectares. A number of officials from government institutions such as the Audiencia (provincial court), the army and regional ministry offices, especially Finance, also bought land.

This local bourgeoisie was active in other provinces as well. In the La Sagra region of Toledo a fifth of the 300 buyers were 'merchants and manufacturers' who acquired 70 per cent of the land. Some, including José Safont, were from Madrid, but most were from Toledo and eighteen local towns and villages. Among the 455 buyers in Granada were 24 merchants, 14 lawyers, 1 manufacturer, 12 doctors, 7 pharmacists, 9 priests, 3 notaries, 3 teachers and 22 military officers. Most buyers on Mallorca were merchants from Palma, although professionals were also important. And of the eight buyers in Soria whom Ortega Canadell could identify two were merchants, one of whom was from Madrid, one a doctor, one a lawyer and one the parish priest of Burgo de Osma.[29]

In Cádiz, the centre of the sherry trade, the bourgeoisie which moved into land ownership was more substantial. As foreign demand for sherry increased after the 1840s the merchants who controlled the trade, and who like the Domecqs, Duffs and Byass were often foreigners themselves, sought to control all stages of the production process and began to acquire the small peasant vineyards in which the grapes they used were grown. They also bought other lands and put them into cultivation, so that the area dedicated to grapes grew by 30 per cent between 1851 and 1870. These families of the Anglo-Andalucian elite which emerged in Cádiz were also active in finance, mining and railroads.

In the end, the largest group of purchasers was composed of the many modest agriculturalists, usually tenants, who were able to acquire smallholdings in or near the thousands of villages across the country in which they lived. These were, for the most part, anonymous men whose only appearance in the historical record was their purchase of land. And in a number of provinces they formed consortiums to make their purchases so that their names are absent even then. As Rueda puts it: 'Their credentials as "simple farmers" says it all: they work their lands living a more or less monotonous life in their ancestral villages, where their descendants will remain.'[30]

These people were present in all provinces although their numbers varied greatly. Even where they were most numerous their share of the land was very small since they each acquired only a little. In Valladolid they accounted for half of all the buyers but they bought only 14 per cent of the land. Their average purchase was 13.5 hectares, compared to 72 for the middle and upper classes, and none of them bought as much as 50 hectares. Valladolid was a province in which the disentailments did not contribute to latifundia, 'but rather the opposite'.[31] Extremadura was a very different place. There were

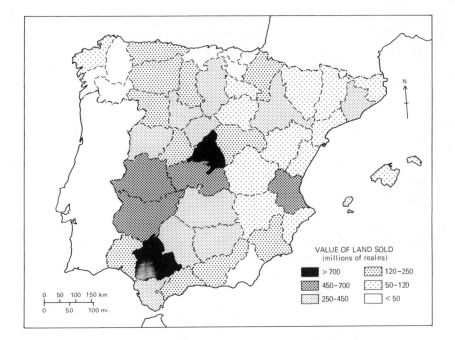

Figure 2.1 *Value of Land Sold in Disentailments, 1836–1895*

1,817 buyers in Badajoz but 1,660, 91 per cent, invested less than 100,000 reales, or a quarter of the total. (On the other hand, the 49 biggest buyers spent over half the total.) Badajoz was a province where the officials in charge of the sales at least attempted to give modest men a chance by dividing large estates into small plots; in the neighboring province of Cáceres, where this was not the case, they did much worse. There 79 per cent of the buyers, 370 people, invested only 4.5 per cent of the total while 5 per cent, 27 people, invested 76 per cent. In Seville, where a sixth of the buyers got over three-quarters of the land, over half acquired fewer than 15 hectares each. The outcome was similar, although somewhat less exaggerated in Madrid, Toledo, Granada and Segovia.

Galicia

The liberal revolution also produced an army of smallholders in the northern region of Galicia, but did so in a more drawn out and complex manner. In Galicia the vast majority of the land was held by peasants on long-term leases known as *foros*. This was one form of 'imperfect property', so characteristic of the Old Regime, which was not affected by the disentailments. There 'the only thing which was sold was the rents and ownership, while the peasant retained use rights – which could not be taken from him – in return for a rent which could not be changed'.[32]

This type of lease was eliminated only in 1926, but by then the process of redemption, in which the peasants bought out their leases and became landowners, was well underway. Initially, in the 1890s, rents owned by the nobility were redeemed not by the peasantry but by merchants, lawyers, money-lenders and better-off farmers, who constituted a new class of rentiers. One such figure was Benito de Soto, a merchant and banker who, in 1905, purchased all the rents owned by the Marquis of Bedana in the Chantada region. By this time, however, the value of the rents, which were paid in kind, had declined markedly from the levels of the mid-nineteenth century and the new rentiers quickly sold out to the peasants, who finally became the owners of the land they had worked for decades. They were also able to acquire the relatively small amounts of land the nobility and hidalgos farmed directly.

The peasants had the means to redeem their leases because of changes in the region's agriculture early in the twentieth century. They began to use more fertilizers and machinery, the latter often purchased collectively through local agrarian syndicates, usually with a Catholic orientation. At the same time the growing demand for meat in the cities encouraged the extension of cattle raising. Finally, the peasants were bolstered by massive remittances – which reached 50 million pesetas annually – from emigrants in America. The rhythm of redemptions followed closely that of remittances. Some emigrants were even buying out leases in Galicia while they were still in Buenos Aires.

But the increased resources the peasants had at their disposal would not have been much use had the rentiers not been willing to sell. That they were was in large part due to pressure applied by the strong and increasingly militant movement of farmers' syndicates known as *agrarismo*. These syndicates, of which there were 954 in the 1920s, used two main weapons to force a solution to the question of the leases: rent strikes and refusal to work for landlords unwilling to have their leases redeemed. The Chantada syndicate, which was founded in 1919, staged a general rent strike the following year which forced the pre-eminent landowner in the region to allow the redemption of two-thirds of his rents immediately and the rest within five years. By the time of the 1926 law scarcely any leases were left outstanding.

Conclusion

What can we conclude, then, about the effects of the disentailments? The first observation is the great diversity of the people who became landowners: they came from virtually every social group. There were, however, very few from the lowest classes which represented the bulk of the population. 'If we exclude the small tenant farmers . . . the presence of members of the lower classes among those who bought land is purely anecdotal: an occasional artisan, laborer, employee, industrial worker or servant . . . the vast majority, the poorest, saw the disentailment take place before their eyes but their participation was all but nil.' Rueda has calculated that the 'lower classes' made up two-thirds of the population of Valladolid and that only ten, 0.02 per cent of them, bought land and the total was less than 150 hectares. Overall only 4 per cent of the people in the province participated in the land sales, even though Valladolid was a province in which the role of small buyers was especially important.[33]

Second, disentailment reinforced the existing structure of landholding. Numerous local studies have born out the argument made by Richard Herr in 1974: 'in an agrarian country a disentailment based on auctions is not going to change the structure of property ownership; rather it will tend to reinforce and exacerbate the existing one, either through greater concentration in the hands of residents of the towns or through an increase in the power of absentees.'[34]

But disentailment did not produce latifundia or absenteeism everywhere. The outcome depended very much on the existing structures of landholding and, as Josep Fontana has stated, 'to the extent that the points of departure were different in different places . . . the final results could turn out to be quite diverse'.[35] Most buyers were clearly local people and most of these bought small plots in their own village or nearby even though they ended up with a relatively small percentage of the land. The disentailments did not 'solve' the agrarian problem, especially in the south, but they did permit large numbers of humble and middling Spaniards to acquire property, and they contributed to building a broad social base for liberalism.

Finally, what effect did disentailment have on Spain's subsequent economic development? This has been a controversial question. It has long been argued that disentailment was a disaster, that it absorbed vast amounts of capital that could have better been used for industrial investment and that it helped preserve a backward agricultural sector which obstructed industrialization. For the great Catalan historian Jaime Vicens Vives the disentailments 'strengthened latifundism to a degree dangerous for the country's economy'.[36] Jordi Nadal has denounced the disentailments in much stronger terms. They hobbled the development of agriculture and played a major role in what he called 'the failure of the industrial revolution in Spain':

> in comparison with the French, for example, Spanish agricultural reform did not aid the formation of a numerous class of small land-owners; and . . . in comparison with the Prussian case, the large estates which were created did not adopt forms of exploitation which were truly capitalistic . . . The mouthful represented by the lands was too big, too much for the digestive capacities of the purchasers. The later lack of financial resources among the purchasers maintained agricultural productivity at its traditional levels . . . Without the creation of cheap surpluses, without the liberation of agricultural workers, the conditions required for the establishment of a dynamic, numerous urban proletariat would be lacking. It would be interesting to know how much this fact contributed to the smallness of industrial enterprises and to the

firm establishment of forms of family business associations. On the other hand, the wretched condition of the country people . . . caused in large measure the lack of elasticity in the demand for industrial products . . . we can have little doubt about this failure [of the agricultural revolution] on the activities of the bourgeoisie and on the development of the secondary sector in general.[37]

Both these arguments have recently come under attack. Fontana has pointed out that the vast majority of land purchases were made with 'government paper which was virtually without value'. The 500 million reales in cash which was invested was about enough to finance one railroad company. The government's continual demands for cash to finance its chronic deficit absorbed much more capital than did the disentailments. We should, he says, pay less attention to those 500 million than to the '30,000 million reales by which the public debt grew, approximately, between Mendizábal's time and the Restoration of 1874'.[38]

Spanish agriculture was not as backward as had been claimed. As we have seen, it was able to feed a growing population and respond to external demands by providing a range of products for export. Rather than drain capital away from industry, it provided capital for investment in other sectors. And rather than being tradition-bound and technologically backward, many Spanish landowners adopted innovations from abroad. (Innovation could come from unexpected directions; in Seville, the aristocracy was prominent in buying new machines.) And if Spanish farmers needed tariffs to shield them from the impact of the crisis at the end of the century, they had their peers in a number of other European countries for company. On this new view, Spanish agriculture is not guilty of failing to fulfill its historical role; even if it did not become a copy of British agriculture, it pulled its weight in the economy, so to speak.[39]

Rural Social Relations

Absenteeism

Absenteeism was a long-standing tradition among the nobility, who lived in the provincial or regional capital or in Madrid, not in the towns or villages where they had their land. Southern Spain increasingly became a foreign country for many, especially the grandees, the members of the highest category of the nobility. By the 1930s

More grandees had been born in the resort city of San Sebastián than in any of the southern capitals. More were native to such French centres of international society as Paris, Biarritz and Bayonne than to all the southern capitals put together . . . But it was Madrid that was the overwhelming favourite of the *grandeza*. There were 177 grandee families – 13 times as many as were to be found in Seville, Córdoba, Granada, Málaga and Jerez combined – centered in that city in the 1930s'.[1]

In the nineteenth and twentieth centuries, absenteeism was increasingly taken up by a section of the non-noble landed elite which emerged from the disentailments. Malefakis has calculated that for the provinces of Cádiz, Córdoba and Seville a seventh of the property in bourgeois hands was held by absentees, not counting those who lived in the provincial capitals, and that this was most common in the richest lands and for the largest farms. Bernal also notes the spread of bourgeois absenteeism in Seville as, one after another, important landowning families took it up:

> Until the middle of the nineteenth century they consolidated their position as large landowners in their places of origin and then, around 1846–50, they began their exodus to the city where they mixed with the mercantile and industrial bourgeoisie and participated in local, regional and, with luck, national politics.[2]

In Alcalá del Río absentees, who comprised between 10 and 16 per cent of the landowners, held more than 60 per cent of the land from 1846 to 1920, and from 1880 to 1901 held 80 per cent or more. For the town of Carmona, also in Seville, absenteeism was more common in 1910 than it was in 1750, although it had declined somewhat between 1750 and 1850. In both those years about one fifth of the landowners were absentee although their share of the town's land dropped from 60 to 48 per cent. By 1910 a third of the landowners were absentee and they held 62 per cent of the land. In part this was because 'the important bourgeois' went to live in Seville and Córdoba and even Madrid.[3] In part they were imitating the nobility, but there was also another factor, one mentioned by Bernal as well: that the increase of social tensions and the spread of violent social conflict led landowners to leave the countryside out of fear.

Some of the increase of absenteeism in Carmona was due to the fact that land there was bought by residents of adjacent municipalities who were themselves farmers. Almost half of the absentee owners in Carmona came from the neighboring towns of El Viso and Mairena del Alcor. These people were not absentees in the full sense of the word, since they could oversee or even work their lands directly. Nor were they necessarily smallholders; the seven brothers of the Jiménez family of El Viso were able to accumulate 2,600 hectares in Carmona alone.

Absenteeism has frequently been blamed for the backwardness of Spanish, especially southern, agriculture. For Malefakis, the main problem with absenteeism was that it led to widespread leasing. In 1933, 29 per cent of all land in the south was leased but over half the land owned by absentees was leased and leasing was most common on the best lands. Large estates were leased intact on short leases to single tenants, known as *arrendadores*, who cultivated them or, in some cases, sublet them in smaller plots. 'The resident *arrendadores* . . . may indeed have been intelligent, technically knowledgeable and interested in expanding agricultural production. Nevertheless the land was in the long run more neglected than if it had not been absentee owned precisely because none of these qualities could enjoy free play. The *arrendador* might cultivate effectively within the existing resources of the farm, but because he lacked security of tenure he could not undertake long-range improvements like the introduction of new crops . . . [Southern landowners] preferred to accept low returns rather than to engage in active management' and did not display the more entrepreneurial spirit of their counterparts in Valencia who developed citrus fruits into an important export industry.[4]

Tenancy was even more common in Old Castile than in the south and the conditions under which it was carried out certainly did not favor agricultural development. The liberal revolution had included changes in the tenancy laws which strongly favored landowners and reduced the protection which paternalistic Old Regime legislation had afforded tenants. Leases were short, generally for three to five years, and required tenants to farm 'according to the custom of the good farmer'. Tenants signed their lease '*a suerte y ventura*', agreeing to pay their rent punctually whether there were drought or other catastrophe, and were sometimes made to renounce the possible protection of Old Regime laws. Where payment was in cash it had to be made in gold or silver; landlords came to accept paper money only slowly. Tenants also had to pay all the expenses attached to the land and this frequently included the one significant direct tax, the *contribución territorial*. And, as Robledo Hernández wryly remarks,

> when the Restoration fiscal system is attacked for the absence of a land survey and tax fraud we should also keep in mind that the large landowners who leased their estates benefited twice over . . . since the little tax assessed on their lands was paid by someone else. The expression 'important taxpayer' was quite a euphemism.[5]

Bernal has criticized absenteeism for the opposite reason. In his view the problem was not that it produced leasing but that the landowners' absence 'did not indicate a rejection of direct exploitation, as it had for the Church and the nobility and which at least permitted a large number of tenants to use the land. The agrarian bourgeoisie continued, in large measure, to direct agriculture at second hand by the use of *aperadores* (administrators)'. Malefakis agrees that the use of administrators obstructed agricultural development.[6] On the other hand, François Heran has argued that such blanket condemnations of the agrarian elite, especially that part of it which had come to land ownership recently, is wrong. 'The physical absence of the landowner did not necessarily mean that he had "abandoned" his land. The Sevillian bourgeois who went to examine his lands a number of times per month was not the same as the grandee who lived in Madrid and visited his Andalucian estates once a year.' Many of the agrarian bourgeoisie had themselves begun as tenants and, he suggests, were not likely to have easily abandoned the outlook that went with it.[7]

Latifundia

Most land in the south and much of it in the center was owned and worked as large farms, latifundia, which generated their own special social relations. When it was not leased, actual management of the land was in the hands of an administrator. Ignacio Vázquez employed four, one for each of his principal estates. A figure of great local power, he is one on whom historians have been unable to shed much light. In his study of Casas Viejas (Cádiz), Jerome Mintz had the son of Alfonso Gómez, the administrator for the Marquis of Negrón, an absentee who lived in Jerez de la Frontera, describe his father's power: 'Every day he would ride out on horseback to one estate or other, depending on what needed to be done. In the evening my father would return home and seat himself in a big armchair and receive petitions. One would come asking for firewood, another for straw; and he would make a decision about each petition.'[8]

Below the administrator there was a small staff of regular employees, known as *fijos*. Alfonso Gómez was in charge of more than 10,000 hectares, including fifteen large estates, which his master owned in the municipality. He was also in charge of the warehouses in town but it was his brother

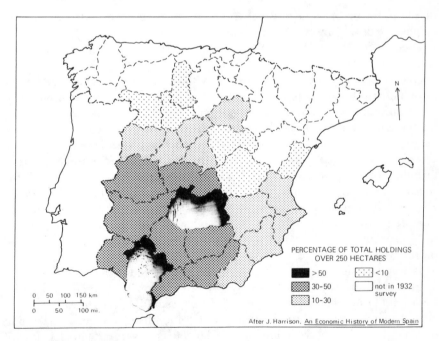

Figure 2.2 *Landholdings over 250 Hectares, 1932*

who really ran them. Each individual estate had a resident manager and a number of foremen. The regular workers included a cook, an ox-drover, a herdsman, a swineherd, a goatherd and a *yeguero* for the breeding cattle. They were employed on a year-to-year basis on a verbal contract and lived on the estate and received rations of flour, chickpeas, oil and some other necessities, in addition to their low, but regular wage. Around 1909 landowners in Casas Viejas added another benefit, allowing workers who did not take time off and who agreed to join a Catholic brotherhood, to cultivate a small plot of land.

With only year-to-year contracts and with their conduct under constant scrutiny, regular workers depended on the goodwill of the landowner, or his administrator, to retain their positions. In cases of social conflict they were under great pressure to show loyalty to their employer. The unpublished manuscript of a local anarchist whom Mintz leaves in anonymity described the Marquis of Negrón's employees as particularly 'fanatic and servile':

> In later years in the house of the Marquis of Negrón the bread was good and complete. Furthermore the campesinos were permitted more animals for themselves, even pigs, which formerly they had not been allowed anywhere. And in this way the fijo campesinos lived well, serving and praising their masters unconditionally . . . Some of them boasted that if anyone tried to get them to join in a strike, they would empty their shotguns at him.[9]

In the town of Palma del Río (Córdoba) landowners armed their regular employees during moments of conflict in the 1930s.

There were, however, very few full-time workers. Most of the work was done by day laborers, known as *jornaleros* or *eventuales*. They made up the largest part of the population in the southern provinces and were most numerous where property ownership was most highly concentrated. In Seville, laborers accounted for 43 per cent of the labor force in 1860, but in some municipalities the figure was over 60 per cent. The situation deteriorated even further after 1860 as the population grew and agriculture entered a prolonged period of crisis. By the 1930s agricultural laborers, including the relatively few *fijos*, made up two-thirds of the peasants in the south poor enough to qualify for settlement under the Republic's agrarian reform. The figure varied from 56 per cent in Extremadura to 67 per cent in eastern Andalucia and 76 per cent in western Andalucia. This compared to 17 per cent on the Cantabrian coast, 33 per cent in Aragon and 41 per cent on the Mediterranean coast.

The outstanding features of the laborers' lives were the irregularity of their work and the misery of their wages. The domination of southern agriculture by a limited number of crops, especially olives and cereals, meant that the peak demand for labor was limited to a few months of the year. According to Malefakis, laborers could look forward to a maximum of 180 to 250 days of work per year; where monoculture was heavy, as few as 130 to 150. According to Bernal the situation was even worse: the average was around 200 days and rarely, if ever, hit 220.[10]

Wage levels were low, usually well below those in other branches of the economy. Bernal has calculated that in Seville, Cádiz and Córdoba money wages remained unchanged over the nineteenth century and that the average wage for an unskilled laborer was 20 per cent lower in 1900 than it had been in 1790. Wages were lowest in the middle decades of the century, which were also the best years for agriculture, and wage levels on the large estates were a third lower than on smaller farms, where skilled workers were often needed.[11] By the twentieth century their wages were well below the national average. In 1919 wages in Córdoba had risen to 3 pesetas while the average for all working Spaniards was 10; at the beginning of the 1930s the gap remained at almost three to one.

Laborers were employed in a number of different ways. They could be hired for the duration of a specific task, generally related to the harvest, in which case they lived in bunkhouses on the estate, *gañanías*, and received some basic foodstuffs such as bread, oil, salt and vinegar. In Casas Viejas these workers spent ten days on the estate after which they returned home for a night. To be hired day by day was more common. Employers tried to employ laborers on a piecework basis whenever possible, especially during the harvest. Such work was done by groups, not individuals. Olive harvesting was done by families while reaping was done by teams who moved from estate to estate. The most common form of work was to be hired for a day for a straight money wage. Such hiring was done each day by the foremen in the town squares where the men assembled hoping to be chosen. For the landowners, this system had the added virtue of dramatizing their power on a daily basis. For Mintz's anonymous anarchist

> The custom of hiring in the plaza was very profitable for the latifundista and their foremen or managers, because those who agreed to go to the field always saw the great number of their *compañeros* who remained behind without work, and so those who had work were submissive and allowed themselves to be easily exploited. If someone who was discontented complained, the foreman or manager responded arrogantly, with great show, 'there are still men waiting in the plaza! Take a walk!' The one who complained was dismissed immediately and would lose the chance to work.[12]

There could be no clearer example of the disciplining power of what William Reddy has called the 'asymmetrics' of monetary relationships.[13]

Levels of skill made a difference to agricultural laborers. Grape cultivation required high levels of skill in all tasks, and olives in some, such as cleaning. Even grains, which in general required fewer skills, could reward the best qualified workers since 'the large estates more often employed those who were good at sowing or cleaning so that they would be at hand when it was time to do those tasks. Skill brought more security rather than higher wages'.[14]

Small-scale farming – by tenants, sharecroppers and smallholders – was most common in the north and east of Spain but it was present throughout the country, even where large estates predominated. Smallholdings were often inadequate to support a family, especially after being divided through inheritance. This was particularly true in the south. We have already seen how Ignacio Vázquez was able to acquire properties distributed as 'patriotic prizes' in the 1820s. The pattern was repeated elsewhere. In 1840, the town council of Pilas (Seville) responded to demands from landless laborers by dividing part of the municipal commons so that 512 people received small plots on emphyteutic leases. Over the next six decades this land experienced both concentration and division. By 1904, 62 per cent of the owners had less than half the original allotment and collectively controlled 8.6 per cent of the land while 14 per cent of the owners controlled 42 per cent and outsiders held 14 per cent. Overall, the number of tiny farms, minifundia, in towns increased continually throughout the nineteenth century, from 175 in 1760 to 472 in 1860 and 639 in 1925. At the same time they covered less and less land; a sixth less in 1925 than in 1854. Unable to support their families on their tiny plots and without access to the common lands which had been sold in the 1856 disentailment, most of these smallholders were forced to work as laborers as well.[15] In Carmona too small plots given to laborers in the nineteenth century did not last long.

Small tenants and sharecroppers were less numerous than smallholders, even in the south, and their situation, outside those regions where emphyteutic-style leases survived, was equally precarious, if not more so. Above all they were at the mercy of economic conditions; when prices were low and rents high their staying power 'was practically nil' yet when prices for farm products rose 'a flood of aspiring tenants converged on the administration offices asking for plots of land. They rarely managed to stay on them after the favorable economic climate changed'. On six estates which Bernal analyzed, fewer than half of the tenants present in 1839 were still there twelve years later, although the survival rate varied from 12 per cent on one estate to 71 per cent on another.[16]

The continuous decline in grain prices from the mid–1830s to the mid–1840s meant that in Andalucia many small tenants were unable to pay their rents, which had begun to rise sharply after 1839, and lost their land to better-off tenants who could. The situation of the small tenant was made even worse by the strong tendency of landowners to do away with rents in kind, which had been common until then, and insist on cash. In the small minority of cases where tenants could continue to pay in kind they survived longer. (Rents on large farms had always been paid in cash.) The decade of recovery which began in 1847 saw the creation of a numerous new set of small tenants. Rents on small farms were higher per unit of land and rose more quickly than those on large ones and landowners responded 'by once again dividing the estates, which had earlier been rented only to a few large tenants, among small tenants, whose numbers increased spectacularly'.[17]

Renting small farms also had what we might call social benefits, helping to 'attach workers to the land and keep them quiet'. Bernal cites a letter to the Duke of Medinaceli's administrator from his steward in El Coronil on this question. After pointing out that small plots return 'half again as much' as the larger ones he noted that

> this should also be considered from a political perspective, since it is not just that in this town ten or twelve people enjoy almost all Your Excellency's property while the rest starve. You may say that this is because they pay for it, to which I reply that the poor will also pay and will do so with higher rents and, I say, other advantages for Your Excellency. [18]

On the other hand, small leases might turn into uncollectable debts which could, in moments of crisis, amount to considerable sums. In 1866 the Duke of Medinaceli ordered his administrators to forgive half the rent of the small tenants. The moratorium was extended in 1867 if the tenants paid the other half of the rent but in the midst of the worst agricultural crisis of the century they were unable to do so. Large tenants also fell behind with their rent but in these cases the landowner did not lose. Large tenants were required to put up collateral, often land or houses, and in cases of non-payment this, or the money raised when it was sold at auction, passed to the landowner, although generally after a court case. [19]

One group of tenants which came to have a high profile during the Second Republic were the *yunteros* of Extremadura. (The name came from the team of mules, *yunta*, which most of them owned.) Stock raising was more important in Extremadura than in other regions, which meant that the demand for farmland was greater there even than in Andalucia. The owner or tenant of an estate would rent part of it to tenants or sharecroppers who would rotate around the estate leaving the fields they had worked to revert to pasture. Leases were short, the *yunteros* had little security, and they competed for leases while vast amounts of land remained uncultivated.

There was, however, a trend away from tenancy and towards direct exploitation of the land at the end of the nineteenth century. The trend applied to many regions of the country, but it did not take the same form everywhere. In Castile, where small tenants were numerous, the share of the land under tenancy fell from 50 to 60 per cent at the end of the century to 40 per cent by 1928 as landowners shifted from the cultivation of grain to stock raising. This switch was favorable to tenants who leased large farms. They were able to consolidate their position, bringing more land under their control. Land which had once supported people was used to support animals and many small tenants were evicted, frequently with the use of force in the form of the Civil Guard. In one town tenants had their houses burned down.

Elsewhere the process followed very different lines. In Mallorca large landowners broke up their holdings after 1870 and began to sell them off in small plots, to the benefit of the small farmers and even some laborers. Large estates in some parts of the island were divided up and sold under a formula known as the *establiment*, under which the buyer put down a small down payment and paid off the rest over a number of years. In Asturias, where peasants farmed most land under *foro* leases as in Galicia, these traditional leases survived the disentailments but many tenants were able to buy out their leases and become landowners. Most remained tenants, however, although they paid their rent to new landlords, usually merchants and civil servants who had succeeded to ownership of former Church lands.

The last part of the country where landowners were able to establish full control over their property was Catalonia. Since the sixteenth century the land used for growing grapes had been under a type of emphyteutic lease known as the *rabassa morta* whereby in return for a fixed percentage of the crop the tenant had use of the land for an indefinite period of time, although by the eighteenth century this had been limited to the life of two-thirds of the vines which the tenant planted and by the end of the century the courts had cut it to fifty years. Eviction required a costly legal procedure and a tenant could freely sell or pass on his lease.

The *rabassa morta* survived into the nineteenth century, but without any consensus as to its duration. Landowners wanted it limited by law; tenants wanted it to be perpetual, or valid for at least 150 years. During the Restoration landowners began to offer shorter sharecropping arrangements and abandon the traditional verbal agreements for notarized contracts. In 1889 they succeeded in having the Civil Code set the duration of the lease at fifty years. The position of the tenants, known as *rabassaires*, continued to deteriorate due to the phylloxera epidemic, a new commercial agreement with France in the 1890s and, in 1906, a Supreme Court decision which allowed local magistrates to order tenants' eviction. Finally, the vines which had been planted after the phylloxera had a lifespan of only twenty-five years so that by 1910 many of the leases began to expire. As a result of these changes 'in many cases landowners succeeded in converting *rabassaires* into simple tenants and sharecroppers. In this way the landed class set the conditions for recovering absolute rights over their property'.[20]

Credit and Usury

Whether they were landowners, tenants or sharecroppers small farmers generally operated very close to the line and frequently needed credit to survive from one year to the next. The state was well aware of the fragility of small-scale agriculture since the Treasury seized 200,000 farms between 1880 and 1886 alone. It also recognized the need to act in its defence, but despite a large number of proposals to provide some sort of public rural credit institution, nothing was done. The period from 1872 to 1919 amounted to 'forty-seven years of projects, reports and debates which produced no solution whatsoever', another example of the weakness of the state.[21]

Credit and other forms of assistance were available to small farmers only in those parts of the country with strong Catholic agrarian syndicates. Catholic organization of the peasantry began in 1902 with the creation of the first Cajas Rurales in Zamora. By 1906 these had won the support of the Church hierarchy and ten years later the Primate of Spain created a national organization, the Secretariado Nacional Católico–Agrario, intended to 'defend farmers from capitalism and ruin . . . to sustain and multiply the class of small rural landowners'.[22] This was to be achieved through the creation of rural syndicates which brought together all those engaged in agriculture. The syndicates would provide a number of important services for the small farmer: the purchase of tools, fertilizer and so on, the sale of his produce at decent prices, loans and, for the tenants, the possibility of becoming landowners. But these organizations were Catholic in more than name only and also sought to strengthen religion in the countryside and prevent the spread of socialist or anarchist doctrines.

By 1920 the Confederación Nacional Católica Agraria (CNCA), which had succeeded the Secretariado in 1917, claimed to have 600,000 members in its 5,000 syndicates. These were far from being evenly spread. They were numerous and strong where small farmers were numerous, and where religious observance remained strong: in Galicia, Asturias, Navarra, Old Castile, León and parts of Valencia. In the south, where neither of these conditions obtained, the Catholic syndicates scarcely existed. The only point at which they had any life, or support from the landowners, was in 1919–21, as a direct response to the widespread revolt of laborers known as the Bolshevik triennium.

The CNCA was particularly concerned to increase the number of small holders. According to the Secretary General 'giving the landless access to a small property, with the hope of being able to increase it by their labor, their economy and their submissiveness, reduces vice, increases virtue and closes the door to revolutionary ideas'.[23] To realize this goal the syndicates purchased land which was then sold or rented collectively. In 1920 they spent 5.2 million pesetas to purchase 10,300 hectares which were distributed among 3,136 people. They also leased 29 large farms, totalling 16,069 hectares, collectively to 6,932 tenants and claimed to have made loans which allowed more than 50,000 others to purchase land. In 1932, José María Gil Robles claimed that between 1917 and 1931 the CNCA had acquired and distributed 29,859 hectares among 9,849 smallholders.

Where such institutions did not exist, and they were all but totally absent in the south where small-scale agriculture was particularly fragile, farmers were left in the hands of money-lenders. These were 'more or less well-off or powerful individuals' who might be better-off neighbors or businessmen or professionals in town.[24] Usury was a prominent feature of life for small farmers. They frequently needed small loans to meet pressing needs such as paying taxes or buying seed for planting. In some provinces as many as 70 to 90 per cent of farmers regularly needed such loans. Rates were generally highest in the cereal lands of Castile and small farmers and tenants paid the highest interest rates of all. If they needed a loan in kind, especially seed, they paid still more. The Provincial Agricultural Council of Palencia reported rates of 20 per cent per month on grains at harvest time and the Mercantile Union of Madrid reported loans of seed which were to be repaid at harvest time at one-and-a-half, two and even three to one. By contrast, better-off farmers could get much lower rates, from 6 to 12 per cent. Through the 'retro', 'a clause by which the buyer agrees to return something to the seller for the price paid' landowners 'gave up farms, which they never recovered, for a price well below their true value'.[25]

Social Conflict

Under the Old Regime the largest and most threatening social conflicts took place in the cities. In liberal Spain the focus of social conflict moved to the countryside. From the beginning of the nineteenth century rural Spain was the scene of repeated protest, very often violent, as the poorer strata of rural society expressed dissatisfaction with the liberal revolution and its results. At one time or another virtually every region of the country was the scene of such protest, but their protests did not always make the same demands. Some wanted to turn the liberal revolution back, others wanted to go beyond it, while still others wanted to get a little more out of it.

Counter-revolution

Unlike France, where the nobility was in the vanguard of the opposition to the revolution, the Spanish nobility generally supported it and the opposition came overwhelmingly from below. In the early part of the nineteenth century this peasant unrest was politically reactionary. As Jaume Torras reminds us, we should not assume that the 'inequalities and miseries' suffered by the peasantry under the Old Regime would make them supporters of *any* alternative system, nor that peasant opposition to liberalism represented support for the Old Regime as it had existed.

> Peasant reaction was not specifically feudal; nor did it imply any supposed radical alternative to the liberal revolution. It should be understood simply as evidence of the peasantry's opposition to the specific manner in which the Old Regime was liquidated. Not just because of the deterioration in the material conditions which the peasantry suffered in the course of the process but also because of the deep frustrations which it inflicted on them. For those who most sharply suffered it, the injustice and misery of the Old Regime did not serve to prepare them for entering a higher stage of historical evolution, capitalist society. For them the alternative to the Old Regime, or rather its negation, could only be the egalitarian project of a paternalistic monarchy in which the intermediaries between the king and his subjects had disappeared. But with the liberal triumph even this utopia was taken from them. The liquidation of the Old Regime, hijacked by the

bourgeoisie, did not bring the negation of that regime but rather its continuation, in the form of subordination and increased inequalities.[1]

Where the weight of the seigneurial regime was heaviest opposition to the existing state of affairs was already being expressed in the eighteenth century. The upheaval caused by Spain's involvement in the wars against revolutionary France, the Napoleonic invasion and the subsequent political uncertainty during the Restoration, the liberal triennium, the 'ominous decade' from 1823 to 1833 and the Carlist War (1833–40) provided ideal opportunities for the peasants to express their dissatisfaction and put forward, albeit in an inchoate way, their own agenda or, as in the case of royalism and Carlism, support explicitly anti-liberal political movements.

In the last years of the eighteenth century and first of the nineteenth the fiscal demands of the state increased under the burden of continual warfare. In parts of Castile the peasantry responded to this heavier taxation, and to rent increases designed to counter the fall in agricultural prices, by reneging on its fiscal obligations, especially to the Church. One rural parish priest complained of the dire straits in which he, and his colleagues, lived in the period 1801–05: 'these days the clergy do not have enough to feed themselves or dress decently. Before the churches were filled with donations and offerings and gifts to charity and the clergy had more and could help the needy.'[2] Moreover, after 1790 when towns in the province began to lease their common lands in order to meet the Crown's fiscal demands they were occupied and cultivated illegally by the peasantry.

There was similar resistance in Catalonia. As early as 1711, but especially after 1774, farmers in the town of Navarcles refused to pay tithes owed to the monastery of Sant Benet de Bages or to recognize the mayors appointed by the Abbot. But this did not represent an attack on the Church; the town had a reputation for conservatism and at key moments the opposition to the monastery was led by the parish priest. The monastery never collected its tithes after 1820: 'its authority and power had ceased to exist well before the liberal decrees of 1835.'[3] Secular lords suffered as well. The Padró, a merchant family which had bought part of a jurisdictional seigneurie from the Duke of Cardona in 1677, was ruined when, in 1814, the peasants refused to pay the dues they owed; the family was forced to launch a number of lawsuits against them.[4]

In Galicia the peasantry was fighting as early as the middle of the eighteenth century against the attempts of the landowners to renew their leases, by witholding rent payments. By the beginning of the nineteenth century this had turned into a 'general rent strike' which left some landowners in debt.[5] Some Basque peasants also began to refuse to pay tithes in the 1780s.

In Valencia, where the seigneurial regime was strongest, there was widespread criticism of it in the eighteenth century, both among the ministers of the Crown and the local population. As rising agricultural and land prices led the aristocratic seigneurs to enforce their rights more stringently, and even to attempt to push their claims beyond those existing in the contracts, there were a number of lawsuits demanding reductions in the amounts to be paid or reincorporation of the areas in question into the jurisdiction of the Crown.

Violent opposition to the seigneurial system emerged quickly. Riots against the draft for the National Militia in August 1801 quickly turned into an anti-seigneurial jacquerie the next month, with the initial demand being an end to the partition of the crops. The main participants were the poorer peasants although 'there is no doubt that the better-off farmers fomented and financed the revolt'. The riots had a standard ritual, beginning with the ringing of bells, a meeting in the square in which the order not to pay the lords was given orally and often followed by shouts of 'Long live the King' and death to the lord. Violence was limited; in some towns the coats of arms on the palaces were destroyed, in others the archives burned and in still others the gallows torn down. The revolts were made in the name of Pep de l'Horta, an imaginary figure, 'given life here and there by whoever dared dress himself as a farmer, cover himself with hat and shawl and shout during a disturbance that whoever shared his crop with the seigneur would die'.[6]

This strong anti-seigneurial sentiment among the mass of the Valencian peasantry would not, however, come down on the side of liberalism. News of the French invasion and the abdication of Ferdinand VII provoked anti-French riots, often led by the clergy, and also gave rise to a spontaneous popular guerrilla war against the invaders. From the beginning these guerrilla leaders clashed with village authorities who collected feudal dues for the nobility. When the French occupied Valencia after January 1812 they enjoyed good relations with the local elites, especially the Archbishop, the cathedral chapter and the nobility. Under great fiscal pressure General Suchet did not enforce Napoleon's Chamartin decree abolishing the seigneurial system. At the same time as the French were increasing the tax burden in the region the nobility were increasing their own pressure.

This did not stop the peasantry from challenging the established order by refusing to pay dues and questioning the authority of the seigneurs. One Valencian lord, the Marquis of Malferit, complained about the flaunting of his rights and authority in what was clearly a charivari in the town of Aieló de Malferit in 1813: 'they demolished the gallows in the presence of the mayor and council, they dressed someone in a ridiculous suit, called him the Marquis and made him oppose the destruction of the gallows, after which they tied him up, put him on a gibbet and rode him through the town covering him with insults.'[7]

In this context, the Cortes of Cádiz decree of August 6, 1811 abolishing the seigneuries was interpreted in the villages as ending the territorial and jurisdictional privileges of the nobility and no further dues were paid. In July 1814 the leading Valencian seigneurs protested jointly to the restored Ferdinand VII:

Ever since the publication of the decree of August 6, 1811 the residents of the villages under my jurisdiction not only attacked that jurisdiction with gross insults . . . but also violently usurped what that decree left to the lords . . . Many even dared to take buildings and property . . . The village of Alberique took from its owner not only the palace and outbuildings where his servants lived but also went so far as to lease at public auction the inn, stores, mills and rooms of the palace. They also took the coat of arms from the portico and inscribed instead Constitution Square . . . As soon as the province was freed from enemy control most seigneurial villages commited the same, and even greater, crimes.[8]

Liberalism, it seemed, had something to offer the peasantry in 1811 but during the triennium, 1820–23, it lost its appeal. Forced to choose between the interests of the anti–seigneurial but landed groups in the region, many of whom were themselves nobles, and those of the peasantry, it chose the former. In many parts of the region the peasants refused to pay dues owing to the nobility and even the tithe, which the Cortes had reduced by half in June 1821. According to the civil governor of Valencia, in July 1822 many people had 'dared to enter the houses of the tithe administrators during the middle of the night, forcibly remove the grain from where it was stored, shamelessly insult their families and oblige them, under threats of murder, to stop collecting and even to return that which they had already collected'.[9] The taxes imposed by the liberal regime also triggered popular opposition. In March 1820 there were riots in Valencia against the tax on products entering the city and the next year against municipal taxes.

The failure of the liberal regime to do anything for the poorer peasantry led to their participation in anti–liberal risings in 1822 and 1823 and later during the Carlist War. Both instances coincided with particularly bad agricultural years in which begging and banditry increased. The royalists were able to attract the peasantry, which had shown its royalist sentiments during the war against the French. Their support was especially strong in those districts in which there were better-off peasants, who were 'the principal support of liberalism'.[10] By March 1823 the royalist commander Sempere had an army of 5,000 men and as he marched towards Valencia he was joined by large numbers of peasants from the Huerta, whose general antipathy to the liberal regime had been exacerbated by the draft for the National Militia.

In Valencia the Carlist War was essentially a repeat performance of 1822–3. As Ardit Lucas states: 'The urban middle class and the affluent peasantry were already definitively liberal while the poorer peasants and the incipient pre-industrial proletariat adhered to Carlism, which became a vague receptacle, with barely any ideological content, of these social tensions.'[11] The Carlist War in Valencia was, then, primarily a peasant war. Carlists came from all over the region but the Huerta, which had supported Sampere in 1823, was a particularly fertile area.

In Catalonia the rising against Napoleon also had a strong anti–seigneurial side. Landowners, tax collectors and usurers were attacked and peasants refused to pay tithes or seigneurial dues and to do military service. Even so, rural Catalonia was soon largely lost to liberalism and offered repeated mass resistance to the liberal revolution. The governments of the liberal triennium quickly found themselves facing a widespread royalist uprising in the Catalan countryside which by the summer of 1822 had turned into a state of civil war.

Torras attributes this to the deteriorating situation of tenant farmers which government policy did nothing to help. The colonial wars and the loss of the American colonies had destroyed the wine and liquor trades, as prices fell and wine exports were reduced to 10 per cent of those of 1792. Peasants had increasing difficulties in finding the cash to pay rents and taxes and any relief offered by the 50 per cent reduction in the tithe was countered by increases in taxes which had to be paid in cash. Moreover, the imposition of the *consumos*, a tax on basic foodstuffs, greatly increased the fiscal burden and provoked loud complaints from small agricultural villages, where the tax fell on the residents and not the non-resident landowners. The disentailment of Church lands favoured wealthy outsiders and led to increasing rents.

The revolt was overwhelmingly a rural one, yet it was not simply a matter of town versus country. Nor was it a struggle between peasants stuck in a subsistence economy and those engaged in production for the market, mostly of grapes, and suffering from its collapse. Torras rejects the attempt to make such a simple interpretation although he does conclude that in general terms there was less receptiveness to liberalism where there was 'dispersed population and a less commercialized agriculture'.[12] The rebels came overwhelmingly from the poorest strata of rural society and they were frequently led by the parish clergy.

Mass peasant opposition to liberalism was a constant in Catalonia. The royalist rising of 1827 against the supposed moderation being shown by Ferdinand VII, known as the War of the *Malcontents*, the Discontented, also received substantial support from the peasants and once again the parish clergy played a central role in mobilizing them. At the peak of the revolt there were as many as 30,000 men in arms, drawn from the same social base as those who rebelled in 1822 and those who would support Carlism in 1833. Carlism found its support in the poorer strata of rural society: small farmers, sharecroppers and laborers. Wealthier landowners tended to be liberals and many abandoned the countryside for the cities. The Carlists never challenged property rights but whenever the Carlist administration collapsed 'all kinds of attacks on "property" proliferated'. However, as the Carlist war dragged on and the Carlists needed to extract men and money they too began to lose the sympathy of the Catalan peasantry.[13] Much of the peasantry remained unreconciled to liberalism: peasants from the mountainous interior of the region played a prominent part in yet another popular revolt against the liberal state, the War of the *Matiners* (the early risers), from 1847 to 1849.

Peasants resisted the liberal revolution in Santander as well. During both the triennium and the Carlist War this resistance converged with the royalist counter-revolution but did not really form part of it. The new liberal regime held no attractions for the province's peasants and instead brought them military service, especially burdensome in time of war, and taxes which increased by 60 per cent between 1820 and 1822. It also brought an attack on their beliefs and practices when it banned burials inside churches and imposed the use of open-air cemeteries. The liberal state also oversaw the deterioration of the peasants' position on the land by allowing the local minor nobility, known as *caciques*, to take control of municipal lands to which the peasantry formerly had had access. The peasants responded by taking to the hills and forming small guerrilla bands. These were distinct from the Carlist forces and acted independently of them. Neither did their attacks on property take political affiliation into account. The property of the clergy, which was overwhelmingly anti-liberal, was one of their favorite targets. These activities persisted in Santander until at least 1845, well after the Carlist War had ended.[14]

However, the greatest example of popular anti-liberalism was Carlism, and its center of gravity lay in the Basque Provinces and Navarre, especially in the countryside. According to John Coverdale, Carlism received the support of a 'cross section of traditional [Basque] society', including most of the cities, and in rural areas and small towns support was 'almost universal'. Liberalism brought sweeping changes to rural life harmful to the peasantry: the sale of common lands, which were purchased by wealthy merchants and nobles, and the threat to long-term leases and inherited rights represented by absolute ownership rights. However, in the Basque Provinces liberalism had other enemies: the clergy and the *jauntxos*, the local lesser nobility whose local political power was based on the regional charter known as the *fueros*. This local nobility differed from that in central and southern Spain in both its nature and its role: 'the region did not abound in powerful or influential nobles. The nobles of the Basque country were of middling rank and fortune. Many of them lived in small towns and were in direct contact with the peasantry [and] many of them supported the Carlist movement.'[15]

These local notables gave peasant anti-liberalism a leadership and an ideology, the 'revolutionary project', or rather the counter-revolutionary one, which made Carlism such a vigorous opponent of liberalism. Their influence did work in the opposite direction too, albeit rarely. In the early days of the Carlist War General Quesada, government commander in the north, reported that some peasants did not support the Carlists because 'they have some good priest to hold them back, or some landowner of upright opinion who has freed them from seduction at the cost of sacrifices and expenses'.[16] Rural liberalism was strongest and Carlism came closest to being a rural class war in the wine-producing region of the Rioja, in the province of Alava, where land was more unequally divided than elsewhere in the region and the loss of common lands was greater. There landowners were the target of Carlist violence and created their own pro-government defence force, the Tiradores de Alava.

Carlism retained its strength in the rural world of Navarre and the Basque Provinces into the twentieth century. During the Restoration the Traditionalist Communion, as the Carlists called themselves, regularly won elections there, especially in rural districts where social patterns changed least. They monopolized Tolosa and Azpeitia, in Guipúzcoa, thanks in large part to the efforts of the clergy and the local landowners. The latter had both economic and moral authority, as the owners of the farms which the farmers leased, as local powerholders and as military leaders in the two Carlist wars. In Alava and Vizcaya, where there were fewer tenants and more smallholders, they retained a moral authority, although in more limited areas of the province. The continuing strength of Carlism in Navarre was shown during the Civil War, when thousands volunteered for the Communion's military forces which fought with Franco's army.

Revolution

Peasant opposition to the liberal state and liberal society took on a politically reactionary color in the north-east, where there was a numerous small peasantry and where religious attachments remained strong enough to serve as an ideological catalyst. In the south, with its mass of landless and near-landless and where the Church had little influence, rural conflict eventually became attached to political movements of the left, especially anarchism.

The alienation of these groups from the liberal revolution was not inevitable. In the 1830s and 1840s laborers and tenants resisted nobles' claims to the land in areas under seigneurial control by witholding rents. These were collective decisions taken at the most fluid moments in national politics at the initiative of local notables such as militia leaders, members of the municipal government and, occasionally, large tenants. The role of the clergy was especially important early on.

However, once the status of the seigneuries was definitively settled in favor of the nobility the peasants were on their own. They responded by demanding the division of municipal lands, which they got in some places, or by occupying land which was either municipally or privately owned. Many engaged in other illegal activities, such as banditry or smuggling. Laborers also protested, sometimes violently, against the use of workers from outside the municipality who lowered wages and took scarce employment. Protest increased 'spectacularly' in the 1860s. Arson was especially common: the number of reported incidents nationally rose from 236 in 1857 to 428 in 1860, 557 in 1863 and 663 in 1870. Landowners requested more protection from the Guardia Civil and fled the countryside for the cities.[17]

The town of Bencarrón de los Condes (Seville) experienced violence as early as the 1830s as unemployed laborers began to steal crops and even 'systematically cut and uproot olive and other trees to sell them for firewood in [Seville]'. Banditry and smuggling were common and frequent robberies left landowners so insecure that many of them sought, and were given, weapons permits from the town council. They also organized posses 'in which residents of Bencarrón and Horcajos and their respective mayors, armed and on horseback, patrolled the nearby fields'.[18]

During the 1850s and 1860s rural unrest in the south was occasionally channelled into political, usually insurrectionary, movements led by radical democrats. A rising in Seville in June 1857, frequently seen as a spontaneous peasant revolt, formed part of a supposed national popular rising planned by the Democrat leader Sixto Cámara. The fierce repression of the rising, which included the execution of ninety-five people, turned a number of towns in Seville into foci of peasant unrest. Likewise, the seizure of the town of Loja by Rafael Pérez del Alamo in 1861 had political not social aims, although the peasants who supported him had their own agenda. During the revolution of 1868 Pérez del Alamo led the revolutionary committee in Carmona which threatened to 'punish those who do not respect private property by stealing wood or olives' and denounced people who could not distinguish between 'liberty and anarchy, democracy and communism'.[19]

The Revolution of 1868 received a great deal of support from the landless, although the meaning they gave it contradicted that of the political leadership. While the new revolutionary authorities, both local and national, spoke and acted in defence of private property, the rural poor responded by occupying and dividing land they considered to have been illegitimately acquired during the liberal revolution: seigneurial lands and commons but not Church lands. In the town of Chucena, for example, as soon as the peasants heard about the revolution they attempted to divide a farm belonging to the Duke of Medinasidonia which had been under dispute since early in the century and which they had already attempted to divide in the 1830s and in 1854.

> In 1868 the occupation was carried out against all the decisions and threats of the Revolutionary Junta. The peasants burned the guard's hut and intimidated and struck those who watched the livestock and forced them to remove the animals from the fields. On October 19 there was a pair of Civil Guards there . . . but in December the peasants put their own animals in the fields and shot those of the tenant.[20]

In December the new government ordered an end to all land occupations and this triggered a series of revolts across the south.

For the rural poor of the south the final disenchantment with radical democracy came in 1848. This disenchantment coincided with the introduction of anarchism into Spain. This new ideology fell on fertile ground; it was, as Manuel Pérez Yruela says, 'the first ideology whose basic message spoke to the problems and long term dissatisfaction of the [rural] working class'.[21] But anarchism did not give rise to sustained protest in the countryside. Rather, rural protest took the form of short, sharp shocks followed by long lulls: the rising at Montilla in 1873, the 'Black Hand' in 1882, the strike wave of 1903–5 and the Bolshevik triennium of 1918–20, a major outbreak of strikes and land occupations triggered by news of the Russian Revolution and deteriorating economic conditions in the countryside.

What accounts for the intermittent nature of southern rural protest? The nature of anarchism itself has often been blamed. Few historians have been more critical than Eric Hobsbawm in his classic study, *Primitive Rebels*. For Hobsbawm Andalucian anarchism is 'the most impressive example of a modern mass millenarian or quasi-millenarian movement'. Although it had advantages, most important of which was its symbiosis with the temper of the peasantry, it had disadvantages which 'were fatal'. Without a proper sense of organization or discipline it was incapable of mounting a serious revolutionary challenge. Hobsbawm recognizes that anarchism had begun to evolve and take on trade union forms but these remained 'shadowy' and ineffective. Anarchism was, then,

> a form of peasant movement almost incapable of effective adaptation to modern conditions, though it is their outcome. Had a different ideology penetrated the Andalusian countryside in the 1870s, it might have transformed the spontaneous and unstable rebelliousness of the peasants into something far more formidable, because more disciplined, as communism has sometimes succeeded in doing. This did not happen. And thus the history of anarchism almost alone among modern social movements, is one of unrelieved failure; and unless some unforeseen historical changes occur, it is likely to go down in the books with the Anabaptists and the rest of the prophets who, though not unarmed, did not know what to do with their arms, and were defeated for ever.[22]

Raymond Carr has made a similar point, describing rural anarchism as 'less an organization than a state of mind . . . a religious movement' whose millennium did not require prolonged struggle or organization.[23]

Others are less critical of anarchism. Victor Pérez Díaz and Manuel Pérez Yruela have argued that anarchism changed – matured? – over time. Pérez Yruela notes that it became less utopian and stressed more limited goals although it was only during the Republic, by which time Socialism had become a major presence in the south, that a significant, ongoing labor movement existed. At the same time, he recognizes that repression was crucial to interrupting this development and that the very nature of anarchism, 'with its direct action, with the image of terrorism and danger it carried', tempted governments to act 'with the slightest motive or even without motive'. And Pérez Díaz points to the scarce resources, economic, political, social and cultural, available to southern peasants as central to making their protest sporadic.[24]

Its organizational informality and ability to capture the insurrectionary urges of the rural poor were great advantages for rural anarchism. It is unlikely that a more discipline-minded movement could have marshalled

Andalucia's landless more effectively. The Socialists, for whom organization and discipline were fetishes, could not. When the Socialists finally gained a mass following in the rural south during the 1930s they had as much difficulty as the anarchists in disciplining their new recruits. Indeed, essentially moderate national leaders, such as Francisco Largo Caballero, found themselves pushed in ever more radical directions by an increasingly militant labor movement and the agricultural workers' union, the Federación Nacional de los Trabajadores de la Tierra (FNTT), was central to this process.

Quiet Protest

Both the counter-revolutionary and revolutionary movements discussed so far challenged the liberal revolution, and the private property in land it created, in a direct and violent way. But there were other, peaceful, protests which, more limited in their objectives, were unlikely to make the jump from court records to the historical record. Such 'quiet' protests have escaped the attention of historians of rural Spain but may have been just as significant as, and were probably more numerous than, the louder and more eye-catching episodes.

On December 24, 1929 the Supreme Court refused to grant two men from the village of Saelices el Chico, in the province of Salamanca, permission to appeal the decisions of two lower courts in a case turning on a dispute over property rights to a piece of common land. The case illustrates beautifully the way in which the redefinition of property effected by the liberal revolution could be the cause of prolonged conflict, even in a part of the country where the peasantry had a reputation for docility.[25] The original suit was brought by some villagers who claimed that a number of others, including the mayor, had in 1925 and 1926 ploughed up part of the common meadow they had used for pasture. They also claimed that land purchases made in 1898, 1912 and 1914 – the last from José María Narváez, Duke of Valencia, a descendant of the great military politician Rámon Narváez – had given them private property rights over a large share of the meadow.

The defendants argued that no such property rights existed, that 'the residents of the village .. had owned the meadow from time immemorial . . . and that it was later declared municipal property . . . and included in the register of public woodlands, belonging to the municipality and not to the plaintiffs' and that they had ploughed the land 'in the belief that they were exercising their rights'. They admitted that in 1897 the state had sold to a number of villagers part of the property, amounting to 6,701 of more than 30,000 trees on it, but that the rest continued to belong to the village. They argued that the residents had subsequently controlled the use of the meadow and pointed to the acquittal in 1914, 1915 and 1916 of one of the defendants on charges of illegally grazing animals on the land in question and to the dropping of a case against him in 1920, when he was mayor, for having removed livestock which was grazing there without permission from the local council. Furthermore, there was no record in the municipal archive that the meadow had ever been divided up.

The plaintiffs won in the court of first instance, in Ciudad Rodrigo. This decision was upheld in the regional court, the Audiencia, in Valladolid, which ordered the defendants to abstain from further infringements on the land in question and to pay the plaintiffs an indemnity of 30,000 pesetas. The Supreme Court refused to hear their appeal. The matter was closed, at least legally, but not in the minds of some villagers. After the Socialists came to power in 1982 one elderly resident of Saelices wrote to Prime Minister Felipe González demanding that these unjust decisions be overturned.

The Second Republic and the Challenge to Property

Throughout the 1920s landowners and the state had two responses to peasant unrest. One was to repress it, using the Guardia Civil or, when necessary, the army. The other, which usually came from municipal governments, was to take the sharpest edge off material misery with such stopgaps as public works projects to provide employment, relief in the form of food or money, or the assignment of unemployed laborers to the wealthiest landowners who would find them something to do and pay them a wage, although one below the norm.

The Second Republic was the first attempt to make the rural settlement produced by the liberal revolution more congenial to small tenants and agricultural laborers. Reformist governments dominated by middle-class Republicans, but including some Socialist ministers, sought to make their lives less desperate and insecure. For the first time the liberal state was calling the absolute rights of property into question. It was also threatening the wealth and challenging the social ascendancy of landowners and large tenants. It paid a high price for it.

The Provisional Government of the Republic, led by the Socialist Labor Minister Francisco Largo Caballero, took a number of measures to alleviate the situation of the rural poor, especially in the south. The Law of Municipal Boundaries required landowners to hire local residents and prohibited them from hiring outsiders. Rural arbitration committees, with representatives of the state, unions and employers, were set up to ensure that labor legislation was not ignored and to serve as a forum for collective bargaining. The eight-hour day was introduced for agricultural work. In case landowners sought to undermine the law by not cultivating their land, a compulsory cultivation decree threatened the expropriation of land which was not farmed 'according to the uses and customs' of the region. Tenants were given new security by a decree which allowed eviction only for non-payment of rent or failure to cultivate the land, and registered labor organizations were given preference over individuals in renting large properties.

These decrees, which were much more impressive on paper than in practice, were intended as stopgaps until an agrarian reform could be legislated. When the Agrarian Reform Law was finally passed in September 1932 it turned out to be highly complex, not focused on the real problem area, the south, and because of its compensation provisions, very expensive to put into effect.

Even so, the law had great potential. Edward Malefakis has described it as a 'revolutionary document'.[26] However, even in its most progressive phase the Azaña government never made use of the law's potential. The first Technical Commission had set a target of settling 60,000 families per year; by December 1933 only 4,399 people had been settled on 24,203 hectares. The situation was exacerbated by the landowners who, egged on by the leaders of the CEDA, soon to become the largest party in the Cortes, did whatever they could to obstruct the reform, refusing to cultivate land, locking out workers and flouting the decisons of the arbitration committees, while telling workers to 'Comed Republica', literally 'eat the Republic'. In the province of Seville alone some 66,000 hectares were taken out of cultivation between 1931 and 1933. The right also managed to seriously weaken a bill, introduced in the summer of 1933, designed to protect tenants and give them the opportunity to purchase the land they rented.[27]

Agrarian reform directed from Madrid was not the only threat to landowners. The loss of local political power to the left was also a danger, as George Collier has shown in his study of the town of Los Olivos (Huelva). There the Socialists took control of the municipal council in May 1933 and used their position to enforce Republican labor legislation, changing the 'relations of employment' and challenging 'the autonomy of agrarian proprietors to manage their own affairs'. The municipal employment office controlled hiring and required landowners to register all jobs there, hours of work were formalized and reduced and the use of machinery was restricted. The Socialist council also carried out important public works projects which improved local life and provided employment. All these initiatives were bitterly opposed by landowners and were reversed when the right regained control of the town hall.

Agricultural reform was slowed even more following the victory of the right in the elections of November 1933. The Law of Municipal Boundaries was repealed in May 1934 and the arbitration committees had ceased to function by the end of the year. The government also introduced a Law to Reform the Agrarian Reform which made further expropriations more difficult and expensive. At the same time there was a return to what Paul Preston calls 'the semi-feudal relations of dependence which had prevailed before 1931' as landowners ignored the laws still on the books.[28] The position of tenants became a major issue while the right was in power. At the end of 1934 Manuel Giménez Fernàndez, the CEDA Agriculture Minister and a sincere social Catholic, introduced a bill making it possible for tenants to purchase land they had leased for twelve years. The bill was fiercely opposed by the Minister's own caucus which succeeded in having anything which curtailed property rights, such as the length of leases, limitations on evictions and 'access to property rights' reduced or eliminated. Giménez Fernández was dropped from the cabinet in March 1935.

At the same time, attempts by the left Republican autonomous regional government of Catalonia to help the Catalan *rabassaires* brought the Generalitat into direct conflict with the conservative administration in Madrid. Had the destruction of the *rabassa morta* lease coincided with the liberal revolution at the beginning of the nineteenth century the *rabassaires* would probably have become Carlists. As it took place at the end of the century, under the auspices of a conservative, constitutional regime, they adopted a different type of protest: federal republicanism. They had organized in 1891 and when wine prices began to plummet after the First World War they did so again, forming the Unió de Rabassaires in 1920. Many of its early leaders were Catalan Republicans of whom the best known was Lluís Companys. During the Primo de Rivera dictatorship (1923–30) the Unió took a moderate line, requesting that the government deal with the *rabassaire* issue as it dealt with the *foros* in Galicia, but to no avail.

During the Second Republic the Unió de Rabassaires was the key to the success of Companys' party, the Esquerra Republicana Catalana, which controlled the regional government after the region was granted autonomy in 1932. Companys acted to reward this crucial constituency by passing the Law of Agricultural Contracts in April 1934. The law was intended to allow the *rabassaires* to acquire ownership of any land they had leased for eighteen years and it was expected that about 30,000 tenants would be able to do so. It also aimed to provide more general stability in the countryside by ending evictions and short-term leases: 'to make all Catalan peasants property owners, within the context of economically viable family holdings, and in this way create a stable society of economically independent and therefore free men.'[29]

However, the Institut Agrari de Sant Isidre, the Catalan landowners' lobby, pressured the national government to challenge the constitutionality of the law. When the Court of Constitutional Guarantees ruled against Companys he had the law passed again in a slightly different form. Finally, in September 1934 Madrid and Barcelona were able to agree on a revised version of the law. The agreement was quickly overshadowed by the attempted insurrection of October 6, 1934 in the aftermath of which the Law of Agricultural Contracts was suspended. It was replaced in May 1935 by a new tenancy law, nominally inspired by social Catholic principles, which made it possible for landowners to easily evict tenants by claiming they planned to cultivate the land themselves. In Catalonia some 1,400 tenants were evicted, including *rabassaires* who had been on their farms twenty, thirty and, in one case, sixty years.

The two years of right-wing government served only to heighten rural conflict in both Catalonia and the south. Following the electoral victory of the Popular Front on February 16, 1936 and the restoration of the regional government the Law of Agricultural Contracts was revived and a decree issued to return tenants who had been evicted after October 1934. As a result of the repression of 1935 the Unió de Rabassaires had been radicalized and moved closer to the parties of the revolutionary left, although without ever abandoning its belief in private property and the family farm. During the Civil War it opposed the collectivization of agriculture which had taken place under anarchist auspices in parts of Catalonia during the summer of 1936, and supported the efforts of the Generalitat to control and then roll back this social revolution. This embroiled it in conflicts, often violent, with the anarchists, the bloodiest of which took place in January 1937 when thirty opponents of collectivization were killed. The *rabassaires* won the battle when the collectives were disbanded after May 1937, but lost their struggle for independence with the defeat of the Republic in April 1939.

In the south, agricultural laborers and *yunteros* responded to the Popular Front triumph by initiating a series of land seizures which the government was forced to sanction. In Badajoz the Socialist agricultural workers' union, FNTT, organized the seizure of 3,000 estates by some 60,000 people. This popular mobilization also compelled the government to revitalize the agrarian reform process. In the four months before the outbreak of the Civil War over 110,000 peeople were settled on half a million hectares. Municipal and local authorities imposed *repartimiento*, assigning groups of workers to large estates regardless of their owners' wishes. There was also a new tone in social relations at the local level. Manuel Pérez Yruela repeats the story of a well-off woman in one village in Córdoba who had her son in a baby carriage when a poor woman, carrying her son in her arms, said that her son should be able to ride too, took the other woman's child out, put hers in and when he had been there a few minutes gave the carriage back. The owner 'was stunned by the lack of respect'.[30] Laborers and small farmers became much more assertive and this frightened the landowners, many of whom fled to the provincial capitals or Madrid. The stage was set for the violent social conflict triggered by the beginning of the Spanish Civil War.

3
Cities and Towns

Just as the liberal revolution brought private property to the countryside, it brought freedom and liberty to the world of manufacturing and commerce. As in other European countries during the Old Regime these activities were controlled by *gremios* (guilds), local institutions to which the Crown had granted the privilege of regulating every aspect of a given trade. However, as the Crown sought to revitalize the economy and restore the country's international position in the second half of the eighteenth century – a sort of Ancien Regime *perestroika* - it found itself following contradictory policies which sought to enhance the status of artisans while seriously damaging their position and that of the institutions which protected them.

Spanish liberals had a much less ambiguous approach. For them the guilds and the regulation of the manufacturing economy which they embodied were not only obstacles to efficiency and progress. They were also philosophically abhorrent, violations of the right to work and of natural and civil liberties. They were prepared to accept the existence of guilds as voluntary organizations with welfare functions so long as the freedom of the individual to carry on the economic activity he wished was respected. Of course this hit at the power of the guilds under the Old Regime, which was based precisely on their monopolistic and regulatory powers. But unlike France during the Revolution, Spanish liberals did not abolish the guilds or prohibit workers from forming organizations.

Stripping the guilds of the privileges which had sustained them cleared the way for the emergence of a manufacturing sector which was not only larger but also contained a very different set of social relations. The world of more-or-less independent, small-scale artisans with a corporate existence, a recognized place in society and the accompanying self-esteem gave way to one of individual workers without any social role or prestige who sought work from employers in return for a cash wage. Former artisans ended up on both sides of the divide, some as employers but most as workers. Most industrialists came from outside the artisanate. The regime of economic freedom gave those with resources, especially merchants, the opportunity to move into new activities and, in time, to constitute a new urban elite. As it allowed the formation of new classes, this freedom also set the stage for the emergence of new tensions and conflicts, and eventually of new organizations with their own demands, either for limits on the economic freedom of the liberal revolution for another revolution to impose a new conception of freedom.

Elites and White Collars

A New Urban Elite

The elite which emerged in Spain's first industrial city, Barcelona, what Gary McDonogh has called the 'good families', resembled its landed counterpart in that it was 'neither a capitalist bourgeoisie nor an aristocratic survival [but rather] an elite composed both of old and new holders of socioeconomic power'.[1] For most of the nineteenth century the old and the new remained apart but in the 1880s they began to coalesce.

The pattern can be followed in the successive generations of one of the city's leading industrial families, the Guells. Juan Guell Ferrer (1800–77) made his fortune in commerce in Cuba and returned to Barcelona in 1836 to start what became a very successful textile business. Guell Ferrer was prominent in banking as well. His heir, Eusebio Guell Bucigalipi (1850–1918), added to the family's wealth and power. He converted the textile business into an industrial colony and was active in insurance and railways. In 1871 he married the daughter of Antonio López, the Marquis of Comillas, and became a director of each of the López companies. He was ennobled, as Count Guell, in 1910. His eldest son, Antonio Guell López (1874–1958) inherited that title and also that of his grandfather and was president of the López businesses. He held a position at Court and in 1930 Alfonso XIII named him mayor of Barcelona.

The first two Guells married women from similar social backgrounds, but for the third marriage became a vehicle for significant social mobility and for the creation of a new elite. The sisters of Antonio Guell López married into the old regional aristocracy. The eldest, Isabel, married the Marquis of Castelldosirus and Baron of Santa Pau, a family whose title dated from 1148 and who before this had married exclusively members of other aristocratic families, to the extent that they often required papal dispensations for consanguinity. Beginning in 1889 women from other leading families of industrialists made similar marriages. And it was women from the new families who married men from the old. Such marriages 'represented the most intensive possible exchange of economic capital for social capital. Titles in general pass through the male line . . . Women of the bourgeoisie, while they would generally not inherit economic investments were the bearers of liquid capital in the form of the dowry'.[2]

Not all industrial regions developed a similar composite elite. In Asturias the old nobility remained aloof from industry and its mentors. In only a few cases did aristocrats invest in industry and in even fewer did they marry into industrialists' families. There was the odd exception, such as the Marquis of Santa Cruz de Marcenado, whose title dated from 1679, who married Ramona Rodríguez Sampedro, the daughter of a financier and conservative politician, but for the most part 'the traditional nobility practised a pronounced endogamy which favored the accumulation of titles'. By contrast, holders of more recent titles found industry – and industrialists' daughters – much more attractive.[3]

Family ties had an important economic role as well. This is clearest in the creation of the López group, known as the *Trasatlánticos*, after the López shipping company, which brought together a series of companies with interlocking directorates 'embedded in a network of social ties and kinship'.[4] The six López companies – Hispano-Colonial Bank, Transatlantic Company, Philippine Tobacco, Spanish Oil Company, Asphalts and Portland Cement and the Bank López-Bru – shared their directors, and most came from a small group of families which were connected by marriage. The López, Guell and Arnús-Gamazo were on all six boards, the Ferrer-Vidal, Sotolongo, Satrústegui and Oñate-Gil on four, and the Carreras, Miralles del Imperial, Girona and Díaz-Quijanos on three. The *Trasatlánticos* formed a cohesive social group in another way as well. They summered together in the coastal village of Comillas (Santander), which was not one of the traditional summer resorts but was the birthplace of Antonio López. By 1927 nineteen palaces had been built there and others and a number of hotels were under construction.

From 1872 to 1932 fifty-two Catalans were ennobled, many of them industrialists and financiers, but neither wealth nor a title provided automatic entry into the Barcelona elite. Indeed industrialists with freshly minted titles were as likely to receive ridicule as acceptance. Acceptance came through the acquisition of skills and tastes, through education and training; through 'socialization in the right code of conduct . . . the influence of [which] transcended the boundary between aristocrat and industrialist to become one of the unifying characteristics of the elite'.[5]

There was a special educational path for the elite. Boys attended the Jesuit schools, which had traditionally educated the sons of the rich and powerful in Spain. (Those poorer children who were able to attend on scholarships were given distinctive uniforms.) In the twentieth century, a university degree, usually in law, became the norm. There was no such established centre for the daughters of the elite but in the mid-nineteenth century the Society of the Sacred Heart was imported from France. The elite socialized together at the Opera and in private clubs and, as we have mentioned, summered together, either at Comillas or at San Sebastián. Even when its members travelled abroad they went to the same places. In the late nineteenth century Vichy was, according to one writer, 'the supreme attraction and indispensable luxury'.[6]

The elite was bilingual in Castilian and Catalan, unlike the rural population and the working class which were predominantly Catalan speaking. However, as immigration made Catalan society more bilingual the elite became less so. By the early twentieth century the elite spoke Castilian, not Catalan, at home, and some women did not learn Catalan at all since they did not need the language to deal with Catalan-speaking workers. The Jesuits, who educated the sons of most elite families, taught in Castilian and some Barcelona priests preached in it instead of in Catalan. In such a basic question as language the elite was markedly different from the bulk of Catalan society.

As the city expanded after the walls were torn down in the 1850s, Barcelona became increasingly segregated. The Rambla de Cataluña and the Paseo de Gracia, new streets which led north from the old city, became residential centers for industrialists and aristocrats. The workers remained in the old core or in the districts around the factories. Güell Park, designed by the great architect Antonio Gaudí, was intended as an upper-class residential district removed from the city and surrounded by walls – having torn down the walls of the old city the elite then considered putting up new ones to protect itself – but it never developed because potential residents thought it too isolated.

The elite was identifiable even in death. The Old Cemetery, which was built in the nineteenth century, had three distinct sections to correspond to social class. The first was the paupers' ditch, the second was the main section with blocks of niches seven high, and the third, the last to be built, was a cloister separated from the main section by an interior wall where the pantheons of the wealthy were located. Prices ranged from a minimum of 50 pesetas in the main section to 600 behind the wall but that only paid for the plot; the mausoleum, often designed by the best architects in the city, had to be built as well. Not all the elite was buried here: the López had a private pantheon in Comillas and Manuel Girona, who gave money so that work on Barcelona cathedral could be completed, was buried in the cloister even though this had been prohibited since the sixteenth century.

The Officer Corps

The army was probably the most important instrument of social mobility in Spain during the nineteenth century. Much more than those of other countries, the Spanish army was open to talent and drew from a broad social base. Raymond Carr has called it 'an instrument for social mobility without equal in Europe'.[7] If rags to riches were possible in nineteenth-century Spain the army was the most likely vehicle.

The requirement that potential officers provide proof of noble blood was eliminated in 1836, but even before this it had been possible to rise through the ranks. During the War of Independence, as the army tripled in size there was a massive influx of such plebeian officers. The colonial wars, the Carlist War and the frequent political crises in which the military were involved produced both a further expansion of the officer corps and a flood of promotions. There were 1,443 promotions in 1843, 921 in 1854 and 2,132 in 1868, all years in which military revolts toppled a government. By the end of the century the number of officers had jumped to 13,000, compared to 6,100 in 1864. For most of the last quarter of the century there was one officer for every 9 soldiers compared to ratios of one to 17 in Austria–Hungary, one to 18 in Italy, one to 20 in France and one to 24 in Germany.

In the second half of the century, and especially after the Restoration managed to get the army out of immediate political involvement, the military career became increasingly institutionalized and the officer corps became increasingly self-recruited. Military academies had a larger role and they favored the sons of officers. Between 1883 and 1893 the General Military Academy reserved half the places for the sons of officers. Those whose fathers had died in action were automatically admitted and did not have to pass the entrance examination. The army became more and more a self-enclosed caste, whose personal ties to other social groups became more attenuated. Officers were much less a part of society after 1875 than before and began to develop a corporate mentality, something which had been absent earlier, and the trend became more accentuated as time went on. After 1900, as an increasingly complex society threw up new dissatisfactions such as regional nationalism and the labor movement which challenged the officers' rigid vision of the meaning of Spain and sense of social order, they came to see the military as the embodiment of the nation and to distrust, even despise, most civilian politicians and liberal politics in general. When the army applied political pressure in the twentieth century it was no longer on behalf of one branch of liberalism against another, but on behalf of corporate interests or 'national' ones, such as order or unity, and against the government and liberal, representative politics itself.

The differences, and similarities, between the two periods can be illustrated in the careers of two officers, one – Baldomero Espartero – arguably the most important figure of the second third of the nineteenth century, the other – Francisco Franco – without doubt the most important figure of the second third of the twentieth.

Espartero (1792–1879) came from a humble background, the ninth child of a wheelwright in the village of Granátula (Ciudad Real). He joined the army as a common soldier during the War of Independence but was able to train to become an officer. He volunteered to fight in the colonial wars in South America where his personal valor won him a number of battlefield promotions. His big opportunity came with the Carlist War, during which he rose to commander in chief, was ennobled twice and named a minister. Espartero's political beliefs were little more than a simple-minded liberalism but he became the idol of the urban lower classes, especially in Madrid, and a leader of the Progressives. He was Regent from 1840 to 1843 and Prime Minister from 1854 to 1856. Following the revolution of 1868 which chased Isabel II from the throne he was a candidate for the Crown. In 1872 he was made a prince, a title normally held only by members of the royal family.

Francisco Franco (1892–1975), the son of a naval officer, entered the military academy after having failed to get into the navy himself. From that point on, his career is similar in a number of ways to that of Espartero. Even though he graduated 251 in a class of 312 his valor allowed him to make a lightning rise during the Moroccan War. He was a captain at 23, a major in 1917, lieutenant colonel in 1923, colonel in 1925 and general in 1926, at 33. His politics were also simple minded, but in his case an authoritarianism based on virulent anti-Communism. He too was the victorious commanding general in a civil war and became the country's ruler. His political skills were much better than those of Espartero and he was able to stay in power for a much longer time, until his death in 1975.

Not all officers shared the same prospects for advancement. Those who began as cadets were much more likely to reach the higher ranks than those who had risen through the ranks. Most officers from lower-class backgrounds fell into this second group. They rarely became generals and most commonly ended up between lieutenant and major. Fernández Bastarreche has summarized the process: 'in all the corps social origin determined a better career for those from military families than for those from the middle class and better for these than for those from the lower classes.'[8] In his analysis of 186 generals, Daniel Headrick found that about a third came from the aristocracy or from families which were important in the military, civil administration or business. The aristocrats were most numerous in the generation who became generals before 1833. On the other hand, only 5 per cent came from what he calls the lower classes and all of those had begun their careers as ordinary soldiers. The rest came from groups in between. Over time an increasing number came out of the military academies.[9]

The geographical origins of the officers followed a clear pattern, one which remained constant throughout the century. The largest number came from Andalucia and New Castile; the smallest from Catalonia and Galicia. The Basque Provinces also produced few officers. In general terms the interior and most rural regions produced most officers while the coastal and most urban ones produced the fewest. Furthermore, Catalonia and the Basque Provinces were the economically most developed regions and the ones where a sense of regional identity was strongest.

What was the officer's place in society? This depended very much on rank. At the top, the generals formed part of the social and political elite. Many were ennobled, especially by Isabel II. Of the 186 generals studied by Headrick, 34 received titles, and some more than one. They also moved into the composite elite of liberal Spain in a number of ways: buying land, serving on boards of directors and holding positions at Court. (This was probably most important during the reign of Alfonso XIII, who prided himself on his special relationship with the army and who liked to take an active role in its affairs.) Marriage was another form of integration: Espartero married the daughter of a wealthy landowner from Logroño. Juan Prim, the military leader of the revolution of 1868, married the daughter of a

Mexican banker and his daughter married into the powerful and wealthy Heredia family.

But Spain had a lot of generals and not all could hope for a title, an heiress or a corporate directorship. In 1896 there were 296 generals, the smallest number since 1825, but still more than in Italy, Germany or Austria-Hungary. Yet those who had to live on their salary did well enough. At mid-century the average salary was equivalent to that of a senior civil servant and a captain general earned as much as a cabinet minister. In the 1880s salaries ranged from 9,000 reales for a brigadier general to 22,500 for a lieutenant general and 30,000 for a captain general, more than their French counterparts and much more than the 12,500 earned by cabinet ministers.

Other officers, including colonels, had a harder time and often could not live on their pay. One English resident wrote in 1845 that officers' 'pay is barely equal to sustaining the appearance of a gentleman. In most of our regimental messes, and at Oxford and Cambridge, it would be considered little better than servants' wages . . . An English nobleman gives his valet as much per annum as the Queen of Spain to a captain in her army'. Two years later an article from *The Times* claimed that 'nothing is more common than to see Spanish officers . . . begging alms in the streets of Madrid after having in vain tried to earn a livelihood as servants in hotels'.[10] On the salary scale announced in 1852 lieutenants earned 550 reales per month, marginally more than a skilled mason or carpenter. Captains received 1,000 reales, majors between 1,400 and 1,600 and colonels 2,300, more than a schoolteacher, who was lucky to earn 650, and similar to university professors and middle level bureaucrats. Even after salaries improved in the 1870s many officers had to find second jobs in order to make ends meet. Still, in provincial garrison towns they cut something of a figure and many officers could find wives from well-off families. In Murcia they often married the daughters of local landowners. Francisco Franco's wife, Carmen Polo, came from a solidly bourgeois family in Oviedo.

In a good many, if not most, cases the officer's life offered little in the way of professional satisfaction. Their usual lot was to be posted to a garrison town where they had little to do. After 1900 many officers, in some garrisons as many as half, had no assignment and some took other full-time jobs. In 1916 the War Minister tried to test officers for their physical and professional condition but he soon had to drop the idea when Artillery and Engineering officers refused to take part. The Barcelona garrison was the first to be tested and there 'some of the officers . . . were in wretched physical condition and could not mount a horse . . . One general asked to be allowed to pass to the reserve rather than be forced to take the tests'.[11]

The Middling Classes

Stretching from the summit of Spain's elite to poorly paid bureaucrats with more pride than prestige or money, the officer corps was far from a homogeneous social category. Likewise, between the working class and the elite stretched a large, diverse and confusing agglomeration which Spaniards called the *clases medias*, the intermediate or middling classes. José María Jover defines them as those who were eligible to vote under the Constitution of 1845, that is those who had a salary of 8,000 reales per year or paid direct taxes of 400 reales, which meant owning property which provided 4,800 reales in income. There were not many of them: 157,931, or 1.02 per cent of the population, in 1858 and 418,271, or 2.7 per cent, in 1865.[12] These were the people whom the moderates saw as allies against further revolution and whom they considered worthy of a political voice. Francisco Pacheco set out the distinction in 1845 between 'the owners, even if in small shares, of the greater part of property, owners of intelligence and ordered force' on the one hand and 'whoever labors to earn his living by the sweat of his brow at an arduous job . . . who is reduced to a scanty wage or an unhappy existence, similar to a machine or a slave', on the other.[13]

Such an approach has the merit of precision but it is far too restrictive and leaves out more than it includes. The cities and towns held large numbers of people – lower level civil servants, shopkeepers, some professionals – who were not workers, or even artisans, but who were not wealthy enough to be voters either, what we could call the lower middle class. Carr has noted the 'instability' in the lower reaches of the middling classes and the practice of *pluriempleo*, moonlighting, which it generated: the 'civil servants and officers who worked as copyists and business agents'.[14] Here we enter the world of genteel poverty and the importance of appearances, satirized by Antonio Flores, of apartments which were poky, dimly lit and poorly furnished, with the sole exception of the lounge for receiving guests:

> Every house has a grand salon . . .which takes up two thirds of the space, monopolizes the light and air . . . Such rooms give the tone and determine the category of the residence and the value of those who live there. Of course the man of the house, his wife and children do not spend time there but that is where the most luxurious furnishings are kept. What does it matter if the lady of the house gives birth to her first born in the darkness of a narrow, miserable bedroom, lying on a modest iron cot if there is plenty of light in the front room and the stuccoed walls reflect the decorations of the grand bed which cost 4,000 reales? . . . Every residence in the capital has one of these rooms *for receiving*, from the clerk with 12,000 reales' income and 12 children to the capitalist with no children but 200 million reales . . .[15]

These are groups about whom we know very little, scarcely even who or how many they were. We can, however, get a sense of their diversity from the range of the direct taxes they paid (See Table 3.1).

We get a similar result if we look elsewhere. Of the 17,770 people listed by Bahamonde and Toro as part of the 'bourgeoisie' in the capital in 1856, over 6 000, more than a third, paid less than 200 reales in direct tax which, on this very rough measure, would have made them ineligible to vote. Another quarter, 4,200, paid between 200 and 500 so that most of them could not have voted either. These groups included 750 of the 1,300 people in the liberal professions – among them over half the lawyers and more than 60 per cent of the doctors – over half of the stockbrokers and business agents and two-thirds of the 5,969 retail shopkeepers, but only one in six of the 824 wholesalers. The distinction between wholesalers and retailers was present in provincial cities such as Murcia. There all eight wholesalers were considered local notables; they belonged to the Casino and participated in government committees. Most of the retail establishments were small, unpleasant shops which carried a wide range of goods. Such shopkeepers rarely employed

Table 3.1   *Average direct tax paid, professions and services: Zaragoza, 1843*

Occupation	Number	Average tax (reales)
Treasury contractors	20	46,487
Administrators of suppressed convents	9	9,147
Landlords	36	3,899
Brokers	8	1,875
Innkeepers	41	1,826
Administrators and employees	44	1,831
Printers	13	1,436
Book sellers	23	1,306
Apothecaries	22	1,206
Teachers (Letras)	8	1,084
Pastry shops	8	1,069
Scribes, courthouse	15	970
Sheep owners	8	790
Surgeons	53	716
Scribes, Ecclesiastical Court	7	671
Architects	9	661
Cafes and refreshment stalls	53	589
Doctors	44	568
Bakers	8	398
Surveyors	7	321
Carters	14	314
Hairdressers	8	306
Teachers, young children	18	301
Barbers	26	253
Coach renters	117	225
Shearers	22	153
Engravers	2	150
Bootblacks	15	150
Grain weighers	32	118
Music teachers	13	110
Total	703	1,357

Source: M.P. Iñigo Gias, *Zaragoza Esparterista.*

anyone from outside the family and many even had other jobs, such as masons or day laborers, themselves.[16]

The nineteenth century saw the consolidation of the major liberal professions such as law, medicine, pharmacy and engineering. These all shared the requirement of university training and during the nineteenth century the professions came to dominate the universities. At the beginning of the century theology was the most popular subject. In 1800, one of every three students at the University of Salamanca and one of every two at the University of Valencia were aspiring theologians. By 1820 students' preferences 'had been revolutionized', and theology accounted for only between 10 and 19 per cent of students at those institutions. The big winners were law, medicine and pharmacy, which was established as a separate faculty in 1845. By 1867/8 almost 50 per cent of all university students were in medicine.[17]

There were some 7,600 university students in Spain in the 1780s, a figure which had changed little by the 1850s. In 1868 there were 12,000 students and by the 1920s some 30,000, a considerable expansion, but one which kept the universities the preserve of the privileged. This was reinforced by the need to pay fees and above all the charge for taking the *licenciatura* degree, the equivalent of a license to practice, which cost as much as 3,000 reales for law and medicine.

Even so the number of professionals increased substantially in the second half of the nineteenth century and first decades of the twentieth. This was less the case for the lawyers, who numbered 5,090 in 1857 and just 5,446 in 1922, than for the doctors and pharmacists, whose numbers jumped from 4,806 and 3,169 to 12,437 and 5,534 respectively. Then there were new professions, such as industrial engineering, which was only recognized in 1850 and by 1913 had 938 practitioners. Yet as they were becoming more numerous, professionals were also becoming less free. Increasingly they found themselves engaged in salaried employment, in businesses for the engineers, in medical assistance societies for the doctors. The extreme case was probably that of the pharmacists, who were reduced to mere dispensers of prepared medicines produced by the drug companies, whose numbers mushroomed by 2,600 per cent between 1891 and 1922. Such threats to the established status of the professions provided the main impulse behind the persistent movement for corporatist organization after 1890.

Many of these professionals, and especially the lawyers, were drawn to Madrid and to jobs in the expanding state bureaucracy. In fact, only two occupational groups within the population of the capital grew during the first half of the nineteenth century. The first were the servants, who increased from 20 per cent of the population in 1757 to 34 per cent in 1857. Visiting Madrid in the 1830s, George Borrow commented that 'perhaps there is no place in the world where servants more abound than at Madrid, or at least fellows eager to proffer their services in the expectation of receiving food and wages'.[18] The other group was the bureaucracy. In 1757, 3,000 people, about 7 per cent of the population, were supported by the state; a century later there were over 10,000 people, 12.5 per cent. As the moderates built their centralized state after 1843 and strengthened the Treasury with tax reform the number of civil servants grew and the amount of money required to support them increased.

Who were the bureaucrats and the politicians? Where did they come from? According to David Ringrose, the recruiting for these elites remained pretty much as it had been under the Old Regime. Most came from the provinces, and family connections and clientelism remained key mechanisms:

> those who aspired to become civil servants acquired a varnish of university education and followed their family and clientelist (caciquil) contacts to Madrid. There they spent a period of probation combining political activity with journalism, law school, apprenticeships in the liberal professions or writers . . . Recruitment adapted to the new political and legal institutions but the sources of political personnel changed little.[19]

Anne Burdick's study of 120 writers and journalists who began their careers in the years 1835–45 shows that 82 per cent were born outside Madrid, that about a quarter had parents who were nobles or *hidalgos* and that virtually all the rest were the sons of professionals. Over 90 per cent of the group eventually held a political or bureaucratic post at one time. Ninety per cent attended university, which confirmed their provenance from the privileged strata of Spanish society, and of these 80 per cent studied law. Very few lived from their writing: Burdick counts only 6 of the 120 who did. The rest held other jobs, usually a number of different ones during their careers. The 120 writers in the sample held a total of 423 jobs, an average of 3.5 each. The most common were journalist (112), writer (107), government employee (104), lawyer (29), teacher (20) and librarian (19), of whom 18 held positions in the National Library or in ministry libraries. While the

Table 3.2 *Annual spending on salaries for State employees, 1850–1935*

Period	Total*	Share†	Period	Total	Share
1850–53	223	49	1892–98	384	38
1854–56	195	42	1899–1905	380	39
1858–62	231	37	1906–12	436	38
1863–68	205	33	1913–18	459	29
1869–74	271	34	1919–23	545	31
1874–79	335	40	1923–29	703	34
1880–85	341	35	1931–35	878	34
1886–91	394	38			

* in millions of 1913 pesetas
† of total government spending in per cent
Source: P. Tedde de Lorca, 'Estadistas y burócratas', *Revista de Occidente*, 1988.

social background, education and geographic origins of these people were similar to their predecessors of earlier centuries the political, bureaucratic and intellectual scene of liberal Spain did have a couple of new features. The first was the near-total absence of the clergy: there were only 3 priests among the 120. The second was the possibility of upward social mobility for men of humble origins. The clearest example was Juan Eugenio Hartzenbusch, who began as a carpenter and ended up as director of the National Library for thirteen years.[20]

The connection between journalism and letters on the one hand and politics and the state on the other was made at the time by Antonio Flores in his collection of satirical sketches *Ayer, hoy y mañana* (1863). The protagonist of 'The mania for jobs, the jobholders, the jobs and those who give the jobs', an ambitious young man from the provinces, tells the deputy from his district that 'letters only serve as a small leg-up towards government jobs; a small announcement one makes to proclaim that there is one more man in the world ready for a place in the government'.[21]

Although both groups were made up predominantly of immigrants, the people who manned the state were very different from those who controlled commerce and industry. The largest groups of Burdick's writers (30 per cent) came from Andalucia and Extremadura and those regions produced 40 per cent of the 202 men who were cabinet ministers between 1833 and 1854. Few of the merchants came from there despite the long commercial traditions of cities like Cádiz and Seville. By contrast the north (Santander, the Basque Provinces and the Rioja) and the central mesetas, which produced a third of the merchants and bankers in the capital in the early part of the century, sent only 10 per cent of the ministers and only 7 per cent of the writers. The divorce between political power and economic power was clearest in the case of Catalonia. From 1833 to 1901 only 24 of the 902 men who sat in the cabinet were Catalans and they served a total of only 3,334 days, not quite ten man-years.

The rage for government jobs, known as *empleomanía*, meant that there were always far more applicants, *pretendientes*, than available positions: 'To be an aspirant for a government post was almost an honoured, and certainly a recognized profession, entailing ritual visits to ministries and the cultivation of the *prohombres* of the party.'[22] Antonio Flores' protagonist, quoted earlier, arrived in Madrid as one:

> They do not come to Madrid as they once did, looking like hayseeds and hoping for a position as page to a grandee . . . Now they come with their hair combed, or as closely as they could manage in the capital of their province, having learned a bit of grammar, spelling, Latin and philosophy . . . carrying a letter of recommendation for the deputy from their district.
>
> If his father is not a voter himself [at this time only 2 per cent of the population could vote] he is the friend of an influential voter and then the letter has been signed by him. The letter merely recommends the young man because, even

> though his father does not vote he makes many others vote and is a great electoral agent . . . He asks only for a modest post which will allow the boy to live comfortably – that is without having to beg – while he devotes himself to a literary career.[23]

Indeed, it was a profession to which many men returned on a number of occasions. A character in Pérez Galdós' novel *Mendizábal* tells the hero that in his 25 years in the bureaucracy he had 'seen fourteen administrations and been dismissed seven times'. With the exception of a few special groups which managed to have the principle of immovability accepted, there was no professional civil service and all appointments were made through patronage, *a dedo* as the Spaniards say. Each time the government changed hands ministers cleaned out their ministries as well as their desks. In his memoirs, Count Romanones recounts that when he stepped down as mayor of Madrid a newspaper announced that 'tomorrow a special train will take the *cesantes*, outgoing civil servants, appointed by the Count home to Guadalajara'. Romanones does not deny the truth of the story; he merely states that 'although the author intended to cause me trouble he in fact did me a lot of good'.[24]

The *cesante* was the alter ego of the *pretendiente* and he too became a recognized figure:

> Those civil servants who are still capable of working but who, due to a reform, a ministerial caprice, a parliamentary recommendation, a word from a subterranean club or the decree of a revolutionary group have been left . . . in the street . . .

> From the most fanatic Carlist to the most radical republican, there is no political group not disposed to produce *cesantes*; all have passed through the sieve, one after another, to populate the immense pantheon reserved for that class . . .

> Since a government job is nothing more than a way of having an income without doing anything, just like a *mayorazgo* used to be . . . talent is irrelevant and . . . the whole business is reduced to whether the person who has the job is a friend or not, which saves the minister or revolutionary junta a lot of headaches.[25]

The author of the portrait, Antonio Gil Zarate, himself a bureaucrat as well as a writer, even identified six subspecies: the *acomodado*, who had independent means, the *industrioso*, who put his knowledge of government to use as a business agent – an early lobbyist perhaps? – the *literato*, who could earn a living as a man of letters, the *económico*, usually an older man with many years' service who did odd jobs and scrimped to get by on the pension due, but often not paid, the *mendicante*, who was incapable of earning a living at anything and finally the *revolucionario*, who spent his time conspiring in cafes hoping for another revolution to return his post. As late as 1880 there was a satirical magazine which bore the title *El Cesante*.

Working Class Formation

The Abolition of the Guilds

In 1813 the Cortes of Cádiz approved a law declaring that 'all Spaniards and foreigners resident in the country can freely establish factories of any kind without requiring any permission . . . [and] can practise any industry or useful trade without having been examined by any guild'. This economic freedom was revoked by Ferdinand VII in 1814 and briefly reinstated during the liberal regime of 1820 to 1823. In January 1834 the government issued new model regulations for the guilds, designed 'to remove the various obstacles which until now have opposed the development and prosperity of various industries'. The guilds still had a role, albeit not their traditional one, as 'groups of men animated by a common desire to stimulate the progress of their industry'. Under the new model the guilds lost all their privileges, were prohibited from enforcing their monopoly over the trade, could not have any rule 'which contradicted the liberty of manufacturing or internal trade' and could not force anyone to join.[1] This decree was overridden on December 6, 1836 when the more sweeping 1813 law was revived, this time definitively.

The vast majority of the guilds disappeared within a short time. But freedom had not killed off a thriving institution. The guilds were already in a bad way long before the liberals came to power. In Catalonia during the eighteenth century 'the history of the guilds' century was one of a great collective decadence . . . a slow and natural death' due to their inability to compete with the new economic forms, especially in textiles, and the failure of the state, both absolutist and liberal, to defend their privileges against this competition. The guilds of Gerona were in such a bad way by the 1830s that in 1836 city officials cancelled the Holy Thursday procession because the guilds could not afford to participate.[2] The situation was similar in Seville where, by the 1830s, the guilds were in a state of 'general calamity'.[3]

Ultimately the crisis of the guilds derived from their inability to compete with new forms of production. This is not surprising in the case of cotton textiles, which was a new industry with a new technology, but the guild system collapsed even in those areas where production was carried on in the traditional way. The silk industry, which was centered in Valencia, is the classic example.

The Arte Mayor de la Seda, the silk weavers' guild, tried to strengthen its grip on the trade in the eighteenth century, toughening up its regulations and enforcing them more thoroughly, but it was unable to prevent the merchant-manufacturer from taking advantage of the economic difficulties of the master weavers and bringing them under his control.

> A number of artisans depended on him. They were often called *fabricantes* although they had nothing more than the name. They brought to the merchant's

dispersed manufacturing their loom, in most cases but one or two . . . Their situation was always precarious and they were often without work . . . Other, semi-independent artisans preferred to buy the raw material themselves and sell the finished product to a merchant, a dangerous approach . . . which often led to debt and, in the end, to the loss of the means of production.[4]

Even some of the well-off masters, who controlled the guild, acted in this way, taking advantage of the difficulties of their colleagues. By 1813, 96 per cent of those looms which were operating were 'on the merchant's account'. The independent master was on the verge of extinction.

The situation in Seville, another traditional center of silk production, was similar. Many of the merchant–manufacturers controlled only a few masters. (In Seville there were 13 who employed 2, and 15 one.) Others had more impressive businesses; the most important merchant-manufacturer in Seville had 50 masters. The most substantial of all was probably Felix Pastor of Valencia. At the end of the eighteenth century he controlled 83 masters and 179 looms. His weaving operations employed some 400 people and all the stages of silk production around 2,000. Pastor became an important landowner and was able to purchase a noble title, marquis, from its previous owner.

As it did in Lyons, silk weaving retained its traditional organization into the 1860s. Production was carried out in their homes by artisans on a small number, usually one or two, of hand-operated looms (power looms were not used in Valencia). They were paid so much per meter for the finished product. They in turn hired journeymen to work with them In many cases the weaver owned neither his workshop nor his loom. Did Valencian weavers react like their colleagues in Lyons, studied by George Sheridan, reducing the number of non-family members and the number of males, whether kin or not, in the household?[5] Only in the 1860s and 1870s, on the eve of the industry's demise, was the artisanal mode beginning to give way to factories located in towns near Valencia which employed women at very low wages. These factories threatened the producer co-operatives which had been established earlier.

The 1836 law established the freedom to engage in economic activities but it did not outlaw associations of producers. Some guilds were able to adapt to the new circumstances and continued to exist after 1836, often as mutual aid societies. Some had made the change earlier; the carpenters of Reus created a friendly society in 1817. In Valencia the carpenters, tailors, bakers and silk weavers continued to have a corporate presence while in Barcelona the shoemakers guild, which was founded in 1212, was still alive on the eve of the Spanish Civil War.

The experience of the silk weavers shows how industrialization did not inevitably mean factory production but could take place within 'the persistence and vitality of small scale units of artisan production . . . Control over raw materials, credit, labor recruitment, work organization and markets' could produce industrialization without proletarianization and the creation of a factory proletariat.[6] The Valencia weavers were not fully proletarianized but their weak and failing grip on the means of production put them but slightly above the line. They too formed part of the working class spawned by the dissolution of the urban guild economy and the development of new manufacturing and extractive activities which had never been controlled by guilds, a working class which survived by selling its labor 'freely'.

The Spanish working class was small in relative terms, as Table 3.3 shows. It was unevenly distributed across the country, forming a series of concentrated enclaves buried in a predominantly agricultural society. The only places with a substantial working class were Catalonia, and especially Barcelona, which was the center of the textile industry; Vizcaya and, to a lesser extent, Guipúzcoa which had iron mining, iron and steel production and shipbuilding; the important coalfields of Asturias; and the light manufacturing and construction industries of Madrid. Third, the working class was highly fragmented: by work experience, regional identity and language, religion and, eventually, ideological affiliation.

Catalonia

Spain's industrialization began with the emergence of cotton textile manufacturing in Catalonia at the end of the eighteenth century. In the early phases, when access to water power was important, much of the industry was located alongside rivers such as the Llobregat and the Ter and home production, by workers who had their own looms and were farmers as well, played a large role. But as steam power and mechanized looms became more important these small centers declined and Barcelona emerged as the industrial capital of the region and the country. Wage labor became the dominant form. The two decades between 1840 and 1860 were the key period for these changes; spinning was almost totally mechanized, half of the weaving was done mechanically and the industry became more concentrated as the number of textile businesses fell from 4,470 to 1,455.

Even so, independent small-scale production remained surprisingly resilient. During the 1840s renting steam power was a common practice: 'Someone

Table 3.3 *Percentage of the labor force in the secondary sector*

	1850	*1910*
Great Britain	48	51.6
France	27	33.1
United States	17	31.6
Belgium	36	45.5
Spain	11 (1877)	18.5 (1914)

Source: I. Katznelson and A. Zolberg, *Working Class Formation* (Princeton, 1986).

built a factory with one steam engine and then leased it to a single individual or, more frequently, to a number each of whom could use a part of the building and a share of the energy produced by the steam.[7] In 1857, a tenth of all weavers in Barcelona, 1,000 men and 100 women, worked at home on manually operated machines. Even within the factories all workers were not at the same level. As it had in Lancashire, the self-acting mule perpetuated a hierarchical relationship between the spinners and the assistants whom they hired and paid.[8]

The number of workers grew slowly in the first third of the century, and contracted during the 1840s and 1850s as mechanization reduced the need for labor. In the absence of any state census between 1797 and 1857 the figures for the first half of the century are estimates or compilations prepared by private commissions. The decline was especially severe in spinning, where the number of workers fell by half between 1839 and 1861. Mechanization allowed women, and especially children, to replace men: the percentage of men in spinning fell from 20 in 1839 to 5 in 1841. The situation in Barcelona itself was a little different. According to Ildefons Cerdá there were 20,683 textile workers in the city in 1857, 13,296 men and 7,387 women, and the numbers in spinning were almost equal. He estimated that fifteen per cent of the workers were under 15 years old.

The industry's ups and downs after 1860 affected the number of workers: there were 70,000 in 1892, 29,000 in Barcelona province in 1905, 168,000 in the region in 1920, of whom 38,000 were women, and 189,000 in 1930, of whom at least 36,000 were women. In the nineteenth century most workers were probably immigrants from the Catalan countryside but after 1914 many came from southern Spain.

Despite growth and mechanization Catalan textile companies remained quite small. In 1841 the average firm had 18 workers per company. This increased to 52 in 1850 and 72 in 1861 but concentration never proceeded much beyond this level. In 1919 there were an average of 52 workers per employer in textiles, 64 in 1923 and 70 in 1927. There were some very large firms, 10 with more than 1,000 workers in 1930 – including one with 4,000 – and 14 with 400 to 500, but they were the exception among the more than 1,700 employers in the industry. Even so, textiles was the most highly concentrated activity in the region after the new public services,

Table 3.4 *Textile workers in Catalonia, 1808–61*

Year	Workers	Year	Workers
1808	100,000	1841	81,168
1833	100,009	1850	75,436
1839	117,487	1861	112,745

such as electricity and public transportation, which had an average of 133 workers per company in 1923. Most other activities, embracing about half of all workers in the region, remained on a very small scale. In the province of Barcelona in 1923 the average employer in metallurgy had 11 workers, in construction and chemicals 15, in paper 20, in printing 12, in food 3.5, in transportation 10, in commerce 2 and in clothing and leather 5. Overall, there was an average of 16.8 workers per business in industry in 1927.[9]

Catalan industry was located predominantly in Barcelona and the surrounding municipalities, many of which were incorporated into the city after 1890, but after 1858 there were also a number of industrial colonies set up in the rural interior, in the Llobregat and Ter valleys. The creation of the colonies was not motivated by strictly economic concerns. Unlike similar colonies which were created in England early in the industrialization process to take advantage of water power, the Catalan colonies were not founded until industrialization was well underway. The first, the Rosal colony in the Upper Llobregat, was established in 1858, by which time self-acting mules had been widely adopted in the cotton mills in Barcelona. Rather, they responded to the weakness of the state which 'provided little economic and political support' and fit in with a broader tolerance of intermediaries between the state and the people, the most significant example of which was *caciquismo*[10]. These colonies were owned and run by industrialists and constituted enclaves of independent authority where what are normally public activities were in private hands: 'Private capital rather than the state . . . provide[d] the basic services – health, housing, schooling and policing'.[11]

Leaving the cities – and their former workers – behind, the industrialists who founded the colonies sought above all else to create a stable and docile labor force. They found it in farm families of the pre-Pyrenean mountain zones with their Carlist political tradition and experience of cottage industry. Whole families joined; sometimes they were ruined smallholders but more often peasants 'who when they got old, or had a lot of children decided to take the whole family to the colony'. Farmers, and frequently sharecroppers, sent one or more children or their wives. Finally, individuals such as non-inheriting sons or daughters seeking a husband went on their own account. Many part-time workers were the children and women from the surrounding farms. Those who had long trips stayed in specially constructed dormitories and returned home at weekends. The Catalan inheritance system, which left the farm to the *hereu*, the first born, produced large numbers of landless children who sought work in the colonies. The availability of work for women and children, one of the standard features of the cotton industry, encouraged large families since a household with lots of children could accumulate numerous wage packets.

In one sense the colonies marked a regression, dispersing industry which had been concentrated in Barcelona into the countryside and away from urban centers. The Amettlá colony which was opened in 1875 was six kilometers from the nearest town. By creating their own, isolated little worlds where their authority was complete some employers sought to free themselves from the turbulence of Barcelona, and especially its labor conflict. (There had been a massive general strike by the textile workers in 1854–5.) An upsurge in labor militancy in 1890 led to a further tightening of the discipline in the colonies with a larger role for the chaplain and a social Catholic approach. The 'classic period of the colony system' was, according to Ignasi Terrades, from 1890 to 1917, but although after 1917 the employers were more concerned with technological innovation than with moral discipline they continued to enjoy the labor peace they had gone to the countryside to find. There were no strikes in the Amettlá colony from 1917 to 1936, and the effects of the Second Republic and the revolution which took place at the beginning of the Spanish Civil War were 'strongly muted'.[12]

In contrast Barcelona experienced repeated and intense social conflict. Indeed, Engels called it the city which had seen the largest number of barricades of any in the world. Much of this involved resistance to mechanization. The first episode of machine-breaking in the city took place in 1824, although there had been one in Alcoy three years earlier. In 1835 the fully mechanized Bonaplata factory was burned, allegedly by workers, although some contemporaries claimed that it was arranged by other industrialists afraid of the competition. The first general strike in Spanish history, known as the 'selfactinas', after the self-acting mules whose introduction it was intended to prevent, took place in the summer of 1854. A number of factories were attacked and machines destroyed. (In smaller cities the violence was instigated by farmers who were seeing their home production disappear, while workers tried to stop them.) In 1870 workers in one factory refused to show women how to use new machines because they feared losing their jobs to them.

Not all movements had such workaday causes. In 1842 the workers joined their employers in rebelling against the government which they feared was going to institute free trade with Great Britain. This led to the city being bombarded in November by the regent, General Espartero. At the end of July 1909 a government decision to mobilize reservists for the colonial war in Morocco triggered a working class uprising. During this 'Tragic Week', as it is known, workers vented their fury on the Church, destroying 21 churches and 31 convents and monasteries.[13]

Between 1888 and 1909 there was also more random violence tied to the anarchist practice of propaganda by the deed. Bombings, especially of the homes of employers whose businesses were being struck, became commonplace in the 1880s and early 1890s. Terror became more spectacular after 1893 when the Liceo Opera House was bombed and 22 people killed. There was an attempt to assassinate the Civil Governor in 1894 and two years later a number of people were killed after a bomb was thrown at the Corpus Christi parade. After a lull from 1898 to 1902 bombings started up again and continued to 1909. There was an attempt to kill Conservative leader Antonio Maura in 1904 and two attempts on the life of Alfonso XIII in 1905 and 1906.

The most imposing strike action in the city came in 1919 with the massive strike against the hydroelectric company known as 'La Canadiense'. This was the first occasion on which the Confederación Nacional del Trabajo (CNT) tried out its new industrial union form of organization. The city was paralyzed, without electricity or trams, for 44 days in February and March before a settlement was reached, but an ill-considered decision to call a second strike, which lasted three more weeks, to get prisoners released led to defeat and was followed by martial law and the arrest of many thousands of CNT members, including most of the leadership. From 1919 to 1923 Barcelona was the scene of a war, known as *pistolerismo*, between gangs of gunmen nominally representing the union and those organized by a German agent and a former chief of police. At its high point, in 1921, there were 228 attacks. The CNT's outstanding leader, Salvador Seguí, was assassinated in March 1923. The power of the gunmen within the CNT led many members to leave and join the new Sindicatos Libres, which were looked on kindly by the authorities. Terrorism combined with repression directed by the military governor, General Martínez Anido led to a rapid decline of the CNT, which would not recover until the Second Republic. [14]

The climax of class conflict in Barcelona came in the summer and fall of 1936. The military uprising of July 18 triggered a sweeping revolutionary movement in the city and across the region as a whole. Virtually all of the largest businesses, both national and foreign owned, were collectivized in the first couple of months of the war and by 1937 the entire textile industry had been collectivized. There are no statistics on collectivization in manufacturing and services but anarchist sources claimed a total of 2,000 businesses. [15]

Asturias

The capital of the coal mining industry was in the northern province of Asturias. There the coalfields produced a working class which in October 1934 staged a massive attempt at social revolution which was put down, but only after two weeks and the efforts of 25,000 troops. The Asturian Commune quickly became one of the major symbols and perhaps the most important myth of the Spanish labor movement. It was, without doubt, one of the most important revolutionary episodes in Europe after the Russian Revolution. The Asturian insurrection has, understandably enough, drawn historians like a magnet but in so doing it has acted as a distorting mirror for the history of the region's working class, presenting it as much more coherent, militant and self-conscious than it really was.

Like their counterparts in the Ruhr, the coal miners of Asturias were fragmented along a number of lines. They were far from being the 'isolated mass' or the 'natural' bearers of solidarity so frequently presented as the miners' fate. [16] In Asturias mine workers were divided by their geographical origins, by their relation to mine work, by their work experience, by their ideological and religious affiliations and by generation. Strong class institutions came late and only as the result of long, laborious effort.

The beginning of large-scale mining in the region in the 1860s made the creation of a labor force a pressing need. Until the First World War the bulk of the workers came from Asturias itself and overwhelmingly from the districts in which the coalfields were located. Until the wartime influx the dominant figure in the mines was the mixed worker, who combined mine work with agriculture. An extensive study of the socioeconomic circumstances of Spanish miners prepared in 1911 by the state Mining Directorate claimed that 60 to 70 per cent of Asturian miners were mixed workers, 'farmers who have their homes and their lands, alternating their work in the fields with that in the mines'.[17] An indirect but particularly interesting testimony to the prominence of the mixed worker comes from the monthly magazine of the Socialist miners' union. In its August 1914 issue, *El Minero de la Hulla* published a story which described the hatred felt by a young miner for the village moneylender who had been able to take away the family farm when the miner's father died. The story illustrates the symbiosis of coal and land among the Asturian working class while the fact that it appeared where it did shows the relevance of the theme for the readership. Even after the First World War the mixed worker remained an important figure. In July 1923 the civil governor reported that 'almost all the strikes called during the summer fit the convenience of the workers engaged in farming. Once the crops are in they go back [to the mines]' and ten years later the Socialist paper *Avance* noted that striking miners were 'involved in the chores of the fields'.[18] The mixed worker was common in other mining zones as well, especially in the Sierra which surrounded the famous Río Tinto copper mines in Huelva.

Mine owners and managers had long resented the predominance of the mixed workers because they were not so dependent on their wages that they were amenable to the industrial discipline their employers tried to impose. Mixed workers did not always show up for work, especially when farm work was pressing. They were also too addicted to religious holidays and to practices such as Saint Monday. At one company on the fringes of the coalfields as many as 75 per cent of the workers stayed home on Mondays and the days following holidays. Employers claimed that mixed workers were lazy, bringing the sloth of the countryside to the mines, and were frustrated by their refusal to respond to monetary incentives to work longer hours or more intensively. Their laments revealed their failure to meet the challenge set out by one writer in 1861: to make miners 'get accustomed to the required subordination . . . and prefer their own interest to their old independence and natural liberty'.[19]

Only the boom of the war years, when the workforce expanded from 18,000 in 1914 to 39,000 in 1920, was able to draw large numbers of immigrants from outside the province into the coalfields, although mine owners had been attempting to do so for a long time. In Mieres, for example, of the 2,206 miners who headed households in 1910, 86 per cent were from the coalfield municipalities and almost three-quarters from Mieres itself. In contrast, between 17 and 52 per cent of the workers employed by six mining companies in Mieres from 1914 to 1934 came from outside the province. The most important sources of immigrants were Galicia, Old Castile and Portugal. Few came from the south or the east.

Even though the vast majority of the wartime immigrants came from Spain itself the presence of large numbers of non-Asturians generated tensions. As early as 1901 there were attempts to physically remove outsiders from the mines and such conflicts increased after 1914. Galicians, who made up the largest contingent of immigrants, were a special target of dislike. Just why this was so is unclear, but there is evidence that Asturians identified *gallegos* with the Guardia Civil. A miners' song from the 1934 insurrection went: 'Inside the bullring/the *gallegos* in three-cornered hats/used us to play bullfighter./Some used sabres/and others whips/ and the policemen from Galicia/kicked us as well.'[20]

This was not unique to Asturias. Anarchosyndicalist leader Angel Pestaña spent his childhood in the mining communities of León and Santander and was impressed by the 'race hatred' he saw there. Once again, the Galicians were the favored target.

> The Aragonese and Navarrese did not mix with the Basques or Asturians, and if they fought among themselves they also formed a group apart . . . from the other regions. When they were attacked by others they came to agreement and defended themselves . . .. Where this 'race' hatred was most notable was between the *gallegos* and the rest . . . The *gallegos* were the butt of all the jokes of that disparate and heterogeneous world; [they] were insulted in every way imaginable, even in songs like these:
>
>> They say that a *gallego* has died,
>> If only twenty more would die.
>> The more *gallegos* who die,
>> The more hides for oil.
>>
>> When the *gallegos* in Galicia
>> March in processions
>> They carry a cat for a saint
>> And an old woman for a banner.[21]

The immigrants had their own networks. Some, such as the Centro Gallego, organized in 1919, and the Colonia Vallisoletana, founded in 1920, were formal. Others were informal grapevines, probably based on kinship, which attracted men from a village to a particular mine. The Tres Amigos mine hired 23 men from La Mezquita (Orense) and 33 from Campo Lameiro (Pontevedra) and among the 2,300 workers hired by the Saus mine between 1914 and 1919, 29 came from Villalón (Valladolid) and 39 from Peñaranda de Bracamonte (Salamanca).

Asturian miners did not live in socially or occupationally homogeneous communities which reinforced solidarity. The province's population had always been widely distributed among numerous small groupings, and the growth of mining, although it did give rise to a handful of large urban centers such as Mieres and Sama de Langreo, did not fundamentally alter this pattern. In 1930, over two-thirds of the population of the seven most important municipal districts in the coalfields lived in centers of 500 people or fewer and only 18 per cent lived in towns of more than 2,000. This meant that many miners lived far from their place of work; trips of six and seven kilometers each way were common. It also meant that miners came into frequent contact with other types of people, especially farmers.

Work itself further contributed to the fragmentation of the miners. There was very little team work, and even when hewers had assistants to help them with timbering and removing coal each worker was paid directly by the company, the hewer on a piecework basis, the others on a straight wage. The varying prestige of the different job categories, and especially the distinction between interior and exterior workers, was a real cause of division. In 1922 the hewers at one mine went so far as to try and create an organization of their own, while at another other workers resisted when a group of well-paid hewers wanted to call a strike, and the meeting nearly ended in violence. Moreover, immigrants were much less likely than locals to become hewers, basically because their tendency to change employers much more frequently was a handicap to promotion.

Different employers treated their workers in different ways. Many, in their determination to create a stable and obedient labor force, made use of paternalistic strategies providing social benefits such as housing, mutual aid societies, medical care, company stores, schools and churches. Only one company, the Hullera Española, which was owned by the Marquis of Comillas, Spain's leading proponent of social Catholicism, offered a comprehensive set of social services and tried to have its workers live in a closed world, similar to those of the Catalan industrial colonies. That goal was unattainable in Asturias because the geographic isolation provided by the river valleys of Catalonia did not exist in the coalfields. The company made one attempt when it created the village of Bustiello from scratch as a model village of model miners. The initial residents were carefully chosen and they were put into identical semi-detached houses which had to be kept up to company-imposed standards. The basic reason for the company's actions was to keep its workers away from unions and labor politics, although publicly it talked about the need to improve their morality.

Hullera Española provided housing, medical care, schools and recreational facilities, and published a magazine intended for the workers. Religion had an important place in the company's social practice. The schools were run by the Brothers of the Christian Doctrine. It restored a number of churches and sponsored religious functions such as the celebrations on Saint Barbara's day – the patron saint of miners – and special Easter missions. The company also paid the salaries of four chaplains whose responsibilities included informing the management of any workers who had unacceptable ideas. The company police force prevented the 'bad press', which included liberal as well as labor publications, from entering its property and closely scrutinized all recreational activities. Mixed dances and nude swimming in the river were prohibited as immoral. Yet despite all its efforts Hullera Española failed to achieve its goal of keeping out Socialist unions.

But labor organization and politics were not inevitably a source of harmony either. The first recorded miners' strike took place in 1873. By 1899 the Socialist trade union federation, Unión General de Trabajadores (UGT) had a presence in the coalfields but the companies were able to destroy the early local unions in 1906–7. The definitive organization of the miners came only in 1910 with the creation of the Socialist Asturian Miners' Union, SMA, which quickly became the dominant labor organization in the region. Even so, the SMA had to contend with anarchist, Communist and Catholic rivals and during the 1920s and 1930s these conflicts were at times violent and occasionally lethal.

The Basque Provinces

Industrialization was most rapid, and most wrenching, in the Basque province of Vizcaya. The rapid expansion of iron mining and the growth of a modern iron and steel industry after 1875 radically transformed Bilbao and its surroundings, known as the Ria. The number of miners increased from fewer than 1,000 in 1870 to 12,000 in 1899. The 2,245 metal workers in 1884 had become 22,000 in 1900. Relatively few of these were Basques; a government report done in 1910 calculated that about a quarter of the province's miners were natives and that the rest were immigrants, predominantly from Galicia, Palencia and Zamora. Unlike in Asturias, immigrants flooded in from other parts of the country immediately, some 60,000 people between 1880 and 1900. Another 19,000 immigrants came between 1910 and 1920. In the minefields many were housed in flimsy barracks built by the companies and purchased food at stores run by contractors and foremen. Others lived in poorly built housing hastily thrown up in the mining towns to meet the pressing need. These new districts lacked basic services such as water, sewage disposal and paved roads and housing was crowded, especially since many families took in lodgers from the vast pool of single immigrants. The situation in the expanding working class districts of Bilbao was no better.[22]

Regional identities remained strong among workers in Vizcaya. Communist leader Dolores Ibarruri, whose husband was a miner, noted how employers used regional loyalties to pit one group of workers against another 'dividing the workers into crews on the basis of their provinces or regions'. Foremen challenged a crew from one region to outwork that from another. These rivalries carried over off the job as well, into taunting songs and even violence.[23] But the greatest tensions were between immigrants and native

Basques. The very fact of such massive immigration, its social consequences and the rapidity with which the immigrant workers, pejoratively known as *maketos*, joined Socialist unions terrified much of the native population.

In Vizcaya, 'where rapid industrialization and massive immigration broke the stability of traditional forms of Basque social life, where traditional culture and identity were seen as seriously threatened'[24], a reactionary, blatantly racist Basque nationalism found its most fertile ground. Basque nationalism was fundamentally a movement of the middle and lower middle classes but it tried to appeal to the part of the working class which was racially Basque. The Basque Workers' Union (SOV) was founded in 1911 and was defined by its nationalism, anti-socialism and adherence to Catholic social principles. By 1921 the SOV had some 2,200 members but few were miners or railwaymen. Most worked in small workshops or were artisans or white-collar workers, although some worked for the important Euskalduna iron company. In contrast, the socialist Metal Workers' Union of Vizcaya, which was founded in 1913, had more than 3,000 members in 1918 and 9,000 in 1920. The Miners' Union of Vizcaya was founded in 1911 with 6,885 members and after a crisis which lasted until 1916 had 6,483 members in 1920.

In the neighboring province of Guipúzcoa the rate of industrialization was more leisurely and the tide of immigration less imposing. The province remained a source of emigration until 1900 but received 38,000 immigrants over the next thirty years. By 1920 people born outside the province accounted for 20 per cent of the population, compared to 27 per cent in Vizcaya. In addition, many immigrants came from the other three Basque provinces; for example, in 1910 half of the residents of Rentería who had been born outside Guipúzcoa came from Vizcaya, Alava or Navarre. Industry was spread more widely than in Vizcaya: 39 of the 90 municipalities had an industrial establishment with more than 49 workers. As immigrants were not concentrated in a limited area and seemed much less of a threat, Basque nationalism had less success.

Businesses were also smaller than in Vizcaya. The most important industry, with 5,776 workers in 1915, was metal, and although there were some large modern companies the average firm had just 40 workers. Arms manufacturing, located in Eibar, had long been a regional specialty and while this gave rise to a large firm such as Orbea and Company with 400 workers, the skills required preserved a large number of small workshops and independent artisans working at home. According to a study done in 1908 some 800 of the 2,400 arms workers were in this last group. The other leading industries were textiles, with 2,698 workers, and paper, with 2,395 workers, both with an average of 75 per business food, 1,471 and 22, and construction, 1,043 and 29. Just over half the workers in textiles and food processing, and a third of those in the paper industry were women. All but 18 of the 403 employees in the state tobacco factory were women as well.[25]

Madrid

Madrid was not an important industrial city but it did have a large manufacturing sector. Consumer goods such as food and drink, furniture, clothing, books and luxury items were produced in a large number of workshops, each of which had relatively few employees. At the beginning of the twentieth century there were 'a multitude of small industries [and] workshops where the boss, the head of the family, is assisted by his wife, his children and a few workers and apprentices'.[26] The 189 businesses engaged in the building and repair of 'devices' employed 1,306 workers, an average of 7 each. The furniture makers had an average of 12 employees, the carpenters 6 and the locksmiths 5. The printers, with 36, and shoe manufacturers, with 90, were larger but still quite small. There were some large businesses with thousands of workers: the MZA railway, the gas factory, the state tobacco factory and the tram companies, but they stood out precisely because they were exceptional.

By 1930 some changes had taken place. There were more large firms, which by the standards of the capital meant those with more than 100 employees, and some even surpassed 500, but these were still few and far between in the important food, wood and metalworking sectors. (Two breweries, Mahou and El Aguila, and a bakery were among the largest businesses producing food.) But these traditional activities continued to be dominated by small producers; food and metalworking enterprises had an average of 10 workers each, woodworking 13.

Commerce was even more atomized. There were some new, large stores, such as the Almacenes Madrid–Paris department store with its 416 employees, but these were still rare. More typical was the vast number of tiny shops with a few employees, when they had any at all. In the food sector alone there were 2,737 bars, taverns and pastry shops, some 7,000 other stores which sold food and an indeterminate number of street vendors. The 8,851 merchants listed as engaged in 'general commerce' employed 24,797 workers, not quite 3 each, the 1,630 members of the association of food retailers had, on average, fewer than 2 employees each and the 4,000 retailers who belonged to the aggressive interest group La Defensa Mercantil Patronal employed an average of just over 3 people each.

The only economic activity which underwent significant structural change was construction. During the 1920s the industry was taken over by a number of large limited companies which put the traditional small contractors out of business.

> The small master builders who had bought a building site which they mortgaged and remortgaged in order to raise the money to allow them to build . . . left the field to the limited companies which had the financial resources to respond to the new demand created by the state's public works projects. These companies, Agroman, Fierro, Fomento de Obras y Construcciones, brought large numbers of workers, often more than 2,000, together on a single site for the first time.[27]

Moreover, the nature of these projects, such as the Madrid subway and the Isabel II canal, allowed the construction companies to hire unskilled workers from among the large numbers of people who migrated to the city in the 1920s while skilled workers had ever more trouble finding work.

These changes had important consequences for the Madrid labor movement and for the political life of the Second Republic. Until the 1930s the Socialist UGT had virtually monopolized the city's unions. The UGT drew overwhelmingly from the skilled workers in the secondary sector, especially construction workers, and was organized on the basis of craft unions in which only the executive had the authority to call strikes; it called them only when negotiations had failed and there was a strong possibility of achieving specific, limited goals.

The UGT tried to incorporate the changes to the city's economy and working class within its traditional structure and practice, but its disciplined, almost cerebral approach, which included a reliance on the state as arbitrator, proved totally inadequate to the new situation in the construction industry. This provided an opening for the CNT, whose style and organization, based on direct action, and a flexible, less hierarchical leadership which left room for workplace assemblies and the strike committees they produced, were the polar opposite of those of the Socialists. This more dynamic approach was successful where there was a mass of unskilled workers which, in Madrid, meant on the construction sites. By the fall of 1933 the CNT had transformed the labor scene in the capital. Strikes took on a new dimension, involving thousands of workers. They lasted longer and became more public, moving out of the private confines of the union hall into public places such as theaters and bullrings. The frequent assemblies encouraged greater participation and produced leaders who were much more at home in the streets than the skilled negotiators of the UGT. The rapid rise of the CNT led to the radicalization of the Socialist unions which in turn produced the radicalization of that wing of the Socialist Party, led by Francisco Largo Caballero, which was most responsive to the moods of the union rank and file.[28]

Organization

While the working class gradually took shape objectively across the nineteenth and twentieth centuries it was slow to produce any sustained forms of collective action, what Ira Katznelson has called the 'fourth layer of class'. When it did the result was distinctive, another piece of the 'comparative puzzles' provided by other European working classes, although sharing important features present elsewhere.[29] Like Germany, Spain had a large Marxist political party with a closely integrated union movement. The PSOE never achieved the size of the German Social Democratic Party (SPD), and Spanish socialists certainly never produced the vast array of ancillary organizations the Germans did,[30] but by the 1930s it was the largest party in the country. Its associated union federation, the UGT, grew slowly and more or less steadily but it became a truly mass organization only in the 1930s when it broke out of its traditional strongholds, Madrid, Asturias and Vizcaya, and won support among the landless laborers of the south. Membership in its agricultural workes' union, the FNTT, soared from 27,340 in 157 locals in April 1930 to 451,337 in 3,319 locals in June 1933. The importance of agricultural workers to the labor movement was a feature which Spain shared with Italy.

Neither Socialist organization established the hegemony enjoyed by the German Socialists, at least before the First World War, because they always had to compete with a vital anarchist/anarchosyndicalist movement, especially after the creation of the CNT in 1910.

The CNT and the UGT drew their strength from different parts of the country, as Figures 3.1 and 3.2 illustrate. Its strongholds were Catalonia and Andalucia, although it also had a presence in Asturias and Madrid. Unlike the UGT, the CNT experienced a number of sharp increases annd precipitous drops in membership, generally tied to government prohibition. Here Spain shares a distinctive feature of the French experience: a labor movement which advocated direct action between workers and employers and largely ignored the question of state power. Only the harsh realities of Civil War, which led anarchists to join governments at both the regional and national levels, forced them to seriously reconsider their position.

There were other unions, Catholic and Communist, and parties, Communist, Trotskyist and Syndicalist, but before the Civil War they were numerically insignificant. By the 1930s, then, the Spanish working class

Table 3.5 *Union membership, UGT and CNT*

Year	UGT	CNT
1888	3,355	
1899	15,264	
1910	40,000	11,000
1914	119,114	
1918	90,000	114,000
1919	160,480	745,000
1920	220,000	
1921	240,113	
1923	210,617	250,000
1929	228,507	
1930	277,011	
1931	958,176	535,565
1932	1,041,531	1,200,000
1936	1,300,000	559,229

Source: M. Tuñon de Lara, *El Movimiento Obrero en la Historia de España* (Madrid, 1977).

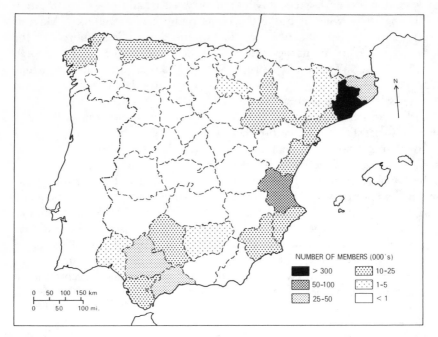

Figure 3.1   *CNT Membership, 1919*

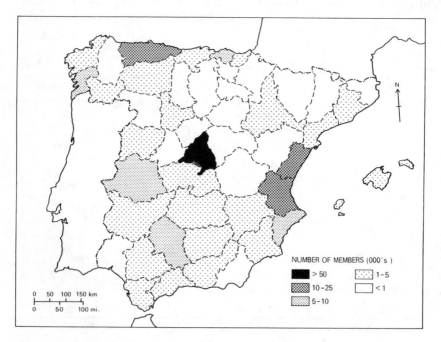

Figure 3.2   *UGT Membership, 1928*

was more or less evenly split between socialist and anarchosyndicalist unions and between a reformist social democratic political party and an anti-political anarchosyndicalist movement which demanded revolution and nothing less.

Both union confederations drew their support from workers in a variety of industrial settings. It is not the case that, as Dick Geary would have it, 'the appeal of anarcho-syndicalism was to certain groups of workers rather than others'.[31] The UGT's first stronghold was amongst the craft workers of Madrid, especially the printers, and until the 1930s Socialist unionism in the capital depended on such skilled workers. Outside Madrid, however, the UGT found its greatest strength among the Asturian miners and the miners and metal workers of Vizcaya who were organized into industrial unions. The CNT drew workers in the small-scale textile plants of Catalonia but its appeal among industrial workers was not limited to such undynamic sectors. It was strong among the workers of the large-scale Asturian metal foundries and the new, large scale construction firms of Madrid. Within Catalonia it also appealed to workers of the largest and most modern enterprises, such as the street railways and electricity companies. Moreover, the power of the CNT as a union lay in its conversion to industrial unionism in 1918. Rather than emphasizing the nature of the industrial setting as the reason for the appeal of anarchism it might be better to stress the place of origin of the workers. In general terms, anarchism had most appeal in those places where there were large numbers of recent migrants from the rural south, such as Catalonia and Madrid in the 1930s. Where there were not (Madrid until the 1920s, Asturias and the Basque Provinces) socialism was more successful.

The pattern of strikes in Spain in the first thirty years of the century fell within the 'startling resemblance' which Shorter and Tilly found for western Europe as a whole. This is shown in Table 3.6.

There were fewer strikes in Spain, but they were somewhat longer and involved more workers.[32] They probably also led to more violence, especially given the government's repeated habit of treating strikes as challenges to public order and bringing force to bear.

Labor conflict increased slowly between 1910 and 1918 before rocketing upward in 1919 and 1920, the most conflict-ridden years before the Second Republic. Conflict began to fall off in 1921 and then dropped radically during the Primo de Rivera dictatorship (1923–30). Repression, including the banning of the CNT and the Communist Party, was partly responsible but the decision of the UGT to co-operate with the regime and its arbitration committees also contributed. The Republic saw unprecedented levels of strike activity, peaking with the failed insurrection of October 1934, once it became clear that the reformist promise of the new regime was being effectively obstructed and culminating, two years later, with the sweeping revolution of the first months of the Spanish Civil War.

Working Class Experience

In the previous chapter we looked at the working class solely from without, so to speak, concentrating on the work it did and the settings in which it did it. How did workers experience their daily lives? What was their

Table 3.6   *Strike characteristics for seven industrial nations, 1900–29*

Country	Strike rate per 100,000 workers	Strikers per strike	Person days lost per strike
Belgium	6.4	400	—
France	7.8	300	15.1
Germany	11.1	290	15.7
Italy	12.1	320	14.2
Spain	6.0	420	23.2
Sweden	18.0	210	40.8
United Kingdom	3.8	1,100	26.7

Source: C. Tilly and E. Shorter, *Strikes in France* (Cambridge, 1974).

Table 3.7   *Strikes and strikers, 1910–34*

Year	Strikes	Strikers	Days lost
1910	246	35,897	1,408,896
1911	311	22,154	364,178
1912	279	36,306	1,056,109
1913	284	84,316	2,258,159
1914	212	49,267	1,017,889
1915	169	30,591	382,885
1916	237	96,882	2,415,304
1917	306	71,440	1,784,538
1918	463	109,168	1,819,295
1919	895	178,496	4,001,278
1920	1,060	244,684	7,261,000
1921	373	83,691	2,802,299
1922	488	119,417	2,672,567
1923	458	120,568	3,027,026
1929	96	55,576	313,065
1930	402	247,460	3,745,360
1931	734	236,117	3,843,260
1932	681	269,104	3,589,473
1933	1,127	843,000	14,440,629
1934	594	741,303	11,115,358

Source: M. Tuñón de Lara, *El movimiento obrero en la Historia de España* (Madrid, 1977).

experience of things such as family, childhood or marriage? These aspects of working class experience are notoriously opaque but one source, working class autobiography, provides us with a window, or at least a keyhole, through which to look.[1]

Five published autobiographies – by Leandro Carro, Dolores Ibarruri, Francisco Largo Caballero, Angel Pestaña and Manuel Vigil – offer us a glimpse of how workers experienced the circumstances of their lives. Of course, they are not representative of the working class as a whole. All were union or party activists. Most came from the north of Spain, none from Catalonia or the south. Only one was a woman.

Work and Leisure

The central experience of working class life was, of course, work but our authors have little to say about it. They tell us about the jobs they held, which were often numerous indeed, and the search for work, but they rarely, if ever, say anything about what their jobs entailed. Largo Caballero was the only exception, describing his work in a box factory, in a book binding shop and in a rope factory. In the last of these 'my responsibilities were to turn the wheel to spin and twist the cords . . . In addition to this I took the cocks to the pit (the master was very fond of cockfighting) as well as taking his horses, mules and donkeys to the drinking trough'. Later on, the seasonality of his trade of plasterer forced him to find other jobs, doing road work for the city or the Diputación, or helping his mother, who had given up domestic service for a precarious independence selling 'things which did not require the immediate investment of much money and which could be easily sold'. As a result, during the winter 'I could often be found in the San Ildefonso market timidly trying to sell servants peppers or tomatoes. I also went to the countryside to pick *cardillos* to sell the next day'.[2] Largo's experience, along with Angel Pestaña's attempt to set up a business selling candy, illustrate both the ongoing desire for some kind of economic independence among the working class and the existence – and probably to a much greater extent than we normally think – of an informal economy outside the routine of regular jobs, what today would be called the 'black economy'.

The skilled men, Vigil, Pestaña and Largo Caballero, seem to have taken pleasure and pride in their work. Indeed, they display what can be called a classic artisanal identity. Vigil was a locksmith. When he completed his military service he turned down the opportunity to become a railroad engineer because 'there was much about the job I did not like, especially the hours of subjection'.[3] The use of that last word, in speaking about work in one of the largest and most modern of all business enterprises of the day, is surely suggestive.

Pestaña had an incredibly varied work experience. Indeed, until he arrived in Barcelona in 1914, when he was 28, his life reads much like a picaresque novel. He worked all over northern Spain in mining and construction, as part of a theater troup, in a flamenco group, in a mirror factory and in France as a *terrasier*, an agricultural laborer, a candy seller and a sandal maker before finding his vocation as a watchmaker. He got into the trade in Algiers through 'a fortuitous accident'. He stayed with it when he moved to Barcelona and very quickly established his independence, setting up shop in his house. Pestaña never actually describes his work but he did enjoy it and considered it an important and valuable part of his life.

> My profession had . . . an important influence in the formation of my character and temperament. Perhaps I was attracted to it by my inclination towards meticulous observation but I am certain that afterwards the profession had a powerful influence on me.
>
> The profession has developed in me the patience, the calm, the serenity necessary to act in all struggles, but especially in social struggles, for the profession of watchmaker requires serenity, calm and patience. Just ask my colleagues.[4]

The trade, in his case of plasterer, was most important of all for Largo Caballero:

> I liked it from the first day. It was considered the aristocrat of the construction trades. Plaster was a luxury which only the houses of the wealthy had . . . The brilliance of the ornaments, the inlay of different color decorations and imitations of all kinds of marble pleased me giving me the sensation that it was not a trade like any other but an art.

He spent some of his time off work making samples and by the time he was 17 he was a master with two assistants.[5]

Given that leisure was much scarcer than labor, and presumably much more treasured, we might expect our authors to talk about it at some length. They do not. Pestaña tells us that on days when rain prevented them from working miners spent a lot of time in their dormitories telling stories, with military service as the favorite topic followed by the 'hardships endured during their apprenticeships, with trips to the brothels in between'.[6]

Newspapers were very important, although the fact that all our authors became political figures may distort the picture here. As a child Pestaña read them aloud to groups of workers, and later, when he worked for the Bilbao-Portugalete railroad, read as many as he could get hold of, borrowing them from fellow workers, even going through their drawers when they were not there. This was how he read his first labor paper. Vigil too was an omnivorous newspaper reader. As a young man he regularly read four Gijón newspapers. Reading was also important to Dolores Ibarruri, although she did not find the labor press enjoyable and 'out of sheer boredom I would let [it] fall from my hands'.[7]

Other forms of working class leisure are almost entirely absent. Pestaña makes a fleeting reference to his father occasionally going to the cafe. He also relates how the Frenchmen with whom he worked as a *terrassier* were amused by their teetotal Spanish workmate who did not 'respect the rites of the sect and carry in his pack a container with at least a couple of litres of wine and the healthy intention of filling it at least twice a day . . . [At the end of the day,] 'one must drink absinthe to finish the day'.[8] Other than this, drinking and drinking places are surprisingly absent. Pestaña also developed an interest in the theater and took a second job in the cloakroom of a Bilbao theater in order to attend more often.

The continued existence of a traditional work routine and leisure practice such as Saint or Blue Monday was in Largo Caballero's eyes one of the 'vices' of his beloved trade. In fact, he expresses satisfaction at having been able to eliminate it, along with piece work: 'Like piece work this custom disappeared . . . Some of us refused to take part in such flings and the good example imposed itself.'[9] Are we seeing here a case of Socialist workers imposing a more modern industrial discipline on craft workers?

Childhood and Education

Working class childhoods were ephemeral. Play is not a significant topic in any of these autobiographies. Dolores Ibarruri talks about it most, recalling how, during vacations, children were left to their own devices, roaming the town and its surroundings and playing, boys and girls together, the same games, jumping onto passing freight cars, hanging from aerial trams and going into tunnels. She also adds that 'we had no toys'.[10]

Most of the authors attended school but only Ibarruri, the only woman in the group, attended for any length of time, until she was 15. Carro had no formal education at all although his father taught him to 'decipher badly' and Pestaña mentions a couple of schools, but he attended for only 'a few months' because he and his father never stayed in any one place for very long. Largo Caballero had only three years of elementary school. Manuel Vigil attended school until he was twelve and could have stayed on longer but he left 'a little ashamed that my younger brother began to work before me'.[11]

This limited exposure to schooling did not reflect a lack of interest in education. Indeed, in at least two cases it occurred in spite of parental encouragement. Pestaña's father, who was completely illiterate, certainly knew the value of education:

> A practical man, he did not want his son 'to be a beast of burden like him' . . . and he got the idea to have me study to be a priest . . . He did not believe in priests or the Church and if he wanted this it was, as he said, because being a priest was a job like that of a miner or a mason, although much more lucrative.

When they were in places without schools, his father had tried to teach Angel himself, making him read 'a set number of lines which he had marked with a pencil after having carefully counted them'. If Angel hesitated or made what his father considered mistakes he was yelled at; 'the third mistake earned me the first blow and thereafter they rained down with each error'. But when Pestaña read newspapers out loud for a group of workers, it was 'one of the few small satisfactions my father's troubled life permitted him'.[12]

Vigil's father, too, encouraged his children to continue in school and Ibarruri describes how mothers strove to have their children receive some education: 'It was a common sight to see the mothers taking their children to the school every morning or afternoon, the mothers almost dragging them along by the hand and the children crying at the top of their lungs.' Even Ibarruri could not get all the education she wanted. Lack of money forced her to abandon teacher training after one year and to become a dressmaker's apprentice.[13]

The most graphic and moving example of the fragility of working class childhood comes from Pestaña. His parents separated when he was very young and when he was 14 his father died, leaving Angel on his own. The child became an adult very quickly indeed: 'I watched the sick man all the first night. At dawn he appeared calm so I lay down a while. During the day he slept a bit and I took advantage to go and play in the street.'[14]

Family: Economics and Sentiment

The basic reason for these ephemeral childhoods was economic need and the centrality of the family economy to the working class. Childhood ended when young people, and they were often very young indeed, went to work to help support the family. Leandro Carro, the second son of a shoemaker with thirteen children, began work at the tender age of 7, as the errand boy in a household goods store and then, at 9, was apprenticed to an iron molder. Largo Caballero also began work at 7, passing rapidly through a variety of jobs before finding his métier as a plasterer. Pestaña began work at 11, starting in the mines as an assistant in the same team as his father. When his father died he found work cleaning trains for the Bilbao–Portugalete railroad.[15]

Vigil's case is the most interesting. His working life began at twelve, when he tried his hand at 'various trades' for two years before settling in as an apprentice in a locksmith's shop. He was not motivated by need but, as we have seen, by a sense of shame that a younger brother was already working. Vigil does not tell us just what was shameful about not working but we can suggest that he felt that he should have been contributing to the family economy as well or that he was not living up to the working class image of a true man, or both.[16]

The one author who did not work as a child was the only woman of the group. Her schooling lasted until she was 15, but then there were few work opportunities for females in mining centers. She herself notes that things were different for boys, that at 10 or 11 'a boy who might be our playmate one day would suddenly no longer be one of us; he would become a wage earner with a role to play in his family and in society'.[17]

Family was crucial to Spanish working class life, but these autobiographies suggest that marriage breakdown was probably quite common. Both Largo Caballero and Pestaña saw their parents separate. Largo Caballero's parents separated when he was 4 because of what he refers to as 'discord in the marriage' and he was left with his mother. At about 3 Pestaña was left with his father after his mother ran off, taking his sister with her. He is a little less reticent than Largo Caballero in describing the situation: 'Although I have never been able to determine the cause there were frequent quarrels between my parents, which usually ended with my father hitting my mother.'[18]

As brief as are the mentions of relations between the authors' parents, they are almost voluminous in comparison to what they tell us about their own married lives, or even about the people they married. Romance and courtship are almost totally absent. Leandro Carro says only that 'on January 31, 1920 Teodora Primo Alonso and I were married in the Ensanche courthouse in Bilbao. We later had two children.'[19] Vigil is no more informative. He was married two months before his twentieth birthday. He, like Carro, says nothing about his wife or how he met her or the nature of their relations before they married, other than to mention that his wish to have a civil ceremony was thwarted by her family. Pestaña, as befits an anarchist, did not marry. He did have a companion but she is mentioned only once, as helping him make a living as a sandal maker, a trade at which he was not very good, while they lived in Algiers. Largo Caballero says nothing at all about his private life.

Neither does Dolores Ibarruri say anything of courtship; she tells us only that she met her husband, a miner, while she was working as a servant and that she was twenty when she married. Other than this all we learn is that he was a union militant and frequently in jail. However, even without giving any details she makes it quite clear that her marriage was far from a happy one:

My mother used to say, 'She who hits the bull's eye in her choice of a husband cannot err in anything'. To hit the bull's eye was as difficult as finding a pea that weighed a pound. I did not find such a pea. May the happy wives forgive me; but each judges the market by the good values we find there . . . I closed my eyes to my surroundings. . . believing that mutual attraction and fondness would compensate for and surmount the difficulties of privation. I forgot that where bread is lacking mutual recrimination is more likely to enter; and sometimes even with bread it still creeps in.[20]

The break-up of a marriage, through separation or, probably more commonly, the death of one of the spouses, would make a difficult economic situation even more desperate. The hardship facing a single parent was particularly intense if that parent was the mother. Dolores Ibarruri faced such problems during her husband's frequent stays in jail. After the general strike of 1917 she sold some of the potatoes they had planted and acquired a pint of milk per day from a neighbor in exchange for mending the children's clothes. She was helped when some of her husband's comrades sent a money order for 50 pesetas but soon was in desperate straits once again and almost sold her sewing machine to raise money. Later on her husband was arrested shortly after having been released from prison and 'I was furious and desperate; we were just beginning to lift our heads above water when once again the privations were going to begin'. Her situation was made more difficult than it might have been by the fact that her own mother had cut her off when she became a Communist.[21]

It would be quite wrong to suggest that the difficulties of working class life inevitably made the family experience an unhappy one. This is particularly true for the relations between parents and children. Through the overall silence, the authors at times reveal a genuine and deep emotional bond, either for their own parents or their children. Pestaña clearly loved his father and did not criticize him for the beatings which punctuated his 'lessons': 'He did not hit me out of cruelty but out of a false sense of what education should be and an excessive love of his son . . . he never forgot me, to the extent that on the rare occasion he went to a cafe he saved the lump of sugar for me.'[22] Vigil certainly appreciated his father's offer to stay in school as long as possible, even if he did not take it up.

Again it is Ibarruri who says most on this score, although in her role as mother rather than as daughter. Her experience was particularly bitter. Of her five children – three of them triplets – only two survived: 'Every day, when I took lunch to my husband at the mine, I had to pass the cemetery where they were buried; each time my heart was torn with anguish . . . It is difficult to measure the amount of grief a mother's heart can contain; it is equally difficult to measure the capacity for resistance that such hearts can acquire.' Later she laments her inability to be a proper mother because of the consequences of her political activity: 'Did I have a right to sacrifice my children, depriving them of a secure and warm home, of the mother's care and affection that they needed so much?'[23]

Women

Ibarruri shows an awareness of the special position of women. She married as a way of escaping the drudgery of her work as a servant yet she found the role of housewife to be an alienating one, as exploitative as wage work but lacking the 'social dimension' it provided.

> My mission was 'fulfilled'. I could not, ought not, aspire to more. Woman's goal, her only aspiration, had to be matrimony and the continuation of the joyless, dismal, pain-ridden thralldom that was our mothers' lot; we were supposed to dedicate ourselves wholly to giving birth, to raising our children

and to serving our husbands who, for the most part, treated us with complete disregard . . .

Although I had no tendency to be nostalgic about the past, I used to long for the time when women worked in the mines. However brutish the work, it offered an outlet no longer available to women in the mining valley; in addition to wages it had added a social dimension . . .

In the mine, the woman was a worker and as such she could protest exploitation together with other workers. In the home she was stripped of her social identity; she was committed to sacrifice, to privation, to all manner of service by which her husband's and her children's lives were made more bearable. Thus her own needs were negligible; her own personality was nullified . . .[24]

The daily problems she faced as a woman, a wife and a mother pushed Ibarruri away from her religious faith and made her susceptible to the appeal of socialism and the labor movement. The Marxist books she began to read were 'a window opening on life' and gave her a way of more satisfactorily explaining her situation. Yet, in spite of this she did not give gender priority over, or even parity with, class in explaining their situation. The solution lay in class liberation through Communism. In recounting how a group of 'missionaries . . . led by . . . the wife of one of the richest mine owners in Vizcaya' came to visit her while her husband was in jail after a strike, offering her a house, land and a job for her husband in return for her returning to the Church, Ibarruri comments that 'when I was a simple village girl, I meant no more to Doña Sebastiana than one of her dogs or cats. But when the village girl is transformed into a Communist woman who engages in struggle . . . the señora is overcome with sudden fright'. And it was Communism that gave her a public voice for the first time:

Ever since my childhood I had liked attending public meetings. . . There were frequent meetings and conferences among all groups in the political spectrum, and . . . I never missed a meeting. I drank in what the orators said, whether Socialist or Carlist, even though I did not understand their political goals. But the musical sound of their language, the sonorous phrase, the impassioned attack, the sarcastic word, the blistering jibe filled me with enthusiasm. Afterwards, at home I would reconstruct the speeches that had impressed me most. As time passed, as I heard those reputed to be great orators, many impressed me unfavorably because of demagoguery or histrionics or lack of simplicity or stimulating content. *Now it was I, a Communist, who was to stand on the platform.*[25]

Even the labor movement and Communism were not havens for women. Ibarruri was an active militant yet she suffered condescension, at least early in her career.

The secretary of the Miners' Union, a well-known Socialist, asked me one day . . . how much I knew about socialism; he asked me what works I had read. I told him, and also mentioned that I was studying *Capital*; he looked at me

pityingly and asked, not without sarcasm: And have you understood any of it
. . . How are you going to understand these concepts if I, who have studied
them for ten years, don't understand them too well?[26]

Religion

What place did religion and the Church have in working class life? Overall,
we see a working class largely alienated from formal religion, for the most
part well before its members discovered labor politics. To judge from their
autobiographies hardly any of them ever went to church. Largo Caballero
makes no mention of religion, even though the limited formal education
he did have was at religious schools. Carro does not admit to having had
any religious beliefs and his experience with the Church is solely one of
conflict. He was publicly excommunicated for his political activities in La
Vera (Navarre) and then, in 1909 or 1910, he fought with a priest over the
type of funeral his father was to have: 'he tried to have him confess and have
a church burial, contrary to my father's will. But in spite of the pressure of
the Church and the authorities he had a civil burial and the people of Pasajes
showed their support, declaring a general strike and going en masse to the
funeral'.[27] Carro also had a civil wedding.

Likewise, for Pestaña, formal religion is totally absent, although he does
give us an enticing glimpse of popular belief in the supernatural when he
describes how a faith healer cured him of cataracts as a child: 'saying prayers
and making many signs of the cross over my eyelids and putting on some
white powder which hurt horribly when she started to rub it in with her
finger . . . In the end I got my sight back.'[28] Vigil's family, or at least his
mother, did have more contact with the Church, but in her case religion
was essentially a way of solving practical problems. When he was three he
and his brother were quite ill, and following the advice of an aunt who
lived in a village, his mother 'offered' them to the Virgen del Socorro, the
patrona of the aunt's village, in return for a cure. As to Vigil himself, when
a friend tried to get him to become an altar boy 'I lit out through the door
and never looked back'.[29]

Again the one exception is Dolores Ibarruri. She received religious education 'at school, at church and at home' and she describes what seems to
have been a fairly deep religious faith which lasted into adolescence: 'My
faith was concentrated on that altar [in the town church]. The sorrowful
mother and her dead child moved me to tears. In that simple figure I
worshipped the living image of the Virgin Mother.' However, her faith
'suffered a deep shock' when she watched the clothes on the statue of
the Virgin being changed: 'My Virgin was like one of those scarecrows
the peasants put in the wheat fields to frighten the sparrows! I watched
them dress the manikin as though I were hypnotized . . . I shivered and my
teacher asked if I felt ill.' Yet she retained some of her beliefs because later
on she describes how they disintegrated in the face of 'the intimate contact

with harsh reality' she experienced as a married woman. Her discovery of socialism banished what was left, although only after a battle, 'as if . . . my Catholic beliefs . . . were determined to leave a shadow, a fear, a doubt in the depth of my consciousness'.[30]

The Meaning of Labor Politics

For Dolores Ibarruri socialism replaced Catholicism as a satisfying way of explaining the world. The labor movement and revolutionary politics were also a solution to her problems as a woman as well as a member of the working class and gave her a public voice she otherwise would have lacked. What did unions and politics mean for the men?

For some they represented a revolutionary change in their lives. For Carro, who was exposed to socialism by his fellow workers, it produced 'a revolutionary transformation in my mind'. It also provided sociability and, perhaps most important of all, recognition of full manhood: 'Spreading clandestine propaganda . . . let me make new friends . . . this and the political conversations I held with apprentices and adult workers . . . made me a man before my time.' At 12 he was arrested during a strike and beaten by the Guardia Civil, 'but the congratulations from workers and apprentices for my strength in not denouncing anyone . . . made me feel a real man with the right to become a member of the Socialist Party'.[31] For Largo, who was 21 when he became a unionist, the impact was equally strong. He was converted overnight after hearing some workers discuss the May 1, 1890 celebrations and 'it produced a radical change in my life. I gave up all entertainments and distractions which did not have a cultural or educational goal'.[32] Unfortunately, he does not tell us what these amusements were.

Pestaña was first drawn to anarchism by an article about a soldier in the Cuban war whose life had been destroyed and who advocated anarchism as the answer to social problems. But he had to overcome the rumors he had heard – from whom? – about the anarchists: 'they held secret gatherings at which they decided who would kill kings, ministers and other important people. The bomb, the knife and death were their laws.' His doubts were overcome when a workmate, 'a good, friendly and affectionate man', admitted one day to being an anarchist and by his example convinced Pestaña 'to work for those ideas about which I knew absolutely nothing'.[33]

The most curious case is that of Vigil. It is really not clear just why he became a Socialist. As a young man he was an active Federal Republican, contributing to their newspapers and serving as librarian at the Casino of the Unión Republicana when he was eighteen. The party's attraction was its advocacy of reforms which seemed to favor workers. One of his friends during national service was a Socialist, but Vigil was not attracted by his friend's explanations and even backed out of an offer to visit Pablo Iglesias. Back in Gijón he was unresponsive to his workmates who tried to get him to become a Socialist and only joined when he returned to Madrid as a reservist and had a number of talks with Iglesias: 'After various interviews, in which he plied me with attention, I was convinced and joined the party.'[34]

What is clear from these five people is that formal ideology played a relatively minor role in drawing them to labor politics. And we are dealing here with men and women who were active militants and leaders, some at the very highest levels – Largo Caballero became Prime Minister in 1936 – for whom we might expect ideology to have been more important than for the rank and file. Rather, it seems that much of the appeal of labor politics lay in the ways in which it helped resolve more basic human problems: giving a woman a social role, making a boy a man, providing new social contacts or providing examples of good human beings. Of course, none of this meant that the commitment of Spanish workers to their political organizations was ephemeral; perhaps quite the contrary. Certainly when the time came to fight in their defence they did so at least as tenaciously and courageously as any workers anywhere else.

4

Identities

Few countries have been more closely identified with Catholicism than Spain. For some, Spaniards and outsiders alike, the Church has been an integral part of the nation's identity, if not the very basis of that identity. Yet, in the nineteenth and twentieth centuries, the Church has been the most controversial institution in the country, struggling to determine how to relate to an emerging liberal society while that society, and the governments to which it gave rise, sought to delimit an acceptable sphere for the Church and religion.

But, as severe as were the difficulties in defining the institutional role and nature of the Church within the new society, even graver was the alienation of an increasing segment of the population from the Church and its ministers, and from religion itself. By the early part of the twentieth century religious belief had ceased to be the common heritage of all Spaniards and turned into yet another point of conflict. In large part this growing 'dechristianization' was a product of the Church's inability to formulate an effective response to the challenges of urbanization and industrialization. But not entirely; its roots lay in certain features of that impressive structure that was the Church of the Old Regime, the consequences of which became evident only when the protective political environment of the absolute monarchy disappeared.

If the identification of Spain with Catholicism was debatable, the identification of Spaniards with their new, liberal state was no less in question. Spanish liberals were not very successful in creating a secular, national identity to supplant the country's long-held religious identity. In fact, one can question the extent to which any nationwide form of identity, sacred or profane, has ever managed to impose itself on top of deeply ingrained local identities of small communities.

The Church, Religion and Belief

In the eighteenth century, the Catholic Church was an institution of great political, economic and social power. There were about 200,000 clergy at mid-century but they were very unequally distributed geographically, with many more in the north than the south. There were also many more clergy in the cities than in the countryside. Old Regime Spain had an urban church in a rural society. The clergy who had direct contact with the faithful, the parish priests, were the smallest part of the ecclesiastical population, greatly outnumbered by the members of the orders and benefice holders who were concentrated in the cities and were most common in the wealthier parts of the country.

The vast wealth of the Church came from a variety of sources. The Church received a quarter of the agricultural income of the Castiles, 45 per cent of the tithes and urban property rents, 70 per cent of the interest on loans and 10 per cent of the livestock. In total, it received 'just over one fifth of all the income produced by the leading sectors of the economy'.[1]

Where did the money go? Certainly not on the salaries of the parish priests, who were miserably paid and frequently had to take on other jobs, such as tutors or administrators for noblemen. The greatest expenditure went on buildings, decoration and 'the splendour of the cult'. This included large numbers of cathedral staff. In 1805 the cathedral of Toledo had 143 ecclesiastical positions, plus a choir of 175, Seville had 137 and Santiago 166. Charity was another major expense, reaching what Callahan calls 'unprecedented levels' in the latter part of the eighteenth century.[2]

During the reign of Charles III (1759–88) there was a government-supported movement for Church reform. However the failure of this program left the Church poorly equipped to deal with the decades of turmoil touched off by the intrusion of the French Revolution into Spain and the radically new political environment which was produced. The institution which emerged from the crisis in the 1840s would be very different from the one that had entered it in 1789.

The Place of the Church

The resistance to the French occupation was fully supported by the Church – which treated it as a crusade – and seemed to reaffirm its role as a leading national institution. The hierarchy supported the election of a parliament in non-occupied territory which, when it met in Cádiz in 1810, had a strong ecclesiastical contingent, 97 of 308 members. Yet when the Cortes passed legislation such as the abolition of the Inquisition, freedom of expression, freedom of the press and reform of the regular clergy, the Church was in opposition. When Ferdinand VII (1808–33) returned to the throne in 1814, the hierarchy hoped to restore the position of privilege that the Church had enjoyed under the Old Regime.

The rift between reformers and traditionalists which had been present in the eighteenth century remained and was even wider than before. Reform came to be identified with liberalism and the reformers within the Church were isolated. In the archdiocese of Toledo, ecclesiastical authorities became concerned with the political behavior of their subordinates and there were a large number of trials of priests who had collaborated with the French or supported the liberals. After 1814 political ideas became an important consideration in the recruitment of priests. The persecution of the liberal clergy increased following the liberal interlude of 1820–3. There was an avalanche of denunciations, and supporters of the Constitution were brought to trial. The best positions were given to older, strongly anti-liberal priests while the liberals were exiled to the least attractive villages.

The experience of 1820–3 drove the Church definitively into the arms of reaction. Initially there was little opposition to the Constitution and most bishops took the oath of loyalty, as did the clergy, although the members of the orders were substantially less co-operative. However, proposals for reform, including the closure of purely monastic orders, drove large parts of the clergy into opposition. Local political authorities began to act against those priests who did not support the Constitution: in Toledo eighty-two were removed from their posts and twenty more listed as disaffected.

Following his second restoration in 1823, Ferdinand annulled liberal legislation and appointed a clerical ultra as his chief minister. He did resist ecclesiastical demands for a restoration of the Inquisition but allowed unofficial Juntas de la Fe to function until 1827. In the last decade of Ferdinand's reign, the majority of the Church supported the government but there was an activist minority, especially strong in Catalonia, which participated in royalist secret societies and turned to the king's brother, Carlos. When the Carlist War broke out in 1833 most of the hierarchy recognized Ferdinand's daughter, Isabel. Support for the rebels came mostly from monasteries and convents in the north and in Andalucia.

Between 1835 and 1843 progressive governments legislated a new, reduced place for the Church and in the process destroyed the institutional base of the Old Regime Church. In October 1835 the monasteries were suppressed and in February 1836 their properties sold. Finally, in July 1837, the male orders were abolished. During the regency of Espartero (1840–3) the government attempted to create a streamlined Church, subservient to the state. The property of the secular clergy was put up for sale and in 1841 a major reorganization of parishes and dioceses was proposed, along with limitations on contacts between the Spanish Church and Rome. Attempts were made to purge politically disaffected clergy by requiring a loyalty certificate to be issued by the civil governor.

Neither the progressives nor the moderates considered the question of the Church as a choice between religion and atheism. Both groups saw religion as important to social order and both sought to find a role for a Church molded by reason. The question at hand was the type of Church, and religion, the country was to have. The progressives attacked what they saw as the excessive size and wealth of the Church, but they never questioned its spiritual hegemony. The Constitution of 1837 made Catholicism the state religion and declared that the clergy were to be publicly supported. Catholicism had an important role to play as a unifying force in a society already divided in a number of ways, a point made by Salustiano Olózaga when he urged parliament to 'do nothing that may lead Spain to lose its religious unity'.[3] The moderates, who came to power following the overthrow of Espartero in 1843 and remained there until 1854, had their own ideas about the relation of the Church to the state and society. For them, the Church had an indispensable role in the maintenance of public order. The clergy had a duty to preach obedience to the laws and resignation to the lower classes.

The moderates emphasized the utility of the clergy, but demanded that the clergy abjure fanaticism, the Inquisition and any political role. It must also meet certain personal and intellectual standards: 'a virtuous, national, Catholic clergy, capable of putting itself at the head of society to uproot through Christian charity the discord among us'. This charity had to be one which respected the established authorities and 'the legitimate inequality of wealth', that is, the existing social order. It was a role that the Church proved willing to take on.[4]

The moderates began to work on improving relations with the Church early in 1844. Exiled bishops were allowed to return and the loyalty certificates were abolished. The next year properties of the secular clergy, which had not been sold were returned. The Constitution of 1845 confirmed Catholicism as the 'religion of the Spanish nation' and bound the state 'to maintain the cult and its ministers'. Negotiations towards a definitive reconciliation began in 1848 and culminated with the Concordat of 1851.

The Concordat affirmed that the 'Apostolic Roman Catholic religion remains the only religion of the Spanish nation to the exclusion of any other religion'. The secular clergy were to be supported by the state and the religious budget was set at one-seventh of total government expenditures. The state also agreed to support the seminaries, permit the Church to hold property and allow a limited number of male orders to function; it also promised that all education would conform to Catholic doctrine. In return, the Pope recognized the land sales which had already taken place, agreed to limited parish and diocese reorganization and affirmed the Crown's right of episcopal appointment. The Concordat resolved the contentious question of Church-State relations but did not settle the question of the place of the Church and its influence in society.

This settlement remained intact until the Second Republic except for the revolutionary interlude of 1868 to 1874. The government suppressed religious communities, prohibited the orders from owning property, abolished the special ecclesiastical jurisdiction and introduced civil marriage and the civil registry. It also proposed to allow freedom of religion. On August 1, 1873, the government of the First Republic announced a plan for the separation of Church and state, in which the state renounced its powers of appointment and let the Church run itself. The law was criticized by clerical opinion and died with the Republic.

The Constitution of 1876 reaffirmed the 1851 settlement but with one significant alteration. Article 11, which dealt with religious matters, was by far the most controversial aspect of the attempt by Cánovas to reconcile all liberal opinion and create a stable political system. Cánovas' solution retained Catholicism as the state religion, and even gave nineteen bishops seats in the Senate, but allowed other faiths to be practised in private. This generated vocal opposition from the hierarchy and even Pope Leo XIII's attempts to rally Spanish Catholics behind the monarchy met with 'rather indifferent results'. By the end of the 1880s the bulk of the Spanish Church was willing to accept the Constitution, albeit without enthusiasm, and the Church continued to push its claims for a larger role in education, censorship and public morality.

There were some elements within the Church which continued to reject the liberal state. In the Rioja, the lower clergy and the religious orders continued to support Carlism. When in 1889 a canon of Santo Domingo de Calzado who had preached against freedom of the press and the 'damned error of liberalism' and called it a sin for Catholics to vote for Liberals, was brought to trial for 'having condemned political liberalism from the pulpit' he was supported by many of the region's clergy. The bishops of the diocese frequently condemned press freedom and in 1883 banned some radical papers.[5] In the Basque Provinces, the clergy preached more frequently just before elections and they preached in Basque in order to attack the government. Funerals were also a common occasion for treating political themes. In 1890, Minister of the Interior Romero Robledo issued a Royal Order on the subject which criticized Basque priests for using Basque to attack the Constitution.

The Clergy

The nineteenth- and early twentieth-century Church was both smaller and poorer than the Church of the Old Regime. But since the changes it underwent did not affect all segments of the institution equally, this much reduced Church did not suffer from all the imbalances of its eighteenth-century predecessor.

The size of the clergy fell by over half between 1797 and 1900, from 200,000 to 87,000. The secular clergy experienced the least change. In 1797 there had been 21,000 priests and 40,000 benefice holders; by the early 1840s there were only 38,000 in all. Their number increased to 42,000 by 1868 only to drop again to 33,000 in 1900, where it remained more or less stable until 1930. The number of parish clergy actually increased over that of the eighteenth century and by the time of the Restoration they represented the largest segment of the ecclesiastical population, although they would fall back at the beginning of the twentieth century to represent only about a third of the clergy.

The regular clergy was much more affected. The War of Independence was a watershed for them. Their numbers had been declining gradually since 1768, but in 1808 had fallen only 16 per cent. Between 1808 and 1820 the population of the male orders fell by 20 per cent and by 1835 it had fallen another 10 per cent, to 30,906. The male orders were abolished in July 1837, but were allowed to return on a limited basis by the Concordat.

The recovery of the male orders was slow, even though the Church took advantage of the ambiguity of the Concordat article governing their activities to introduce a number of orders. In 1867 there were only 1,500 monks in the country. The real revival of the orders took place during the Restoration. Thirty-four new male orders appeared after 1875 and 115 monasteries were founded. They had 22,000 members by 1910.

The female orders and congregations did not have so turbulent a history. They were largely ignored in the process of reform and Saez Marín, commenting on the scarcity of data about them in the early nineteenth century has written that 'it seems as though the governments set up a barrier of sacred respect around this group of women who voluntarily took a standard of living well below a decent level'.[6] The decree of July 1837 did not dissolve these orders, although it reduced the number of houses and ended all recruiting, a ban which lasted until 1851. According to the religious budget, there were 12,000 nuns in 1842, 11,600 in 1854, and 16,700 in 1867. The female orders actually led the revival of the regular clergy after 1875. Forty-one new orders were founded during the Restoration and by 1900 there were over 42,000 nuns, making up almost half of all the clergy.

The revival of the religious orders was heavily dependent on the support of wealthy benefactors. After 1880 the Jesuits of Toledo were dependent on aristocratic donations. The Jesuit Colegio de Chamartín, in Madrid, was opened at the request of the nobility; the land was given by the Marquis of Pastrana and the building financed by his wife, who sold a Rubens to Baron Rothschild to pay for it. When she died in 1892 she left the order 20 million pesetas, about half the government's annual budget for the Church.

The elite of Bilbao was particularly active in promoting these activities. The University of Deusto, which was founded in 1886 owed its existence to a number of leading industrialists who created a limited company to acquire the land. A commercial and engineering college was set up in a similar way thirty years later. Both were run by the Jesuits who undertook to train a new Catholic elite. Members of the elite also sponsored religious schools and other institutions for the workers and their children, such as the primary school in Deusto run by the La Salle brothers and the attached mutual aid society, savings bank and recreational center. Taken together this represented an attempt 'to create and control a securely Catholic world of entertainment and financial benefits as well as instruction'.[7]

The increased importance of clergy with pastoral duties was surely a positive change, but other imbalances of the past remained: unequal regional distribution and unequal remuneration. Large areas of the country, in particular the south, remained as neglected as they had been in the eighteenth century, if not more so. Clergymen remained very thin on the ground in Andalucia throughout the nineteenth century. In 1859 there was an average of 729 people per parish across the country but in Badajoz there were 2,216, in Almería 3,207, in Málaga 3,667 and in Cádiz 7,493! In 1932, the Archbishop of Seville blamed the shortage of clergy and the excessive size of parishes for contributing substantially to what he called 'apostasy' in the province of Huelva. At the other end of the country, in Asturias, Father Sarabia, a famous missionary, listed the shortage of parish clergy and the excess of benefice holders as one cause of 'our Catholic decadence'.[8]

The abandonment of the south was not a new problem, but the failure of the Church to respond to urban growth was. The Church proved unable to create new urban parishes to keep pace with population growth and the development of working class suburbs. In 1858, the city of Barcelona, with a population of 184,000, had sixteen parishes while Granollers, with 32,000, had thirty-nine. The parish structure of the country's largest city remained unchanged after 1877: in 1907 a number of parishes had over 50,000 residents and some more than 60,000. Two years later there was an average of one priest and coadjutor for 10,000 workers.[9]

At the beginning of the twentieth century, the parish of San Esteban de Carabanchel Bajo, in Madrid, had one priest for 16,000 souls and in 1930, Puente de Vallecas, also in the capital, had five priests for 80,000. This did not reflect an absolute shortage of priests, however. At the same time, the central Madrid parish of Santa Barbara, with a population of 20,000, had sixteen priests. The differential is a clear reflection of what Cuenca Toribio has described as a strategy aimed at 'the spiritual reconquest of the leading elements' of society which concentrated the clergy in the central city parishes.[10]

The parish clergy continued to be poorly paid and poorly trained. In the 1820s three-quarters of the parish priests of the archdiocese of Toledo earned less than the 5,000 reales that the Cortes of Cádiz had determined as adequate for rural clergy. Incomes ranged from 1,650 to 15,000 reales and some of the poorer clergy were forced to engage in activities like raising pigs in order to get by. Cathedral canons received more than parish clergy. In 1851 the Nuncio summarized the situation prevailing before the disentailments: 'the common opinion about the wealth of the clergy . . . is due to the unequal distribution of the resources. To put it bluntly, this idea was based on the situation of the upper clergy, part of which was very wealthy. With regard to the parish clergy, which was very poor, it was totally erroneous.'[11]

In fact the material position of the Church had been declining since the late eighteenth century, even if the final blow did not come until the disentailment of 1837. The income of the Archbishop of Toledo fell from 6 million reales in 1800 to 2.9 million in 1823. Ferdinand VII made use of Church revenues and abolished others, such as the feudal baronies in Catalonia. This hurt monasteries, like Poblet, but was welcomed by their subjects, who 'for good measure refused to pay the tithe and other obligations they had traditionally paid to the monks'.[12] In other parts of the country the Church suffered from the refusal of much of the peasantry to pay the tithe, a problem shared, as we have seen, by the nobility. In Guipúzcoa this resistance had begun in the 1790s and by 1831 the amount collected had fallen by almost a quarter. By the time the tithe was legally abolished in 1837, it had largely ceased to exist in fact.

The disentailments destroyed 'the old and substantial patrimony of the Church in Spain almost entirely', as the Nuncio put it in a confidential circular in 1853. The Church's independent income was replaced by government payments known as the *clero y culto*. The same system was established by the Concordat, and the Nuncio, for one, was satisfied with the level of support which he estimated to be about that produced by the Church's properties and the tithe prior to 1836.[13]

The Concordat did not improve the situation of the lower clergy. In Barcelona, only about a third of the clergy were paid out of the state budget, a third held benefices and the rest had to live off fees collected for services. During the Restoration, income continued to be badly distributed: the bishops and canons, who made up 3 per cent of the ecclesiastical population, received 15 per cent of the ecclesiastical budget. The capitular clergy was reduced in size, but remained 'a class apart . . . through eligibility requirements that excluded the vast majority of the parish clergy'.[14]

The educational, and even moral, level of some of the rural clergy at the beginning of the nineteenth century left a lot to be desired. In Toledo in the 1820s many rural clergy had only a limited education, merely taking the tonsure without becoming full priests. In 1829 the Nuncio reported to Rome that the rural clergy were frequently ignorant and behaved scandalously. The bishop of Calahorra issued a pastoral in 1816 in which he attacked the all too frequent behavior of his priests: 'They say mass and pray but often lightly, without devotion or any understanding of what it means. The rest of the day they are idle . . . they do not study and never pick up a book, or even a spiritual book, or even know of their existence.'[15]

The Concordat, which established central seminaries, did not substantially improve the level of ecclesiastical education and training. The theological faculties had been closed between 1845 and 1852, so that the new seminaries, and their students, had no contact with the universities and were intellectually isolated. Seminary education was also deficient in pastoral training. The number of seminarians increased from 16,000 in 1853 to 23,600 in 1867, but not all of these became priests and not all the students were capable of doing so. In the 1850s the Bishop of Barcelona complained frequently about their intellectual ability and lack of application.

As deficient as a seminary education might have been, not all priests enjoyed even that. The plan of study written in 1852 added a 'short course' of three years of Latin, one of philosophy and two of theology designed to produce priests for rural parishes. The normal training lasted fourteen years. The plan was justified on the grounds that 'not all those who become priests need these studies since there are in the Church many ministries for which such instruction is not necessary and because not all of them can afford it or have appropriate intellectual gifts'.[16] The diocesan bulletin of Toledo 'published a series of articles describing each and every gesture the priest should make during Mass, an indication that some clerics lacked even this basic knowledge'. After examining the sermon collections and other books used by the clergy in the Rioja, Sainz Repa concluded that their cultural level was lamentably low.[17]

At the start of the twentieth century the alternatives to a lengthy stay in a seminary, usually between the ages of twelve and twenty-three, had been eliminated. Like so many other aspects of Catholic life the world of the seminarian was a closed one, both physically and intellectually. According to Lannon,

> it was usual for students to be visited by their families only at set times, while other visitors were discouraged and required special permission. Mail was read on its way in and out by priests in charge of discipline. Even during vacations a kind of isolation had to be constructed: seminarians were warned against going to the cinema, the evening stroll or political meetings, reading novels or the secular press, and dressing or behaving in a 'secular' way.[18]

The actual instruction did little to prepare them for an urban and industrial world which most seminarians, coming as they did largely from the villages and small towns of Castile, found alien.

Problems of discipline remained as well. In the 1860s the bishop of Burgos attempted to eliminate abuses among his parish priests, while at the same time, the bishop of Tortosa made ample use of domestic missions run by the orders to compensate for the shortcomings of his clergy such as 'the shortness of numbers, their reluctance to follow episcopal directives and their deficient formation'.[19]

Parish Life and Proselytism

The inadequacy of clerical education and training was revealed in the poverty of parish life. At the beginning of the nineteenth century, the best prepared priests in the archdiocese of Toledo sought positions without pastoral responsibilities, and those who remained parish priests were incapable of executing their pastoral tasks properly. In the 1830s Jaime Balmes had written about the need to create a new clergy which would undertake 'continual activity' in the parish and would reach out to the faithful. Instead, the pastoral training given priests after 1850 emphasized quite the opposite: 'a pastoral approach . . . which was based on the supposition that the faithful should go to the church attracted by the virtue of the priest. Beyond the classic visits to the sick the priest's ordinary ministry did not take place outside the church, the sacristy or the confessional.'[20]

In their pastorals, the bishops of the Restoration emphasized the care of souls and the incorporation of the parish clergy into this task. The parish priest was to be 'the protagonist of Christian life'[21] but it would seem that in large parts of the country this was not the case. Sarabia described the poverty of religious life in Pola de Lena, Asturias, at the turn of the century in the following way:

> Starting with a healthy, moral and traditional atmosphere we see a rachitic Christian life dominated by routine. Communion barely existed . . . only two old women every now and then. There were sermons only once or twice per year, on Corpus Christi and on the day of the patron of the parish church, Saint Martin.

> We children never had catechism and I never heard any explanations, either in school or at church. It all came down to learning the Astete [catechism] by rote.

At Easter 'there was no preparation at all. I have the sad conviction that the vast majority of those confessions and communions had more of sacrilege than dignified observance.'[22] The situation was similar in Huelva during the 1930s. The archbishop of Seville reported in 1932 that the priests functioned badly outside the sacristy and that parish life lacked any vitality. In many places there was not even a Sunday sermon and catechism was not properly taught.[23]

If pastoral life in the parishes was stagnant, the Church did display some energy and even innovation in another activity, proselytism. In Toledo, the apostolic missions were revived immediately after the Napoleonic War but the great fillip to missionary activity came in the 1840s with the efforts of Antonio Claret. Named apostolic missionary in 1841, Claret undertook to preach throughout rural Catalonia, in Catalan. He also made use of the modern propaganda technique of the massive distribution of printed material.

Claret had come up with the idea of establishing a religious publishing house to produce materials to assist in the task of proselytism, and in 1848 the Bishop of Seo de Urgell created the Librería Religiosa. Between 1848 and 1866 the Librería, which had an office in every provincial capital and an agent in many smaller towns, printed 2.8 million books, 2.5 million pamphlets and 4.25 million catechism sheets and flyers. Many of the pamphlets were written by Claret himself and his most popular work, *The Sure and Straight Road to Heaven*, went through four editions and 14,000 copies in Catalan and forty-eight editions and 41,7000 copies in Spanish. The flyers were mostly devotional, written in verse or reprinting popular songs addressed to the Virgin and the crucified Christ. The overall tone of the published material was 'polemical, conservative and little interested in scientific discoveries'.[24]

During the Restoration, and especially after 1900, the Catholic press developed into a significant force. An Apostolate for the Press was created in 1891 and in that year there were 248 Catholic publications including 35 daily papers, but they were found in only 22 provinces. By 1910 there were over 400 publications, including 64 dailies, in all but ten provinces and by 1913 there were 750 publications. A Catholic press agency, Prensa Asociada, was set up in 1908.

Missions became a major instrument of the revival of Church activities following the signing of the Concordat. The bishop of Barcelona in the 1850s saw the missions as preparation for his own visits to the parishes. He created five missionary teams which visited at least thirty-five towns in ten months. As we have seen, the Bishop of Tortosa used missions in the 1860s as a means of overcoming the inadequacies of his clergy. But the bishops were not alone in promoting missionary work. The Marquis of Comillas made use of them at his coal company in Asturias, where management arranged for the Jesuits to run missions to encourage the workers to fulfil their Easter obligation.

The missions were of various lengths, usually between one and two weeks. The center piece was preaching, with the sermons designed to achieve mass confessions and communions. The pardon of enemies was often the most emotional act. The missions also contained other activities such as processions with local images, dawn rosaries and sermons designed for special groups, such as women, the young and workers. In the smaller centers, the missions, with their ceremony, were a major event and drew large numbers of people but they were less successful in the cities. As early as 1850, the missions were making little impact in the city of Barcelona itself.

Preaching was considered an important activity, and rightly so in a country with a high illiteracy rate. Following the Napoleonic War the clergy of Toledo were encouraged to preach frequently in order to create a 'new climate which helped the Church influence those groups which threatened to break away from ecclesiastical control'.[25] The bishops of the Restoration emphasized preaching in their pastorals and issued norms regarding both form and content. Concern over the poor quality, and even absence, of sermons in many parishes led to the publication of vast numbers of collections of sermons – at least 133 volumes – to help those priests who were unable to prepare their own homilies.

The Mind of the Church

Sermons and pastoral letters offer an excellent window through which to glimpse the mentality of the Spanish Church in the nineteenth century. The pastorals of the archbishop of Toledo after 1814 abounded in jeremiads against new ideas, and this closed mindedness can be said to have characterized the hierarchy, and indeed the Church as a whole, throughout the century. In 1854 the bishop of Barcelona issued a pastoral which was endorsed by the other Catalan bishops, in which he 'fulminated against Protestantism, secular culture, religious tolerance, liberty of expression and "theatre, dances, cafes" and sundry other evils'.[26] And this in Catalonia, where the Church would first confront the problems caused by industrialization and the emergence of a working class! Although the Spanish Church was not entirely monolithic, up to the Civil War, and well beyond, it was dominated by a single outlook which has been well described by Frances Lannon:

> Competition from other ideologies was never tolerable, and could not be when they were automatically categorized as both erroneous and evil . . . Such an interpretation was inherently anti-pluralist and anti-democratic. Moreover, these political preferences were all the firmer for being derived not from a political or economic analysis that could be modified, nor even from scriptural images and texts that could be argued over, but from a static ecclesiology which repelled complexity and ambiguity.[27]

An analysis of the pastorals of the bishops of the Restoration has revealed a pessimism about the religious condition of the country, consciousness of social change which had to be addressed and a fear of liberalism as the cause of 'everything wrong with society'. The bishops defended the Pope's claim to temporal power, advocated an 'indissoluble link' between the secular and ecclesiastical authorities, claimed the right to censor all types of publication and interpreted all attacks on the religious orders as attacks on the Church itself. They saw Spain's defeat at the hands of the United States in 1898 as a divine punishment for a nation gone astray.[28]

José Antonio Portero has analyzed a number of collections of sermons published throughout the nineteenth century and has found a stable and consistent outlook which differs very little from that of the bishops.[29] The sermons were characterized by a homogeneous ideology which left no room for dissent: it rejected all thought not grounded in religion and demanded the total submission of society to the Church. Renovating Catholic currents from elsewhere in Europe had little success in Spain and the domestic ones were few and lightly supported.

As the preachers saw things, the Church possessed the truth and this eliminated any need for tolerance of other faiths. Science could be acceptable, but only so long as it did not question faith. Reason alone was destructive of both religion and society and had to be limited by faith. No distinction was drawn among new intellectual trends, all of which (positivism, rationalism, krausism and socialism) were considered to be products of Protestantism.

Politics, like science, had to conform to Catholic ideas. Liberalism was rejected out of hand and its two concommitants, liberty and equality, were rejected as irrelevant for Catholics, whose duty was to obey divine and human authority and for whom the only equality that mattered was in the eyes of God. Defense of the political order included defense of the social order. Social inequality, in either a society of estates or a society of classes, was divinely ordained.

The preachers' analyses of society were simplistic. There were only two social groups: the rich and the poor, each of which had specific obligations to fulfill in order to achieve salvation. The wealthy had their riches in order to practice charity, the poor their poverty in order to work and express acceptance of their condition. (We have already seen how such ideas about philanthropy were undergoing substantial change among lay people in the nineteenth century.) Preachers modified their social analysis somewhat in order to incorporate a middle class tied to finance and industry. This change required a re-evaluation of labor, which passed from being a punishment for original sin to a form of religious exercise, like prayer.

The sermons did criticize those members of the middle class for whom making money obscured Catholic values and who stimulated the rebelliousness of the lower classes by failing to live by those values. They did not, however, go on to question property and social inequality, which always remained Christian virtues. Whatever social discord existed could be relieved by once again injecting Christian ideals into social relations. The best way to do so was through giving alms which, by definition, took place within a framework of inequality, 'the duty owed by the wealthy in return for the submission that the poor should show'.[30]

Frances Lannon's study of the seminary of Vitoria casts light on this mentality and on the shortcomings of the clergy of the Restoration Church. It also helps explain the impermeability of the institution and its continuing alienation from the society in which it had to function. Discipline was strict and the seminarians' contacts outside it, even with their families, were controlled. Students were not allowed to attend other educational institutions; they were totally isolated intellectually. Their training emphasized Thomistic philosophy and this 'philosophical language set' prevented any meaningful intellectual discourse with other groups. Attitudes to the social question were simple-minded: loss of religious belief was the cause of all problems. In short, the Vitoria seminary was

> a Catholic educational institution deliberately enclosed within its own moral and intellectual, as well as physical boundaries. The pedagogical stress lay on as total a separation as possible from outside influences, regarded more often than not as inherently pernicious. As one student wrote as late as 1930 . . . the seminary was a nursery where tender shoots are preserved from the suffocating atmosphere of an unhealthy world.[31]

Attempts which were made in the late 1920s and early 1930s to add new subjects to the course of study, change educational methods and take a closer, more serious look at social phenomena did not survive the Civil War. The experiments ceased and the staff was purged.

Her study of the Society of the Sacred Heart in Bilbao reveals another aspect of this isolation from society as a whole. The order ran a school for the daughters of the local bourgeoisie and another school for poorer students who could not pay fees. The schools were adjacent but there were separate doors, uniforms, teachers, first communion groups and even separate seats at mass. Both the convent and the schools had limited contact with the world beyond their walls: the only paper received was the Integralist *Gaceta del Norte* and that was read by the Superior who passed news on to the sisters. Students were not prepared to sit state exams which meant that texts and syllabi were free from state control while teachers were not required to have any university training. The sodalities for the laity drew former students and the women of the local elite and their activities were all held on convent property.

The schools used texts designed for Catholic schools in general as well as some produced especially for them. Both offered an integralist version of national history and politics little removed from the Syllabus of Errors. Liberalism was condemned as a sin and the cause of the nation's defeat in 1898. As late as 1929 a catechism produced for general use in Catholic schools taught that liberalism was 'a very serious sin against the faith' and that it was 'a mortal sin' to vote for liberal candidates. The convent was one example of what Lannon sees as the Church's attempt to 'create an enclosed world, a counter community separate from and defined over against the wider community in which it existed'.[32]

The Church was never able to get much beyond this emphasis on alms and charity, and the reintroduction of Catholic ideas into social relations in general, when dealing with the ever more pressing 'social question'. Even in Barcelona, the locus of Spanish industry, Catholics seemed unable to transcend instinctive reactions and pat answers. In the 1850s the response of the bishop to labor unrest was to put himself unreservedly on the side of established order and preach resignation to the workers. As he told the Civil Governor, what was needed was 'religion and repression'. The Catholic paper *El Ancora*, whose editorial staff included two future bishops, could only look backwards when dealing with this issue: 'nostalgia for the guilds of the past and criticism of industrialization, polemics against socialism and communism and proposed solutions based on an idealized past'.[33] Even in 1916 when the Primate published a pastoral letter criticizing the injustices of capitalism for the workers he was capable of little more than invoking the country's Catholic tradition. The Church was aware that industrialization presented a potential danger, but it had no idea of how to confront it. The Church was, in William Callahan's phrase, 'puzzled by a society in ferment'.[34]

The Church and the laity were increasingly active in charity and welfare work during the Restoration, both through the religious orders and lay associations. It did make other attempts to deal with social problems. In the 1850s P. Francisco Palau ran a School of Virtue which sought to instruct workers on the social question and during the Restoration a number of groups were created with the purpose of indoctrinating the working class: female congregations such as the Servants of Saint Joseph, the Daughters of Saint Joseph, the Servants of Mary and the Ladies of the Catechism, as well as educational and recreational groups for the workers, known as Workers' Circles.

Leo XIII's encyclical *Reurum Novarum* (1893), which called for a Catholic-inspired response to the injustices of capitalism, including Catholic unions, elicited considerable interest among Spanish bishops, who commented on it in twenty pastoral letters. There was, however, little practical response and the attempts which were made to develop a Catholic presence in the world of labor were, with only limited exceptions, failures. Catholic unions, undermined by their close ties to employers, who were suspicious and mistrustful of all union activity, and their subsequent inability to act as genuine labor organizations and defend the economic interests of their members, did not succeed in challenging those of the Socialists and anarchists. Spain did not have a 'white Bolshevik' like Miglioli in Italy, but it did have dedicated and able organizers like Pedro Gerard, Gabriel Palau, José Gafo and Maximiliano Arboleya, all of whom belonged to religious orders, but even these were not allowed to succeed. Despite a plethora of initiatives, conferences and organizations, by 1919 'actual achievements in winning industrial workers to the Church, or effectively mobilizing those for whom it had always remained significant were extremely slight'.[35]

The experience of Father Maximiliano Arboleya and the Catholic miners' union in Asturias is a case in point. Arboleya's problem was that the parameters for Catholic unionism in the region were set by the Marquis of Comillas, owner of one of the largest mining companies and the leading lay exponent of social Catholicism in the country. (It was Comillas who had formed the Central Catholic Action Committee in 1894 as a response to *Rerum Novarum*. He also owned the Trasatlántica shipping company, whose vessels were described by one clerical admirer as 'floating parishes'.) The two men had totally opposite conceptions of what Catholic unionism meant, as Arboleya explained in his notes of a conversation with the Marquis in December 1916:

> Here he produced in me a sad impression when I saw the total certainty with which he said that I was completely wrong and that this was because I did not know the workers, although I have lived among them all my life . . . He told me that it was good for the workers that their associations be as closely tied to the employers as possible and that the workers themselves agreed with this and wanted the employers to participate.[36]

Any Catholic union at the Marquis' company had to fit in with the management's goal of preventing the spread of 'socialism' and from the beginning Catholic unionism in the region had one overriding objective: to serve as a prophylactic against the labor movement.

In April 1901 the chaplain of the Hullera Española asked Arboleya's advice on how to avoid the growth of socialism in Aller, where the company had its mines. The answer was that only unions which copied the methods of their rivals could be successful and that the paternalism practised by the company would be a failure. But Arboleya was unable to put his ideas into practice: 'My ideas made me much more dangerous than Pablo Iglesias [the founder of the Socialist Party] himself since he did not have to wear a habit to justify his socialism.'[37] In 1912 Arboleya returned to Aller in response to an invitation from the company's management to write the statutes for a Catholic workers' organization which was to be independent of the company. However, his plan was promptly rejected in favor of one developed by Father Palau which was more mutualist in orientation.

In 1918, a broader based Catholic miners' union, the Spanish Catholic Miners' Union, was established and within a year claimed to have 2,260 members. However, it was incapable of retaining, let alone moving beyond this initial success and by 1932 its membership had been halved. Even at the Hullera Española the Catholic union could not better its Socialist rival. In September 1934, Arboleya was lamenting the 'almost total lack of strength of Catholicism among the workers'.[38]

The failure of Catholic unionism in Asturias was fairly typical of its fate in industrial regions. The efforts of the Church in the countryside were more successful. The most outstanding example was Navarre, where during the early twentieth century a network of 156 rural syndicates, in which priests were active, was put together. These Navarrese syndicates formed part of a national organization of Catholic agricultural associations called the Confederación Nacional Católica Agraria (CNCA), which had been created in 1917 to bring together the large number of such bodies which had emerged since 1902.

The syndicates were 'inter-class' bodies which brought together large and small landowners, tenants and sharecroppers in order to harmonize relations among them and defend 'agricultural interests'. They also sought to help the troubled smallholder of the northern part of the country through collective action such as the purchase of tools and fertilizer and the acquisition of credit at reasonable rates of interest. In addition, they had 'moral' aims: encouraging religious observance and preventing the spread of revolutionary ideologies into the countryside.

The success of their efforts was concentrated in areas where levels of religious observance had remained high and the Church well integrated into local life. The organizations grouped together within the CNCA were concentrated in the north, and the national organization had its roots in Old Castile. The distribution of the 450 syndicates existing in 1909 reflects broader patterns of religious practice we will examine shortly. The latifundia south was conspicuous by its absence. Syndicates were established there in any number only in 1919–20, as a conscious response by the CNCA, backed by absentee landowners, to the widespread unrest which had begun in 1918. Both this support and the syndicates evaporated once the danger had passed.

Belief and Disbelief

The failure of the Church's rather meagre initiatives on the social question was a symptom of a much deeper phenomenon: the alienation of large parts of the population from official Catholicism. Prime Minister Manuel Azaña could anger Catholic public opinion in 1931 by stating that Spain had ceased to be Catholic, but if his remark was impolitic it was not inaccurate. Even some churchmen recognized that many Spaniards were lost to the Church and lamented the fact in print. The author of *The Apostasy of the Masses*, which was published in 1936, asked whether the country was still Catholic, and answered with a chilling no: 'Only small minorities of authentic Catholics, whose strength varies by region, are on the side of the Church. The vast majority of ordinary people are not ours, they are indifferent or they are against us.'[39] Three years later, Father Sarabia would echo Azaña's remark in the title of his book, *Is Spain Catholic?*

Recently, William Callahan has gone even further, asking not only if Spain had ceased to be Catholic by the 1930s, but if it had ever been so. He argues persuasively that a process of 'accelerated dechristianization' got underway about 1850 and quickly produced regional patterns of religious observance. By 1869, the 'regional character of Spanish Catholicism [was] already in place'.

> The Church was strongest in areas of large peasant populations who had reasonable security of land tenure and lived in numerous small villages with a strong sense of communal life. It was weakest in the great latifundia lands of Extremadura, La Mancha and Andalucia, where a rural proletariat lived in desperate economic

circumstances. And already by 1869 the weakness of the Church in metropolitan areas was becoming evident.[40]

1869 provides such a visible dividing line because of the petition campaign undertaken by a lay organization to protest the government's proposal for religious toleration. Using the parish clergy as agents, it collected 2.8 million signatures across the country. In eighteen provinces over a fifth of the total population signed, and with the exception of Alicante, all were in the north. The total hit 40 per cent in the Balearics, Guipúzcoa, and León and 59 per cent in Navarre. In sixteen, mostly southern provinces, less than a tenth of the population signed.

There are not the parish and diocese-level studies of changes in religious practice to reveal the rhythm and pattern of dechristianization, but we have some indications from the province and city of Logroño. The massive abandonment of religion, as measured through fulfilment of the Easter duty, came after 1843, and especially in the 1870s when it fell below 70 per cent for the first time. By the end of the century, observance was down to 40 per cent, and in some years less. Men were much less obervant than women and children: about 20 per cent of all those complying were males. The decline affected only a small area of the province, the commercial agricultural zone on the right bank of the Ebro, while areas of small peasant agriculture were much less affected. Lisón Tolosana found something similar in the Aragonese town he studied: there was a sharp decline in the number of people fulfilling their Easter duty from 1826 on, so that by the middle of the century 'the Church had lost control of the village'.[41]

Evidence for the south is fragmentary, but compelling none the less. Missionaries who travelled through the region between 1890 and 1918 were appalled by what they saw. Francisco de Tarín called the south an 'atlas of dechristianization' and in one part of Seville a group of missionaries was stoned in 1899. According to Peiró, in many places in the diocese of Cuenca, Toledo and Ciudad Real, attendance at mass and Easter obligation was around 5 per cent.[42]

Religious practice was clearly divided along class lines. One archbishop of Seville described the wealthy as 'pious' but said that the lower classes 'are ignorant of Christian doctrine, do not go to church, profane the holy days and live in concubinage'. In the Sevillian town of Bencarrón, most agricultural laborers were indifferent or hostile to religion, which they saw as belonging to the upper classes.[43] Jerome Mintz found a similar pattern in Casas Viejas: 'Religious observance . . . was sharply circumscribed. The masses said on Saturday night and Sunday morning were attended by men and women of the upper classes . . . by those dependent on them . . . and by the defenders of the social order. Few campesinos ever attended mass.' Likewise, most peasants bypassed the confessional, and many ignored sacraments such as marriage and baptism.[44]

In the province of Huelva, which was part of the archdiocese of Seville, religious practice was almost non–existent by the late 1920s. On average, only 20 per cent of the women and 6 per cent of the men met their Easter obligation, half the burials were non–religious, civil marriage was frequent and there was an almost total absence of religious vocations. There was a general ignorance of religious doctrine and in many places religion had been turned into folklore. Among the reports sent to the archbishop by the parish priests in 1932, the following, from the town of Niebla, is fairly typical:

> Number of inhabitants, 2,027. State of morality and Christian life: leaves much to be desired. There is abundant drunkenness and the Christian life has been largely abandoned. Sunday mass: 99 per cent of the men are absent. Women are little better: 90 per cent are generally absent. They do their Easter obligation in the same numbers. Last rites: almost all the sick ignore them . . . Six communions are administered daily and twenty weekly. There are four notorious cases of concubinage. Christian education: bad, much ignored by parents.[45]

The situation in urban working class areas was equally bad. In 1908, one year after the opening of the only church in the Barcelona suburb of Coll–Blanch, the priest gave only eighty communions per month. Attendance at special subsidized spiritual exercises for workers was very low: 55 in 1906, 46 in 1907 and 77 in 1908, including only one in the populous working class district of Hospitalet. In the dioceses of Barcelona and Vic, the rates of reception of last rites and baptism within a week of birth (something the Church considered an important obligation) both fell after 1900. The percentage of those receiving last rites fell from 52 per cent in 1900 (already a low figure) to 46 per cent in 1920 and 40 per cent in 1935. The percentage of babies baptized in the first week dropped from 30 per cent in 1900 to 15 per cent in 1920 and 10 per cent in 1935. The situation was little different in Asturias or Madrid.

Religion lost ground in the south and the big cities because these areas were neglected by the Church and because the lower classes saw the Church as the supporter of the social order. In those areas where religion remained strong, we might suggest that it was due to the close connection between religion, the Church and its ministers, and local life. William Christian has pointed out that in the mountain villages of Santander, until the late nineteenth century in some places and until the 1930s in others, the parish priests were 'local boys without a great deal of education. They often kept cows themselves and sometimes wore regular work clothes'.[46] Likewise, Martin Blinkhorn has commented on the popular nature of the Church in Navarre, usually considered the most Catholic region of the country, where parish priests were usually locals who were well integrated into the community. This is a factor which has not been studied, but is likely to have been of great importance in preserving or reinforcing the role of the Church. Priests were recruited primarily from the rural lower classes of the north, regions with the highest levels of religious observance and, in turn, these regions stood the best chance of having priests who were part of the community. On the other hand, the distance between priest and the local community was greatest where religious feeling was weakest.[47]

Along the same lines, the relation between high levels of religiosity in the rural areas of Catalonia and the Basque Provinces and the ability of the clergy to function in the local language is undoubtedly important. The role of language was recognized by churchmen: Claret's works were published in Catalan as well as Spanish and the catechism written by the Bishop Costa y Borras of Barcelona was published in a bilingual edition. Yet he himself hoped that Catalans would learn Spanish better: 'this contributes to providing the appropriate polish to people and things when they leave this region.' He also ordered seminarians to speak only in Spanish 'so that they become familiar with that language'.[48] After 1875 Catalonia had a native episcopate which came to be closely identified with regionalist feeling.

The situation was even clearer in Mallorca. There Catalan was the language in which the Church communicated with the mass of the faithful in both sermons and instruction of the catechism. In 1898 the bishop established a chair of Mallorcan language and literature and Mallorcan history at the seminary and four years later offered a prize for the best book on the life of Christ 'of a popular character written in good Mallorcan'. When in 1902 the government banned the teaching of catechism in Catalan in the public schools, the bishop of Mallorca joined with his colleagues in the Catalan-speaking dioceses to protest. Their protest clearly stated the connection between religious observance and the local language:

> The recent Royal Decree on the teaching of the catechism in Castilian damages the spiritual interests of these dioceses in an extraordinary and irreparable way since Castilian is not the language of the people. On the one hand it obstructs the understanding of dogma and the duties of Christians, on the other it will confuse and torture the minds of the children who are taught less in school than at home where the superior teaching of their mothers will necessarily be turned into a continual correction of religious education badly understood in a language which the family does not use, a language which all understand badly and in which they never succeed in expressing their feelings.[49]

Changing Forms of Observance

Religious observance as measured by attendance at mass and other religious services declined sharply in large parts of the country during the nineteenth century. Where observance remained strong, the nature of religiosity did not necessarily remain static. Rather, both the forms and content of religious practice evolved over the course of the century. One of the most marked changes was the spread of devotionalism. Devotions mushroomed during the nineteenth century. According to William Callahan this was due to the decay of the parish liturgy and the decline of the corporate religious life of the Old Regime which had been expressed in the *cofradías*. Devotionalism also allowed an individualistic style of religion, more consonant with liberal society.[50]

Devotions were encouraged by the hierarchy. The most important were the Marian cults, which were bolstered by the declaration of the Immaculate Conception as dogma in 1854. Missionaries helped found rosary societies, and by 1900 there were Marian associations in all cities and parishes. Another rapidly growing cult was the Sacred Heart of Jesus, which was promoted actively by the Jesuits. The inauguration of the Cerro de los Angeles, outside Madrid on May 31, 1919 opened an expansive period for the cult which lasted until the Second Republic.

Devotions waxed and waned in popularity over time as new ones were introduced to an area by missionaries or through religious publications. In the Santander valley studied by William Christian, the cult of the Sacred Heart was not introduced until 1910. The growth of cults devoted to Mary and Jesus brought with it a decline in the veneration of the saints. The strength of various devotions was reflected in changing patterns of naming children. The popularity of certain Marian cults: la Inmaculada, de los Dolores, del Pilar, del Carmen, was revealed in the appearance of composite names such as María del Carmen. Christian found a drop in devotion to the saints in general after 1858 and a corresponding increase for Jesus and Mary. Jesus was first used as a name in the valley in 1858, two years after the Sacred Heart was made a feast of the Church. There were very few simple 'Marías' after 1880.[51]

Christian also describes a wide range of devotions based around shrines. Most dealings with the divine took place through shrines, and this was the only type of religion practised by men. The nineteenth-century Church, unlike that of the previous century, was disposed to integrate this popular and folkloric side of religion. The popularity of shrines experienced periods of expansion and contraction, with contractions corresponding to periods of economic hardship. Shrines specific to the valley were more consistently popular than either regional or national shrines, indicating once again the connection between religion and local life. Mintz found something similar in the Andalucian village he studied: the peasants who shunned services in the church were drawn to local shrines.[52]

Religion took on an increasingly individual emphasis in the second half of the nineteenth century. New catechisms emphasized faith, hope, charity and good works and new devotional works stressed private devotion and portrayed salvation as an individual matter. Spiritual exercises, a more individualized form of mission dominated by the Jesuits, and spiritual direction became popular after 1880, especially among the middle classes, fitting in well with the Church's strategy of attracting the elites.

One major form of religious expression during the Old Regime, the con-fraternities, had an unequal history during the nineteenth century. They were still very active during the reign of Ferdinand VII but declined after their properties were sold in 1841. In the second half of the century there was a revival of religious associations, but these were voluntary and not defined by corporate status as were the confraternities of the Old Regime. Most of the vast number of voluntary associations which were established all over the country were engaged in some form of charitable work: the distribution of food, clothing and medicine – but never money – to the poor, the provision of home relief to the sick, homes and schools for orphans and the children of the poor, workshops to provide employment and even a home to preserve the morality of young female servants, and this in 1883!

Anticlericalism

One new development was the emergence of violent popular anticlericalism, especially in the cities. In the eighteenth century there had been occasional outbursts in rural areas prompted by disputes over rents and jurisdiction, that is springing from the Church's role as landlord and secular authority. Already by the 1820s the prestige and popularity of the Church was declining, no doubt a result of the Church's wholehearted association with political reaction following the restoration of Ferdinand VII in 1814.

This development was particularly marked in Barcelona, in whose surrounding countryside the clergy, and especially the orders, supported royalist rebels in 1822–3 and again during the Carlist War of 1833–40. In 1834 some of the city's monasteries were stoned during the celebrations for the new constitution, the Estatuto Real, and there were frequent satires, particularly in the theater, where the clergy were presented as perverse and as a threat to the state.

Verbal anticlericalism has long formed a staple of Spanish popular culture. Bartolomé Bennassar reports that a collection of proverbs published in 1627 contained almost 300 directed at the clergy which revealed 'an unequivocal hostility to both secular and regular'. A second such collection, published in 1953, contained 217 proverbs about the orders, some of which were so rude that the editor felt the need to moderate their language. In the middle of the nineteenth century both George Borrow and Theophile Gautier commented on this phenomenon and in the 1850s the bishop of Barcelona frequently petitioned the civil authorities to stop the sale of obscene religious images such as one of 'the Baby Jesus between two nymphs in extremely immoral and provocative poses' as well as satirical theatrical performances directed at the clergy.[53]

This tradition continued into the twentieth century. In June 1909 a complaint by a parish priest in the Asturian coalfields led to the prohibition of parts of a music hall performance in a local workers' cafe. The production was called the 'Turn of the Century Opera' and the offending skits were entitled 'the Anarchist' and 'The Village Priest'. In his study of the Andalucian village of Casas Viejas in the 1920s and 1930s, Jerome Mintz found 'two contrasting accounts concerning religion: the written histories of the well born and the oral tradition of the peasants'. The second tradition saw the regular clergy as greedy, oppressive and immoral and accounted for the abandonment of the local monastery by claiming that the outraged shepherds had killed the monks to avenge their oppression.[54]

There was also a lengthy history of anticlericalism in literature, going back, as Julio Caro Baroja has shown, to the medieval period. And this found expression across the literary spectrum. In the middle of the nineteenth century Eugène Sue's *The Wandering Jew* stimulated the appetite for scurrilous portrayals of the clergy. Benito Hortelano, who was a publisher and a political progressive, relates that in 1845–6, 'I was soon inundated with authors proposing similar works, among them an ex-Dominican. . . carrying a manuscript entitled *Mysteries of the Jesuits*.[55] Similar books were published in the 1880s, among them *The Secrets of the Confessional*, which included an orgy in a monastery. But anticlericalism was also a prominent characteristic of the highest levels of Spanish literary art. Many of the greatest modern novelists and playwrights made this the theme of their work. For some, such as Vicente Blasco Ibañez, Pío Baroja and Benito Pérez Galdós, easily a peer of Dickens, it was a prominent theme. 'Clarín's' *The Judge's Wife*, probably the greatest Spanish novel since *Don Quijote*, is about a priest who falls in love with one of the women from whom he takes confession.

Not all anticlerical sentiment was expressed in such harmless ways. Violence, against clerics and especially against religious buildings, also appeared. The first incident came in Madrid in July 1835. Rumours that the Jesuits had poisoned the city's wells led to a riot and the killing of seventy-eight monks. Anticlerical violence in the 1830s was, in William Callahan's view, closely tied 'to the political struggle between liberal and ecclesiastical interests' and subsided once the battle had been largely won, with the suppression of the monasteries in 1837.[56] However, anticlericalism was a genuine sentiment of the urban lower classes, particularly in Barcelona, where it emerged once again in violent form in the Tragic Week of July 26 to August 1, 1909. A general strike called to protest the sending of troops to fight a colonial war in Morocco turned into a spontaneous outburst of church and convent burning. Street fighting left 112 dead and 21 churches and 31 convents were burned in Barcelona alone. Other religious targets included schools, welfare institutions and workers' centers. Priests, monks and nuns were not harmed, but the workers did display what Joan Ullman has called a 'macabre curiosity' about the nuns and their lives – and deaths:

> They left intact certain rooms which they believed contained proof of the tortures perpetrated in cloistered convents. Hundreds of curious visitors later visited the tiny windowless cubicles and the 'infamous martyrdom room', containing a metal bed whose frame consisted of perforated tubes connected with gas pipes. They viewed the open tombs that revealed the corpses of nuns tied hand and foot, with heavy scourges beside them.[57]

Another bout of church burning, this time in Madrid and various southern cities, took place in May 1931, apparently triggered by the opening of a monarchist political club in the capital, and left 21 convents destroyed. And immediately following the military rising which triggered the Spanish Civil

War there were numerous attacks on churches and other religious buildings throughout the Republican zone as well as widespread killing of ecclesiastics which cost the lives of 4,184 priests, 2,365 monks and 283 nuns.

The Quest for a Secular Society

Despite their repeated conflicts with the Church, Spanish liberals were rarely hostile to the institution itself and never to religion. They sought merely to find it a place within and compatible with a liberal political and social order. Some elements within the Church felt that it was not being allowed a sufficiently influential role in national life but they found the settlement made by the Restoration tolerable, even if it fell far short of meeting all their desiderata.

In its religious legislation the Second Republic was qualitatively different from all preceding constitutional regimes. With only a handful of exceptions the founders of the new regime, and especially middle class Republicans such as Manuel Azaña, were hostile to the Church in a way that their nineteenth-century forerunners had not been. They saw the Catholic monopoly of religious life as a fiction and the social influence of the Church, especially in education, as an obstacle to social progress. In their religious policies they sought not merely to put limits on the social influence of the Church but to eliminate it altogether. Religion was a private matter, tolerable if it supported itself and stayed within the walls of church buildings; when it strayed beyond those confines it was not. Republican leaders sought to create a modern, secular society in which religion was reduced to a strictly private matter.

Beginning with the Provisional Government, Republican administrations acted quickly and energetically to realize their goal. Within two months the government had abolished compulsory religious education, prohibited Corpus Cristi processions and required all elementary school teachers to have a university degree, a measure which hit the nuns who taught in private schools. It also declared freedom of religion.

The Republican Constitution of 1931 defined the new place of the Church. It declared, for the first time ever, that Spain had no official religion and that government financial support for the clergy, a fixture since the 1851 Concordat, was to be ended within two years. The religious orders were to be driven out of education, industry and commerce and limits were imposed on how much property they could own. Over the next two years these principles were given force through enabling legislation. In January 1932 the Jesuits were dissolved and their property nationalized, cemeteries were secularized and divorce legalized. In June 1933 the highly controversial Law of Congregations demanded that the religious orders withdraw from primary and secondary teaching by the end of the year. This last measure must be seen in the context of an aggressive education policy which strove to make public, secular education much more widely available than it had been.[59]

The place that the Republic had legislated for the Church was much more in line with its actual weight in Spanish society than the role it claimed for itself.

At the same time, those measures did not respect democratic principles nor were they politically wise. Important measures, such as the Law of Congregations, as well as more minor ones, such as the ban on religious processions, went well beyond what could be consistent with the separation of Church and State. And harassment by leftist local governments, such as the imposition of a tax on the ringing of church bells, only added to the impression that the Republic was bent on persecuting the Church. This provided the issue around which the opposition coalesced and built a mass base, among the smallholding peasantry, which it might otherwise have lacked. The main right wing party, the CEDA, presented Republican religious legislation as an attack on the family and property as well as on the Church. It was, said party leader José María Gil Robles, a threat to 'Christian civilization. . . We are faced with social revolution'. The Church, which had been ill-disposed to the Republic from its inception, used similarly militant language. When Franco rebelled against the Republic it gave the Church the opportunity to fight a new crusade; it was an opportunity that the Church did not waste.

The Limits of the State

The divisiveness generated by the Catholic Church would have been much less important a problem had Spanish liberals built a state capable of claiming the loyalty, or at least the acquiescence, of the population. Nineteenth-century liberals were not indifferent to the need to build a strong state but their vision of what the state should be and do was inseparable from their idea of whom it should represent. The two great groups of liberals, moderates and progressives, differed sharply over how far political rights should reach and this affected their visions of the state. The struggle was decided in favor of the moderates in 1843. From then until 1931 they held power more or less continuously and erected a state in their image. Advocates of extremely limited political rights – the Constitution of 1845 created an electorate of less than one per cent of the population – and rigidly conservative on social questions, the overriding function of the state was to preserve their position and protect them from a people they feared.

Thus the process of state-building in Spain only partially resembled that described by Charles Tilly as one of the fundamental features of nineteenth-century European history:

> states took on responsibility for public services, economic infrastructure and household welfare to a degree never previously attained. The managers of national states shifted from reactive to active repression . . . All these activities supplanted autonomous local or regional notables and put functionaries in their places. As a consequence, notables lost much of their strength and attractiveness as intermediaries in the attempts of ordinary people to realize their interests.[1]

The Spanish liberal state did have some pretensions in the fields of education and social welfare but before the Second Republic it did not seriously attempt to realize them. Even more important, the Republic's centre-left governments (April 1931–September 1933 and February–July 1936) sought, for the first time, to uproot local powerbrokers, the *caciques*, who had mediated between the national authorities and ordinary Spaniards. This attempt to bring the state into more direct contact with the population was intimately bound up with the reform of agrarian structures and, together, these two projects were the most important components of the peaceful revolution which provoked the military revolt which began the Spanish Civil War.

The Liberal State

Through the eighteenth century Spain was governed by an absolute monarchy. Like the other continental powers, and unlike England, there existed no representative body which could limit the power of the Crown. Even so, the monarch was far from exercising absolute authority. At the most basic level the area where the Crown exercised direct jurisdiction covered less than half of the national territory and included about half the population. In the rest of the country jurisdiction was in the hands of members of the nobility or of the Church. In the Basque Provinces and Navarre, the Crown had to contend with regional privileges, the *fueros*, which were vigorously defended by assemblies dominated by the local gentry. Finally, in many places municipal government was firmly in the hands of the nobility or local oligarchies which the monarchy could not dislodge.

The power of the Crown was also limited by the existence of a congeries of privileged individuals and institutions such as the Church, nobility, guilds, universities and cities. Many of these privileges were honorific, such as the right of grandees to keep their heads covered in the presence of the king, but others were more practical and undermined the ability of the state to function effectively. By far the most important of these related to taxation. The clergy and the nobility enjoyed exemptions while in some regions taxes could not be raised without the consent of the regional assembly which meant, in practice, that they could not be raised. The state went vastly into debt to finance the wars and this debt contributed substantially to the ultimate collapse of the Old Regime.

The fragmented nature of the Spanish state was well described by Pablo de Olavide, one of the outstanding figures of eighteenth-century enlightened reformism. It was

> A body composed of other and smaller bodies, separated and in opposition to one another, which oppress and despise each other and are in a continuous state of war. Each province, each religious house, each profession is separated from the rest of the nation and concentrated in itself . . . Modern Spain can be considered as a . . . monstrous Republic of little republics which confront each other because the particular interest of each is in contradiction with the general interest.[2]

This fragmentation persisted despite the efforts of eighteenth-century Spanish kings and their ministers to make the term 'absolute monarchy' more of a reality. Their actual achievements were limited and the outbreak of the French Revolution put an end to the reformist project, but their efforts did not go for nought. As Raymond Carr has observed, 'it was as architects rather than as builders that the Caroline bureaucrats bequeathed to liberalism this program . . . there is no reform of the nineteenth century, no reforming attitude of mind, that cannot be traced back to one of the servants of Charles III'.[3]

For the first three-quarters of the nineteenth century the fundamental cleavage within Spanish liberalism ran between the moderates and progressives. They differed on such crucial questions as the origin of political sovereignty and the proper extent of the franchise. They also disagreed in important ways on the nature of the state, such as local government and the maintenance of law and order. Both models of the state were essentially centralist, but there were important differences of degree. With their support among a much broader range of the urban population, the progressives' project was distinguished by its concern to provide greater freedom and power to local institutions by means of elected municipal governments and a citizens' militia under local control. In contrast, the moderate vision was of a totally centralized and hierarchical structure with political rights for the few. It had no place for municipal autonomy or an independent armed force such as the militias. This vision descended directly from the ambitions of the enlightened reformers of the previous century. It shared their concern for efficiency, prosperity and order.

The principal architect of the moderate state was Javier de Burgos. Determined to overcome the weakness of the central state, which he saw as the chief failing of the Spanish monarchy, and drawing inspiration from France, de Burgos designed a structure which, if anything, exaggerated the French model of uniformity and intense centralization. For de Burgos, 'the liberal state was, above all, centralization. What he called the protective action of government, or the "omnipresence of the administration" consisted of "removing at once the thousands of obstacles and promoting, with a single and enlightened impulse, great prosperity . . . Those charged with doing this must form a chain which starts with the head of the administration and ends with the last local policeman" '.[4] The moderates won out. After 1843 their model was put in place and remained standing, with only the brief interludes of 1854–6 and 1868–74, until the creation of the Second Republic in 1931.

The state structure dreamed of by the eighteenth-century reformers was built fairly quickly. The abolition of the seigneuries in 1837 restored direct jurisdiction over the entire territory and population to the Crown. In 1841 the customs barriers were moved from the Ebro River to the border with France, ending the duty-free status enjoyed by the Basque Provinces. The codification of the laws began in the 1840s and the decimal system was adopted for weights and measures in 1848, although it was not effectively in place until about 1880. Regular censuses began in 1857 and civil registers for births, deaths and marriages were instituted in 1870.

The division of the national territory into provinces and the appointment of agents of the central state to govern them had begun with the Cortes of Cádiz but came and went with the liberals, suspended' in 1814, revived in 1820 and suspended again in 1823. The new internal divisions were established definitively by de Burgos during his tenure as Minister of Development from October 1833 to April 1834. His decree of November 30, 1833 did away with the traditional divisions and replaced them with forty-nine provinces, modelled on the French *départements*. He also created an official, eventually called the civil governor, as the agent of the central government in each province. The *Instrucción* to these new officials outlined their wide-ranging responsibilities: statistics, welfare, education, economic development. However, these always remained essentially political, rather than administrative, positions and in practice the development functions were subordinated to the politically relevant duties, such as the maintenance of public order and 'the policing of liberty: meetings, associations, the press and strikes'.[5]

This was an important step but it was not enough to fulfil the moderate vision, which required that the authority of the central government reach directly into every town and village. For this reason, and because the political strength of the progressives lay at the local level, the moderates were determined to undermine local government autonomy by increasing the power of the mayor and converting his office into an appointed one. They did so in 1845. The Muncipal Government Law gave the Crown the power to appoint mayors and deputy mayors in all county seats with more than 2,000 residents. In all other places they were appointed by the civil governor. It also limited the number of elected town councillors to half of the total plus one. The rest were appointed by the Crown. This system whereby the mayors were transmission belts for the authority of the central government was retained during the Restoration in its Municipal Law of 1877.

The moderates also created a unified, although not a particularly effective fiscal system. Although the country was chronically in debt in the nineteenth century, a result of the Napoleonic and Carlist wars, and found the conditions under which it was granted foreign loans ever less favorable, liberal governments did not use their powers of taxation to remedy the situation. Taxes were blatantly regressive and collection terribly inefficient, and both of these conditions favored the propertied groups on whom the system depended.

The face of the system of taxation in liberal Spain was set in 1845 with the fiscal reform carried out by Alejandro Mon y Santillán. The foundation stone of government revenues was a new tax created by unifying a number of existing taxes on land and agriculture. Although agriculture was by far the principal source of wealth throughout the nineteenth century, this land tax accounted for only 20 per cent of total revenues between 1850 and 1890. The other principal direct tax, on manufacturing and commerce, brought in only 4 per cent of revenue over the same period. The bulk of government income came from indirect taxes, which bore most heavily on the less well off. The most important were taxes on consumption, including the heartily detested *consumos* on food. These were especially important for local governments and from 1876 to 1905 they provided between 87 and 100 per cent of all their revenues. In the same period indirect taxes accounted for 36.6 per cent of revenue for the national government and direct taxes 37.2 per cent. Monopolies and services provided 19.1 per cent, properties 4 per cent and other sources 3.1 per cent.

In part the tax burden had this profile as the product of conscious government policy. An equally, if not more, important factor was the incapacity of the state to determine, let alone collect, what it was owed. An agency to assess agricultural wealth on a national basis was created in 1846 but it was quickly decided that the compilation of a national survey would be too time consuming and expensive. Instead, government chose to rely on 'the assessments of their properties presented by the taxpayers themselves', not exactly a reliable source of information. The result was that an estimated half of all taxable wealth went undetected and despite widespread recognition of this massive fraud, nothing was done to prevent it. Evasion, like the tax system itself, was unequal: the wealthy and those with political influence, locally or higher up, got away with far more than anyone else. A similar situation prevailed with regard to the tax on industry and commerce: each association of industrialists or merchants in a municipality was assigned a quota and each member assigned a share. In practice the more powerful members of each association shifted the bulk of the burden to their less influential colleagues.

The governments of the Restoration were able to improve Spain's international financial standing by whittling down the national debt but because they did so without changing the fiscal system they were unable to increase revenue enough to provide much in the way of public services. From 1882 to 1895 expenditures on debt servicing increased by 22 per cent while other expenditures dropped by 11 per cent. Even with such austerity, governments were incapable of balancing the budget and continually took out new loans. The trauma of the Spanish–American War led to a fiscal reform which instituted a direct tax on certain forms of income but this was little more than tinkering and the deficits soon returned.

As a result, the levels of public expenditure in Spain were among the lowest in Europe. In the 1850s the Spanish government spent 7.76 francs per person compared to 65.2 in Great Britain, 33.3 in France, 17.2 in Prussia, 15.3 in Portugal and 11.2 in Sicily. Spain remained at the bottom of the table at the end of the nineteenth century and into the twentieth. Public spending did not reach 10 per cent of Gross Domestic Product, a level which France, Germany and Britain achieved in the 1880s, until the twentieth century and by that time the figure for Britain, Germany and even Italy stood at 16 per cent.

Even so, the composition of government spending, at least as measured by expenditure on wages and salaries, shifted significantly during the Restoration. The share devoted to the military dropped sharply while those

Table 4.1 *Debt as percentage of public spending, 1890–1920*

	UK	Germany	Italy	Spain
1890	18.2	nil	31.6	33.6
1900	7.0	nil	34.4	33.0
1910	7.4	5.6	25.0	34.5

Source: P. Tedde de Lorca, 'Estadistas y burócratas', p. 29.

Table 4.2 *Public spending per capita, 1890–1920 (constant prices)*

	Great Britain	Germany	Spain
1890	100	100	100
1900	189	145	91
1910	164	194	105
1920	358	283	152

Source: P. Tedde de Lorca, 'Estadistas y burócratas', p. 29.

ministries providing public services such as education, labor and commerce and industry became much more important, moving from 4 per cent of total spending on wages and salaries in 1875 to 16 per cent in 1923.

Centralization was one watchword of Spanish liberals. The other was homogeneity. The special jurisdictions and special privileges for social groups or parts of the country, so characteristic of the Old Regime, had no place in liberal Spain, where all Spaniards and all regions of Spain were to be equal before the state. Liberals were, however, prepared to make occasional exceptions. One, as we shall see, was the preservation – and extension – of a special legal jurisdiction for the military. The other was the recognition of the regional charters of the Basque Provinces and Navarre. The preservation of the traditional privileges of the region within a constitutional polity had initially been proposed by local liberals who hoped to maintain the fiscal benefits they entailed. In the concluding days of the Carlist War the question of the charters became entangled in the political struggle between moderates and progressives and the possibility of constitutional change. The charters were confirmed by a law passed in October 1839 although they were to be modified so as not to conflict with the constitution. The right of the provincial Juntas to approve or reject national laws was abolished, and the provinces were made subject to conscription.

In the case of Navarre the modifications were made by a law passed in August 1841, but even then the region was allowed to retain its fiscal autonomy and control over local government financing. Since any changes in the province's tax liability had to be negotiated, Navarre's contribution to the national treasury became progressively smaller. In 1842 Navarre contributed 0.37 per cent of the government's revenues. By 1860 it contributed only 0.27

per cent, and by 1935, 0.12 per cent. As María Cruz Mina remarks, this was a major breach in the principle of equality:

> the Navarrese, like the Basques, refuse to talk about privileges and prefer to talk about historic rights or foral rights. But in a state with equality before the law . . . the situation remains one of privilege with respect to citizens without *fueros*, and especially when it is tax exemptions which are at stake.[6]

The situation of the Basque Provinces was settled after the Carlist War of 1875. The Law of July 21, 1876 made Alava, Guipúzcoa and Vizcaya subject to national taxation and conscription. However, the privileges of the region were not totally destroyed. In February 1878 a system of financial agreement was put in place which left the region in an advantageous position. In 1889–90, for example, the three Basque Provinces ranked 45, 48 and 49 in tax per capita. While the national average was 21.72 pesetas per person no Basque province paid over 12. The Treasury assessed a total contribution for the provinces and then left it to the Diputación to collect it. The advantage was especially great for the regional elites who controlled the Diputaciones, since they were able to slough the burden of direct taxation elsewhere.

Another major breach in the principle of equality, and one which was the source of much discontent, was the obligation to do military service. In 1837 the existing system of recruitment, which included total exemptions for privileged estates, was replaced by one nominally based on universal service. However, service could be avoided by a cash payment of 1,500 to 2,000 gold pesetas or by providing a substitute, which cost from 500 to 1,250 pesetas. Both cash redemption and substitution were abolished in 1912 and were replaced by a system in which the length of service could be reduced for cash payment; from three years to ten months for 1,000 pesetas; to five months for 2,000.

Needless to say, not all Spaniards had the same opportunities to avoid military service although many did everything possible to liberate their sons from it. According to Nuria Sales, 'families who were far from prosperous stretched themselves to the limit of their material possibilities'.[7] We can get a sense of this from a note sent by officials in Murcia to the Captain General of Andalucia: 'There have been and always will be abuses in every province. Every year people use every resource to free their sons: influence, friendship, bribery, lies.'[8] There were clear regional differences in the frequency of cash redemptions, substitutions and quota payments and these were clearly related to social structure. Where 'work was less poorly paid, where smallholders were more important than laborers and short-term tenants, where society was less polarized and the middle classes were stronger' more people bought their sons out. Thus, Catalonia, the Basque Provinces and Madrid had very high rates while Andalucia, parts of Castile and Galicia had consistently low ones. On the other hand, Galicia had the highest desertion rate, desertion serving as 'the alternative to an impossible redemption in cash'.[19] In Asturias, another region with low redemption rates, avoidance of military service was a factor which contributed to very high rates of emigration. And, as Table 4.3 shows, evasion increased as time went on, hitting unprecedented levels following the start of the war in Morocco in 1909.

While there were numerous critics of the system there were also many who defended it. Among the arguments in favor of redemption was that 'the children of the well-off classes were not physically prepared for the rigors of army life and were morally incapable of bearing the weight of military discipline'.[10]

The widespread desire to escape military service created opportunities for new businesses: companies offering insurance against the draft and agencies providing substitutes. Many of these enterprises were run by prominent politicians and public figures, aamong them Pascual Madoz, Ramón Mesonero Romanos, the Duke of Alba, the Archbishop of Toledo, and the descendants of Christopher Columbus. The Marquis of Comillas provided a similar service for employees who had worked for his coal mining company for five years, lending them the money to avoid military service. The money provided to buy a son out of military service was supposed to be used to attract volunteers and persuade soldiers to re-enlist but the financial straits of the government were such that it was spent on such basic items as barracks and weapons. Only a small percentage of those who paid for redemption were actually replaced by volunteers. Since those soldiers who did join voluntarily were eligible for disability pensions and pensions for widows and orphans, and therefore potentially quite expensive, the government kept them out of places where they could come to harm, such as colonial wars, and sent the draftees instead, even though they were less well trained.

In places where regional charters had once protected young men from the draft, local authorities often arranged collective substitutions. The city of Pamplona ran a Draftees' Society and there was a similar organization for the Baztan and Elizondo valleys. These plans were much cheaper than the

Table 4.3 *Avoidance of military service, 1895–1914 (Percentage among total eligible for service)*

Year	%	Year	%
1895	2.7	1905	10.5
1896	3.6	1907	9.7
1897	4.1	1908	10.5
1898	4.6	1909	10.3
1899	5.6	1910	11.5
1901	7.2	1911	12.8
1902	7.2	1912	18.9
1903	7.2	1913	20.8
1904	11.9	1914	22.1

Source: S. Payne, *Politics and the Military in Modern Spain*, p. 481, fn. 57.

commercial operations, from 250 to 330 pesetas compared to 750 to 1,500 in 1877. When Basques were made subject to conscription following the abolition of the *fueros* in 1876 a number of cities in the region set up collective substitution schemes.

The inequities produced by the ability of some Spaniards to avoid military service did not go unnoticed by those who could not afford to and their resentment could occasionally lead to violence. The outstanding example took place in Barcelona in July 1909, following the mobilization of reservists for the war in Morocco. As the soldiers were marched to the port on July 18, disturbances broke out.

> The ceremonies attendant upon the embarkation seemed calculated to excite the populace, not least because they conjured up sad memories of soldiers leaving for Cuba eleven years earlier; the transport ships were the same, the property of the 'clerical' Marquis of Comillas. Government officials, accustomed as they were to formulating public policy with no regard for public opinion, made no conciliatory gesture toward the reserve soldier nor toward his family, left with no means of support. Instead officials gave speeches on patriotism, while socially prominent women, whose own sons were able to pay the 1,500 peseta fee necessary for exemption from conscription, distributed religious medals . . . The spark that set off the violence was the distribution of medals and cigarettes by the society ladies. Some of the soldiers disgustedly threw the medals into the water as men and women in the crowd began to shout 'Throw away your guns.' 'Let the rich go; all or none.'[11]

This was the prelude to the Tragic Week.

Law and Order

One fundamental area of state-building on which all Spanish liberals agreed was the question of public order. Throughout the nineteenth century and into the twentieth, whatever the regime in power, there was 'a preponderance of military institutions and juridical techniques enmeshed in administrative and governmental activity, especially in the field of security and the police'. The responsibility for this lay not so much with ambitious military men as with civilian political leaders, 'incapable of presenting their own minimally efficient alternative to sustain the State'.[12] As a result, according to Manuel Ballbé, nineteenth-century liberals produced 'a specific authoritarian state structure', or, as Joaquín Lleixà puts it, a 'pseudo-state'.[13]

During the Old Regime, Spanish administration had a more military flavor than did that of other European nations. The military had a central place in daily affairs. The Captains General were the ultimate authorities so far as law and order was concerned. Military commanders had the right to declare states of war. Military jurisdiction could be applied to civilians in such areas as lack of respect for military authorities. Most of this was kept on by Spanish liberalism, beginning with the Cortes of Cádiz which chose, as Ballbé puts it, 'authority over liberty': the Constitution of Cádiz did not contain a declaration of rights and freedoms but did include special laws relating to public order.[14] And even though the Constitution forbade any special legal jurisdictions, the extensive military jurisdiction contained in Charles III's military regulations remained in force. The institutions which were responsible for law and order, the army and the militia, were military in character. These features – militarized policing agencies, the preservation of military jurisdiction and the absence of any effective guarantee of rights of expression and assembly – were present in all nineteenth-century liberal regimes. Nor was there any evolutionary trend in the other direction. By the early twentieth century public life in Spain was more militarized than ever before and the country had its first military dictatorship in 1923.

Between 1820 and 1823 governments limited the right of assembly and extended military jurisdiction to cover expression of ideas and assembly. The triennium was also responsible for an innovation which would become an ongoing characteristic of liberal Spain, the use of military men to fill civilian offices, especially civil governorships. In his struggle to create a civilian administration on the French model Javier de Burgos ran into military opposition which succeeded in reducing the scope of the powers of the civil governors. The main point at issue was police power, which de Burgos had intended to go to the civil governors. In the end he was compelled to concede precedence to the Captains General, even though he was well aware of how this weakened his nascent state structure. Writing in 1841 he lamented that 'the Administration's commands were not accidentally disrupted but habitually contradicted while its principal agents were reduced to spectators or unwilling accomplices to systematic aberrations'.[15]

During the 1830s Spanish constitutions failed to guarantee basic democratic rights and military men continued to have, and use, the authority to declare states of exception on their own. After 1843 the moderates created a law enforcement agency, the Guardia Civil, consonant with their vision of the state, but they also revealed their fundamental agreement with the progressives on the question of law and order. The Constitution of 1845 kept the public order provisions of the progressives' Constitution of 1837 and they retained, and invoked, the 1821 law extending military jurisdiction over civilians. Officers continued to fill civilian posts, Captains General remained superior to the civil governors and states of exception were used frequently against political opposition.

The brief interregnum known as the progressive biennium, 1854–6, did not attempt any significant changes. The draft constitution failed to guarantee the right of association and decrees were used to dissolve political clubs and close down newspapers. In June 1855 the Captain General of Barcelona dissolved all worker organizations to preserve public order. When the moderates returned to power they added sedition and riot to the crimes to be tried under military law. Similar patterns prevailed during the revolutionary interlude of 1868–74. Although the new constitution 'recognized and regulated' the right of assembly, governments quickly reverted to using states of exception to throttle political opposition. The 1821 law on military jurisdiction was revived in 1869; a special jurisdiction for the military was retained, and civilians were subjected to it for offences such as insults to soldiers. A new Public Order Law was passed in April 1870, and although the Constitution required that a special Law of Suspension be passed before the government could declare a state of exception it was ignored. From then on 'the utilization of states of war to resolve problems of public order would once again be the norm'.[16] Under the First Republic (1873–4), little changed. Military men continued to have a high profile in the administration, in part due to efforts to reduce the deficit, and constitutional guarantees were frequently suspended.

The Restoration brought little change. The Army Law of November 1878 stated that one of the key tasks of the military was to defend the state against its internal enemies. It made the Guardia Civil an integral part of the army and made insults to the Guardia a crime under military law. In 1886 a Liberal government passed the Law of Military Justice putting insults to 'analogous institutions' and disrespect to military authorities under military jurisdiction. Both Conservative and Liberal governments made frequent use of states of exception: forty-six between 1874 and 1911. The reach of military law over civilians was increased even more by the infamous Law of Jurisdictions (1906). In November 1905 a mob of some 200 army officers attacked the print shop of a satirical Barcelona newspaper. The government resigned and its successor, unwilling to incur the wrath of the military, passed the law which made insults against army officers a crime to be tried in military courts. In 1912 the Liberal Prime Minister, José Canalejas, added a new weapon to the public order arsenal when he militarized the railroads in order to break a strike.

The growing intensity of class conflict, especially after 1917, led governments to rely increasingly on both the Guardia Civil and the army to preserve public order. As a result the regime became ever more dependent on the military and ever more liable to pressure from it, as the episode of the *juntas de defensa* revealed. From 1917 to 1920 the Juntas (trade union type organizations of middle ranking officers based in the peninsula, which sprang up to protest low pay, proposed military reforms and the battlefield promotions of officers serving in the Moroccan War) were more or less able to dictate terms to successive governments because, as Carolyn Boyd has written, 'the King and his government were fearful of losing military support at a moment of political and social crisis'.[17]

One thing no Spanish government before the Civil War did do was create a professional, non-militarized police force. Juan de la Cierva, a Conservative politician who had served as civil governor of Madrid, described the police of the capital as

> a dangerous conglomeration of agents appointed and dismissed independently and capriciously by the governor and the Minister. They had no security whatsoever

and were not required to have any special qualifications. With salaries of less than 2,000 pesetas per year you can imagine what would come of their being in contact with all types of criminals and all types of corruption.[18]

The absence of a professional police force had especially grave consequences in Barcelona, which was hit by two spates of terrorist bombings between 1888 and 1909. Despite increasingly severe legislation, few cases were ever solved and in 1907 the city of Barcelona took the unusual step of calling on an officer from Scotland Yard, Inspector Charles Arrow, to head a special anti-terrorist unit. The leaders of the Second Republic doubted the loyalty of the existing paramilitary police, and created a new force, but it quickly took on the same military character as the Guardia Civil. But then with a name like the Assault Guards, perhaps that should not have been a surprise.

National Militia and Guardia Civil

While Spanish liberals had a shared concern for the maintenance of law and order they did not agree on the nature of the agency to be entrusted with this important task. This difference of opinion grew out of the differences in their visions of the state, differences which were, in the last instance, based on the differing social composition of their political constituency. Drawing much of their support from the urban artisanate, the progressives consistently advocated democratically elected municipal governments and the existence of a militia independent of the central government. Militias were present at all stages of the liberal revolution from 1808 until 1843 and during the two subsequent revolutionary interludes of 1854–6 and 1868–74. Although the moderates were responsible for the suppression of the militias in 1843 and again in 1856, and for their definitive elimination after the Restoration, they had not always been opposed to them. Liberals of all stripes supported the militias which were formed after 1808, and those liberals who supported the regime of Joseph Bonaparte backed the Civic Militia which he created in 1809. Both forces were socially segregated, not taking anyone below the level of master artisan.

The disagreement over the militias emerged after 1820 and centered on the issue of their social composition. Moderates wanted the militia restricted to the middle and upper classes; their rivals wanted them open to all. The militia which was organized in Madrid following the revolution of 1820 required its members to pay for their own uniforms and as a result most of them were 'high level employees, merchants, property owners and master artisans'.[19] The law of June 1822 which created the National Local Militia required potential members to be 20 years old and own property or have some other known source of livelihood but also left the town governments discretion in recruitment.

As the militias became much more democratic after 1833 they made the moderates increasingly uncomfortable. In Madrid, 40 per cent of the militia men were artisans, 18 per cent came from commerce and 15 per cent were property owners. When the militias were re-established in 1854 artisans made up 38.5 per cent of the militia of the capital, salary earners 18 per cent, merchants 17 per cent and white collar workers 16 per cent. Following the revolution of 1868 the Madrid city council created the Volunteers of Liberty, open to all citizens, and by 1872 almost a third of all members were workers. The Minister of the Interior, Práxedes Sagasta, who would lead the Liberal Party during the Restoration, began almost immediately to try and assert his authority over the militia of the capital.

The militias were finally, and definitively, suppressed following the Restoration. In this new political context, with substantial political consensus, the struggle for political power between the two liberal families gave way to a shared concern for social stability provoked by the chaos of the First Republic and the appearance of revolutionary working class ideologies and organizations. The militia no longer had any place or function. Indeed, it represented more of a threat than anything else. As Pérez Garzón remarks:

> A militia made up of property owners no longer made any sense, since the bourgeois liberal State had created more reliable institutions to safeguard the regime of property. They did not want a *complete* National Militia because . . . in that historic moment national had become synonymous with *popular*... From an institution of property owners it had turned into a proletarian force.[20]

The moderates' conception of the state required a reliable law enforcement agency. Clearly the National Militia would not do, for it was, after all, both beyond the control of Madrid and dominated by the lower classes. By November 1843 the militias had been disarmed. They were replaced, in March 1844, by a new force, the Guardia Civil, which would become 'an armed elite at the service of the civilian administration'.[21] The original idea was for the Guardia Civil to serve as a civilian counterbalance to the army in questions of public order and to further strengthen the state structure. This concept ran into immediate and substantial opposition. When the decree which created the force was put to the Cabinet there was, according to the minutes, 'a heated debate' over whether it was to be incorporated into the army. The decree revealed the victory of the civilian position. It also announced the moderates' distrust of the lower classes:

> The government requires a force which is always at its disposition to protect people and property and in Spain, where war and civil disturbances make this an even greater need, society and government have only the Militia and Army to protect them, both of which are inadequate to do the job completely . . . This civilian corps offers the added benefit that since the Militia will be relieved of this most difficult part of its duties *it can be organized . . . to exclude certain classes whose admission was tolerated only because the active character of the Militia has led many well established people to avoid serving in it . . .* At the same time, the civil force will allow the Army to avoid frequent interventions in popular acts . . .

which, by excessively strengthening the military within the state do not favor the constitutional system.[22]

This victory was extremely short-lived. In May the Duke of Ahumada, 'perhaps the general with strongest aristocratic roots and most identified with the moderate counter-revolution', was appointed Director of the Guardia Civil, but he made his acceptance conditional on its operating along completely different lines. It was to be totally dependent on the Ministry of War, militarized, and segregated from society at large both juridically, by a special statute, and spatially, through residence in barracks houses. Ahumada's terms were accepted in a decree issued by Prime Minister Narváez. The new decree did not repeal the original one, even though the two conceptions of the Guardia Civil which they contained were almost totally contradictory. Both ministries, War and Interior, issued regulations for the corps, the former 'written so that one would say that the Ministry of the Interior simply did not exist, nor any dependence on the civil authorities'.[23] The latter set of regulations put the Guardia under the orders of the civil governors, their agents and even mayors, but this had little real meaning. The process of separation from the civil authorities was completed in 1878 when Cánovas made it an integral part of the army.

The Guardia Civil began as a small force but expanded rapidly, in both numbers and territorial reach. Following the roads and railway lines, the force reached the level of county seat and then that of the individual town and village. Expansion at the local level was especially rapid during the Restoration. In 1846 the Guardia Civil had 514 posts and 7,135 men; in 1876, 1,585 and 14,858; in 1880, 1,966 and 16,149; and by 1898, 2,179 and 19,105. The Guardia Civil brought the central state directly into the furthest reaches of the country. It absorbed all police functions and displaced the numerous local, fragmentary security forces of the Old Regime.

The Guardia Civil also took over the functions of the various rural guards, which numbered some 18,000 men in the 1860s, although the large number of people required and the opposition of agricultural pressure groups in important regions of the periphery, such as Catalonia and Valencia, who wanted a non-militarized and locally controlled force of specialists, made this a slow process. In 1876 the Guardia Civil was given responsibility for the maintenance of law and order in the countryside. In the late nineteenth century, with the growth of the labor movement, the force came increasingly to be used against strikes, which were more often seen as threats to public order than as legitimate forms of protest.

The expansion of the Guardia Civil was the foremost example of the growth of the liberal state in Spain. At the same time, however, it can also be seen as marking a crucial limitation of that state: an essentially suspicious, if not openly hostile, attitude towards the bulk of the population. This is evident in the widespread hatred of the Guardia Civil among ordinary Spaniards. In large part this was a product of the ideology of the force, which was one of unambiguous social conservatism. The *Guía del Guardia Civil* published statements such as 'in all towns there are people notable for their position, their wealth – and even if they do not have that – for their honour . . . These people are identified with the Guardia Civil' and 'One needs more virtue to be rich than to be poor.'[24] Landowners competed to have posts built in their localities and often paid for them themselves, as according to one former Director of the Guardia, they would also pay for medical care and even equipment and living costs. This was no less true in industrial areas. The Hullera Española, a major coal mining firm in Asturias, paid for the Guardia barracks in Ujo where it had its head office.

The limitations were implicit in the separation of the Guardia Civil and their families from the rest of the population by housing them in barracks and in the attempt to do everything possible to prevent their developing ties with the community where they were posted. It was stated explicitly by General O'Donnell in a circular of 1854: 'The distribution of the Guardia Civil in over 1,000 detachments amounts to a fully military occupation of the entire national territory.'[25] There could be no more eloquent statement of the ultimate weakness of the Spanish state, which lacking any other effective unifying institution relied so heavily on what Lleixà has called the 'domination, not the direction, of the ruled by the rulers'.[26]

Education and Language

Thus far we have emphasized the repressive nature of the liberal state, but Spanish liberals also recognized that the state should provide certain services for the population. Education was the most important of these. From the Cortes of Cádiz on, they assumed education was a responsibility of the state. The Constitution of Cádiz proclaimed that every village should have a primary school and this basic idea was contained in a series of education laws and plans during the nineteenth century: in 1821, 1836 and 1845. The public education system was given its definitive shape in 1857 with the passage of the Moyano Law, which remained in force for over a century.

The Moyano Law made primary education obligatory for children up to the age of nine and free for those who could not afford to pay. The schools were to be financed by the municipalities, not the central government, but Madrid set the syllabus and determined the books to be used. Central government funding for primary education remained minimal: between 1850 and 1875 education never accounted for more than 1.13 per cent of the budget and by the 1870s it had fallen to 0.55 per cent. The state's financial commitments did increase in 1900 when it created, for the first time, a Ministry of Education and turned teachers from municipal employees into civil servants.

In France, at least under the Third Republic, public education was seen as crucial to the development of national unity and to the defence of the tradition of the Revolution. Both these goals could be furthered by 'the extinction of particularisms', of which the most threatening were languages other than

French. According to Eugen Weber, 'the Third Republic found a France in which French was a foreign language for half the citizens.' However, by 1914 a 'determined assault against provincialism', in which the schools had a central role, had succeeded in imposing French over the various patois and stimulated a sense of French nationalism.[27]

Spanish liberals also sought to create linguistic as well as administrative uniformity in a country facing the problem of particularisms and the vitality of patois and languages other than Spanish: Gallego, Basque and Catalan. Schools were to be the basic agents of this program. All education plans and laws included language as a fundamental part of the curriculum, and that language was Spanish. Other languages were actively discriminated against. In 1851 the civil governor of Barcelona banned instruction in Catalan which was, he said, increasing 'in violation of the rules and contrary to what in every way is best'. In 1902 the government issued a decree announcing sanctions against teachers who gave religious instruction in languages other than Spanish.

The war against non-official languages was much less successful in Spain than in France. Indeed, if anything, these languages were getting stronger, especially in the twentieth century, when they became the rallying cry for political movements for autonomy or even separation. Why was this? One reason was that the Spanish state was much less effective in creating the basic agent of linguistic uniformity, the schools. As Albert Balcells has argued, Catalan persisted in general use 'due less to any conscious and active resistance on the part of Catalan speakers than to the grave deficiencies of the educational system'.[28] In Barcelona, the public, or state, school network was smaller and enrolled fewer students than the private one. By 1922 the public schools had an enrolment of 16,000 students while private schools had some 50,000. Religious orders had a particularly strong presence in the private sector: 325 of the 560 schools in Barcelona in 1918 were religious. Only 74 were public. The situation in Madrid was similar: in 1908, there were 135 public schools and 311 Catholic ones, and the Catholic schools enrolled four times as many students.

Schools were only part of the problem, however. In his discussion of France, Weber attributes the decline of patois after 1880 to a number of factors in addition to the extension of schooling by the Ferry Laws: Protestant missionary activity, the spread of the printed word, military service and the increasing incorporation of the rural population into national life, as 'national society became more significant than local society'.[29] In Spain these factors either did not exist or did not have the same effect as in France.

There is no evidence, for example, of any significant Protestant missionary activity in Spain. If the experiences of George Borrow as related in *The Bible in Spain* were at all typical such activity was not likely to be very productive. Military service, which was such a powerful agent of linguistic unity, was much less important in Spain. In two of the areas where languages other than Spanish were strongest, Catalonia and the Basque Provinces, the rates of avoidance of military service through cash redemptions and quota payments were highest; in the third, Galicians had the highest rates of desertion. Thus one shortcoming of the liberal state contributed directly to another.

The effects of the spread of the printed word were, from the point of view of castilianization, ambivalent at best, particularly in Catalonia. Catalan was a language with a strong literary tradition and the nineteenth century saw a remarkable revival in the literary use of Catalan, known as the *Renaixença*. While most of the books written by members of the Catalan elite between 1850 and 1939 were in Spanish, Catalan was rapidly closing the gap. Even though the industrial elite of Barcelona became increasingly castilianized over the nineteenth century Catalan remained the language of home and factory. With a predominantly Catalan-speaking working class Catalan was 'necessary for the economically and politically active males of industrial families'.[30]

Throughout the nineteenth century there was a vital popular literature in Catalan. Many of the chap-books were in Catalan, especially those dealing with contemporary or recent historical themes. One Barcelona shopkeeper recalled in his memoirs that in the early 1840s city workers and militiamen sang political songs in Catalan and that one particularly popular one was published in a newspaper called, curiously enough, *El Centralista*. Another pointed to the use of Catalan in popular theater in the 1860s. 'Not only out of patriotism but also to make it easier for the bulk of the audience, for the most part of modest social position, to understand, Barcelona authors who wrote for the *salas con alcoba* made great efforts to do so in Catalan.'[31] In their study of Barcelona in the 1850s Josep Benet and Casimir Martí found that the city's working class spoke little Spanish and that accounts of trials in which workers participated as either witnesses or defendants show them speaking in Catalan.[32]

Finally, the economic and social changes which Weber sees as contributing to the triumph of French had the opposite effect in Spain, in large part because while in France patois was spoken in rural, less developed regions, in Spain it was precisely in the most developed areas, Catalonia and the Basque Provinces, where non-official languages were most deeply rooted and where important political movements for regional autonomy emerged. Catalan nationalism was substantially the expression of the frustration of an industrial bourgeoisie in its attempts to claim a share of political power in the state. Basque nationalism was strongest in Vizcaya, the most industrialized of the three Basque provinces, where it expressed the fears of the petty bourgeoisie and indigenous working class that the massive immigration of non-Basques triggered by the industrial take-off after 1876 would cause the destruction of traditional social values.

Caciquismo

The gravest weakness of the liberal state was its failure to penetrate into all corners of the nation and touch all its citizens directly. Of course it did collect taxes, administer laws and draft young men for the army, but even in these most basic tasks the state tolerated the existence of local powerholders who both helped it and circumvented it in its functions. These intermediaries were known as *caciques*, a word derived from the American Indian term for a village chief. The *caciques* 'did not derive their tenure or their power from the goodwill of superiors in a governmental hierarchy. They retained room for maneuver on behalf of their own interests. Much of the work of national authorities therefore consisted of negotiating with [them]'.[33]

The persistence of these intermediaries between the state and the citizen cannot accurately be ascribed to any failure of Spanish liberalism but rather must be seen as the product of conscious decisions. *Caciquismo* is most closely identified with the Restoration monarchy (1875–1931), the most stable and long lived of the constitutional regimes of the nineteenth century. Following the social upheaval, civil war and political chaos which characterized the period 1868–74 political leaders were concerned above all to establish a system which guaranteed order. The architect of the new regime, Antonio Cánovas del Castillo, was an admirer of the British parliamentary system in which he saw the peaceful rotation in power of the two political parties as the foundation of that country's success. He had also learned the lesson of Spain's own earlier constitutional experiments: that political peace demanded the accession to power through peaceful means of the principal opposition party.

Acting on these insights he oversaw the drafting of a new constitution which would claim the acceptance, if not the devotion of the Liberals as well as of his own Conservatives, even though this meant temporarily alienating some ultra-Catholic elements. The Constitution of 1876 drew on elements from both moderate and progressive constitutions. Catholicism was declared the state religion but private practice of other faiths was allowed. Sovereignty was said to reside jointly in the Cortes and the Crown. Cánovas' approach proved successful, especially when Práxedes Mateo Sagasta, the leader of the Liberal Party (which was itself a melange of political factions), accepted the Crown as the arbiter of power. Once this had happened the two parties could alternate in power by using the royal prerogative to dissolve parliament regardless of the actual distribution of seats. The king did not appoint a government because it held a majority but instead appointed a Prime Minister who was given a dissolution and the opportunity to manufacture a majority of his own. Cánovas and Sagasta reached a formal agreement, known as the Pact of the Pardo, in 1885 according to which the Conservatives would step down and advise the king to appoint the Liberals.

This agreement to periodically alternate in power totally perverted the British parliamentary model which Cánovas so claimed to admire because it depended for its success on systematic electoral management which robbed political democracy of any real meaning. These 'made' elections were based on the prior agreement between the leaders of the two dynastic parties, but such agreements made in Madrid, while a necessary part of the system, were not sufficient to make it work. National political leaders could not impose their decisions at the local and regional levels but had to make arrangements with the *caciques* at those levels in what Javier Tusell has called a 'pact with reality'.[34]

The making of an election was a complex business. It began in the realm of high politics, among party leaders in Madrid. The key figure was the Prime Minister, who controlled the administration and made the final selection of candidates, although the actual arrangements were made by the Minister of the Interior. (One particularly able minister, Francisco Romero Robledo, earned the nickname 'the Great Elector' for his efforts.) However, even at this rarefied level decisions could not be taken quickly or easily. A number of groups had to be taken into account and given a certain amount of satisfaction, above all the leaders of the various factions within the governing party, and the leader of the opposition. Even some representatives of the non-dynastic opposition, such as Republican Emilio Castelar, were allotted seats. The key word was negotiation. As the two dynastic parties became more and more factionalized in the early twentieth century the process became that much more difficult. By 1923, the last year in which an election was held under the Restoration system, 'a Liberal Party which was divided into tiny groups confronted the Conservatives who were themselves extraordinarily fragmented'.[35]

Not all the electoral districts in the country were equally at the disposition of the fixers in the capital. The principal difference among them lay in the degree of control enjoyed by the government on the one hand and the local powerholders on the other. Those most open to the discretion of the government, the majority, were known as *disponibles, muertos* or *mostrencos* – literally, available, dead or strays – although even here there would be some influential person who had to be assuaged. These districts were often given to candidates, known as *trashumantes*, who were parachuted in. The second type of district was where the *caciques* were sufficiently strong to prevent the government from freely choosing a candidate. In some cases they became rotten boroughs, totally controlled by a single person, such as the Duke of Tamames who held the district of Ledesma in eight elections between 1886 and 1903.

Finally there were the *independientes* or *emancipados*, where the mobilization of the electorate had done away with control by both the government and the *caciques*. This was most easily done in urban areas where a well organized party practising mass politics could quite easily be successful. Alejandro Lerroux's Radical Party was able to control local government in Barcelona in the early years of the twentieth century with only 10 per cent of the vote. Caciques did not try to compete in the realm of real politics. According to Joaquín Romero Maura,

> For the *cacique* controlled press the spectacle of candidates going out to solicit real votes could only be compared to publicly asking for political charity. Any

cacique who did so would have been admitting that his base of support was precarious or even illegitimate. There are almost no known examples of *caciques* who seriously fought against modern political parties with a similar organization of their own.[36]

Once the *encasillado*, the list of candidates for all parties, had been finalized another set of negotiations began, this time between the government and the local party elites. The civil governor acted as intermediary. His job was to placate both parties and assure the required result with as little violence as possible, although this was not to be ruled out. The experience of Fernando de León y Castillo provides a particularly graphic example of this.

> I was defeated in the next election . . . I went to the Canaries to campaign personally but the governor of the province, who had definite instructions to have me defeated at any cost, went with the captain general to Lanzarote in a warship, where I was going to win easily. He arrived in Arrecife to intimidate. He immediately summoned all the socially and politically influential people of the island and demanded that they vote not for me but for the government candidate and threatened to arrest them all, put them on the warship and send them immediately to Fernando Poo.
>
> I did not want to put my friends in a difficult position, because the threat of deportation would have been carried out, so I withdrew my candidacy.[37]

This, however, would have been an extreme case. There were other kinds of fraud and coercion, many of them quite picturesque, which were generically known as *pucherazos*. These could include last-minute changes in the location of voting stations, locating the polls so as to discourage turnout, for example in an epidemic hospital, on the roof of a building or in a pigpen. Voters were arrested on election day, hired gangs used to cast votes for the dead, known as *lázaros*, who had been included on the voters' lists, and government officials sent out to harass possibly unfriendly voters, for example by having surveyors re-check property lines. Government employees could also be encouraged to vote for the official candidate. As picturesque as such methods were, the system did not depend on them, at least not before 1900. (Thereafter, increased electoral competition from regenerationists, Radicals, Socialists and regionalists required increasing use of the *pucherazo*). As Varela Ortega notes, 'we should not let the ingeniousness blind us to the fact that, all in all, there were few such cases'.[38]

The reason was that most of the time the elections were so well prepared that such fraud was not necessary. Such preparation was possible because of the highly centralized nature of the Spanish state which gave the central government great influence on local and provincial governments. Civil governors could turn mayors into electoral agents of the government party quite easily. Often threats were enough; when they were not, mayors could be fined. In the last instance, an uncooperative town council could be suspended for some minor irregularity and replaced by a government delegate.

Caciquismo depended on the local influence of specific individuals and their ability to translate this into political support. This required the existence of a fairly sophisticated and highly centralized state from which a wide range of favors could be extracted. Romero Maura has described the confluence of local and national factors which contributed to Spanish *caciquismo*:

> A local phenomenon to the degree that well entrenched local bosses were an invincible enemy for any minister who tried to confront them instead of negotiating . . . A phenomenon also closely tied to centralism: the municipalities and provincial administrations of that Spain of few resources had fewest of all . . . For an infinity of material things, but also for numerous administrative questions, local people depended on decisions which could only be taken in Madrid, and in these matters intervention by a *cacique* was vital.[39]

The local level was the most important. In the towns and villages the local *cacique* was, in Tusell's words, 'the summit of the clientalistic pyramid and the true monopolizer of political life'.[40] The *cacique's* ability to deliver the vote depended on his ability to provide favors for his clients, or *amigos politicos*. These favors – jobs, building permits, tax exemptions or exemptions from military service – did not come from his personal wealth but from his influence with the administration. They had to be seen to be something only the *cacique* could achieve, not as something the state provided as a matter of course to its citizens. Such favors were, however, illegal and meant that taxes were not collected and government decrees not enforced. Yet the fact that the men in government were also party leaders and that the number of deputies they could command depended on keeping the local *caciques* sweet – for a *cacique* could always switch his allegiance and that of his clients to another party – prevented them from doing anything about it. Such illegalities and inefficiencies were the price they were willing to pay for a political system which worked smoothly. These favors did not just go to the *cacique* and a small group of friends and relatives alone; they were fairly widespread and touched people of all social classes. Perhaps the most important favor received by ordinary people was exemption of a son from military service, which could be achieved by means of a falsified medical certificate or a false declaration of height.

Although the Restoration system became more difficult to manage after 1898, and especially after 1914, as a much broader part of the population was mobilized politically, it did not evolve towards a more authentic democracy. When the dynastic parties began to become more responsive to public opinion and legislate accordingly the system was brought to an end by the Primo de Rivera coup of September 1923. Primo declared war on the *caciques* in the name of national regeneration but his political vehicle, the Unión Patriótica, incorporated them rather than uprooting them. The *caciques* were still firmly in place in many rural areas during the municipal elections of April 1931 which led to the proclamation of the Second Republic. The monarchists actually won control of more municipalities than did the Republican–Socialist coalition, but these were almost exclusively small towns and villages where the old methods could still be used. The king and his advisers knew that where the public had been allowed to speak freely it had come out unambiguously against the monarchy.

The Meaning of the Republic

Most historical writing on the Second Republic has emphasized the attempts by the centre-left governments led by Manuel Azaña to legislate reformist solutions for some of the most pressing national problems: they army, the place of the Church, regionalism, the land question. While such a focus is not misplaced it does tend to overlook an important aspect of what the Republic was about, the extension of the state. This may sound strange today, when the dominant ideology proclaims the state as the archenemy of the freedom of the individual, but in a society in which important functions remain largely under the control of private, autocratic organizations or individuals, the extension of the democratic state can be a progressive and liberating experience.

The Republican experiment can be interpreted in this way, as an extension of the state, the substitution of private power by public power. This was clearly true of the legislation restricting the functions of the Catholic Church, especially in the field of education. When the Republic was created in April 1931 there were some 350,000 children in religious elementary schools and more than one million children without any school at all. Republican governments acted aggressively to change this situation, offering to provide at least half the construction costs of all new schools and to pay the salaries of the teachers. In March 1932 the Education Minister was claiming that 7,000 schools had been built, and another 2,500 were up by the end of the year. A five-year plan called for the number to reach 27,000. (This compared to a rate of 500 schools per year between 1909 and 1931.) Refresher courses were made available for qualified teachers who had been doing other work and some 15,000 people applied in 1931.

The Republic also tried more unorthodox approaches to end the cultural isolation of many small communities. In May 1931 it created the Teaching Missions Trust within the Ministry of Education. This organization arranged for touring teams, usually of university students, to take classic and more modern culture into small towns and villages. There were theater companies – including García Lorca's 'La Barraca', choirs and the People's Museum, a collection of replicas of great works of art. There were also less high-brow contents. According to one participant:

> The true missions . . . were those which we students and poets made to villages which often did not have electricity, armed with a movie projector, comic and educational films, a gramophone and records . . . At nightfall, in the school

or in the square we organized an accessible and agreeable program of poetry readings and various commentaries . . . finishing off with one of the famous silent films of Charlie Chaplin . . .[41]

Other Republican legislation worked in the same direction. It was also true of some of Azaña's military reforms, such as the suppression of the Captains General and the incorporation of military into civil justice. In a curious way it was also the case with regional autonomy; by creating a Catalan regional administration, and later a Basque one, the Republic brought the state closer to a previously disaffected part of the population. Agrarian reform also contributed. On the most superficial level it represented the assertion, however timid, of the state's right to change property relations in the name of the public good. At a deeper, and ultimately more important, level it threatened to break the control over local life exercised by the landed oligarchy. A newly mobilized rural population sought to wrest control of local government from the elites and use mass politics to end the rule of the *caciques*, as George Collier has shown for a village in Huelva.[42] This was particularly true after the victory of the Popular Front in February 1936. The landless began to display a new assertiveness: 'In every respect, economic, religious, political and in everyday relations, the workers wanted to demonstrate the power and support which the electoral victory had given them . . . The attitude, the new tone, was more important than the actual number of violent conflicts.'[43] The extension of the democratic state deep into the countryside had contributed to making, if only temporarily, a world turned upside down. It would take three years of civil war and a brutal repression to right it again.

Communities

Village Community

The primary locus of identity for most Europeans before the nineteenth century was the village. This was, as Jerome Blum has put it, 'simultaneously an economic community, a fiscal community, a mutual-assistance community, a religious community, the defender of peace and order within its boundaries and the guardian of the public and private morals of its residents'.[1] Such corporate villages were common in Spain, especially in the north. And they could survive in practice well after they had been fully incorporated into the centralized structure of the liberal state.

The village was composed of its *vecinos*, which translates as 'neighbors' but actually had the sense of 'citizens', and their families. The status of *vecino* was generally limited to men, and those who were married heads of housseholds and who worked the land. The village was thus 'a federation of houses, not of persons', with the male head of the house as its voice. Citizens formed part of the village's self-government, the council, and they and their families had a share of communal resources. For young men the passage to full citizenship was marked by marriage, although in some places they had to pay for the privilege by giving a feast.[2]

The village council, *concejo*, acted as a form of local government. There were officers, the most important being the headman, chosen either through election or by rotation, but the council was supreme. It was the council which determined local laws and regulations. The headman presided over the council and served as the voice of the village law, which was essentially customary. Moreover, the headman did the work of the state in the village, most importantly collecting taxes.

With their fetish for centralization and homogeneity, liberals were inevitably the sworn enemies of such systems of local government and they imposed a uniform system of law and of municipal government based on the creation of municipalities out of formerly distinct villages. Even so, villages in León 'continued to govern themselves according to the older forms of customary law' and even 'revised and updated the texts in which the customary law had come down to them'.[3]

The basis of village life was the collective exploitation of communally owned economic resources, land and forests. In Santa María del Monte communal land was extensive, between 50 and 70 per cent of the total, and was used in a number of ways for the benefit of the villagers. It was available for use as kitchen gardens, for pasture, for threshing, and to provide land for those who needed it due to population growth. At the end of the 1860s the village began to clear woodland and distribute it in lots, *suertes*, to residents, but 'with the condition that the *suerte* corresponding to each [resident] be held by him for the days of his life, remaining afterwards for the *concejo* so that the *concejo* may dispose of it and give it to the next [resident]'.[4] Later, however, new plots were given on an inheritable basis. This development eventually produced conflict between the poorer villages who needed land so as to be able to establish their children as independent farmers and the wealthier ones who did not want to lose their access to pastures. Even with these clearances woodland remained and villagers received lots so they could collect wood. Use of the woods was governed by 'a complex set of rules and regulations' and in 1870 the village hired one of the residents to act as forest guard. The communal sense survived even in the face of the liberal redefinition of property rights as the village as a whole participated in the disentailments, purchasing lands it 'had traditionally administered or held in leasehold' and then splitting them into equal shares.[5]

Villagers were also subject to communal labor, the *hacendera*. These tasks included building or maintaining roads, irrigation systems, boundaries and pastures. Often their compliance was not entirely voluntary and coercion was necessary, as the following account from the early part of the twentieth century shows:

> Along with the notice given in council . . . the [*hacendera*] is convened by a characteristic peal of the bells which the [headman] himself or the guard of the fields repeats several times to goad the lazy, aside from the shouts, excitations and even insults he directs at them as he passes through the street, and at times even entering the houses by main force, if necessary, 'to drag the people out'.
>
> When by dint of bell ringing, notices, and threats all the [citizens] who are to carry out the *hacendera* are gathered at last the [headman] draws up a list or head count, then gives his orders for the execution of work.[6]

The village also functioned as a 'moral presence'. Citizens were required to appear at meetings of the council, which were regularly held on Sunday. The major purpose of these meetings was to announce violations of customary norms of behavior or of regulations governing land use. 'This was at once a public confession of sin and a public shaming . . . It was very embarrassing to have one's name read . . . the custom of publicizing how one had erred was often worse punishment than the fine.'[7]

Villagers were also required to attend funerals, votive masses and rogations and to take in the wandering poor. Religious practice was frequently closely tied to local community. This was most clearly so in the case of the celebration of the patron saint, which was special to each village, but it could have many other manifestations.

The connection between religious observance and local community was present even in less tightly knit places, such as the town of Bencarrón, in the province of Seville. Purely religious activities declined in importance, but those associated with one of the town's two *hermandades*, or confraternities, retained and even increased theirs. The confraternities were founded in the middle of the eighteenth century and were originally purely religious organizations, but in the nineteenth century they became associated with the division of the town's population into two matrilineal *mitades*, halves. Within the confraternities there was traditionally a conflict between the members and the priest over how much control the latter was to have. The priest, who was seen as a representative of outside authority, was often relegated to the role of religious counsellor. The association of membership in one of the *hermandades* with family helps explain the apparently contradictory behavior of some of the residents, who during the 1930s could be members of revolutionary organizations and anti-Catholics while maintaining respect for the Virgin of their confraternity.[8]

Such religious practices, which were not part of the official liturgy and which escaped the control, and often even the approval, of the clergy and the hierarchy, were important in Spain. Many of the most vital aspects of religiosity belonged to this sort of popular or local religiosity. Perhaps the most imposing were, and are, the Holy Week processions, especially in

Seville, which Lannon describes as 'a uniquely genuine religious phenomenon precisely because of their popular character, largely independent of the doctrinal and disciplinary structures of the Church, and immersed in a communal rather than individualistic culture of group or neighborhood tradition'.[9]

This situation would appear to confirm a warning given by the anthropologist Susan Freeman to avoid considering all events which have some religious content 'as if all their parts were expressions of religious fervor' and to keep in mind that many such events, and perhaps those which retain their popularity more than others, contain non-religious elements which can help account for their survival. She points out the case of the Asturian shrine festivals, *romerías*, which contain a 'variable balance . . . between their elements of religious observance and of picnics'.[10] Did the Asturian industrialist Francisco Gascue suspect something of this nature when, in 1883, he complained about the attachment of the local mine workers to numerous religious celebrations which reduced the number of work days to only 250 per year? 'The saint of the parish, the festival of the hermitage of one place, the patron of another, of the house of the neighborhood . . . If it really were devotion which moves these people to so much religious activity the custom would be excusable, even respectable. The worst of it is that there is no such devotion.'[11]

Protest

Just as religion formed part of a local, village-based culture, protest too was contained within cultural forms. And these could persist well after the broader culture had begun to deteriorate. The two most important forms of protest were the charivari and the food riot.

We have no study of the Spanish version of the charivari, the rituals of public ridicule of those individuals who violated local norms of behavior, but such rituals surely existed. Earlier on we mentioned one example in the context of the anti-feudal revolt in Valencia at the beginning of the nineteenth century: residents of Aielo de Malferit 'demolished the gallows in the presence of the mayor and council, they dressed someone in a ridiculous suit, called him the Marquis and made him oppose the destruction of the gallows, after which they tied him up . . . and rode him through the town covering him with insults'.[12]

This charivari has made the historical record because it formed part of a direct challenge to the political and social authorities in a way that most others did not, confined as they were to chastising violations of long-established patterns of – usually moral – behavior within the local community. Food riots, by contrast, are much more visible to the historian because they were much more visible, and threatening, to state authorities, from whom they generally demanded certain kinds of action.[13]

Events in Gijón during the subsistence crisis of 1854 conformed to the standard pattern: on November 21 two ships destined for Nantes were being loaded with grain when groups of men appeared, threw sacks of grain to the ground and ripped them open. When another cargo was being loaded later that day large crowds pelted soldiers with stones. The response of the mayor was to ask the civil governor to provide money for public works and for a ban on grain exports, 'a measure which, even if it is not at all in harmony with general theories, is now absolutely necessary and is the only one which may spare us from the conflict which is surely approaching'. The civil governor immediately provided money for public works, organized subscription at the parish level and, a few days later, made available 60,000 reales so that the city could purchase grain.[14]

Food riots became less frequent after 1868, due to increased grain production and improved transportation, but they did not disappear. (Neither did they disappear in France.[15]) Spiralling food prices provoked major epidemics in 1898 and 1904–5. The Socialist labor movement opposed food riots on both occasions. In 1904–5 it attempted to channel the protests into more organized and less violent forms, giving them 'a strong political charge'.[16] It was unable to do so but was more successful in 1916 when, in response to the inflation triggered by the First World War, socialists and anarcho-syndicalists jointly organized a campaign to demand cheap food.

There were at least eighty-one disturbances in May 1898. Most took place in 'second level urban centers, especially those with close ties to the countryside'.[17] Andalucia, Extremadura, Murcia and the two Castiles, along with the most important mining zones, in particular Asturias, were the regions most hard hit. The leading cities, Madrid, Barcelona and Bilbao, were spared due to preventative measures, such as the provision of municipal canteens, taken by the local authorities. The disturbances shared the main features of the classic food riot of the Old Regime: they were spontaneous and without any real organization, short, violent and informed by a sense of 'moral economy'.

The riots were brief. Most lasted only a day and very few lasted more than two or three. They also had a local geography. They often began at a market – the Gijón riot began on the docks where fish was sold – or at a place where food was exported, such as the port or the railway station. From there they proceeded to the homes of people believed to be speculators and to public buildings such as the town hall or the courthouse. (In Burgos the local authorities and merchants were able to defuse a riot by making 6,000 kilos of bread available 'at an affordable price' and promising not to export any grain.) Foodstuffs were frequently seized and given away or sold at a price below that of the market, as in Gijón where rioters applied the 'just price' to cocoa, coffee and cinnamon taken from the chocolate factory owned by a leading political figure. The riots occasionally had an anticlerical element: in Talavera de la Reina (Toledo) a number of churches were sacked and sacrilegious acts committed. The rioters failed, however, in their attempts to burn convents. In Tarazona the bishop was stoned by the crowd when he called on them to return home peacefully.

The most frequent demand was the reduction or abolition of the *consumos*, the hated tax on foodstuffs, and the collection points, *fielatos*, and their archives were frequently destroyed. The *consumos* were collected in four different ways: by the local government directly, by agents of the national Treasury, by agreements with local economic organizations or by leasing the right to collect them to a private individual. This last was by far the most inflammatory, and disturbances were frequently directed against the tax farmers.

The riot known as the 'Sanjuanada', which took place in the important Asturian coal mining town of Mieres on June 22, 1897, nicely illustrates a number of these themes as well as showing the persistence of traditional forms of protest in one of the most modern sectors of the economy. For a number of days there had been rumors of discontent among the miners over a recent increase in the *consumos*. On the morning of the 22nd workers from two mines marched into the city collecting new demonstrators as they went. They were led by a man on horseback who carried a black banner with the slogan 'Down with the *consumos*! Death to the mayor!' (According to one account the banner had no slogan at all.) A crowd of some seven to eight thousand people, dominated by some 2,900 striking miners – and, one supposes, their wives – gathered in front of the town hall shouting 'Down with the rogues and idlers. Down with the *consumos*!' The mayor, accompanied by the local judge and the commander of the Guardia Civil, met a five-person delegation which demanded 'energetic measures' to assure that merchants gave full weight as well as periodic checks of their scales, inspection of meat, a requirement for bakers to indicate the weight of their loaves and the lowering of the *consumos*.

The mayor agreed to the first three demands and promised to look into the other two but then trouble broke out. According to his report the crowd tried to break into the town hall and someone fired pistols at the Guardia Civil, who returned fire, killing two and wounding seventeen. However, according to the conservative paper *El Carbayón*, Francisco Martínez, who had been farming the *consumos* for a number of years, threw a bottle into the crowd injuring a demonstrator and this triggered violence. Another paper, the *Eco de Mieres*, said that Martínez had shouted that the workers had enough money. In any case when Martínez left the town hall the crowd followed him to his house 'with whistles and other unpleasant signs'. There was more violence there when one of the women of the house allegedly flung boiling water on the crowd in the street. Martínez was taken off to jail as the crowd demanded, but more as a protective measure than anything else. At seven in the evening more Guardia Civil and two companies of infantry arrived by train from the provincial capital but by then the riot had fizzled out.[18]

Women were prominent in these riots. They often initiated the disturbances, as in Gijón where their complaints about the price of hake led to a number of strikes, attacks on the city hall, mills, and the home of a leading grain merchant as well as on a number of stores and the homes of notables.

Rioters were sometimes led by women and on at least one occasion women alone were involved: 'in Badajoz . . . the men had not joined in and were the target of catcalls'.[19] On at least two occasions, once with axes and once with knives, women confronted the soldiers sent in to put down the disturbances.

These were extreme examples of what Temma Kaplan has called a 'female consciousness [which] centers upon the rights of gender, on social concerns, on survival' which, while fundamentally conservative because it accepts the sphere defined for women, can have 'revolutionary consequences [when] women demand the rights that their obligations entail' and make use of their networks to carry out collective action. Kaplan provides some examples for Barcelona, most importantly what she calls the 'women's insurrection' of January 1918 when fuel shortages and rationing provoked attacks on coal trucks, marches to the office of the civil governor to demand price controls, one of which led to nineteen women being shot, and strikes by female factory workers who also attempted to draw out female sales clerks at the city's department store. They also attacked music halls 'in an apparent attempt to reduce fuel consumption . . . Up and down the streets of pleasure . . . popularly known as the Paralelo . . . women with sticks broke down doors, smashed mirrors and sometimes succeeded in persuading bar girls and cabaret dancers to join them'.[20] Pamela Ratcliffe makes a similar argument for the importance of neighborhood connections in women's collective action, violent, cultural and recreational, in Gijón in the early twentieth century. Even the cigarette makers, who had a strong, work-based, almost artisanal, identity, owed much of their high profile to their activities in the working class district of Cimadevilla.[21]

From Play to Leisure

Village society did not conceive of leisure as an activity separated from – and in opposition to – others. Instead, play was fully integrated into the overall life of the community. The point has been made by anthropologist Victor Turner: 'It would be better to regard the distinction between "work" and "play", or better between "work" and "leisure" . . . as itself an artifact of the Industrial Revolution, and to see such symbolic-expressive genres as ritual and myth as being at once work and play or at least cultural activities in which work and play are intricately inter-calibrated.'[22] This was the case for festivals, such as those of the local patron saint.

But even isolated and traditional villages might occasionally enjoy, and pay for, leisure activities, in the form of travelling entertainers. There must have been hundreds, if not thousands, of such people wandering around the countryside but they have left little trace. Fortunately a few bothered to petition the authorities for permission to do so or, curiously, for tax exemptions, so we know of their existence. It must have been a special occasion when Joaquín Elecegui, 'known as the Spanish Giant', arrived in a village in 1833 to 'exhibit his person', or in 1856 when the brothers Marcelino and Prudencio Serrano passed through so that Marcelino could 'display his left hand, which is colossal'. Perhaps even Francisco Contreras, 'the phenomenon without arms' might go on tour to show his 'tricks with firearms using his feet'.[23]

The emergence of leisure time and of commercialized entertainments to fill it is part of the larger tendency to separate work from other aspects of life, characteristically a product of urbanization and industrialization. In Spain leisure became increasingly commercialized in the nineteenth and twentieth centuries and most such commercialized entertainments were available to members of all social classes, at least in the cities.

Opera was the most socially exclusive. The most famous cultural institution in Barcelona, and perhaps in the whole country, was the Liceo opera house, which opened in 1847. The Liceo was the child of the city's new industrial elite and constituted a challenge to the aristocratic Theater of the Holy Cross which had functioned since 1587. The Liceo was set up as a corporation supported by leading financiers and industrialists, such as Manuel Girona, president of the Bank of Barcelona. The lowest priced tickets were quite cheap; but boxes were sold at higher prices, and passed from one generation to another, and the theater was run by a commission of those who purchased them. In 1847 a private club for box owners, the Círculo del Liceo, was added. The Liceo was destoyed by fire in 1861 and rebuilt within a year. The theater, like the city itself after its expansion in the 1860s, was segregated by class. The second floor – first balcony – the *planta noble*, housed the boxes of the elite but the orchestra and the second balcony were also prestigious locations. The third and fourth balconies were less prestigious but still respectable while the top balcony, known as the *galliner*, chicken roost, was the one left to poorer music lovers – students and workers. The original building had, according to one folklorist, carried social segregation a step further:

> it is said that the associates were people of position who felt disdain and lack of consideration for the common people to the extent that in building the theater . . . they were deeply concerned that those who sat in the upper floors could not descend to the orchestra or lower floors where the builders [sic] had their seats and boxes. Because of this the first theater had no communication between upper and lower floors. If someone in the house wanted to go from a higher floor to a lower, or vice versa, he had to exit to the street.[24]

Like most major European cities, Madrid and Barcelona had commercial pleasure gardens, although Madrid was somewhat laggard. In 1834 Mariano José de Larra lamented the absence of such recreational institutions, which he blamed on the absence of a commercial, financial and industrial middle class, the preference for other entertainments, especially bullfights, and a general reluctance to have fun in public. The Jardín de las Delicias, the first of a large number of pleasure gardens, was opened that same year and was well received. Most were short-lived but they were constantly replaced by new ones. Some, such as the Jardines del Paraíso, required substantial investments to build the manicured gardens and tree-lined promenades, but none was in the same category as the great ones of London or other European capitals. All the pleasure gardens provided cafes and restaurants and offered a range of entertainments. Dancing, concerts and theater were the most common but there were also circus, pantomimes, cosmoramas and cicloramas, shooting ranges, billiard rooms, velodromes, roller skating rinks and in one, the Campos Eliseos, a small bullring in which nighttime bullfights were held.

Most served an affluent clientele but some others, like the Eliseo Madrileño which opened in 1860, drew more modest people, such as shop clerks and seamstresses. Still others saw their customers change over time. By the 1890s the Jardines del Buen Retiro, which had been operating since 1872, became popular with less well-off people, a development which was possible because the admission price had remained unchanged at one peseta. At least one paper found this distasteful, noting that 'at what was once the center of culture and recreation today the gentlemen must mix with a crowd of children and riffraff . . . We will now do without the Jardines; that most agreeable meeting of all that was most distinguished in Madrid, that tone, is gone forever'.[25] The last of the nineteenth-century pleasure gardens closed in 1904.

Of course, the elites had their own private leisure facilities. The most widespread – there was at least one in virtually every town of any size – was the private club known as the *casino*. S.T. Wallis, an American who travelled through Spain in the 1840s and 1850s, gave this description of the Círculo in Málaga: 'It is supplied with the principal English and continental papers and is, of course, the center of commercial intelligence . . . For those who enjoy billiards and cards there are the needful facilities, together with reading rooms for the silent and conversation rooms for the social.'[26] The description of the 'Gentlemen's Club' of Vetusta, the thinly disguised Oviedo of Leopoldo Alas' *La Regenta*, is less flattering:

> The servants of this establishment wore uniforms like those of the urban police . . . All the servants had bad manners, inherited like their uniforms. Indeed they had been provided with uniforms so that there should be some way of telling that they were servants . . .
>
> Beyond the hall there were three or four passages converted into rooms for waiting in, conversing in, playing dominoes in – all haphazardly mixed up together. Further on there was another, more luxurious room . . . the meeting place of the gravest and most important personnages in Vetusta . . . Silence must reign here and in the next room as well, if possible . . . [It] never saw the light of day: it was always sunk in murky shadow . . . The reading-room, which also did duty for a library, was narrow and not very long. The library itself was a walnut-wood bookcase of no great size, built into the wall. The wisdom of the society was there represented by the Royal Acacdemy's *Dictionary* and *Grammar*. The purchase of these books had been motivated by the recurrent

disputes between members who disagreed about the meaning and even the spelling of certain words . . . In the bottom door of the bookcase there were works which provided more substantial instruction, but the key to that section had been lost.

A new form of commercial leisure which emerged in the 1880s and quickly took Europe by storm was the cabaret. According to H.B. Segal this began as 'an informal grouping of artists . . . who felt a need to come together, preferably away from the eye of the public and critic alike' and had 'a certain elitist character'.[27] The first was the famous Chat Noir in Paris, which opened in 1881 and spawned numerous imitations. The cabaret's Spanish home was Barcelona, where the Quatre Gats opened in January 1897, advertising itself as a beer hall, tavern and hostel. It was founded and supported by a group of artists who had been part of the Parisian bohemia – Picasso exhibited there in 1900 and participated in other ways – but also drew on artists attracted to Catalan nationalism. Like cabaret generally, the Quatre Gats also favored 'small art forms' such as shadow shows and puppetry and for the latter it drew on a Catalan puppet tradition which, like so much of Catalan culture, had been revived in the second half of the nineteenth century. The Quatre Gats was distinctive in one important way in that it 'openly sought the presence of the public, among whom it hoped to gain favour for the new Catalan modernist paintings represented by its participants'. The Quatre Gats closed in 1903 having survived longer than most other European cabarets.[28]

Football was introduced into Spain at the end of the nineteenth century by British sailors and Englishmen involved in mining as well as by Spaniards who had studied in England. Foreigners were often involved in the first clubs, which were created in the 1890s: Athletic de Bilbao (1898), FC Barcelona (1899) and Real Madrid (1902). They created a national federation and a national championship in 1902. This soon received the sponsorship of Alfonso XIII who offered the Copa de su Majestad el Rey. A professional league was created in 1928. The leading teams came to be identified with their cities but even more so with their regions, especially Catalonia. FC Barcelona quickly became identified as a Catalan club in contrast to the local rival Real Club Deportivo Español, which was considered 'a Castilian team which had deliberately chosen a name which Catalans found mocking and provocative'.[29] Before a game in June 1925 fans booed and hissed as a British Royal Navy band played the national anthem, the *marcha real*. The military governor responded by closing the stadium for six months.

By the 1920s football had become very popular with the working class. The Hullera Española mining company in Asturias provided equipment and a playing field for a company team, which was coached by the monks who ran the company schools. In 1926 the Asturian miners' leader Manuel Llaneza lamented youth's lack of interest in the union which he blamed on their occupation with 'football, bullfighting and the tavern' and the following year the leaders of one important union lodge denounced the young who were, they said, interested in nothing but the tavern and 'that damned vice of football'.[30]

The most important of the new forms of commercial leisure was, of course, the movies. The first moving pictures were shown in Spain in May 1896 and they very quickly became a popular form of entertainment. At first movies were added to programs which featured a number of different acts but they soon became an entertainment in their own right. The first cinemas were improvised in basements or were 'primitive sheds' known as *barracas*. These could be found in all parts of cities like Barcelona and Madrid, but especially in the working class neighborhoods. By 1910 Barcelona had over 100 cinemas and according to one estimate 160 in 1914. There were also a number of larger, more luxurious cinemas, located in the center of the city – in Barcelona along the Ramblas – with segregated seating and different admission prices which catered to middle class audiences uncomfortable with the tackiness and rowdiness of the *barracas*. Some of these had over 1,000 seats and one had 3,000. The movies had even penetrated the countryside: one Baltasar Abadal arranged showings in a number of villages in Catalonia. By 1914 there were more than 900 cinemas in the country and by 1931 more than 3,000.

Some saw cinema as a threat. The government implemented prior censorship of all movies in 1912. According to the bishop of Barcelona the darkness offered an opportunity for immoral behavior and in 1920 the state Director General of State Security ordered that men and women be seated in separate sections of the movie houses, a measure that was as unenforceable as it was ridiculous. In 1915, when a carpenter employed by the Hullera Española opened a cinema, the company president demanded that all films be subjected to prior censorship and had him warned that he would be fired 'if he shows morally questionable films or allows immoral behavior'. The company doctor was commissioned to act as censor and a guard was stationed in the cinema at all times 'to preserve order and morality during the performances'.[31]

Opera, cabarets, football and cinema were found across Europe but the most popular entertainment of all in Spain was a domestic product which, with one minor exception, did not exist outside the Ibero–American world. That, of course, was the *corrida*, the bullfight.

Bullfights had long been a part of important public celebrations, such as royal weddings or the accession of a new monarch, and they continued to fill this role in the nineteenth century. In 1811 King Joseph Bonaparte celebrated the birth of Napoleon's son with a general illumination of Madrid and free entry to the theaters and bullfights. For the *corrida* on March 31 'all the seats and boxes will be open so that people can sit in them first come first served without any preference or distinction. Only the Royal Box will be reserved'.[32] In 1823 five residents of Alcalá de Henares were given permission to sponsor a bullfight 'to commemorate the liberation of King Ferdinand VII and his family with public activities which express our joy'.[33] Three years later the city, lacking the money to carry out urgent repairs to its water supply system, requested permission to hold a bullfight to raise the funds. In 1843 a number of leading noblemen, including the Duke of Osuña, sponsored a series of *corridas* to help celebrate the wedding of Isabel II.

While continuing to fulfil these ceremonial or symbolic purposes, bullfighting also quickly developed into a business. Indeed, it was probably the first example of commercialized mass leisure in western society.

As early as the first decade of the nineteenth century the city of Madrid leased its bullring and the right to stage *corridas* to a private entrepreneur who was chosen through a process of tendering bids. The money went to the city's hospitals. In 1811 the ring was leased for two years with the contractor having to agree to hold twenty-four fights per year. Similar practices were used in other cities but the lease was for a much shorter period, usually for the few days of the annual fair, *feria*. The city of Valladolid placed the following advertisement in May 1861:

Bullring for Rent

The city of Valladolid is renting its bullring for the four bullfights to take place during the fair next September. Bids will be accepted until July 10 in the office of Domingo Fernandez. No bid under 70,000 reales will be accepted.

Last year the same bullfights produced 102,535.68 reales revenue with 138,531 reales in unsold tickets.

As well as the benefits accruing to this type of spectacle from the Palencia, Alar del Rey, Reinosa and Santander railroads this year there is the added advantage of having the 40 kilometre San Chidrían–Burgos line open.[34]

The bulls were not always so attractive a proposition. In 1861 the city of Salamanca would have gone without bullfights during its *feria* had not the city's merchants taken on the task late in the day. Season tickets were available but those who wanted tickets to a single fight ran the risk of having to deal with *revendedores*, scalpers. Most cities saw few bullfights. In 1932, 219 were held, but in only three cities, Madrid with 32, Barcelona with 24 and Valencia with 18, would they have been anything like a regular weekly event. Seville, a capital of bullfight enthusiasm had only 6; Salamanca and Pamplona, whose San Fermín festival was made famous by Hemingway, 4 each. Seven other cities had 3, 15 had 2 and 49 but one.

The bullfighters were professionals who had to pass through an apprenticeship as *novilleros* before becoming fully-fledged matadors. They were among the first modern professional athletes and public idols. The best could become wealthy as well as famous: Mérimée reports that in 1859 Cúchares donated twenty head of cattle and fifty sheep to support the war in Morocco. Most came from the ranks of the artisanate, especially in Seville, although Madrid also produced a number of bullfighters. By the twentieth century, and probably before, they had agents, *apoderados*, who looked after their affairs. The bulls were raised by wealthy landowners although we do not know whether, or to what extent, this was a profitable activity. By the

1930s there were two organizations of bull breeders, the established Unión de Criadores de Toros, which included such famous names as the Domecqs, and the newer Asociación de Criadores de Reses Bravos.

Bullfighting was big business. The author of a pamphlet attacking the *corrida* published in 1876 estimated from 40 to 50 million pesetas were spent each year on bullfights and that most of it was spent by workers. (This did not count the harm to the economy when they took a day off work to attend.) Defenders of the spectacle countered with the argument that the bullfight was good for local business. But business was not always good. In 1933, for example, commentators were lamenting the state of affairs: the number of bullfights had fallen from 249 in 1931 to 219 in 1932. Only a few bullfighters excited the public and putting others on the program was a sure way to lose money. More worrisome was a general lack of passion for the *corrida* as other sports, football and boxing, as well as politics competed for attention. The company which ran the Madrid bullring had done very badly while the balance sheets in Barcelona had turned out better but only because of the major innovation of paying the matadors a percentage of the gate instead of a seet fee.

The authorities were constantly concerned about the threat of disorder at the bullfights. The public frequently responded to cowardly bulls, or bullfighters, by throwing, as an 1846 proclamation by the mayor of Madrid put it, 'oranges, rocks, hats or other projectiles which interrupt the *corrida*'.[35] Mérimée, on the other hand, suggested that the authorities were really not so bothered about such disorder and that within limits they were prepared to tolerate it. 'In the bullring' he wrote in 1830, 'and only there, the public commands as if it were sovereign and can do and say whatever it likes.'[36]

One other traditional leisure activity, cockfighting, retained its popularity through the nineteenth century. This was a common feature of village festivals although one foreign visitor reported that by the early twentieth century it was 'tending to disappear in many parts of [the country]'. Cockfighting was not just a rural or small town entertainment: as late as 1876 Madrid had a *circo gallístico*, cockfighting ring. Fernández de los Ríos' *Guía de Madrid* (1876) described the *circo* as 'comfortable and elegant' which suggests that its clientele reached into the upper classes.[37]

The working class enjoyed all these forms of entertainment to a greater or lesser degree but the classic form of working class leisure in Spain, as it was everywhere in the industrializing world, was the tavern. The tavern offered male companionship but it also provided some forms of entertainment such as gambling and what we might call music hall performances, although the evidence for this is limited. A series of musical skits titled 'The Turn of the Century Opera' performed in one tavern in the Asturian mining town of Moreda drew the ire of the parish priest, who had the commander of the Hullera Española company police check it out. The policeman disapproved of two characters, the 'Anarchist' and the 'Village Priest' and told 'the owner that these two roles could not be repeated and he promised they would not'.[38]

Taverns were constantly denounced by middle class moralists and by the more respectable elements of the working class itself. For the former the tavern was a seedbed of immorality which threatened both the worker's performance on the job and the social order. One mine manager in Asturias blamed alcohol for turning the miner from his usual 'quiet, honest, submissive, intelligent, tranquil and good-humored self' into a brawling ruffian 'not fit for work'. [39]. More ominously, these commentators made a direct connection between the tavern and 'socialism'. For the manager of the Hullera Española, taverns were 'havens for propagandists of strikes and even murder' while the *Boletín Oficial de Minería y Metalurgia*, a government publication, urged mining companies to provide social services in order to draw workers 'from the taverns and so-called "workers' circles" where they do nothing but plan strikes'.[40]

This connection was not so clear for many labor leaders. Manuel Vigil, an early Socialist organizer in the region, also criticized the miners' fondness for the tavern. 'Although they are not drunkards,' he wrote in 1900, 'in general the workers like to drink and do consume relatively large amounts and this does them no good. They do not do it out of vice but because the world they inhabit provides no other relaxation than that offered by a bottle and a deck of cards.'[41] The third issue of *El Minero de la Hulla*, the monthly magazine of the Socialist miners' union, published a story, 'The Young Girl's Triumph', which described the havoc wrought in the working class home by alcohol. Organized labor attempted to establish an alterative locus for working class leisure in the Casas del Pueblo and *ateneos*. These offered lectures, theater and choral groups and libraries. (The Casa del Pueblo of the Asturian miners' union in Mieres had a library of 17,000 volumes at the outbreak of the Civil War.) Anarchists were particularly interested in theater which they saw as a first rate propaganda instrument. In fact the first Spanish presentation of Ibsen's *The Doll's House* was given in Barcelona in 1896 by an anarchist theater group. Where they existed Catholic unions had similar institutions, the Círculos Católicos (Catholic Circles), although in Asturias at least these were mostly funded by sympathetic employers.

Symbols

The liberal state failed to create a ritual or set of symbols which might have stimulated a strong national feeling. It failed to 'invent tradition'.[42] One British observer noted this in the 1870s: 'The state has tried of late years to consecrate to idle parade a few revolutionary dates, but they have no vigorous national life. They grow feebler and more colorless year by year because they have no depth in the earth.'[43]

Early Spanish liberals were well aware of the strength of such rituals and symbols. May 2 (Dos de Mayo), and the 'founders of Spanish liberty', were first commemorated in 1809. Two years later the Cortes of Cádiz decreed that May 2 would be a national holiday 'in honor of the first martyrs for the freedom of the nation . . . and to excite the valor and patriotism of the nation to imitate their heroism, patriotism and love of our legitimate sovereign'.[44] It continued to be celebrated even after Ferdinand VII was restored to the throne and returned the absolute monarchy, although as a 'day of strict mourning'. Indeed, the great virtue of May 2 as a national holiday was its political versatility. It could be used by liberals and reactionaries both, and it could be given differing political meanings as the invitations sent by the city council of Madrid in 1835 and 1836 show: the former was to commemorate those martyred for 'their love and loyalty to their legitimate sovereign'; the latter to commemorate those martyred for 'their love of liberty and national independence'. Hatred for the French played a large part in the popular memory of May 2: Louis Teste, a French journalist who travelled in Spain in the early 1870s, noted that the holiday 'no longer serves as a pretext for violence against Frenchmen living in Spain' and that he had been able to walk around Madrid speaking French 'without being harassed at all'.[45]

The Dos de Mayo, then, would seem to have been ideal raw material for a patriotic holiday, but subsequent liberal regimes seem to have done little to realize its potential. In 1812 the Cortes of Cádiz ordered that a monument be built, but it was not completed until thirty years later. Also, the celebrations were left in the hands of the municipal government of Madrid and the day came to have little resonance outside the capital. And although Hay said that May 2 was the 'only purely civic ceremony I ever saw in Spain', the official celebration had a strong religious component, including mass at the San Isidro church. By the 1850s there was not much enthusiasm, even in Madrid. According to the author of *Memoria histórica del dia 2 de mayo de 1808 en Madrid*, (1852), lately there had been 'a decline in the attendance of those who were invited and . . . the crowds in the streets through which the parade passes and in the Prado [where the May 2 monument is located] are less numerous'. Teste said that the 1872 celebration lacked any excitement and 'seemed more like a funeral'.[46]

The lethargy of political authorities in nurturing such symbols of secular nationalism stands in contrast to the energy and enthusiasm with which the symbolic representation of Spain's religious identity was promoted, and not just by the Church. These efforts were most intense in the first two decades of the twentieth century, coinciding with, if not caused by, the spread of class conflict and the breakdown of the *turno* system of the Restoration.

To commemorate the centenary of the War of Independence Alfonso XIII bestowed the honors of the rank of Captain General on the Virgin of Pilar, in Zaragoza. In 1917, he decreed October 12, the day of the 'discovery' of America, as a national holiday, but the date was also associated with an appearance of the Virgin and the holiday was frequently known as the 'Day of the Pilar and of the Race'. Finally, two years later, on May 30, 1919 and in the presence of the entire government, Alfonso consecrated the country to the cult of the Sacred Heart of Jesus while he dedicated a monument, '28 meters in height with a 9 meter high statue of the Sacred Heart with its right hand blessing and accepting the offering of the nation', built on the Cerro de los

Angeles, a large hill 14 kilometers from the centre of Madrid, and supposedly the geographic center of the country. This ceremony was the culmination of a campaign begun in 1915 in which smaller statues were 'erected in hundreds of towns and villages . . . with as much pomp and representation of local authorities as possible. They appeared in provincial government buildings and even on hill tops'.[47]

The weakness of secular national feeling was by no means inevitable. Indeed, Spanish national identity could flourish in the most unexpected places, such as villages of the Catalan borderlands. There, by the 1820s, peasants and villagers who shared the Catalan language and close social ties with villagers on the French side of the border were already 'divided by their adopted nationalities as Frenchmen and Spaniards'. These identities, Peter Sahlins argues, were not imposed from the center nor were they dependent on the disappearance of earlier, local identities. Rather, the defense of local boundaries in the context of state consolidation and a blurred international border allowed villagers to build themselves a national identity which was not obstructed by but indeed 'drew strength from . . . enduring expressions of local identity'.[48]

The villages of the French and Spanish Catalan borderland had long engaged in disputes over boundaries and use rights, particularly grazing. Occasionally these were settled amicably, more frequently through litigation. Such disputes multiplied in the eighteenth and nineteenth centuries as population growth and increasing taxation made it more pressing than ever for villages to defend their resources. To do so they increasingly turned to their national states. In the process they began to identify their opponents as *gavatx*, a highly pejorative word for Frenchmen, and subsequently themselves as Spaniards. This new national identity was negative and limited, or 'contextual and oppositional: a statement about the "otherness" of their neighbors across the boundary [which] appeared in the context of communal struggles'.[49]

If this was the basis for the development of a secular national identity it was a restricted one. Certainly, a secular national identity did not displace a religious one before the Civil War. In that conflict, both sides tried to make use of the symbolism of the Dos de Mayo, but Franco had the symbolism of Catholic Spain, which while not shared by all Spaniards retained its resonance for many, on which to draw as an ideological cement for his various supporters. The Republicans had no such symbols to help overcome the even greater divisions in their camp. In the war of symbols, as in the war of armies, the religiously defined state vanquished its opponent.

5

The Franco Regime and After

A Belated Miracle

When the Civil War ended on April 1, 1939 Francisco Franco took control of a country devastated by three years of military conflict. The human losses were staggering: over half a million dead and another half a million in exile. Many thousands more were to die in the postwar repression. The destruction of the economy was no less thorough. Agricultural production was a third below prewar levels and the number of livestock reduced by 30 to 40 per cent. Transportation had been devastated: a tenth of shipping and about 40 per cent of railway equipment had been destroyed. Industry, which had been retooled for military needs and had had to suffer a shortage of raw materials, especially in the Republican zone, was disrupted. Real per capita income would not regain its prewar levels until 1952.

From Autarky to Liberalism

The initial response of the Franco regime to this situation was to adopt a fascist-inspired policy of autarky: rapid industrial expansion in the context of national economic self-sufficiency, a policy which would remain substantially unchanged until the late 1950s. This strategy was embodied in two early pieces of legislation: the Law for the Protection and Development of National Industry (October 1939) and the Law for the Regulation and Defense of National Industry (November 1939). The object of the former was massive import substitution. By granting privileges to firms declared to be of national interest it would encourage the domestic production of goods that were being imported. The second law required all public enterprises and all private firms receiving government support to use domestic inputs whenever they were available. This strategy was reinforced by highly protective tariffs, import controls and controls on exchange rates.

The second key element of the regime's economic policy was enhancing the role of the state. Such an approach was not novel in Spain. Primo de Rivera had tried it in the 1920s, but the instrument chosen by Franco to implement it was based on a foreign model. The Instituto Nacional de Industria (INI), created in 1941, was a copy of Mussolini's IRI. It was intended to undertake the development of industries related to national defense and those in which the private sector was unable or unwilling to get involved. The INI first turned its attention to fuels, fertilizers and electricity but soon moved into transportation, iron and steel and automobiles, among many other fields.

Autarky applied to agriculture as well. Here the outstanding example of the regime's policies was the creation of the National Wheat Board in 1937 to provide a guaranteed market and price for the country's grain crop. The policies were a failure. Prices were fixed so low that throughout the 1940s as much as half of the crop was sold on the black market, where prices were two to three times higher. Nor did Spain ever achieve self-sufficiency in grains. It remained dependent on substantial imports, the vast majority from Juan Perón's Argentina. Even so, there was a significant drop, between 30 and 50 per cent, in per capita consumption. The 1940s were known as years of hunger for a reason.

These policies proved incapable of creating the self-sufficient industrial economy for which they had been designed. In fact, they had great difficulty in restoring the economy to where it had been in 1936. By 1950 production of iron and steel, ships and fertilizer was still substantially below 1931 levels and the standard of living had fallen 17 per cent since 1940. Industrial output did begin to grow in the 1950s, but did not make the breakthrough into sustained growth. Traditional structures and technology remained unchanged: in 1958, 85 per cent of all firms had fewer than five employees and 73 per cent of industrial enterprises were using equipment that antedated the Republic! Even though real wages remained 15 to 25 per cent below those of 1936 production costs were high and exports stagnated.

By 1959 the country faced imminent bankruptcy. Only then, with the survival of the regime on the line, were the technocratic ministers affiliated with the Catholic lay order Opus Dei permitted to fundamentally change the course of economic policy. The Economic Stabilization Plan announced in June 1959 marked the death of autarky – although not of government intervention, which would be retained through the formulation of Development Plans – the creation of a market economy and the reinsertion of Spain into the international economy. The main lines of the plan were a reduction in public expenditure, the rationalization of government controls, the establishment of gold parity for the peseta and the liberalization of trade and foreign investment. The impact of the liberalization measures was felt immediately: a severe recession which made possible a dramatic improvement in the balance of payments. The stage was set for the Spanish 'economic miracle' of the 1960s.

The Miracle

From 1960 to 1974 the economy grew at an unprecedented rate, an average of 6.6 per cent overall, 9.4 per cent in the industrial sector. Only Japan matched these figures. Productivity rose an average of 5.9 per cent, 7.5 per cent in industry.

Spain ceased to be primarily an agricultural economy: employment in the agricultural sector fell from 41.7 per cent of the labor force in 1960 to 23.1 per cent fifteen years later, while industrial employment rose from 31.8 to 36.8 per cent and employment in the service sector from 26.5 to 40 per cent. Likewise, the weight of agriculture in the economy as a whole declined. In 1959 it still accounted for a quarter of the Gross Domestic Product. By 1970 it had fallen to only 15 per cent. The automobile industry, the core of modern industrial economies, barely existed before the 'miracle'. SEAT, jointly financed by the INI and the Italian automobile giant FIAT, was created in 1950 but at the end of the decade Spain was producing only 36,000 vehicles per year, and exporting none. By 1973 Spanish factories turned out over 700,000 vehicles, of which more than a fifth were exported.

This amazing economic transformation – and the social transformations it spurred – was dependent on the confluence of three outside forces: foreign investment, tourism and emigration.

With the dismantling of autarky, foreign capital flowed into Spain in vast amounts. In 1960 there had been $40 million invested. By 1965 this had grown to $322 million and by 1970 to $697 million. The most important source, the United States, was responsible for 40 per cent of this investment, followed by Switzerland (21 per cent) and West Germany (11 per cent). Foreign investment has provided a boost to the traditionally undercapitalized Spanish industry. It has also given the country access to advanced technology, vital for a country which invests very little in research and development: 0.34 per cent of GNP compared to 2.7 per cent in Britain and 1.5 per cent in West Germany. Foreign investment is concentrated in the most dynamic sectors of the economy and in the largest firms. Forty per cent of the 500 largest Spanish firms have some foreign participation and this accounts for about one-eighth of their net worth.

The presence of so much foreign capital has contributed to the physionomy of the industrial and service sectors: a modern, dynamic component of large firms grafted onto the pre-existing world of predominantly small companies. While the average number of workers per industrial company did increase from 5.85 in 1962 to 13.47 in 1978, very small companies have continued to predominate. In 1975 over 89 per cent had fewer than 50 workers. The permanence of the old was even more striking in commerce: in 1980, 90 per cent of retail establishments had fewer than 4 employees and new forms such as self-service and supermarkets were still relatively rare.

The economic 'miracle' also left traditional regional disparities intact as the concentration of economic activity continued and even grew more intense. The Development Plans of the 1960s minimized investment in infrastructure so that by and large industry located where this already existed, although Madrid, Zaragoza, Valladolid and Pamplona did emerge as industrial outposts in a largely agrarian hinterland. By 1967 Catalonia, the Basque Provinces and Madrid accounted for half of the industrial labor force and by 1975 over half Spain's GNP was generated in these three regions plus Valencia and Zaragoza. Between 1966 and 1973 ten provinces received over half the investment. Thirty-two per cent of the jobs created were in three provinces, 70 per cent in eleven. Massive internal migration reduced the difference in per capita income between the wealthiest and poorest provinces from 4.18 to 2.4 between 1955 and 1977, but this camouflaged the growing poverty of the poorest areas.

The second of the external forces driving Spain's economic growth was tourism. Beautiful beaches, warm weather and bargain prices made it the prime target of the mass tourism generated by general European prosperity in the 1960s. Tourism quickly became the country's most important industry. Six million tourists visited the country in 1960. By 1982 the number had risen to 42 million, more than one tourist for each Spaniard. In 1960 receipts from tourism were $297 million (US); by 1982 they amounted to more than $7 billion.

The third force, emigrant remittances, was also dependent on European prosperity. The growing economies of France, West Germany and Switzerland created a demand for unskilled labor – well paid by Spanish standards – which attracted millions of Spaniards, as well as Portuguese, Italians, Yugoslavs and Turks. The Spanish government seized on this as a way of exporting unemployment as well as earning large amounts of foreign currency and assisted emigrants in leaving the country. In 1965 they were sending back $362 million and in 1973 $1.1 billion.

Agriculture

The demands of industrial development had a significant impact on the regime's agricultural policy. Following the Civil War the government quickly reversed the agrarian reform of the Second Republic and restored the social and economic hegemony of the landed elite. This was accompanied by an ideology which emphasized the values of rural life, invoking them as the embodiment of national values. The only attempt to deal with the problem of the landless peasantry was through the process of colonization, but this affected only 50,000 people between 1939 and 1965. The Law of Manifestly Improvable Farms passed in 1953 made possible the expropriation of non-cultivated arable land but it was left unenforced.

Government policy served to preserve the social status quo in the country-side into the 1960s. The program of concentrating smallholdings undertaken in the 1960s was designed to reinforce the viability of small-scale agriculture, and the conservative values associated with it, particularly in the Castilian heartland. It also served to preserve a traditional, limited series of crops. The creation of state marketing boards, and especially the National Wheat Board which was left untouched by the Stabilization Plan, established guaranteed prices for crops such as wheat, wine and olives, stifling experimentation with new crops. It even encouraged the spread of wheat cultivation to new areas. As a result of these rigidities, Spanish agriculture was unable to adapt to increasing demands for meat and dairy products stimulated by greater prosperity. Meat consumption rose from 25 kilos per person in 1964 to 59 in 1974, that of milk from 63 liters to 96, but livestock production lagged far behind. In the early 1960s agriculture had a slightly favorable balance of trade; by 1975 it was running a deficit of $1 billion. At the same time, the government was forced to spend millions of dollars in buying up excess wheat, wine and olives.

However, with the first Development Plan of 1964–7 the government's attitude to the countryside changed radically. Rather than keeping people on the land in order to preserve traditional values, it was now essential to move them to urban areas to participate in the industrialization of the country. At the same time, agriculture itself was to be modernized and industrialized. This meant the decline of both the rural labor force and the small farm. Between 1951 and 1970 some 3.8 million people left rural areas for the cities. This rural exodus meant the disappearance of large numbers of farms: between 1962 and 1972, 319,000 agricultural enterprises disappeared. These disappearances were limited to farms of under 50 hectares. In fact, during those ten years, over 336,000 of these smaller farms vanished while the number of farms over 50 hectares actually increased by 17,000.

Even so, the productivity of Spanish agriculture remains desperately low by European standards. Capitalization (investment per acre) is about a fifth of the OECD average and mechanization has lagged as well. This reflects the continued presence of many small farms – in 1975, 95 per cent of all farms were under 10 hectares – as well as the scarcity of rural credit. The use of funds by the Cajas de Ahorros (Savings Banks) is regulated by the government, which consistently channels them into the industrial sector, thereby contributing to growing regional disparities.

The Crisis

The Spanish 'miracle' has been unable to resist the general crisis of the international economy. Growth all but stopped after 1973, revealing the special fragility and artificiality of the boom of the 1960s. Spain's dependence on primary imports, especially energy, was much greater than that of EEC countries: 72 per cent of total needs compared to 22 per cent in 1976, and the government did not take any steps to curb energy consumption after the oil shock of 1973. Energy jumped from 13 per cent of total imports in 1973 to 42 per cent in 1981. Productivity levels remained well below European levels, a symptom of the continued weight of small firms. Inflation rates were substantially above those of other OECD nations after 1973 although after coming to power in 1982 the Socialists have brought them down to levels similar to those elsewhere in Europe.

The most visible sign of the intensity of the crisis is unemployment. The level of employment actually fell in the decade after 1974. The unemployment rate jumped from 3.2 per cent in 1974 to 12 per cent in 1980. By the end of 1987 it was above 20 per cent and the number of unemployed had passed three million. Youth has been especially hard hit. This is a Europe-wide phenomenon but of greater gravity in Spain where, at the end of 1984, there were some 800,000 young people without work.

Spanish governments have been helpless before this intractable problem, and it may be that no improvement will be possible without a major trans-formation of the country's productive apparatus to improve productivity. The government of Felipe González has taken this route since 1982 and has found it a painful one. The reconversion of the iron and steel and shipbuilding industries, mostly located in Euzkadi, Asturias and Galicia, has provoked frequent demonstrations and even violence. The prediction made by one American economist in 1982, that 'Spanish society must accept the fact that the restructuring of the productive apparatus may eliminate more jobs than it will create . . . [and] if Spanish productivity is to rise, Spain's economy may have to endure in the foreseeable future an even higher rate of unemployment than that existing in 1980', is being borne out.[1] Even the economic growth of 1986, 1987 and 1988, which has been so rapid as to have been called a 'second economic miracle', has been insufficient to much reduce either the numbers of unemployed or the levels of unemployment. The 1980s and 1990s may well be characterized by the coexistence of high growth and massive unemployment.

Men, Women and Children

At present Spain's demographic patterns are closer to those of other major European countries than at any time since the mid-nineteenth century. In the 1980s, the national rates for population growth, mortality, natality and life expectancy are closer than ever to French, German or British levels, although significant regional differences remain. Spain does not yet have a single national demographic system. This represents a continuation of the trends which began at the very end of the nineteenth century, but it has not been a steady evolution. The decline in death rates continued throughout, but the decline in birth rates stalled until the 1960s, so that the population continued to grow rapidly until very recently, from 25.9 million in 1940 to 38.5 million in 1984.

Death

Since the Civil War mortality rates have had two main characteristics: steady decline and regional diversity. The overall death rate fell from 14.3 per thousand in 1941–5 to 7.4 in 1984. But the rates remained far from uniform across the country. In 1976, when the national death rate was 8 per thousand, provincial rates varied from a low of 6 in Madrid to a high of 12 in Lugo and Teruel. The sharp drop in the national rate, which moved Spain from being among the countries with the highest rates to among those with the lowest, had been mostly completed before the economic boom of the 1960s.

On the other hand, infant mortality rates, which are considered one of the best indicators of a country's level of development, long remained among the highest in Europe. Infant mortality rate did decline throughout the post-Civil War period but until the mid-1960s it remained more than 50 per cent higher than the rate in France. However, from 1965 to 1980 infant mortality was reduced by 75 per cent so that in 1980 there was virtually no difference between the Spanish rate (11) and the French (10). This dramatic improvement has been the product of a higher standard of living and the widespread availability of quality medical care.

Despite the overall improvement, regional differences remained 'abnormally acute', to use Nadal's phrase.[1] In 1967 infant mortality in provinces like León, Ciudad Real and Cuenca was twice the national average and three times as great as that in Castellón and Guipúzcoa. In general terms the interior, and especially Castile-León and Extremadura, remain what in the 1950s Arbeló called 'a veritable cemetery for babies'.[2] This reveals once again the tragically large differences in regional levels of development.

Birth and Birth Control

The long term decline in the birth rate which had begun to decline slowly but continuously early in the twentieth century was halted, or at least slowed, during the twenty-five years after the war, when birth rates fluctuated between 20 and 23 per thousand. The rate fell below 20 only in the late 1960s and thereafter fell sharply, to 18.6 in 1975 and 13 in 1984.

The existence of this lengthy plateau between 1940 and 1964 has led Diez Nicolás and J.M. de Miguel to reject the idea of a 'systematic' decline in natality in the twentieth century and to argue that this interruption was due to changes in attitudes towards family size which were caused by the ideology of the Franco regime in favor of large families, offering prizes for the parents of large numbers of children. Whatever its cause, the presence of this plateau, at a time when death rates fell by almost half, led to 'a demographic explosion similar to that produced in other European countries in the second half of the nineteenth century'.[3]

Two factors, both coinciding with the economic 'miracle', explain this surge: an increase in nuptiality and a lowering of the age at first marriage. The percentage of women between 15 and 49 who married increased substantially, from 47.2 per cent in 1940 to 59.3 per cent in 1965. Nuptiality rates peaked between 1955 and 1960 when, according to Amando de Miguel, they represented the highest figures in Spanish history. Nuptiality remained high until the mid-1970s, when it began to drop dramatically. If the upsurge in nuptiality after 1955 was due to the economic 'miracle', as de Miguel argues,[4] we can assume that the severe crisis which began after 1975 and has yet to relent, especially as regards youth unemployment, contributed to the fall off in marriage rates.

Age at marriage has fallen since the Civil War. The average age actually rose in the immediate postwar years, hitting its peak in 1945, at 29.6 for men and 26.1 for women. From that point on it began to decline steadily, reaching 26.8 and 24.2 in 1979. The percentage of women married in all age groups rose between 1940 and 1970, but it rose most in the 20- to 24-year cohort. While the age at first marriage remained high by European standards, the gap between Spain and its neighbors closed substantially after 1965. In 1980 the difference between the age at which people in Spain married and that at which people in Britain and France married was less than half as large as it had been only fifteen years before.

Even though both nuptiality and age at marriage evolved after 1955 to favor population growth both the birth rate and the marital fecundity rate dropped at the same time. The rate of marital fecundity, which had fallen steadily from 1900 to 1936, rose from 1950 to 1968 before beginning to fall once again, and dramatically after 1976. In 1968 marital fecundity was 2.98; by 1981 it was 1.99, below replacement rate. The average family size, which had risen steadily between 1900 and 1940, fell notably after 1960, from 4 to 3.02 in 1975. Clearly, the use of birth control was spreading. Even so, birth control was much less practised in Spain than in other countries even in the late 1970s and Spaniards made considerably less use of more modern methods. Of course, the fact that birth control was illegal until 1978 contributed to this.

Despite widespread knowledge about the various methods of birth control, in 1977 just half the married women made use of one, compared to figures of 90 per cent in the more advanced countries. The were significant differences among women based on age, place of residence and educational levels. Married women under 34 were much more likely to practise birth control than those over and the use of birth control methods was directly related to both the size of the place of residence and levels of education. In general, 'the situation in Spain in 1977 is (*mutatis mutandis*) very similar to that of the United States in 1960'.[5]

In the late 1970s birth control remained a matter for men. A survey by the National Institute of Statistics showed that 59 per cent of the methods were used by men, 28 per cent by women and 13 per cent by both together. Relatively few Spaniards used more modern, secure methods. In 1977 fewer than a quarter of Spanish couples used the pill, IUDs or sterilization, compared to three-quarters of American couples. (The figure for the United States in 1965 had been 38 per cent.) When it came to the pill, Spain was 'one of the few western countries in which the pill was *not* the most popular form of contraception . . . and where coitus interruptus remained the most utilized method'.[6] The profile of the woman who in 1977 was most likely to use the pill (and least likely to use coitus interruptus) was under 30 years of age, living in a big city – and especially in Catalonia – having a university education, whose husband was an executive and who was a non-practising Catholic or a non-believer. The woman most likely to use coitus interruptus or no method at all was over 40, lived in a town of 10,000 people or less, in Galicia, Asturias, Andalucia or the Canary Islands, had a primary education or less, whose husband was an agricultural laborer and was a practising Catholic. While religion was clearly a factor in determining birth control practices, 'not even practising Catholics follow the Church's doctrines on birth control'.[7]

The Place of Women

The question of birth control shows that since the Civil War the position of Spanish women has been different from that of other European women. Spain is not, as an early issue of *Ms* magazine would have it, 'the birthplace of machismo'[8] but if there is *any* legitimacy in seeing it as a particularly 'macho' country it derives from the Franco period.

The situation of women in liberal Spain was very similar to that of women in other industrializing western nations, but after the Civil War Spanish women found themselves in a very different, and less favorable, position. They lost their political rights, the suffrage they had achieved in 1933 – a loss which was shared by Spanish men as well – but the changes went far beyond politics. Given free rein by the Franco regime, the Church was finally able to impose its moral vision on Spanish society as a whole. This Catholic traditionalism, underwritten by the state, severely limited the place of women, relegating them to a sphere defined as narrowly, and perhaps more so, than the women's sphere of the nineteenth century. Women could aspire to marriage and motherhood but little more.

The Franco regime literally turned back the clock on the legal position of women. It restored the Civil Code of 1889, which made married women legally subordinate to their husbands, as well as some provisions of the Criminal Code of 1870. The latter established a double standard for adultery – the husband's affairs had to constitute a 'public scandal' before they qualified – and permitted a father or husband to kill his unmarried daughter or his wife for staining the family's, or rather his, honor if he caught her *in flagrante delicto*. The regime added something of its own in the 1938 Labor Charter, the first of its Fundamental Laws, which promised to 'liberate married women from the workshop and the factory'.

Women, at least those of the middle and upper classes, found their world, and especially their contacts with men, severely restricted. Only one month after the end of the Civil War the government banned co-education and the ban remained in effect for thirty years. There was also a general re-assertion of parental authority after the war, keeping children on a tighter rein and, as Josefina Aldecoa put it, 'the boys with the boys and the girls with the girls'.[9] The official political organization, the National Movement, had its Sección Feminina, which was responsible for 'Social Service', the girls' version of national military service. This was intended as a 'formative' experience, for the girls involved in it and through them for Spanish society as a whole. For six hours per day for six months, single women and childless widows between the ages of 18 and 35 did physical education, took courses in religion, cooking, family and social formation, sewing, domestic science and economy, child care, singing and national syndicalism at the Escuela del Hogar (School of the Home) and did volunteer work in offices or hospitals. Any woman who wanted to take part in state examinations or get a job with the government had to have a certificate of having done her social service and after 1945 the certificate was needed in order to get a driver's license or a passport and to join cultural and sports organizations.

Courtship was very tightly controlled – almost ritualized – collective and highly public. The first stage was often the *paseo*, which has been well described by the novelist Carmen Martín Gaite:

> In every Spanish city there was a main street or a square where the now obsolete ceremony of the *paseo* (promenade) took place at fixed times. From one to two in the afternoon and nine to ten at night groups of girlfriends got together to go for a walk . . . and arm in arm, studying the boys, both those they knew and those they did not, more or less openly and talking quietly about them, promenaded peacefully and unimaginatively . . . In the Plaza Mayor of Salamanca [where Martín Gaite grew up] the girls walked clockwise and the boys counter–clockwise. Since both groups walked at about the same, generally slow, pace you knew that for each lap around the square you would have two opportunities to see the person with whom you wanted to exchange glances and you could even calculate with a fair degree of accuracy just where the fleeting encounter would occur . . . If a group of boys approached a group of girls so that a member of one could 'accompany' a member of the other they always changed direction to walk with the girls; they never made the girls walk in the same direction as them.

Girls went to the cinema in groups, but this still left some possibility of contact with a boy since 'the "companion" of a specific girl who was still tied to her gang of friends could find out they were going to the movies the next day and suggest that they leave a ticket at the box office with his name on it'.But movie houses were even more suspect in Franco's Spain than they had been at the beginning of the century and they were closely supervised. In some places the management responded to improper behavior by 'projecting on the screen a warning to "the occupants of row such and such", not mentioning the seat number but with the threat to do so if they did not behave'.[10]

Parents were aware of possible suitors for their daughters and directed them to those they saw as serious and promising, which meant those from good families and those with good economic prospects. Engagements frequently lasted for years and were often according to Martín Gaite, 'a tense and unpleasant stage, with no surprises beyond that of their own often weak and insincere conversation'. The main problem for a woman was to control her fiancé's passionate impulses.[11] The irrevocable step was the ceremony of asking for the woman's hand, which took place a few weeks before the wedding and was sealed with an exchange of gifts.

The legal and economic position of women improved over time and with the return of democracy is once again similar to that of other European women. A number of major legal reforms took place under Franco. The double standard for adultery and the definition of the residence as the 'husband's home' were done away with in 1958. Three years later gender discrimination for all employment except in the judiciary, the military and the merchant marine, was done away with, equal pay was mandated and men lost the right to avenge their honor by killing a wife or daughter who stained it. In the waning months of the Franco regime husbands lost their legal status as the 'head of the family'. This change marked a 'decisive step' for Spanish women as 'the essence of the patriarchal family was attacked'.[12] Wives could now work without their husband's permission and no longer owed obedience to them.

The legal position of women improved even further under the constitutional monarchy. The Constitution of 1978 prohibited discrimination on the grounds of gender and this was confirmed in the Workers' Statute of 1980. The 1978 reform of the Criminal Code put married women on an equal footing with their husbands in the administration of property and control over children. Divorce was legalized in 1981 and abortion two years later.

Few women worked before 1970 but since then they have become a much larger part of the work force, jumping from 15.8 per cent in 1950 to 29.2 per cent in 1977. Spanish women were still less likely to work than women elsewhere in Europe but by the end of the 1970s the difference was not that great. The 28 per cent of women in the work force in 1979 compared badly to the 44 per cent in Denmark and the 45 per cent in Sweden but quite well with the 32 per cent in France and West Germany. Those women who did work earned less than men did but the difference was less in Spain than in most other parts of Europe.

The women's movement developed slowly but the years 1974-7 saw an unprecedented 'expansion of feminism: new groups, meetings, radio programs, round tables, lectures, articles. A true effervescence, dynamic and full of enthusiasm . . . spreading from Madrid and Barcelona to Andalucia, Asturias, Galicia, the Basque Country, Valencia'.[13] Even so, the public presence of the women's movement has been sporadic at best. Many of the organizations proved ephemeral. Women have also been active within the political parties and have had something of a presence there. They made up 12 per cent of the candidates in the 1977 and 1979 national elections and 4.5 per cent of the successful candidates in each. One woman, Soledad Becerril, held a ministerial post in the UCD governments and two now sit in Felipe González's cabinet. These are small figures in absolute terms but they are probably quite respectable in comparison to the situation in other countries. At its January 1988 congress the governing Socialist Party voted to reserve 25 per cent of all spots on party committees and candidate lists for women.

Migration

Regional demographic differences remained significant. In 1965 three regions, Aragon, Asturias and Galicia, had natality rates below 17 per thousand while three others, Andalucia, Murcia and the Canary Islands, were above 23. While the general trend has been for the more industrialized regions to have lower birth rates than those which have remained dependent on agriculture there have been some reversals. As internal migration brought large numbers of young people from the countryside to the cities the birth rates of provinces such as Palencia, Salamanca and Zamora, which had been very high from 1940 to the mid-1950s, began to drop rapidly after about 1955. At the same time, provinces such as Barcelona, Madrid and Vizcaya saw their birth rates reverse themselves and increase again.

As we have already mentioned, one of the bases of the development plans of the 1960s was the transfer of population from the rural world to the urban, from agriculture to industry and services. In fact, since 1959 the Spanish population has indeed displayed a remarkable geographic mobility. Between 1962 and 1976 some 5.7 million Spaniards moved from one province to another while in the fifteen years following the Stabilization Plan over 3 million left the country altogether.

The Franco period saw a major change in the direction of Spanish emigration. Emigration was prohibited from 1939 to 1946 and when it resumed Latin America retained its position as the favored destination. However, the levels of movement were substantially below what they had been earlier in the century as the Latin American republics began to apply new immigration policies based on a careful selection of immigrants. By 1965 the number of returnees exceeded the number of emigrants. The new selectivity of the target countries worked a major change in the demographic and professional structure of this migration. Industrial workers and technicians outnumbered agricultural workers and the number of women and children involved increased dramatically.

As the possibility of emigrating to Latin America shrunk in the mid-1950s the growing economies of western Europe opened a new door for Spanish emigrants. The response was massive: close to 2 million people left between 1962 and 1976. The most popular destinations were Switzerland (38 per cent), West Germany (35 per cent) and France (21 per cent). In addition, 1.5 million people went to France as temporary agricultural workers. In 1978, about a million Spaniards were living elsewhere in Europe.

The demographic composition of this flow was very different from that to Latin America. It was composed overwhelmingly of economically active males. The non-active component was only one per cent compared to the 53 per cent for the Latin American migration, reflecting the temporary nature of the migration and the reluctance of the European states to become saddled with a new resident population. Like those Spaniards who had gone to America before the Civil War, those who went to Europe after 1959 were predominantly unskilled. Over a quarter were agricultural workers and 38 per cent were artisans, industrial workers and laborers. Many of this last group were construction workers only one short step removed from the rural world.

Unlike America and North Africa, Europe drew people from every single province. Andalucia, a region which had participated only minimally in previous migrations, became the most important source, followed by Galicia, Valencia, Castile and Murcia. Emigration was most intense in those areas which retained the highest birth rates – and consequently a young population – and the lowest cultural levels.

Demographically the European flow was quite distinct from the transatlantic one. Women were much less important: 15 per cent of the European emigrants between 1964 and 1977 compared to half of the American emigrants. In terms of professional status the differences could not have been more marked. Of those who went to Europe in this period 95 per cent were agricultural and industrial workers, 4.7 per cent service and clerical workers and only 0.2 per cent managers and technicians. Of those who went to America, just over half were workers and just under half were in the other two categories.

Despite the importance of emigration during the 1960s and 1970s, it was overshadowed by the dramatic internal movement of population occasioned by the economic 'miracle'. According to official figures, which undoubtedly understate the degree of mobility, some 5.7 million Spaniards moved from one province to another between 1962 and 1976. And this figure does not include the large number of people who began to leave the countryside almost immediately after the Civil War: some 700,000 in the 1940s and 2 million in the 1950s driven out by the steep drop in agricultural real wages or by political reprisals.[14]

This movement took many millions from country to city, occasioning the decline in the agricultural work force. It also effected a significant spatial redistribution of the national population, which has followed the growing concentration of economic activity in a very small area of the country. This is not new, but rather the continuation on a much greater scale of developments which had begun before the Civil War. Zones of traditional agriculture, located predominantly in the center, have lost population, in some cases to such an extent that observers have lamented the 'progressive desertization' of the interior. During the 1960s twenty-three provinces, covering 60 per cent of the national territory, lost population.

The two Castiles, which had been all but totally excluded from the process of industrialization, were the hardest hit. Old Castile (now the autonomous region of Castilla–León) declined from 2.85 million people in 1960 to 2.55 million in 1977; New Castile (Castilla–La Mancha) from 1.38 to 1.04 million. Every corner of these regions was touched. In the course of the 1960s 95 per cent of the municipalities of Castilla–León lost population and some were totally depopulated. Five provinces, Avila, Palencia, Segovia, Soria and Zamora, had less population in 1975 than in 1900! It is precisely here, in the heartland of the conservative smallholding peasantry, that the regime's abandonment of its ideological commitment to the rural way of life and values in favor of headlong industrialization has had its most disastrous effects.

These developments are but the most visible symptoms of the widening economic gap between the industrial and non-industrial regions of the country. Migration has helped reduce the differentials in income per capita between the richest and poorest provinces from 4.18 to 2.4, but it has done so by concentrating the bulk of the population in the wealthiest, most vital areas. Of all capital invested in the country between 1966 and 1973, 59 per cent went to the ten wealthiest provinces and only 1.5 per cent to the ten poorest.

The movement from agricultural areas to urban ones has had as a logical corollary the growth of the urban population. Since the Civil War the importance of population centers of fewer than 50,000 people has fallen steadily, although the decline has been most marked for the smallest centers. In 1940 over a third of all Spaniards lived in municipalities of fewer than 5,000 people; by 1975 only 19 per cent did so. At the other extreme, the percentage of the population in centers of more than 100,000 people rose from 19 to 37 per cent. Even in areas such as Castilla–León, which have largely been bypassed by industry, urban population has increased markedly; by at least 70 per cent in all nine provinces between 1950 and 1975 and by over 100 per cent in seven of them. The very largest cities have grown fastest: Madrid, Barcelona, Bilbao, Valencia, Zaragoza, Seville, Málaga and Murcia accounted for half of all population growth between 1960 and 1970.

Many small centers have disappeared entirely. There were 547 fewer population centers in 1970 than ten years earlier. Small hamlets in poorer agricultural areas have been hardest hit. In 1966 Julio Caro Baroja reported reading a newspaper article which indicated that over 100 abandoned villages were for sale in Spain, and in November 1984 *El País* reported that there were over 2,000 abandoned villages and another 3,500 on the verge of being abandoned.[15]

Table 5.1 *Population distribution by size of municipality, 1940–70*

Size of municipality	1940	1950	1960	1970
Fewer than 5,000	36.0	33.5	28.9	22.3
5,000–10,000	15.1	14.4	14.3	10.9
10,000–50,000	23.9	31.5	21.1	22.3
50,000–100,000	5.3	6.2	11.9	12.1
100,000–500,000	10.8	11.9	13.6	18.8
More than 500,000	8.3	12.1	14.2	17.9

Source: J. Nadal, *La población Española*, p. 245.

Anthropological studies provide specific examples of the exodus. In the Castilian mountain village studied by Stanley Brandes, population fell from 1,303 in 1940 to 805 in 1970. The vast majority of those who left were between 21 and 40.[16] In Tierra de Campos, also in Castile, emigration affected all parts of the rural community: all age groups, but especially the young, all professional sectors, but especially agricultural workers, and both sexes. It touched all communities, but especially those with fewer than 500 inhabitants. Even in areas where emigration has been traditional, such as Susan Freeman's Valdemora, it has become much more generalized. In 1960, 85 per cent of the younger males had left, compared to about half of the two previous generations. Three-quarters of the migrants went to Spanish cities.[17]

In Andalucia the impact of emigration differed somewhat. In the twenty-five years after 1950 the population of Estepa, in Seville, fell from 11,855 to 8,100 in spite of a large natural increase. Movement within the country touched all social classes while the movement to Europe was dominated by agricultural laborers. Some 86 per cent of the town's emigrants came from the agricultural proletariat. In the Córdoba agro-town of Fuenmayor the mechanization of agriculture intensified the chronic unemployment problem, giving rise to what David Gilmour has called a perpetual migration of men.[18]

In the Basque villages studied by Greenwood migration has taken the form of 16 to 18 year olds leaving the farm for laboring jobs in the city even though local agriculture has become much more profitable. In some villages this has resulted in many farmsteads being abandoned while in others farmers have been able to incorporate non-agricultural activities into their lives.[19]

In all cases, the rapid growth of the cities has taken place in a political context in which no plans or controls were applied and in which greed and corruption were left unchecked. Urbanization was governed by the 1956 *Ley del Suelo* which, in theory, was intended to limit speculation in urban property but which actually contributed to it. According to Linares Sánchez the law was shaped by the 'urbanizing obsession' of a time when 'apartment blocks were built in the middle of the country, without paved streets, often without lighting and almost always without schools'. Developers were allowed to build at high densities, so that Spanish city centers, which already had among the highest population densities of any in the world, became even more crowded. Old buildings were replaced by new ones and old, large apartments gave way to new, smaller ones. Madrid, which was surrounded by 'intrinsically inexpensive land, undeveloped empty land' suffered from speculation.[20] Few green spaces were left anywhere.

Towns in the Greater Barcelona region, such as Cornellá and Sabadell, saw their populations double, triple or more in twenty years with depressing results:

> Unauthorized barrios grew up on the outskirts without electricity, transport or drains. Towards the end of the fifties the Mayor of Sabadell calculated that out of a total of 200 kilometres of streets in Sabadell 48 km were unpaved and without drains. 'The growth of the suburbs', he wrote, 'was completely uncontrolled.

They looked like . . . the far West'. Indeed, some of the new barrios were given nicknames such as Kansas City.[21]

By the 1980s Spain's demographic patterns were very similar to those of European nations generally considered more advanced or developed. The mortality rate had declined to the point when it was one of the lowest in Europe and even infant mortality, which had remained stubbornly high into the 1960s, was at the same level as in France. Fecundity also fell into line. By 1981 the Spanish rate was below replacement level and only marginally higher than that of France or Great Britain. Nuptiality rates, which had been high in 1960, were slightly lower than those in France and Italy by 1981. There were some respects in which Spain continued to stand out: Spaniards continued to marry later than the French or the English, although not Italians, and the frequency of the use of birth control was relatively low and the types of methods used relatively traditional, although in both cases the gap between Spain and its neighbors was narrowing. In demographic terms, then, Spain was truly a European nation.

The Land

Agriculture contributed much to Spain's industrial development – armies of workers, growing markets and substantial amounts of capital. In turn industrial development had a major effect on both agriculture and rural society. Agriculture became a much less significant part of the national economy and provided a smaller share of employment at the end of the Franco period than it had at the beginning. By 1975 agriculture contributed less to GDP in Spain than it did in Italy. In 1940, 52 per cent of the work force was in agriculture, a slight increase over the pre-Civil War rate but in 1977 the figure was 21 per cent. As a result, agriculture and the social conflicts which it generated were politically much less important in the 1970s than they had been in the 1930s, particularly in the regions of large estates. Writing in 1971, Juan Martínez Alier described one 'remarkable success for the Franco regime and for the landowners': that 'the thorny problem of *latifundismo* may now disappear painlessly from Spanish politics'.[1] This prediction turned out to be true: in post-Franco democratic Spain land reform has not been a significant political issue. Its newly acquired low profile can best be measured by the fact that the central government has not dealt with it at all, but left it to the autonomous regional government of Andalucia and that when the question appeared in the press it was never on the front page.

The Crisis of the Smallholder

The Nationalist rising against the government of the Second Republic received its most important mass support from the smallholding peasants of Old

Castile. The Franco regime proclaimed an ideology of the 'sovereignty of the peasantry', which emphasized the values of rural life and exalted smallholders as the embodiment of true Spanish values.[2] The regime's interventionist agricultural policies, and especially the National Wheat Board, did serve the interests of this group, although perhaps less than they did the interests of the large landowners. However the the changes in the economy which followed the Stabilization Plan of 1959 made the position of the smallholder more precarious than it had ever been.

The crisis of the smallholder was detonated by the massive migration from the countryside to the cities and abroad. This produced a rapid increase in wages which pushed up production costs. Owners of large farms could compensate by mechanizing production, which they did in vast numbers, especially after 1960. The number of tractors increased from 25,000 in 1955 to 228,700 in 1969. In 1962 farms of over 100 hectares, which represented 1.8 per cent of all farms, accounted for 36.7 per cent of all tractors and 61 per cent of all mechanized harvesters in the country.

The difference in production costs between mechanized and non-mechanized operations was greatest for winter grains, the most widespread crop, especially in Castile. During the 1960s the balance between costs and prices shifted to such an extent that it was no longer economically rational to farm winter wheat on a non-mechanized basis, but many farms were too small to justify the purchase of a tractor. In these circumstances the small farmer could only survive by severely exploiting himself and his family. This bind was well expressed by Victor Pérez Díaz in a phrase which cannot adequately be translated: 'la explotación familiar lo es así a doble título: una familia explota la tierra "explotándose"'.[3] The smallholder's standard of living declined relative to that of other groups, to the point when it was little better than that of the agricultural laborer. And these changes were not taking place in a vacuum: 'While the maintenance of the small farm demands austerity from the members of the family modern means of communication and the mobility of the population mean that new ways of life and styles of consumption become attractive and new necessities are created, even in the remotest corners of the countryside.'[4]

A survey of the 'material and cultural levels of families' done by the National Statistical Institute revealed the extent to which small farmers, and not agricultural laborers, were the worst-off sector of the rural population: in the wealthiest and poorest provinces alike, when it came to the possession of such amenities as running water and a toilet in the house and owning refrigerators, washing machines, television sets and cars, only for the last did the farmers have a clear advantage, and even there this was not always the case. More laborers than farmers owned a fridge in Santander, Logroño, Valencia, Jaén and Huelva, more owned a washing machine in Santander, Valencia and Orense, more owned a television in Gerona, Santander, Valencia, Jaén and Tenerife and more owned a car in Santander.

The government tried to counter these developments with two policies: concentration of landholdings and aid to co-operatives. The first was intended to make small farms more efficient by concentrating the various small holdings of farmers into larger units. The initiative for concentration had to come from the farmers themselves and required a petition signed by 60 per cent of the landowners holding at least 60 per cent of the land in the village. The vast majority of such petitions, 74 per cent, came from Castile, even though the problem of fragmented holdings was less severe there than in Galicia, Asturias and Santander. By 1973 some 3.6 million hectares had been reapportioned. The second policy was to encourage the creation of co-operatives through the granting of favorable credit terms and access to machinery which would have been uneconomical or totally out of the reach of individual smallholders. This approach was much less successful than the concentration of holdings. After promising beginnings many co-operatives broke down due to disagreements among the members. In 1970 only 0.1 per cent of all Spaniards engaged in agriculture were members of co-operatives.

These policies were not sufficient to halt, or even slow down, the exodus from the countryside, especially of small farmers. In 1970 there were 75,000 fewer landowners and 300,000 fewer laborers than there had been five years before. Five years later the number of laborers had fallen by another 235,000 while the number of landowners had fallen by 680,000. Overall, smallholders declined from 23.3 per cent of the rural population in 1965 to 13.8 per cent in 1975.

Those who remained had recourse to a number of strategies to keep their heads above water. The most important of these was to split one's efforts between the farm and employment in a non-agricultural activity, giving rise to the increasingly widespread phenomenon of part-time agriculture. The importance of this varied according to the size of the farm and the region of the country. Farmers who owned fewer than 5 hectares earned 51 per cent of their total income off the farm and 36 per cent of their total income in non-agricultural activities. For owners of larger farms these other sources of income were less important. Non-agricultural work was most frequent in those regions where alternative employment was most readily available, such as the Basque Country, where it accounted for 48 per cent of total income, Asturias and Santander (39.7 per cent) and Logroño and Navarra (33.2 per cent), and less important where it was harder to find, as in León (19.3 per cent) and Galicia (21.5 per cent), or where employment in agriculture was available, as in Eastern and Western Andalucia (22.3 and 19.1 per cent), Levante (19 per cent) and New Castile (16.6 per cent).

Latifundia

Social conflict in the rural south was a principal detonant of the Civil War. Such conflict was frequent in the nineteenth century, but took on a new regularity and intensity in the twentieth. As Paul Preston has remarked, 'no single area of social or ideological confrontation during the 1930s matched in scope or impact the agrarian problem'.[5] The Civil War itself was significantly, if not exclusively, a struggle for power – and property – in the regions of the large estates. The victory of the landowners was unconditional. Wherever the Nationalists established control the power of private property and its previous owners was reasserted. This was a violent and bloody process. The agrarian reform of the Republic was reversed and the institutions of the landless, their unions and political parties, were liquidated. So were many men and women, both leaders and followers. There began what George Collier has aptly called 'the uncontested reign of property'.[6]

The Francoist state was more interventionist than any in the modern history of Spain, yet this intervention provided the landed elite with a greater freedom than they had known previously. The state was unambiguously and actively on their side, the autonomous resistance of the rural working class had been destroyed and would not be allowed to reappear, and in the aftermath of three years of civil conflict the rural proletariat was larger than it had been before. Wages fell and a more intensive rhythm of work was imposed. These conditions led landowners to undertake a basic restructuring of the social landscape. During the war itself they began an assault on tenants and sharecroppers and brought ever-increasing percentages of the land under their direct cultivation. In the the 1930s some 70 to 80 per cent of the latifundia in Andalucia were rented; by the end of the 1950s over 60 per cent were directly cultivated by their owners.

This ran counter to the Nationalist position – and that of the agrarian right during the Second Republic – in favor of rural tenancy. In this, at least, political allegiances made little difference: Nationalist supporters were not spared from eviction. In February 1938 the newly appointed Director General of Economic and Social Land Reform noted that 'a multitude of reports of evictions, especially of people who had fought for the Nationalists, have rained down on the ministry'.[7]

These changes undoubtedly had much of revenge against those who had challenged their property and their position during the Republic. They also made good economic sense. In spite of the relatively low level at which the new regime fixed prices for agricultural products, the difference between prices and wages, which accounted for the largest part of the landowners' costs, was very much in the landowners' favor from the end of the Civil War well into the 1950s. Costs were further cut by the fall in the use of expensive inputs, such as tractors and fertilizers, after 1939. The widespread black market meant that large producers generally received prices much above those set by state marketing boards. The end result was that the large estates were much more profitable after the Civil War than they had been before.

The political situation did not permit agricultural laborers to resist the reduction of their wages through organization, and for some fifteen years after the Civil War they had little alternative to staying where they were. However, once emigration or migration to the cities became viable alternatives, vast numbers of laborers seized them. Movement replaced resistance, but the result was the same: rising wages for those who remained. The index of rural wages, which stood at 424 in 1950 against a base of 100 in 1935, spiralled upwards, to 1,125 in 1960 and 5,030 in 1972 while the wholesale price index just more than doubled. Real wages increased by 83 per cent in the 1960s alone. Traditional, labor intensive farming methods gave way to more capital intensive, mechanized agriculture, especially on the large estates. Beginning in the 1950s the composition of rural society changed dramatically. In 1950 half of all people active in agriculture were wage earners; by 1970 the figure had fallen to 29 per cent.

These developments had two significant effects on the way landowners used their estates. The first was to affect decisions on which crops were to be planted and which cultivation tasks were to be performed. In his classic study of the large estates in Córdoba, Juan Martínez Alier found that rising labor costs had led landowners to move to less labor intensive crops, even on irrigated lands. The result was increasing unemployment. On non–irrigated land summer crops were abandoned in favor of fallow. Whatever the crop ultimately decided on, there were also a number of tasks which landowners considered dispensable, at least at high costs for labor, and which were often done away with. These included weeding wild oats on wheat land, clearing shrubs on the *sierra*, hoeing and earthing olive trees, pruning and harvesting fallen olives.

The second major effect of the rise in wages caused by migration was a return to the tenancy practices largely abandoned after the Civil War. In spite of its economic efficiency many otherwise 'profit oriented' landowners in Córdoba were reluctant to grant tenancy contracts 'because this means a loss of prestige', preferring to use piecework instead of time payment in order to reduce costs. However, by the early 1960s tenancy and sharecropping had made a major comeback. In the absence of any official statistics Martínez Alier estimated that in 1964–5 such arrangements accounted for almost half of the crops on irrigated land. Landowners found that labor productivity jumped by 50 to 100 per cent and that output also increased. For their part, laborers were eager to take on tenancies, which meant secure work and the chance to increase their incomes.[8]

Not all landowners were convinced by the arithmetic of tenancy. 'Many landowners refuse to consider [it] as just a form of incentive wage; it is also a new land tenure arrangement and this has non–economic implications', such as being an admission of professional incompetence or defeat. Even among those landowners who accepted tenancy there was a reluctance to use the name. The revival of tenancy in the 1960s was accompanied by 'a range of new labels' such as *contrato de sociedad* and *participación en beneficios* (profit sharing).[9]

The changes caused by massive migration did not eliminate the chronic problem of seasonal unemployment, a product of the fluctuating demand for labor produced by the principal crops cultivated in the south: wheat and olives. Mechanization further reduced the average number of work days per year, from between 180 and 220 before 1936 to between 90 and 150 in 1970–3. In some places this meant that many laborers 'spen[t] at the most only three or four months in the pueblo . . . with family and friends; the rest of their time is spent wandering about the region in search of a daily wage, most often alone'.[10] Moreover, based on his interviews with estate owners in Córdoba, Martínez Alier drew the conclusion that they were less likely to '"invent jobs" for a few attached laborers' in the 1960s than they had been before the Civil War and even into the early 1950s.[11]

The Franco regime did attempt to provide a 'solution' to the agrarian question: colonization. A law passed in April 1949 allowed the National Colonization Institute (INC) to expropriate, with indemnification in cash, land beyond the amount the Institute had determined as the allowable maximum. The scope of the program was further reduced in 1952 by another law which exempted farms, whatever their size, declared by the Ministry of Agriculture to be 'exemplary agricultural enterprises'. Expropriated land was settled by *colonos*, tenants, who were required to follow standards of cultivation set by the INC. In order to actually become landowners the tenants had to pay the Institute the price of the land plus interest according to a schedule the INC set. Colonization proceeded at far too slow a pace for the program to serve as a solution to the agrarian problem. By 1960 some 200,000 hectares had been settled and by 1965 only 49,645 tenants had been placed on farms, and of these only 8,600 had managed to acquire full title. By comparison, the Second Republic's agrarian reform, which was much criticized as a cumbersome and inadequate response, put 4,399 farmers on 24,203 hectares in sixteen months and settled another 110,000 farmers between March and July 1936. In addition, most of the new farms were small, under 8 hectares, precisely the size of farm which was becoming increasingly unviable.

The large estates functioned much the same as they had before the Civil War. Some were managed by their owners, others by a hired administrator who was resident on the estate. All of the estates around the town of Fuenmayor were managed by administrators; the landowners were never directly involved and had no contact with either the workers or the field managers. The administrator hired the field managers who in turn hired the laborers, generally in the principal squares of the towns. David Gilmore provides a good description of the process in Fuenmayor (Córdoba):

> the laborer walks to the plaza in the evening before dinner . . . Leaning against a wall, he loiters, smoking and chatting with his friends, until at last he is approached by a field manager. The man, acting on instructions from the bailiff, walks up randomly to the group of workers and says 'Look here, man, what are you doing tomorrow? Do you want to work?' The worker responds in a disinterested tone, 'Well, what kind of work is it?' The manager replies that he needs some men to weed sunflowers in the cortijo 'San Juan'. The worker, feigning indifference, asks 'Is it day wage or piecework?' The manager then bargains with him about the working conditions and the daily wage (an upper limit having been set by the bailiff), and if a price is agreed on, the manager tells the laborer where to go in the morning. The next evening, after work, the laborer returns to the same plaza at about the same time and waits for the same manijero to approach. The

manager asks if the worker wishes to repeat the following day, and the worker either agrees or replies that he has found better work elsewhere.[12]

Such a system was convenient for the field managers, but the laborers saw it as more dignified than the alternative, going to the estate to offer oneself (*brindarse*). The bargaining described by Gilmore is a product of massive migration; into the 1950s, when there were far more workers than available work, this was not possible. By the mid-1970s the situation had so changed that workers could sometimes wait in a favorite bar for the field manager to come to them.

Casual laborers hired for more than a day at a time often lived on the estate, sleeping in dormitories. Generally these were segregated by gender and very few had separate quarters for married couples. The conditions in these dormitories were, in the 1960s, similar to those in the laborers' own homes, except for the degree of cleanliness. The food, for which the laborers paid out of their wages, was also similar and prices were somewhat lower than those in the stores.

For laborers, work was very much a family affair. In Fuenmayor at the beginning of the 1970s, entire families, including children as young as 8, were employed cotton picking, which was done on a piecework basis. This took place in the autumn, so that these children missed many days of school. In 1971 a local teacher did a study and found that over a quarter of all the children in the town had done agricultural work 'which required a prolonged absence from the classroom'.[13]

Women retained a significant place in the rural work force, performing up to a third of all work in the early 1960s. Some agricultural tasks, especially those which were relatively light and required stooping and bending, such as harvesting olives, were long considered women's work. In addition, land-owners found it advantageous to employ women: they earned less and were considered to be more docile. Laborers held as part of their concept of *unión* that women should not work while there are men who are unemployed, a position which was supported by the regime.

As in the past, the vast majority of agricultural laborers were hired on a day-to-day basis or, usually during the harvest, for a specified longer period of time. There were also a certain number, about 10 per cent during the 1960s, of permanent employees: the administrator, foremen, tractor drivers, timekeepers and cooks. These people had year-round work, a major incentive in an economy with chronic seasonal unemployment, and might also receive special favors, such as cash or other presents, plots of land or a helping hand in dealing with the state administration. Family ties were often crucial in attaining these positions: 'in most estates there are lineages of permanent labourers, relatives of the main overseer or of some older permanent labourer, occupying the best position.'[14]

Even at work there were few, and sometimes no relations between land-owners and laborers. The landowner was infrequently on the estate and contact was 'reduced to the barest bones of the cash nexus'. There was one significant exception to this, the awarding of the *aguinaldo*, Christmas gift, at the end of the olive harvest. This was a traditional practice, but not one that was inevitably followed. When the gift was given it was preceded by a 'little social ritual' but since this 'places the labourer in a supplicant role' it was left to the women to perform.[15] Laborers clearly understood that this was a gift in the sense described by Marcel Mauss: 'The great acts of generosity are not free from self-interest . . . To give is to show one's superiority . . . To accept without returning or repaying more is . . . to become a client and subservient.'[16]

Laborers generally viewed society as divided into 'we' and 'they', with the performance of manual labor as the point of distinction. Their vision of society was affirmed on a daily basis. The sharp separation of landowners and laborers continued to permeate life in southern towns. Landowners had their clubs, the Casino de Labradores, laborers their neighborhood bars. Landowners went to church, laborers generally did not.

In Fuenmayor (Córdoba) these distinctions were even more visible. Even when the two groups found themselves in the same building the landowners managed to keep themselves apart. The movie theater had three different ticket prices and segregated seating until 1967. When this was eliminated landowners began going to see movies in other towns. Landowners had long had private pews in church. In 1968 the parish priest abolished the practice and the landowners went elsewhere to pray. That same year they abandoned their confraternity rather than accede to the priest's request to include laborers in the processions. This priest did not last long and the private pews were restored as soon as he was replaced. During Carnival, when laborers achieved a minor inversion of the social order by revelling in the streets of the center of Fuenmayor, many landowners would leave town. There were a number of incidents of violence against landowners who were less discreet.

Rural society in the south revealed little of the integration through patronage claimed by the prominent anthropologist Julian Pitt-Rivers.[17] There is little evidence of landowners attempting to act as patrons to their workers, especially the day laborers. There is even less evidence of the workers, either casuals or *fijos*, recognizing the landowners' right to interfere in their lives or of their repaying patronage with loyalty. The society generated by the large estates is dominated by class relations, unmediated by patronage. Even so, that society has been a relatively tranquil one ever since the Civil War. In part this is a product of the war itself and the laborers' knowledge that the Franco regime was not shy about using force. This 'internalization of political control' created ambivalence towards labor or political militants, the 'men with ideas', at least into the 1960s.[18] But this was not the only reason. The laborers' own values contributed significantly to the stability of the large estates. 'Laborers have', according to Martínez Alier, 'values which would result in conduct directed at doing away with *latifundismo*; they also have values which would result, and sometimes do result, in reforms . . . improving the laborers' situation as to wages, employment and conditions of work; and finally they have values of conformity.' Their concept of *cumplir*, 'fulfilling the obligation to do one's job with the required degree of diligence' according to commonly understood standards, leads them to work within a situation they do not see as legitimate.[19]

Finally, and most important, the material misery of the laborers and the private tyranny of the landowners, which produced the conflicts which played so large a part in causing the Spanish Civil War, were both much reduced – albeit not totaly eliminated – during the years of the Franco regime. This was, as we have said (see p. 221), a major achievement, but it was not the result of any conscious actions by the regime. Unable to organize to challenge the landowners, laborers resisted with their feet once the opportunity arose. For those who remained wages rose and material conditions improved and, of at least equal significance, landowners ceased to enjoy the over-supply of labor which had allowed them to treat the laborers as disdainfully as they had in the past.

It is fair to say that the agrarian problem was resolved during the Franco years, but it is misleading to say that it was resolved by the Franco regime. It would be more accurate to use the Spanish reflexive form and say that the problem *se resolvió*, took care of itself. Whatever the reason, this has been a very significant development and one of the principal reasons that Spanish democracy has been more secure in the 1970s and 1980s than it was during the 1930s.

Cities and Towns

During the life of the Franco regime, and especially after 1959, the center of gravity of the Spanish economy moved from agriculture to industry and services, and the center of gravity of Spanish society moved from the rural to the urban world. These shifts were accompanied by changes in class structure and social relations.

The Growth of the Working Class

One of the most striking changes has been the expansion of the working class. Formerly but a small part of the labor force and geographically confined to a small number of enclaves, by 1976 it accounted for 28 per cent of the active population and was spread across the entire country. There was also a significant shift within the working class itself, with skilled workers taking a much more prominent place. Well over half the unskilled workers were in the construction industry, the classic field of employment for recent immigrants from the countryside. In manufacturing, skilled workers outnumbered the unskilled by thirteen to one.

It is difficult to measure the material position of Spanish workers against that of other European workers. It would seem that in general they are less well off than those of Germany but that their situation is not very different from that of workers in France or Italy. The share of wages in the national income, 58.6 per cent in 1974, was almost identical to that in France and Belgium, 59.2 per cent, and very close to that in Italy, 60.9 per cent. In 1975 Spanish workers had noticeably longer hours than those in most other European countries, but a decade later they were on a par with the French and ahead of the Germans.

The labor movement also experienced major changes. The pre-Civil War unions had been liquidated by the Franco regime and most of their leading militants had either been killed, gone into exile or put in jail. The only labor organization permitted was the official, fascist-inspired Organización Sindical (OS) of so-called vertical unions which brought together all workers and employers in a given branch of the economy. Strikes were illegal and remained in the Criminal Code until 1975. Collective bargaining within the official union structure was allowed in 1958 but the government retained, and used, the right to impose wage settlements. The regime did produce some social legislation which favored workers: social security, family allowances and, most important, the 1944 Law of Labor Contracts which made it virtually impossible for a business to fire workers. (This law came under concerted attack by business leaders in the 1980s and was diluted by the Socialist government in the name of providing greater flexibility in the labor market.)

Despite the legal prohibitions, both strikes and free labor unions re-emerged, especially after 1958. The early 1960s saw a number of major strikes, including the 1962 Asturian miners' strike. Between 1964 and 1974 there were some 5,000 strikes and in the last year of the Franco regime alone there were 3,156. At the same time a new, independent labor organization, the Workers' Commissions, Comisiones Obreras (CCOO), appeared at the end of the 1950s, first in Asturias and the Basque Country and then spreading to other parts of the country. The CCOO began as *ad hoc* committees pressing immediate, concrete demands in individual factories. In large part this was a response to the legalization of collective bargaining within the OS which gave a new significance to shop stewards and factory committees. The CCOO worked within the framework of the official unions and, as Joseph Foweraker has argued, this symbiotic relationship was central to their success: 'The real process of the progressive representation of labor demands . . . could not have emerged or developed outside the OS . . . the commissions were born and grew by *colonizing* the institutions of the OS and in particular its various representative committees at plant, provincial and regional levels.'[1] By 1966 the CCOO had won about half the posts in large factories and that year they held their first national assembly. Two years later they were made illegal but even so, in the 1975 syndical elections they took some 40 per cent of all posts.

The historic union federations, the Socialist UGT and the anarchosyndicalist CNT, refused to work within the OS and also distrusted the CCOO, which they saw, with only partial justification, as under Communist control. As a result, when the ban on labor organizations was removed after Franco's death the CCOO emerged as the strongest union in the country even though it had split into three in 1976 when its Communist leadership was acknowledged. The UGT quickly recovered and was able to overtake the CCOO in both membership and support in the elections for shop stewards and factory committees which are held every two years. At the same time both the UGT and the CCOO lost members from the high point of affiliation in 1978 but the decline was less severe for the Socialist federation. By 1981 only some 15 per cent of the labor force was unionized, well below the figure for most European countries, and even that of France, whose 20 per cent of unionized workers in the 1970s put it at the bottom of the European table.

The ideological make-up of the unions is now radically different from what it had been before the Civil War. The labor movement remains divided between two dominant organizations – which between them account for 80 per cent of all unionized workers – and one of these two is still the Socialist UGT. But the other is not the anarchosyndicalist CNT. This still exists – there are in fact two CNTs – but it now carries very little weight. Its place has been taken by the Communist CCOO. Achieving a major profile in the labor movement is something which, before the Civil War, was beyond the Communists' ability. There are also a number of other unions but they are small and not too significant at the national level. At least one, the Euzko Langilleen Alkartasuna–Solidaridad de Trabajadores Vascos (ELA-STV), which is associated with the Basque Nationalist Party, Partido Nationalista Vasco (PNV), carries a lot of weight at the regional level.

The tremendous upsurge in strike activity which began in 1974 was intensified by the promise of political change after November 1975. Spain led all European countries in the number of working days lost to strikes in 1977 and 1978 and it led in the number of work days lost per thousand employees from 1977 to 1979. The late 1970s was, moreover, a period of unusually frequent strikes almost everywhere in Europe. Strike activity began a precipitous decline in 1980.

The dramatic decline in strike activity in the 1980s has been a fairly general pattern in Europe, and the United States, but in Spain it was intensified by the consolidation of the political situation and the constructive role which the two dominant labor organizations played in it. During the transition

Table 5.2 *Results of union elections, 1978–82*

	1978 %	1980 %	1982 %
CCOO	34.6	30.8	32.8
UGT	21.7	29.3	36.7
Other unions	13.4	22.8	18.3
Unaffiliated	30.4	17.2	12.0

Source: G. Prevost, *The Spanish Labor Movement*, in T. Lancaster and G. Prevost, *Politics and Change in Spain* (New York, 1985), p. 131.

Table 5.3   *Strikes: working days lost per 1,000 employees, 1975–9*

	1975	1976	1977	1978	1979
Spain	205	1,438	1,907	1,361	2,288
Italy	1,732	1,599	1,026	631	1,620
UK	265	146	448	413	1,273
France	226	290	209	125	2,071
West Germany	3	19	1	115	18

Source: International Labour Organization, *Bulletin of Labour Statistics*, 1986.

political leaders of both the left and center sought to cool out social conflicts through national agreements covering wage increases, employment and social legislation. The UGT and CCOO went along with this approach for the most part, even though it did provoke internal dissent at times. The first of these agreements, the Moncloa Pact of October 1977, was signed only by political leaders, Prime Minister Adolfo Suárez, Socialist leader Felipe González and Communist leader Santiago Carrillo, but the unions did adhere to it. In January 1980 the UGT signed the Acuerdo Marco Interconfederal with the principal employers' organization, Confederación Española de Organizaciones Económicas (CEOE), and the next year both UGT and CCOO signed the Acuerdo Nacional de Empleo.

The Growth of the Middle Class

The other major shift in class structure has been the expansion of the middle class through the growth of the professions and the appearance of a 'new middle class' of technicians and white collar workers. These groups, professionals, technicians, administrators and employees in commerce, grew faster than any others, jumping from 14 to 21 per cent of the working population between 1965 and 1975. This has led José Felix Tezanos to conclude that 'these are the

Table 5.4   *Evolution of occupational groups, 1965–75*

	% increase
Professionals	89.7
Administrative, commercial and technical employees	54.6
Entrepreneurs and managers	51.2
Service workers	43.1
Supervisors and skilled workers	37.2
Self-employed	−6.7
Agricultural workers	−30.4
Farmers not employing others	−38.5
Unskilled workers	−49.7

Source: J. F. Tezanos, *Estructura de clases y conflictors de poder en la España postfranquista* (Madrid, 1978), pp. 194, 196.

only sectors which are expanding rapidly enough to permit us to talk about an authentic social transformation'.[2]

This new middle class is much more heavily made up of employees than was true of the traditional middle class, who were defined to a considerable extent precisely by their independence. In this sense they are much more like workers. This is increasingly true even for members of the liberal professions, who more often find themselves in salaried positions in large organizations. As the greatly expanded universities turn out large numbers of aspiring professionals they will be more likely to experience unemployment. In 1975–6 there were some 22,000 students enrolled in pharmacy, 47,000 in law, and 70,000 in medicine! At the beginning of the 1980s there were already more than 10,000 unemployed doctors. Of course medicine is a traditional glamor field but new ones such as telecommunications and electrical engineering emerged in the 1980s and should attract large numbers of students. The deterioration in the position of white-collar workers and professionals has led to unionization and strikes, some of which, like the teachers' strike of 1988, have been long and bitter.

The Church, Religion and Belief

The evolution of the Church and its position in Spanish society during the Franco years was, seen from the perspective of its struggles in the nineteenth century and the first four decades of the twentieth, both surprising and ironic. With Franco's victory the Church had before it what it had been struggling to attain since the crisis of the Old Regime: the full power of the state in supporting its religious monopoly and enforcing a unity which did not exist naturally. This system, which was known as National Catholicism, was embodied in the Concordat of 1953. Yet within a decade of this long sought after achievement significant elements began to withdraw from the Church's marriage to the Franco regime in pursuit of a more democratic system in which Catholicism would have to survive on its own merits. The Church itself became more pluralistic, less isolated and less controversial than before but did so at a time when its actual social influence was less than at any time in the country's history.

Church and State

The Church very quickly baptized Franco's rebellion a crusade and supported it unequivocally and with negligible internal dissent. The most complete statement of the position of the institutional Church was the 'Joint Letter of the Spanish Bishops to the Bishops of the Whole World' of July 1, 1937. The letter, which bore the signatures of all but five of the country's bishops, repeated the interpretation of the war as a religious struggle in which the Church had been the principal victim of the fury of one of the contending parties. The Republic had attacked religion itself and this made the war an 'armed plebiscite'.

> The one side was attempting to suppress God, whose work must be accomplished
> by the Church in the world, and the Church herself was suffering immense harm
> . . . such as perhaps no institution has ever before suffered in history; the other
> side, whatever may be its human defects, was striving to keep alive the old spirit,
> both Spanish and Christian.

The bishops excused the 'excesses' of the Nationalists as the inevitable, if lamentable, product of war, but made it clear that they were qualitatively different from those committed by the other side: 'To kill for the sake of killing; to destroy for the sake of destruction; and to make a principle of despoiling non–combattant opponents both on the field and in civil life: that is what can be affirmed of one side and cannot without injustice be imputed to the other.' They also denounced the Basque Catholics' support for the Republic as illegitimate and accused their leaders of blindness and ignoring Papal pronouncements forbidding Catholics to have anything to do with 'Communism'.[1] Even the execution of fifteen priests by the Nationalists when they occupied the Basque Provinces in the fall of 1937 elicited no significant protest from the Church. In addition, 450 Basque priests were removed, imprisoned or exiled and the use of Basque, and Catalan, from the pulpit was prohibited.

Franco quickly repaid the Church for its support by abolishing all Republican legislation which had undermined its social role, such as the legalization of divorce and the restrictions placed on the religious as teachers. These were unilateral acts of a well disposed government, but the Church remained determined to extract from the new regime a guaranteed position of privilege such as it had not enjoyed since the eighteenth century.

The relationship between Church and state was delineated in the Agreement between the government and the Vatican of June 7, 1941 which included the confessionality of the state, that education at all levels be consonant with Catholic teaching, state support for the Church and the prohibition of unilateral government legislation on matters touching religion. On the key issue of appointments, the agreement established a complex selection procedure in which both Madrid and the Vatican had a say. Finally, the Concordat of 1851 was to remain in effect until a new one could be negotiated.

The Church's hand was strengthened by the defeat of Germany in the Second World War. In his first major cabinet shuffle, in the summer of 1945, Franco introduced a number of key Catholic figures into the government, including Alberto Martín Artajo, President of Catholic Action, as Foreign Minister. Franco's concern to strengthen his ties to the Vatican gave the Church the leverage with which to extract the confirmation of its privileged position within the state. This confirmation was embodied in the Concordat of August 27, 1953, which was itself an elaboration of the 1941 Agreement.

The Concordat was the basis for what was known as National Catholicism. The state proclaimed the Catholic identity of Spain and enforced the Church's religious monopoly in return for which the Church justified the existence of the regime. The basic principle of the Concordat was confessionality: all laws were to be measured against the yardstick of Catholic orthodoxy and no other religion was to be allowed to show itself in public in any way. Article 1 recognized Catholicism as the official religion of the nation, Article 2 granted the Church the freedom to operate without any restriction and Articles 19 and 20 provided state financing of the Church. Canon marriage was recognized in Article 23, Article 26 dictated that all education had to conform to Catholic dogma and morality, and empowered the bishops to assure that this was the case, and Article 27 imposed compulsory religious instruction at all levels. The Church was guaranteed a presence in the press and radio by Article 29, while Article 34 guaranteed Catholic Action the freedom to pursue its activities under the direction of the hierarchy.

The Church was forced to accept a degree of state intervention in its internal life, but the concessions it made fell far short of the historic practices of Spanish regalism. The Church regained full control over the appointment of parish priests and retained a voice in the selection of bishops. The procedure outlined in the 1941 agreement was retained: the Nuncio and the government would make up a list of at least six candidates, from which the Pope would choose three, from which the Head of State would make the final choice.

The Concordat remained in force until it was ended by agreement on December 4, 1979 and the place of the Church in national life was redefined by the new democratic Constitution of 1978. Long before this, however, significant opposition to the privileges granted by the Concordat had emerged at all levels of the Spanish Church. The touchstone for this opposition was the Second Vatican Council and the December 1965 Encyclical *Gaudium et Spes* which, by proclaiming the right of workers to form their own unions and attacking single party regimes, called the Francoist political system into question. The initial response of the hierarchy, a collective letter of June 29, 1966, was to exempt Spain from the encyclical's strictures, but the 'uncoupling' had already begun. A new generation of bishops began to speak out against aspects of the political and the social situations, denouncing the conditions of agricultural laborers in the south, criticizing confessionality, supporting freedom of association and condemning the trial of sixteen Basque nationalists in Burgos in 1970.[2]

The desire of the Church to distance itself from the Franco regime was most dramatically illustrated in September 1971 in the proceedings of the first Joint Assembly of Bishops and Priests. The Assembly clearly delegitimized the relationship between Church and state born of the Civil War in a 'scathing indictment of Francoism . . . [which] advocates that the Church should sever all relations with the Franco regime, that the Concordat should be drastically revised and that the Bishops should resign their seats in Cortes'. It also approved a resolution asking for forgiveness for the Church's role during the Civil War.[3]

Dissatisfaction with the position of the Church emerged more quickly and more strongly within the lower clergy, especially those priests whose involvement in Catholic Action had brought them into contact with the working class and those in the Basque Provinces where the regime's prohibition of the Basque language could only antagonize a clergy in a region where religious vitality was due, in some degree at least, to the use of that language. By the mid-1960s so many priests were engaged in illegal union activities, including working with the Communists in the Workers' Commissions, that a special prison had to be built for those who were arrested. The extent of the clergy's dissatisfaction with the existing situation was revealed in a poll taken in 1970: 62 per cent were opposed to the Church's position on social and economic questions, and among those priests under 30 the figure was 86 per cent. Only 19 per cent favored confessionality; 55 per cent were against it and only 26 per cent felt that separation of Church and state would be worse.

By 1973 the hierarchy as a whole had moved into a position of opposition, although a powerful Francoist minority remained. In January an episcopal letter questioned confessionality and advocated religious liberty while reclaiming the Church's freedom to pronounce on social and political questions. The latent influence of the Francoists was revealed in the Collective Letter of April 1975, the first such document since July 1937. The letter issued a 'muted call' for trade union freedom and civil rights, but did not openly denounce the regime. It called for religious tolerance but asserted the superiority of Catholic belief. However, as Norman Cooper states, it did contain 'an explicit emphasis on the need to set Spain on a new path of reconciliation, finally putting an end to postwar enmities'.[4] This was made clear by Archbishop Tarancón in his homily at the mass celebrated to begin the reign of King Juan Carlos, in which he stated that the Church would not favor particular political options and demanded freedom for all.

The first step in redefining Church-state relations was taken in July 1976, when Juan Carlos renounced his right of presentation to episcopal appointments. The Concordat was replaced by a series of four partial agreements, covering the legal position of the Church, which came into force at the beginning of 1980. On the crucial issue of finances, the agreements called for state financing of the Church to end in 1983 when it would be replaced by a 'religious tax' levied on all declared Catholics. However, by the summer of 1984 the tax had not been instituted due to so-called technical problems. In 1985 the Church was scheduled to receive $74 million from the state.

Article 16 of the new Constitution declared that there would be no state religion but that the government would 'take the religious beliefs of Spanish society into account and will in consequence maintain appropriate co-operation with the Catholic Church and the other denominations'. The bishops were not entirely happy with the Constitution because it did not definitively rule out divorce, and although it did proclaim the freedom to found schools it did not provide that the state would fund private schools. Prior to the referendum on the Constitution held on December 6, 1978 the episcopacy announced its support for the document although nine bishops, including the Primate, publicly dissented, claiming that the Constitution did not guarantee freedom of education, sufficiently support family values, did not totally ban abortion and did not mention God by name.

The Church accepted democracy and even pluralism but did not renounce its goal of defining Spain's moral standards. Its main concern after the Constitution came into force was to achieve favorable legislation on social issues such as education, divorce and abortion. In March 1980 the Church succeeded in having its interpretation of freedom of education enshrined in the education law passed by the Unión del Centro Democrático (UCD) government: that the state should support private educational institutions financially while respecting their belief system and allowing them total autonomy from public control. The Church mounted an impressive campaign of mass opposition to the Socialists' Education Bill, Ley Orgánica de Educación (LODE), which created parent–teacher councils in the schools and guaranteed the freedom of expression of teachers in the classroom as well as limiting the freedom of private schools to choose their students, but despite a constitutional challenge the bill became law in 1985. (It is noteworthy that the Spanish Church was much less successful than its French counterpart in obstructing a major Socialist education project, the Savary law. In France the law was withdrawn altogether and the minister resigned.) The Church also lost on the other two issues. Divorce was legalized by the UCD in 1981. The Church roundly criticized the bill at the time for allowing divorce by mutual consent, but the number of divorces actually taking place was much lower than anyone anticipated. The Socialists legalized abortion in limited circumstances in 1984. When the first legal abortion was performed in Oviedo, in August 1985, both the doctor and the woman involved were excommunicated.

The Mind of the Church

It is clear that the Spanish Church is no longer the virtual ideological monolith that it was before the Civil War. Moreover, not only have new intellectual trends made their appearance, but the mainstream is now far removed from the distrust of liberalism and the intransigent insistence on a state-supported monopoly in religious and moral matters which characterized it before Vatican II.

Immediately after the Civil War the Church continued to strive for religious unity. The Primate, Cardinal Gomá, talked of 'divine totalitarianism' and the preferred style of religious practice was mass, public expressions such as popular missions and national pilgrimages. National Catholicism was based on the identification of Spanish being and Catholic being, and the claim that '99.5 per cent of Spanish society is Catholic and remains loyal, at least in its thoughts, to the millenarian religion of its parents'.[5]

The claims of religious unity were not, of course, based on assessments of actual levels of religious practice or belief and at least some members of the

Church recognized and admitted the futility of attempting to impose such unity. As early as 1950, Enrique Tarancón, then bishop of Solsona, wrote in his *Diocesan Bulletin* that 'the crusade atmosphere and the rejection of laicism has not taken root. The official position has changed but that of the people has not. For a moment it seemed as though a really religious and Christian national Catholicism was emerging but it has not turned out that way'.[6] Still, the dominant tone of the highest levels of the Church remained, through the 1950s, that of the crusade and national religious unity.

Resistance to these views came first from the lower clergy. The parish clergy was, as it had long been, predominantly rural and northern in its origins. In 1970, 56 per cent had spent the first five years of their lives in towns of fewer than 2,000 people and another 27 per cent came from towns of between 2,000 and 10,000. At the same time, there were clear signs that priests were having much more success in coming to terms with the modern world than had their pre-Civil War predecessors. A poll of clerical opinion taken in 1971 produced results that revealed an 'approximation to the leftist position of the Spanish intelligentsia'.[7] If priests felt more at home in the contemporary world, they were also less sure about religious doctrine and about the means of expressing their faith. A survey done in 1974 revealed that 39 per cent of priests were unsure of theology and 51 per cent were unsure on moral questions. There was also a massive increase in the number of renunciations by priests in the 1960s: from 163 in 1963 to 3,700 in 1969.

In part this was due to a much greater openness to trends in foreign Catholicism than had been the case before 1936, itself undoubtedly a product of the ferment stimulated by the Second Vatican Council. An important indicator of this development was the sharp increase in the publication of religious works from outside Spain in the 1960s. In the two decades following the Civil War the available religious literature had been produced almost entirely by Spaniards and included such nineteenth-century works as Claret's *Camino Seguro*, which had its 181st edition in 1959. By 1965 only 10 per cent of all works of dogma and 33 per cent of all other religious works published in Spain had been written there. Also, after 1965 large numbers of Spaniards began to receive clerical training abroad.

For all the talk of religious unity some elements in the Church recognized, and had recognized even before the Civil War, that a large part of the Spanish population were nominal Catholics at best. The position of privilege codified in the Agreement of 1941 and the Concordat of 1953 was taken as an opportunity to 'rechristianize' the country and make unity a reality. At first it seemed that this might be possible: the 1940s were a period of 'great religious effervescence' marked by the construction of seminaries and the rebuilding of churches, a flourishing of vocations and high attendance at Mass.[8]

The characteristic religious form of the decade was the popular mission, what Orensanz has called an expression of 'total religiosity'. Missions were preceded by information campaigns in the press and on radio and an open letter from the bishop. The mission could last up to twelve days in a large center with full daily schedules which included preaching, confession and communion and ended with a collective ceremony. Missions also revived the great public ritual of the Inquisition, the *auto de fe*, although the victims were no longer human: 'They consisted of burning in the central square the greatest possible number of pornographic or simply dangerous books, magazines and photographs.'[9] The missions also blurred the boundary between Church and state, which was only appropriate in National-Catholic Spain, as local political authorities received the missionaries and took part in most of the acts.

For a moment it appeared that these efforts were having their effect, but in the long run they proved a failure and religious unity remained as much a chimera as ever. There is even evidence that the momentary success of the 1940s was itself artificially inflated by coercion. Martínez Alier has reported that in Andalucia agricultural laborers were required to attend mass in order to get work. In Asturias few were fooled by increased church attendance among the region's workers. As Arboleya reported, 'everywhere, even in some farming villages, the priests and committed Catholics tell me that things are great and there is no danger of backsliding "so long as the soldiers are here". In addition to maintaining public order they have managed to fill the churches with workers'.[10]

Forms of Observance

Genuine or not, the effervescence of the 1940s and the recovery of observance it stimulated were short-lived. Thereafter previous patterns of observance, or non-observance, reasserted themselves. Rogelio Duocastella found that after 1950 there was a stabilization and even a decline in religious observance. Based on figures from the Catalan dioceses of Vic and Barcelona, rates for the reception of last rites and the baptism of children in the first week of life fell. He also found a drop in attendance at Sunday Mass and fulfilment of the Easter obligation. Even the conservative, Catholic heartland was not immune. In Ciudad Rodrigo (Salamanca) in 1951 only 42 per cent of the men and 55 per cent of the women attended mass. The decline in attendance at Sunday services continued so that by 1972 only 35 per cent of those under canonical obligation to do so attended. In 1983 the FOESSA Foundation's *Informe Sociológico* reported that advance data from a new survey put the figure at 28 per cent.

But the national figures hid, as always, regional, class and gender differences. In 1980 the religious map of Spain differed little from what it had been more than a century before, with an observant Spain divided from a non-observant one roughly in the middle of the peninsula. The highest rates of attendance at mass were registered in Astorga, Burgos, Palencia, León and Osma-Soria, the lowest in Cádiz, Seville, Almería, Jaén, Badajoz, Ciudad Real, Murcia and Valencia. Duocastella found that in rural areas attendance at mass varied from a high of 90 per cent in the Basque Provinces (excepting Vizcaya) to 80 per cent in Galicia and Asturias (excepting the coalfields), 60 to 80 per cent in Castilla-León, 20 to 40 per cent in New Castile and Extremadura and less than 15 per cent in Andalucia. In Madrid attendance was about 40 per cent in the center of the city but fell in areas where the population was made up largely of immigrants from non-observing rural regions. In Barcelona some working class suburbs had rates as low as 2.5 per cent. The rate for Bilbao was 54 per cent, high for an industrial city but well below the figure for the region as a whole. In general, rates for the cities were lower than those for the surrounding countryside except for the south, where the situation was reversed. Women accounted for about two-thirds of those attending with little variation from one diocese to another.

The rural south remained one of two great black holes of Spanish Catholicism. There was a direct relation between religious practice and social position. In 1968 Linz and Cazorla found that while 80 per cent of large landowners and 64 per cent of farmers employing laborers were practising Catholics, only 43 per cent of independent farmers without employees, 36 per cent of renters and 14 per cent landless laborers were. Urban levels of observance were higher than rural ones in all Andalucian provinces except Málaga, and lowest in the agrotowns with a large population of agricultural laborers.[11] A Catholic Action survey in the 1960s found that 90 per cent of agricultural laborers called themselves anticlerical, 50 per cent of the males never attended mass and that the majority did not take their first communion until forced to do so during their military service.

Local studies confirm these patterns. In Bencarrón (Seville) most landless laborers were indifferent or hostile to religion, which they saw as the property of the wealthy. In his study of the *campiña* region of Córdoba, David Gilmour found that although church attendance was generally low it was especially so among the poor. There was a direct relation between wealth and observance and these class differences were given tangible form and reinforced by the Church itself. Gilmour reports that 'laborers stress that the rites of baptism, marriage and funeral were divided into three classes, based upon cost' and that the local cemetery was divided into three sections, each with a different price. Poor women worshipped not in the church but outside the town limits at a non-official chapel which was not frequented by priests. The lay brotherhoods were also class based. In the mid-1960s there were two in town, each of which had 150 members: La Verdadera Cruz, all of whose members were large landowners, and La Humildad, which included large landowners, other landowners and members of the local middle class. Laborers joined neither and the two brotherhoods for the poor had disbanded in 1963 due to a lack of devotion and falling revenues. Laborers were hired to carry the floats of the brotherhoods in religious processions but in 1973 they refused, and La Verdadera Cruz had to import specialists from Seville.[12]

The relation between religious observance and local identity continued to operate in many areas. In Bencarrón the religious acts organized by the two brotherhoods, which themselves were based on the division of the town's population according to the mother's family, retained their importance in the

1970s while those organized by the parish priest were much less successful. The position of the priest was ambivalent at best: he was expected to perform the necessary rites but to keep out of other aspects of local life. Susan Freeman found a similar situation in the Castillian village she studied, where the most important religious rituals were those associated with collective activities which emphasized not dogma but the 'harmonious participation in collective ritual'. Purely religious rites were quite secondary: most villagers confessed and took communion only at Easter and attended mass only on fiestas. The formal Church had little place in the village's community life and the priest had no significant role in local affairs. Indeed, he was 'usually roundly disliked' and Easter confession was heard by a priest imported from outside.[13]

Forms of observance have continued to change. In the Castilian village studied by Stanley Brandes the traditional baptism practice and the 40-day quarantine of the mother were replaced by a large ceremony in which the mother participated, mourning became less severe and shorter than it had been in the 1950s and first communion came to be celebrated in a more elaborate way. Moreno Navarro found that first communion became an important ceremony only after the Civil War as part of the attempt to 'rechristianize' the population, whereas before 1936 only baptisms and weddings had been celebrated. According to Susan Freeman, in rural Castile local shrines have fallen into disuse, an observation confirmed by William Christian in his comments on the disappearance of 'the sense of divine participation in the landscape' which had marked popular religion in the region in an earlier time.[14]

Orensanz has described the change from the 'total religiosity' of the 1940s to an increasingly personalized religion as the dominant trend in Spanish Catholicism since 1950. The most successful of the manifestations of personalized religion were the *cursillos de cristianidad*, Courses on Christian Life, with their emphasis on the mystical, spiritual content of the Church. The courses were a major innovation in religious style for Spain, with 'many resemblances to the evangelistic techniques of Protestant fundamentalism; they were informal, emotional, proselytizing and utterly preoccupied with personal salvation attained through a born again experience'.[15] The courses took place in groups of thirty, as far as possible away from normal life. The members were seen as spiritual leaders and chosen carefully. The directors and most of the participants were laymen. In total there were 5,744 courses attended by 197,334 people – 26,086 women and 171,288 men.

The second great weak spot of the Spanish Church was the working class. In 1957 a survey carried out by Catholic Action revealed that only 2.9 per cent of workers belonged to any religious organization, only 8 per cent attended mass regularly and only 29 per cent fulfilled the Easter obligation. On the other side, 41 per cent declared themselves to be opposed to religion, 90 per cent anti–clerical and 86 per cent said that their religious observance was limited to baptism, marriage and death. (The connection between religion and rites of passage appears to be the one great strong point of Catholicism in Spain: in

1981, 96 per cent of all marriages were religious and 95 per cent of all children born were baptized.)

The physical presence of the Church in working class areas remains weak, as it was in the late nineteenth and early twentieth centuries. Resources and personnel remained unevenly distributed and little has been done to correct the situation. Indeed, in the 1960s the trend to what Duocastella calls micro- and macroparishes continued. Microparishes, with fewer than 500 people, accounted for half of all parishes in the country in 1965 and claimed priests who were needed elsewhere. Macroparishes, with more than 10,000 people, were far too large for effective pastoral work, especially in working class suburbs which did not have chapels or other religious institutions.

The Clergy

The size of the clergy grew substantially between 1945 and 1981, from 87,770 to 129,811, but this impressive number of religious hid a chronic shortage of parish priests. The number of priests increased only slightly after 1945, from 22,913 to 23,039 in 1981, but their relative weight in the religious establishment as a whole fell from 21.4 to 17.7 per cent. The ratio of population to parish clergy grew from 1,228 to one in 1961 to 1,900 to one in 1981. Stanley Payne describes a 'steady and unabated' decline in the diocesan clergy since 1969 but the relative shortage was evident well before then: in 1959 there was one parish priest per 1,336 people in Spain compared to one priest per 766 Catholics in Switzerland, 917 in Ireland, 1,090 in France and 1,125 in Germany.[16] The other side of the coin was a massive increase in the size of the regular clergy. In 1945 there were 15,953 monks and 48,904 nuns; in 1981 the figures were 28,350 and 78,422 respectively.

Geographically the clergy remained clustered in the north, avoiding the large cities and the southern provinces. In 1964 Vitoria had 275 people per priest, Pamplona 372 and Lugo 491 while Barcelona had 2,555, Madrid 3,447, Ciudad Real 3,094 and Cádiz 3,169. Ten northern dioceses had fewer than 500 residents per priest and twenty-three more between 500 and 1,000 while all southern dioceses had at least 2,000 and four more than 3,000. In 1957 there were 1,741 parishes without a resident priest, a major improvement over the immediate post-Civil War situation, but the absence of pastoral attention was more widespread than this figure indicated. In Orera, in the diocese of Jaén, only 3.4 per cent of the population of 17,257 had the benefit of regular Sunday services, 6.8 per cent received two or three masses per month, 40 per cent two or three per year and 50 per cent received nothing at all.

New Currents

Some elements within the Church were conscious of its weakness among the working class and of the need to open new roads of pastoral work in order to achieve the 'reconquest of the workers' it desired. The basic point was that improved material conditions would make the workers more receptive to religion. The Church criticized the lack of Christian spirit of the upper classes which had kept the workers in such precarious material conditions, but without much effect. In Málaga, Bishop Angel Herrera created a Social School to inform the clergy on social questions and also encouraged the formation of an 'agrarian employers' association' to help ease the situation of the rural working class. This effort was a failure, as the landowners refused to co-operate. In 1959 Herrera blamed the failure on an 'anachronistic seigneurial concept of property' which was prevalent across the south.[17]

Another innovative approach, based on the Belgian Young Christian Workers of the 1920s, did succeed in giving the Church a foothold in the working class through the specialized branches of Catholic Action: Hermandades Obreras de Acción Católica (HOAC) and Juventudes Obreras Católicas (JOC). The national organization was controlled by Christian Democrats but in 1959 they were replaced by a new left-leaning leadership, more concerned with trade union and political questions. These organizations were radically different from the rather diffident attempts to penetrate the world of labor before 1939: 'where they had been pious, under firm hierarchical control and organized from the top down, the JOC and HOAC of the late fifties and sixties were a genuinely grass roots phenomenon, profoundly involved in working class concerns like wages and working conditions and utterly convinced that these matters were as central to Christianity as saying prayers and going to Church.' This Catholic labor movement reached its peak in 1962–6, when it participated in and was able to influence the Comisiones Obreras, illegal workers' commissions which were emerging at the time. However, conservatives in the Episcopal Conference were able to rein in the movement and bring it under their control, and by 1969 much of its vitality had been lost.[18] The membership had never been large compared to those of other Catholic Action agencies, 12,000 for HOAC and 70,000 for JOC, but they were located precisely in those places where the Church had long been weakest: the industrial regions of Bilbao, Catalonia and Asturias.

Catholic Action and its agencies were always kept under the control of the hierarchy. New forms of lay association such as parish-level Christian communities, like Caritas and Justicia y Paz, which are independent of such control, also appeared. There are also some super-parochial organizations such as the Comunidades Cristianas Populares, which have left-wing political affinities and accept liberation theology, as well as charismatic movements. In 1980 a Church survey produced a map of 640 small Christian communities in thirty-five dioceses.

Despite all the ferment, at the time of Franco's death the Catholic Church retained what Payne calls an 'imposing' role in education and the media. In 1975 it controlled a radio network with fifty stations; eight daily newspapers; and 700 periodicals, about a quarter of the total published in the country. Its presence in education was even greater. Payne estimates that the Church controlled about 25 per cent of all schools, in the mid-1970s. In 1975–6 Church schools enrolled

31 per cent of all pre-school children, 23 per cent of all elementary, 21 per cent of secondary and 14 per cent of pre-university students in the country.[19] The educational efforts of the Church were concentrated on secondary education which, until the late 1960s, remained the preserve of the middle and upper classes. In 1970, 20 per cent of the students in church schools came from households with a monthly income of over 30,000 pesetas, compared to only 7 per cent for the public (fee-charging) schools, and while 41 per cent of the students in the state schools came from homes with monthly incomes of less than 10,000 pesetas, only 21 per cent of the students at the religious schools did so. Likewise, over half the church schools were located in better off districts. It was here, in the Church schools, that the large number of regular clergy were employed. In 1980 most of the 100,000 regulars were teaching 23 per cent of all the country's students. And not all were working in Church schools; important public institutions such as the Universidades Laborales were run by religious orders until the mid-1970s. The Jesuits ran the Laboral in Gijón (Asturias) until 1977.

During the Franco years a new instrument of Catholic influence became very prominent: the Opus Dei. The Opus was founded in 1928 by José María Escrivá de Balaguer, although its public existence began only in 1939 when it started to recruit students in Barcelona and Madrid and Escrivá's book, *El Camino*, was published. In 1943 the Opus was recognized by the Vatican as a 'communal institution' and four years later it became the first of the Secular Institutes.

The thrust of Escrivá's collection of 999 maxims is to unite religiosity and daily life, with an emphasis on obedience and achievement. Men with talent are urged to achieve whatever position they can. The Opus' outlook is modern in its approach to economic development but the organization was firmly rooted in the old Church. The Opus has often been seen as a more modern strain within Spanish Catholicism but according to Frances Lannon, Escrivá's *Camino* 'is elitist, male, individualist, hostile to sexuality, silent on economic and social problems. It belongs not to the new currents of *aggiornamento* but to the Crusade Catholicism in which it developed'.[20] The Opus always emphasized education. It was able to control the Scientific Research Council and through it establish a dominant role in the academic world. One estimate claimed that a quarter of all university posts filled between 1939 and 1951 went to members of the Opus. It also established its own institutions of higher education: the University of Navarre and the Business School in Barcelona, both of which have much better facilities than the public universities.

The Opus is hierarchically organized with three classes of members. Those with a university education can be either numeraries or supernumeraries depending on whether they take the vows of chastity, poverty and obedience and live in Opus residences; those with less education or with a physical defect of some kind are oblati. The Opus is also secretive: members are enjoined to be cautious in mentioning it to outsiders. From the beginning this secrecy aroused the suspicion of other elements within the Church.

The emphasis on education and worldly achievement meant that Opus members were well placed to fill important positions in the economy and the administration. This potential was realized in an impressive manner in 1957 when Franco shuffled his cabinet and brought in five experts linked to the Opus, including the Minister of Commerce, Alberto Ullastres, who would play a crucial role in designing the economic policies which led to the Spanish 'miracle' of the 1960s. The period 1957–73 has been called the 'era of the Catholic technocrats' and some writers have gone so far as to talk of an Opus conspiracy to control the state,[21] a charge only encouraged by the secretiveness with which the organization surrounds itself. While the Opus has lost direct political power since the assassination of Carrero Blanco in 1973 it remains firmly entrenched in the administration, the university and the financial world.

By the end of the 1970s Spanish Catholicism was far from the intransigent monolith of the pre–Civil War era and the first decades of the Franco regime. Vatican II administered a shock which unleashed new energies and made the Church a more vital institution than it had been for a long time, bringing it closer to parts of society with which it had had little contact. With vitality came unprecedented fragmentation. At the same time it relinquished the official privilege which had been the source of so much of its power and influence. The Church still presents its moral vision as the best for the country as a whole but, having come to terms with democracy and pluralism, it no longer takes rejection of its guidance as an assault on its very existence.

The Extension of the State

The Franco regime was founded on the military conquest of one half of Spain by the other and buttressed by repression throughout the thirty-six years of its life. During the first months of the Civil War the great Spanish philosopher Miguel de Unamuno told the generals in a famous speech that '*venceréis pero no convenceréis*', to conquer is not to convince. The rapidity and thoroughness with which Spaniards disowned Francoism once given the opportunity proved him right, but the unpopularity of the Franco regime as a system of government should not blind us to perhaps its most important accomplishment, one which constitutes one of the principal paradoxes of the period: the extension and legitimation of the state. The Franco regime brought the state into the lives of ordinary Spaniards to a degree and in a way the liberal state never had, and that contact was far from limited to the tax collector, the police – political or otherwise – and the recruiting sergeant. Under Franco the state took on a new economic role, becoming more interventionist than at any time since the enlightened despotism of Charles III. At the same time it expanded the range of the services it provided, such as education, health care and social security. Spaniards have complained and continue to complain loudly about the cost and quality of these services, but few question that the state should provide them.

In political terms the Franco regime constituted a major break in the long Spanish tradition of constitutional government, but there were at least two important continuities between the two: the vision of a highly centralized state and the militarization of law and order.

Centralization and Autonomy

The motto of Franco's Spain was 'One, Great and Free', and the order of the words was no accident. The component of the reformist program of the center-left during the Second Republic which most antagonized the military was the granting of regional autonomy to Catalonia in 1932 and the likelihood that it would be granted to the Basque Provinces as well. To most officers the existence of regional autonomy, even in as diluted a form as it took during the Republic, represented the disintegration of the fatherland. Franco dealt harshly with Catalonia and the Basque Provinces: their autonomy was revoked immediately, their languages banned from the schools and the press and the names of streets and towns castilianized. The hatred of autonomy was so strong that when the Nationalists conquered the Basque Provinces in 1937 they shot a number of priests and cancelled the special fiscal privileges of Vizcaya and Guipúzcoa. The publication of books in Catalan was permitted once again in the mid-1940s, but Catalan was kept out of the electronic media. All special treatment for the regions, with the exception of Navarre, which had fervently supported the Nationalist rising and which was allowed to retain its own special institutions, were suppressed and cultural uniformity imposed.

Franco sought to carry centralization, which was one of the hallmarks of Spanish liberalism, to its logical extreme and make Spain a culturally homogeneous nation, something which no Spanish government had ever achieved or, for that matter, even attempted. But Franco not only failed to eradicate the linguistic and cultural diversity of Spain; if anything, his attempts to impose uniformity led to the revitalization and spread of regionalist sentiments. In the so-called historical nationalities, Catalonia and the Basque Provinces, autonomy came to be seen as the necessary concomitant to democracy. The political leaders who made the transition to democracy following Franco's death realized that some form of autonomy was inevitable and included it in the Constitution. However, the possibility of autonomy was not limited to the historic regions. The Constitution proclaimed the 'indissoluble unity of the Spanish nation' as well as the 'right to autonomy of the nationalities and regions'. This was very much a compromise between the regionalist parties and what Spaniards call the 'state level' ones, although the inclusion of the word 'nationalities' was fiercely opposed by conservatives.

At the same time the government sought to balance those two regions by making autonomy available to all others as well. The result would be an unusual state structure, a decentralized but not a federal state which Spaniards have designated as the state of the autonomies. The Constitution prescribed a two-track mechanism for its attainment. The fast track, contained in Article

151, allowed parliamentarians of a region to bring an autonomy statute to the national legislature without a prior referendum on the question. This applied to Galicia, Catalonia and the Basque Provinces, historic nationalities where pre-autonomy regimes, a sort of shadow regional government, had been established. The Basque and Catalan statutes were approved by parliament in the fall of 1979 and by referenda in October. Regional elections were held in March 1980. Galicia got autonomy in April 1981 and held its first elections the following October. The second, slower track, applied to all other regions of the country. The first such statutes were approved in December 1981 (Asturias and Cantabria), and by May eleven more were in place and elections for all thirteen had been held. Spain today has seventeen autonomous communities plus the African enclaves of Ceuta and Melilla.

Although the basic principle of regional autonomy was accepted early in the transition, construction of the new state was not easy. The actual transfer of authority from Madrid to the regional governments was very slow and marked by frequent controversy. More important, in the period of crisis which followed the attempted coup of February 23, 1981 the two leading parties, UCD and the Socialists, agreed to regain control over the process and in July presented the Organic Law on the Harmonization of the Autonomy Process, known by its acronym, LOAPA. This provoked widespread opposition in Catalonia and the Basque Provinces, where it was as seen as an attempt to reduce their autonomy to the same level as that of other regions, and eventually led to a decision of the Supreme Court that parts of the law were unconstitutional.

Despite these problems, and not infrequent griping at the grass roots level about the cost of the new governments – which was particularly acute in Castilla-León when it was discovered that the president of their government had a higher salary than the Prime Minister – autonomy has taken root. The regional governments are exercising authority in crucial areas such as law enforcement – Catalonia and the Basque Provinces have their own police forces – and education. The Basque and Catalan governments have been able to assert the place of their languages in the schools, the civil service and the media to an unprecedented degree.

The creation of the state of the autonomies is a major break from the Spanish liberal tradition and one which has undoubtedly increased the legitimacy of the state by recognizing and incorporating the heterogenity of the country. There is, however, one aspect of this problem which has remained impervious to solution, the question of Basque terrorism. This has been the gravest threat to Spanish democracy and it is one of Franco's most important legacies.

Basque nationalism was originally a conservative, Catholic and even racist reaction to industrialization and the consequent influx of immigrants from other parts of Spain. Through the Republic and Civil War it remained conservative and Catholic, dominated by the Basque Nationalist Party (PNV). In the 1950s however, the party's youth wing took a more radical turn and in July 1959 they created a new organization, Basque Land and Freedom, best known by its acronym, ETA.

From its beginnings ETA was subject to complex ideological debates and recurring schisms. It was very quickly influenced by new ideological currents, especially those of Third World nationalist struggles, and came to advocate armed struggle for independence. It committed its first violent act, derailing a train, in 1961. Seven years later ETA assassinated its first victim, a police inspector widely known as a torturer. The blunt methods of repression following that killing generated much public support for the organization, especially among the region's youth. The 'Burgos Trial' of sixteen *etarras* before a military court in December 1970, which produced nine death sentences (later commuted) and over 500 years of prison sentences, was probably the key event in this process. The trial was accompanied by a three-month state of emergency: 'House searches, unlimited detentions, banishment and censorship of mail were to be even more unrestrained than usual. The link between the trial, the wide persecution and the Basque people could hardly have been established more graphically.'[1]

The most spectacular of ETA's operations and the one which most contributed to the dissolution of Francoism was the assassination of Franco's handpicked successor, Prime Minister Admiral Luís Carrero Blanco in December 1973. However, following the death of Franco and the beginning of the transition to democracy, ETA continued to act as if nothing had changed. ETA split once again in 1979; ETA–Militar remained devoted to the armed struggle alone while ETA-Politico-Militar accepted political action as well. The establishment of the regional government in 1980 did not end terrorism. Although ETA itself has always been a small organization, never having more than 600 members between 1959 and 1981, the radical nationalist option continued to enjoy widespread support.

Herri Batasuna (HB), which was founded in 1978 as a coalition of radical nationalist groups and which is considered to be the political arm of ETA-Militar, almost immediately became the strongest nationalist party after the PNV. In the national elections of 1979 HB received 13 per cent of the vote and won three of eleven seats in the region. In 1982 it took only two seats but in 1986 took four and received almost 250,000 votes. In the first regional elections, in 1980, HB won eleven seats and 18.3 per cent of the vote. The PNV, by contrast, took twenty-five seats. In the regional election of December 1986, HB increased its number of seats to thirteen. There is a stubborn significant minority of people in the Basque Provinces who remain violently alienated from the democratic state, and while it is unlikely that ETA terrorism will manage to provoke a military coup, a full solution to the Basque problem is also unlikely.

The Maintenance of Order

The Franco regime did not need to invent any new methods for the preservation of law and order, as it was able to carry over the practices and institutions of the liberal period. The differences were a matter of degree alone: 'The Francoist institutional plan for public order did not break any new ground but followed, although much more firmly, that already laid out in the nineteenth and twentieth centuries.'[2]

Policing remained militarized. The Police Law of 1941 created a new force, the Policía Armada (Armed Police) – later known pejoratively as the *grises* (greys) after their uniforms – to replace the Republic's Assault Guard. Like its Republican predecessor the Policía Armada was commanded by military officers on active duty. The military status of the Guardia Civil was reasserted in its 1942 regulations, which declared the force 'one of the corps which make up the Army' and by the creation, in 1940, of a general staff manned solely by army officers. Finally, the regime continued to make great use of military jurisdiction which brought a wide range of offences by civilians under the auspices of military courts. Membership in communist or masonic organizations was made a crime in March 1940 but this law also cast its net much more widely, against all who 'spread ideas which threaten religion, the Fatherland and its fundamental institutions or social harmony'. This was followed by a law of November 15, 1953 which created special military courts to apply the 1940 law. Another law of 1943 delared a number of public order offences, such as participation in meetings or strikes in public services, to constitute military rebellion and subject to military courts under military law. (In one case in 1960 Jordi Pujol, now the head of the Catalan government, was convicted of military rebellion and sentenced to seven years for having distributed regionalist propaganda.) In 1945 the Military Code of Justice made verbal injury to the armed forces, including the police, an offence under military law.

The role of the military was not much affected by the major changes in public administration which took place at the end of the 1950s as part of the strategy of economic development. The new Public Order Law which was published in 1959 – until then Franco had used a law passed by the Republican–Socialist coalition in 1933 – appeared to point to the substitution of civil for military jurisdiction in a number of areas. In practice it led in the opposite direction, to the famous decree of September 1960 on 'banditry and terrorism', which defined the following as acts of military rebellion: the spreading of 'false news' designed to disrupt public order or insult the state, the government, the army or other institutions; participation in meetings with those same objectives; and participation in strikes which disrupted public order. In 1963, following a highly critical attack by the International Commission of Jurists and the international protest against the execution of Julián Grimau (for military rebellion during the Civil War and 'ongoing rebellion' afterwards) the government created a new set of civilian courts to apply the public order laws, the infamous Public Order Tribunals (TOP).

From 1968 to 1971 the TOP shared jurisdiction over acts of 'banditry and terrorism' with military courts. In 1971 military courts lost their jurisdiction once again, but did retain the power to try cases of insults to the armed forces. The TOP continued to function until December 30, 1976, more than a full year after the death of Franco. In 1975 and 1976 alone they tried over 10,000 cases. This practice did not die with Franco. As late as 1978 there were 148 cases of civilians tried by military courts, including one against the prestigious Catalan theater troupe Els Joglars, four of whose members were sentenced to two years for 'public and written injuries against the Armed Forces' in a play which dealt with military trials.

Since 1976 democratic governments have managed, against strong opposition from within the police, the army and some sectors of society, to change the situation somewhat. Yet Spanish police forces remained military in nature and Spain remained a highly policed society. In 1986 there was one policeman for every 300 citizens (although this figure does not count the 37,000 municipal police or the regional police). Only Italy, with one policeman for every 246 people, had more.

Article 8 of the Constitution of 1978 separated the armed forces from the police and defined the military's mission as 'guaranteeing the sovereignty and independence of Spain, defending its territorial integrity and constitutional order'. The military was not to have a policing function; the 'protection of the exercise of rights and liberties and the guarantee of the security of the citizenry' were left to the police. This represented a fundamental change, making 'the new police institutions the antithesis of what [the police] have been in our history'.[3] The Constitution also restricted the jurisdiction of military courts to strictly military matters and the Supreme Court subsequently ruled in favor of the civilian courts when conflicts over competence arose. This was a major change, although the fact that military authorities continued to claim the right to try civilians was a hold-over from the past.

The Constitution speaks clearly enough, but subsequent enabling legislation was less forceful. The Police Law of 1978 did not demilitarize the Policía Nacional, (which was nothing more than Franco's Policía Armada renamed and reclothed), but it did restrict military jurisdiction. Most important, offences committed against members of the police and the Guardia Civil were to be tried in civilian, not military courts. Another law passed in December 1978 put all offences stemming from the exercise of constitutionally guaranteed rights, including 'insults to the armed forces' in the media, under civilian courts. These changes met with resistance from some military authorities, who claimed the right to try cases of insults to the Guardia Civil or injuries caused to members of the Policía Nacional during demonstrations. In January 1980 the editor of *Diario 16*, one of the leading newspapers in the country, was brought before a military court for an article which accused a General Torres Rojas of conspiring against the government. (In October the Supreme Court sent the case to the civilian courts; General Torres Rojas played a leading role in the abortive coup attempt on February 23, 1981.) These conflicts were ended by a reform of the Military Code of Justice at the end of 1980.

The need to deal with the seemingly intractable problem of Basque terrorism which, by 1986, had claimed over 500 victims, mostly members of the police and army, led the government to bring in a tough anti-terrorist law which permitted suspects to be detained for ten days without being brought before a court. This can be seen, however, as part of a more general response by governments in the 1980s to the phenomenon of terrorism and, given the seriousness of the problem in Spain, quite a measured one.

Reform of the police forces themselves has been much slower than the reform of the laws. The Policía Nacional retained its military character and its officers still spend two years at the military academy. The status of the Guardia Civil remains ambiguous. The National Defence Law of 1980 did not define it as part of the army but did leave it, at least partially, under the authority of the Minister of Defence. The Socialists added to this ambiguity with a 1986 law which stated that the regulations of the Guardia Civil were based on military regulations. One writer has seen this as 'having legally consolidated its military character, which had been in doubt throughout the democratic transition'.[4] However, in 1987 the Socialists took the unprecedented step of appointing a civilian to command the force.

The State and the People

During the Franco regime the state came to touch more Spaniards in more, and more varied, ways than ever before. In part this was the product of ideology, in part of demagogy, and in part of a rather hurried response to economic and social changes provoked by the regime's changing policies.

The unprecedented breadth of state intervention in the economy which took place after the Civil War was clearly ideological, following both Nazi and Fascist models and the indigenous interventionism of the Primo de Rivera regime. Agriculture was controlled through fixed prices and marketing boards. The Instituto Nacional de Industria, INI, symbolized the new place of the state in the industrial and service sectors. Despite the reorientation of economic policy towards liberalism at the end of the 1950s, the Spanish state retained a prominent role in economic life. The National Wheat Board remained an imposing institution, while the INI has kept its fingers in an astounding range of pies: 'from golf clubs to cars, from iron and steel to luxury hotels, from technologically sophisticated ships to the products of artisans'.[5] Between these government corporations and the bureaucracy the state is far and away the largest employer in the country. In 1984 the public sector employed 1.3 million people, one out of every eight working Spaniards.

After they came to power in 1982 the Socialists attempted to reduce the economic role of the state. They began to prune the INI. Inefficient steel and shipbuilding operations were subjected to 'reconversion' which destroyed large numbers of jobs and produced major protests, especially in the north, and a number of companies were sold off. Volkswagen was allowed to buy a controlling interest in SEAT, the automobile maker. Even so, eighty state corporations and their 600 subsidiaries employed some 200,000 people in 1986. The Socialists also attempted to make the labor market more flexible, reducing job security by making it easier for firms to fire workers and expanding the scope of temporary employment contracts, a move strongly opposed by the unions. Still, government regulation of economic activity can reach levels some find suffocating: in 1984 Carlos Ferrer Salat, president of the most important business lobby in the country, claimed that it was necessary to have forty-two permits to build a house in Barcelona!

The Franco regime also created a welfare state. The health service, while the target of frequent criticism, took medical care into the furthest corners of the country and gave countless villages resident doctors for the first time. The social security system provided both unemployment insurance and old age pensions. Even the official unions, the *sindicatos*, contributed to making Spaniards look to the state: they had 'provided the only mechanism through which most workers could improve their living and working conditions. In addition to collective bargaining and legal advice the State Union had offered an astonishing range of services' such as housing, worker co-operatives, schools and leisure clubs.[6] But the most important, and beneficial, aspect of the extension of the state was education.

The Second Republic had marked the most determined attempt to assert the priority of the state in education. In this, as in so much else, the Franco regime moved even more strongly in the opposite direction. Franco's National Catholicism gave the Church a greater role in many fields, education among them, than it had enjoyed since the end of the Old Regime. Education had never been so strongly influenced by the Church as during the twenty years after the Civil War. In the 1960s, however, the regime began to reassert the role of the state, although without contesting the legitimacy of the Church's role. As educational opportunities expanded dramatically, surpassing anything that had existed before, the state provided many of the new schools. The expansion of the state school system continued after 1975, although the Church was able to solidify its schools by winning large, and expanding, subsidies from the state. Despite its very real problems, by the mid-1980s the educational system was larger and more extensive than ever, offering more services to more Spaniards and more closely associated with the state.

The availability of education increased dramatically at all levels. The number of elementary school students stood at 2.35 million in 1939–40, 150,000 fewer than in the last year before the Civil War, and did not return to the prewar peak until 1943–4. Enrolments began a slow but steady rise in 1948–9 and by 1974–5 some 4 million students were in elementary school. The school leaving age was raised to 14 in 1964 and by 1974 virtually all children between the ages of 6 and 14 were in school.

The changes at the secondary and university levels were even more impressive. During the Republic the number of students in secondary schools had increased by over 60 per cent, from 76,000 to 125,000. After the Civil War the number grew slowly, reaching 261,000 by 1953–4. In February 1953 the high school curriculum was reorganized into two successive stages, each of which provided its own certificate, and this change helped keep more students in school to the leaving age of 14. Ten years later the number of high school students had almost tripled and by 1970–1 it stood at 1.5 million. The number of universities increased from 12 in 1960 to 30 in 1983 and the number of students attending them mushroomed from 37,000 in 1940 to 650,000 in 1980. The percentage of 18 to 25 year olds attending university jumped from 2 in 1960 to 17 in 1980. Moreover, more students from humble backgrounds were able to attend. In 1979–80, 40 per cent of university students had parents who had no more than elementary education.

As secondary and higher education became much more accessible, the proportion of female students also increased markedly. At the end of the Franco regime they accounted for just under half, 48.8 per cent, of secondary students and by 1982–3 they were 54 per cent. Within the high school program, the percentage of women increased with each successive year. At the universities women went from only 14 per cent of the students in 1939 to 44 per cent in 1979.

For the first twenty years or so of the Franco regime the role of the state in education was reduced. Education 'was seen as a responsibility which lay with society and in which the state need only assist . . . Of course the Church was the only force capable and allowed to take over the teaching function'.[7] This is not to say that under Franco the state withdrew entirely. First the schools had to be 'purified' of the 'contamination' caused by the Republic. School libraries and the teaching profession were purged during the Civil War and those teachers who remained in their posts were required to take courses 'in order to saturate their spirit with the religious and patriotic content which inspires our Crusade'. Religious education was made obligatory and all teaching was required to conform with Catholic principles. Political indoctrination, under the rubric of Formation of the National Spirit was introduced and remained on the curriculum until 1976, although to judge by political developments it was quite ineffective.

Once ideological standards had been imposed the state did reduce its presence. The weight of public elementary schools decreased throughout the life of the regime, from 80 per cent of all elementary students in 1946–7 to 60 per cent in 1975–6. At the secondary level the public sector virtually collapsed: 70 per cent of secondary school students attended public schools in 1931 but by 1943 only 30 per cent did so. There were only six more public high schools in 1959 than there had been in 1939.

This trend was reversed in the 1960s. Responding to the need to create a school system suited to a rapidly industrializing economy, the government undertook a complete re-evaluation of the education program and produced the 1970 General Education Act, the first such piece of legislation since the Moyano Law of 1857. The General Education Act included a clear statement of 'the educational function of the State' and led to a remarkable expansion of the public school system, most dramatically at the secondary level. In 1960–1 only 15 per cent of high school students were in public schools. Fifteen years later the figure had almost tripled. For COU, the university preparation year, over two-thirds of the students were in public schools.

This trend accelerated greatly after the death of Franco and by 1983 two-thirds of all secondary school students were in the public system. The public schools were even able to recover a little ground at the primary level, increasing their share of the student population from 60 to 63 per cent between 1975 and 1983.

It also appears that the prestige of public schools increased. A number of polls taken between 1965 and 1975 revealed that the percentage of people who felt that the public schools were better than religious ones increased from 16 per cent to 47 per cent. This is in spite of the fact that private schools often have better facilities. According to José María Maravall, Minister of Education in the Socialist government from 1982 to 1988, public high schools were only half as likely as private ones to have a laboratory and two-thirds as likely to have sports facilities or school libraries.[8]

One significant new departure made by the democratic regime has been the promotion of education in languages other than Castilian. Despite its drive for homogeneity the Franco regime did permit private schools which taught in Basque and Catalan. These were particularly numerous in the Basque Provinces, where the first *ikastolas*, Basque language schools, were opened in 1960 and spread rapidly. This development was another of the ironies of the Franco period, since 'more children studied Basque or in Basque in the primary schools of the region in the last 25 years of the regime than had done so from the beginning of time until 1950'.[9] Since 1978 the *ikastolas* have been officially recognized and subsidized by the regional government and have begun to move towards integration into the public school system, while Basque was made an obligatory subject in the public schools. By 1981–2 two-thirds of all students in public pre-schools and elementary schools were studying the language. The situation is even more advanced in Catalonia. Catalan was made a required subject through secondary school in 1978 and by 1980–1 95 per cent of all high school students were being taught the language and its literature. Education either partially or totally in Catalan also spread and by 1980–1 was being offered by about a quarter of all schools in the region, although with strong variations from one district to another.

How does public education in Spain compare to that in other European countries? According to UNESCO statistics, at the end of the 1970s enrolment rates were similar to those elsewhere in the EEC. There was virtually no difference at the primary level but the range was much greater at the secondary level, where Spain's figure of 67 per cent was similar to that of Greece (69) and Italy (73) but further behind the UK (77), France (78), Holland (82) and Belgium (86). The expansion of the university system allowed Spain to move from tenth place to seventh, and ahead of the UK, in 'gross schooling rate, the number of students compared to the total population'.[10] Spain had the highest rate of female enrolment at all levels.

Despite the growth of the public sector since 1970, private education retained a relatively strong presence. In 1982-3 about a third of all elementary and secondary school students were in private schools, many more than in Italy (15 per cent), Germany (12 per cent), France (8 per cent) and the UK (7 per cent). There were, however, some countries in which the private sector was much more important still, such as Belgium and Ireland, where they accounted for 55 and 88 per cent of the students.

In spite of increases in the budget Spain spent relatively little on education. In 1976 Spain was at the bottom of the European table in terms of education spending as a share of GNP with 1.9 per cent, compared to 2.3 per cent in Greece, 3.3 per cent in Portugal and France, 4 per cent in West Germany, 4.1 per cent in Italy, 5.3 per cent in the UK and 8 per cent in Sweden. This low level of expenditure means, among other things, that facilities are poor. The situation of school libraries at the end of the 1970s was 'nothing less than a disgrace'.[11] Spain was last, with 0.3 books per student, compared to 0.9 in Portugal, 10.8 in Roumania and 25.6 in Sweden. The amount of money dedicated to scholarships and grants to students who remain in school after 14 has shrunk sharply, from 16 per cent of the education budget in 1965 to 3 per cent in 1980. Spain also compared very poorly here, spending one-twentieth the amount of the UK and one-fortieth that of Germany.

While expenditure on education and other public services is ultimately a political decision, it is also subject to the constraints imposed by the total revenues available to the state. The Spanish state has been, and remains, a relatively poor one. The Franco regime retained the reliance on indirect over direct taxes which had been set out in 1845 and, moreover, it permitted wholesale evasion of those direct taxes which it did impose. In 1965 total tax revenue amounted to only 14.7 per cent of GDP, the lowest figure of any OECD country, and little more than half the OECD average of 27.4 per cent. By 1975 the percentage had risen slightly, to 19.6 per cent, but Spain's relative position remained unchanged. Spain stood out equally with regard to the weight of personal income tax in overall taxation. In 1965 income tax accounted for 14.3 per cent of tax revenue compared to the OECD average of 26.3 per cent. Ten years later the Spanish figure was virtually unchanged and Spain had been overtaken by Italy.

The first democratic government instituted a fiscal reform in 1977 which put a new emphasis on the direct taxation of income and began to reduce the opportunities for evasion, although these remained substantial for anyone not on a straight salary or wage. The result was to increase the amount of revenues available: between 1975 and 1985 both the percentage of GDP taken in taxes and the weight of taxes on personal income rose by almost 50 per cent but the Spanish state still remained relatively poor. Within the OECD only in Japan and Turkey did taxes account for a smaller share of GDP.

Table 5.5 *Total tax revenue as percentage of GDP in 1985*

Country	%
Sweden	50.5
Denmark	49.2
Norway	47.8
Belgium	46.9
France	45.6
Ireland	39.1
United Kingdom	38.1
West Germany	37.8
Canada	33.1
Portugal	31.1
United States	29.2
Spain	28.8
Japan	28.0
OECD	37.2
OECD Europe	38.9
EEC	39.8

Source: OECD, *Statistiques des Recettes Publiques des Pays Membres* (Paris, 1987).

Overall, the democratic tax collector put his hand further into the average Spaniard's pocket than Franco's ever did. This is one aspect of the extension of the state about which few are happy and for which becoming more like other Europeans has been of little comfort.

The Consumer Society

The economic 'miracle' brought with it rising standards of living and levels of consumption. These, in turn, produced a change in values, as urban employment and city living became much more prestigious than their rural counterparts. Through the nineteenth century Spaniards of all classes strove to acquire land; since 1960 they have striven to abandon it. Farmers' sons have refused to take land in inheritance and many younger farmers have had difficulty in finding wives. The young have been the most eager to leave. Miguel Delibes, one of Spain's leading novelists, captured this situation in a powerful image when he described those few young people who remained in the villages as having 'their bags packed, that is spiritually absent, ready to flee at the first opportunity'.[1] The same situation is expressed in the advertisement an agricultural college has placed in the Salamanca bus station: 'To be a farmer is a profession not a life sentence.' They have fled to the cities, to a society of high consumption and to a culture which is increasingly international in nature.

The Degradation of Rural Life

The full impact of these developments can best be seen at the village level, and there through the work of anthropologists. The exodus from Benabarre (Huesca) included many small farmers pushed out by 'a very substantial breakdown in the traditional economy'. Farmers began to have trouble finding heirs for their land and young men could not find wives 'as local girls [became] increasingly unwilling to marry into peasant households'. Some went so far as to advertise for wives in agricultural journals and Church-sponsored magazines. The standard of living of the small farmers was little better than that of the laborers. Young people were no longer prepared to accept the spartan life to which farmers were condemned.

> In the last two decades they have been exposed to a series of cultural influences which have drastically altered their view of what constitutes proper living. What the parents considered a reasonable standard of living now appears to their offspring as abject poverty . . . traditional agriculture . . . is not capable of providing for the new consumer goods, diversions and educational demands which have become minimal expectations in the last fifteen years.[2]

In the Basque village studied by David Greenwood the unprecedented profitability of agriculture stimulated by industry and tourism in the surrounding region was unable to prevent many farmers from abandoning their farms because 'agriculture . . . no longer satisfies their ideals of dignity in work'. The young were especially loath to commit themselves to agriculture: parents have had to 'entice a child' to take on the farm. In Echalar, another Basque village, many young women emigrated temporarily to France to find work. There they developed new skills and new tastes which made them reluctant to marry a farmer and return to village life. William Christian found that few of the young women in the villages in Santander which he studied were interested in marrying farmers and that the rate of marriage to outsiders had jumped sharply since the 1940s.[3] Residents of Valdemorra, in Castile, saw the emigration of children and the depopulation of the village as 'desirable ends' while 'none of the young girls in the village wants to marry a farmer. All instead look forward to an easier life in a town with at least one movie theater and a husband in a salaried position'.[4]

The devaluation of rural life is strikingly clear in Los Olivos (Huelva). There emigration and changes in agriculture produced nothing less than a 'transformation' of the village in the 1960s. The landowners who remained could no longer afford to hire agricultural laborers and had to use family members in their place. Other members of the family took on occasional work, such as domestic piecework for clothing manufacturers. Many of the migrants returned on their vacations, bringing back money which they used to modernize their houses in the village. The former laborers are now usually better off than the landowners for whom they had once worked.

Los Olivos, in short, has ceased to be a place in which the owner of agrarian property reigns supreme. More than likely, he has abandoned most of his parents' land, has applied for public-works unemployment relief, and has joined one of the crews building a retired person's or emigre's pueblo home. Meanwhile, the former landless worker or poor smallholder who left for blue-collar work in the city more than likely has visited the pueblo to talk about his bettered fortunes. He may even be one of those who employs the sons of those for whom he and his parents once labored. In the course of a generation, history has inverted the postwar order.[5]

Television and radio were a principal cause of this wholesale dissatisfaction with village life. Well before television sets were within the means of most individuals, rural Spaniards had been exposed to this unprecedented window on the world through state sponsored *teleclubs* in the villages. The Ministry of Information gave a television to the village which then set aside a room, frequently in the town hall, where it was set up for public viewing. By the 1970s the ownership of a television set had become the norm for Spanish households, even in the countryside. In 1975, 79 per cent of all homes and 63 per cent of the homes of farmers and agricultural laborers had a television.

Christian argues that in Santander television 'has greatly abetted the reorientation of families away from the village toward the city' and Hansen suggests something similar for the Catalan countryside. 'Instead of the traditional saving and reinvesting [for land] habits of the Catalan peasant, consumerism offers the peasant youth instant escape from the drudgery of agriculture and more intimate contact with metropolitan lifestyles.'[6] Lisón Tolosana includes the media in his explanation for the opposition of young people in Belmonte de los Caballeros to traditional practices.[7] It is also worth noting that autonomous regional governments in both Catalonia and the Basque Country very quickly established television networks which broadcast in Catalan and Basque.

The Rise of Consumerism

Industrialization brought a rising standard of living and with it new levels of consumption. Average income jumped from $290 (US) in 1955 to $497 in 1965 and $2,486 in 1975. Necessities ate up a declining share, leaving more for discretionary spending. Both the production and ownership of consumer goods such as televisions, washing machines, telephones, and especially cars, multiplied. By 1983 Spaniards had still not reached the levels of many other Europeans but they were getting there.

Spain became a consumer society but there were sharp regional differences in the ownership of consumer goods. In prosperous regions such as Catalonia, the Basque Country and Madrid at least 85 per cent of homes had a television and a fridge and 35 per cent a car in 1975. In poorer regions such as Extremadura, Galicia and Andalucia televisions were found in betweeen 57 and 77 per cent of homes, fridges in between 36 and 65 per cent and

Table 5.6   *Structure of personal spending, 1958–74*

	1958	1964	1973–4
Food	55.3	44.7	38.0
Clothing	13.6	14.9	7.7
Housing	5.0	7.4	11.6
Household	8.3	9.2	11.1
Surplus	17.8	19.9	31.6

Source: M. Navarro López, 'Pautas de consumo en España y diferencias regionales' in M. Fraga, ed. *La España de los años 70* (Madrid, 1979) I, 815.

Table 5.7   *Possession of selected consumer goods per 1,000 population*

	Televisions 1979	Cars 1983	Telephones 1983
Belgium	297	331	417
West Germany	317	400	572
France	292	372	544
Italy	231	345	405
UK	327	318	520
Spain	253	228	352

Source: EEC Statistical Office, *Review, 1975–1984.*

cars in between 19 and 25 per cent. Such items were also more likely to be found in larger population centers than smaller ones. In cities with more than 50,000 people 90 per cent of the homes had televisions, 89 per cent had fridges and 41 per cent had cars. By contrast, in villages of fewer than 2,000 people only 50 per cent of the homes had a fridge, 60 per cent a television and 24 per cent a car.

Increased consumption has also taken less tangible forms. Foreign vacations have become commonplace: in 1977 some 8 million Spaniards took their holiday abroad. Middle class Spaniards such as school teachers now go on shopping weekends to London and take their holidays in such exotic places as Tunisia and Turkey. The English language has been a major consumption item at least since the 1970s, as the proliferation of private language schools makes clear, but in the mid-1980s intensive residential language programs for young people, primarily in England but also in the United States, at prices around $3,000 per month, became increasingly popular.

The Internationalization of Culture

The decline of rural life had a cultural as well as economic dimension, as traditional local activities and festivities yielded to a more homogeneous, national – and even international – culture, especially among the young.

Barrett found a decline in recreational activities such as football teams, the orchestra and street dances in Benabarre. The youth were the least interested in village tradition. 'Apathy is only displayed toward "traditional" events or elements of community culture such as processions, skits and folklore. On the other hand, all fiesta events which are part of contemporary urban culture are popular and gain active support.'[8] During the 1950s and 1960s the young men of the Aragonese town of Belmonte de los Caballeros began to 'revise' a number of traditional practices, rejecting the demands of the municipal council and rejecting maternal interference in the choosing of wives.[9]

In the Castilian village of Becedas there was 'rapid loss of traditional cultural values' due to emulation of urban practices and the abandoning of some local practices which were seen as backward. The traditional baptism, which was attended only by the mother and three other women, was replaced by the large attendance usual in the cities; first communion celebrations became more elaborate, and mourning became less severe and reduced in duration. The number of religious processions was cut during the 1960s from fourteen to five and villagers took to consulting a doctor instead of a *curandero*.[10] Susan Freeman found something similar in the Castilian village she studied. Fewer traditional celebrations were held and those which remained were 'celebrated with less vigor than before'. Moreover, she saw new styles of life evolving within the *pueblo*: women had ceased to take an active role in agriculture, marriages between cousins, designed to merge properties, were now looked down on as mercenary and inferior to matches motivated by love, and the traditional practice of newlyweds spending a year living apart in their parents' homes had been abandoned so that newlyweds now generally live together and alone.[11]

In some places traditional practices were more resilient, changing their form while retaining their basic content. This has been the case of the ideal of the multi-family farmstead in villages in or near the Asturian coalfields. As more and more village men went into the mines they built three- or four-story apartment buildings occupied by the builder and his descendants and in-laws. 'In this way the ideal of having the family "under one roof" has been reconciled with resources acquired in the more modern sectors of the economy.'[12]

Commercialized leisure activities have also changed. Cinema has become much less popular. Through the 1940s Spain had more cinema seats per capita than any country in the world except the United States and those seats were frequently filled. After 1965, however, both the number of cinemas and attendance began to drop, from 9,029 and 400 million in 1965 to 5,178 and 273 million in 1974. Most of this decline can be attributed to television, which was introduced in 1956.

The other significant change was the spectacular rise of football, which surpassed bullfighting to become the national passion. Football was used by the Franco regime both as a social tranquillizer and a stimulant to national pride, especially in the 1950s when the national side and clubs such as Real

Madrid had a run of international success. Aside from filling the stadia, Spaniards spent vast amounts of money on football. They bet $117 million on the pools between 1963 and 1973 and bought specialized newspapers and magazines. *Marca*, with its circulation of 400,000, was the most widely sold periodical in the country for many years. In spite of all the money they generate, the football clubs are far from being run on business principles and many ran up huge debts as they spent millions to buy foreign stars such as Maradona (Barcelona) and Bernd Schuster (Barcelona and Real Madrid).

More recently the interest in professional sports broadened to include basketball. There has long been a Spanish league but the silver medal Spain won at the 1984 Olympics produced a quantum leap in the sport's popularity. In 1988 Spanish television carried the finals of the NBA championship between Los Angeles and Detroit complete. The new status of basketball was confirmed in October 1988 when McDonald's sponsored an invitational tournament in Madrid featuring Real Madrid and the Boston Celtics. The trophy was presented by Prince Felipe, the heir to the throne.

The importance of football and basketball illustrate the growing internationalization of culture. This development is most advanced among Spanish youth, who are fully integrated into an international, commercial popular culture based on rock music. Spain had its own domestic products: on the one hand Marisol, an attractive blonde intended to be a cross between Doris Day and Linda Ronstadt, on the other a group such as Los Bravos whose 'Black is Black' was an international hit; but foreigners were dominant. Beatlemania, and the Beatles, arrived in Spain at about the same time as in the rest of Europe, followed by the Rolling Stones, 'los Roling' to Spanish youth, and the rest of the British wave of the mid-1960s. Twenty years later only the names had changed. All the major rock stars pass through Spain on their international tours; in the summer of 1988 alone Spaniards flocked to see Michael Jackson and Bruce Springsteen as well as the Amnesty International tour featuring Springsteen and Sting.

There are two common denominators to the changes in leisure: it has become much more commercialized and it has been integrated into an increasingly homogeneous international – and American-dominated – leisure world. The first change is a matter of degree, the second is a fundamental shift. Spain was never culturally isolated but the scope and extent of the penetration of foreign influences in unprecedented. (Spain is also far from unique in undergoing this experience but it is probably more exaggerated there than elsewhere.) English words are invading the language, especially in such high quality and trend-setting venues as *El País*, the country's leading newspaper. In the summer of 1987, for example, when the word was still unfamiliar to many North Americans, one of the paper's regular columnists, Juan Cueto Alas, used the neologism 'dinks' (Dual Income No Kids) without any explanation. And, it is said, Madrid was the first city in Europe to have all of Wendy's, Burger King and McDonald's.

Conclusion

Seen solely from the surface of political events the history of Spain since 1800 appears as an unbroken litany of short-lived governments, military coups and civil wars. The culmination was, of course, the Spanish Civil War of 1936 to 1939. Moving from internal to international affairs, the story becomes one of military defeat, loss of empire and increasing international irrelevance.

Such a perspective leads naturally to pessimism, to a belief that Spain and its people had somehow failed, to a sense of Spanish distinctiveness. Yet it is legitimate to ask whether the modern history of Spain is any less edifying than that of Germany or Italy, with their fascist regimes, of France, with its frequent revolutions and the savagery of the anti-Communards, or even of England, whose violence was, for the most part, directed outwards to a colonial world. And, to highlight a little-noted fact, Spain was the only large European state to remain aloof from the general butchery of the two world wars.

All this is to say that Spain, along with every other western European country, has had its problems responding to the big changes of the last two centuries. These big changes have been the same in every case, for Spain as for France or Germany. To come back to what I said in the Introduction, in the nineteenth and twentieth centuries Spain was fully a part of the European mainstream. It experienced the fundamental trends of historical development in Europe. Inevitably, the responses were not identical. Spain was not a copy of any other continental country, let alone of England, but it was unquestionably a member of the western European family. Economic historians are now revising the traditional view of French economic development to argue that its industrialization was not retarded compared to that of England, but that it was qualitatively different. By the early twentieth century France had reached roughly the same place as England, although by a very different route.[1] The same can be said of Spain. By the 1980s it too had become an advanced industrialized society, comparable to any in western Europe. The Spanish road was longer and more circuitous, but ultimately it led to the same place.

What were these big changes, these fundamental trends of historical development in Europe? They are to be found not in the realm of high politics and diplomacy but in that of economic development, social change and the relation between state and society. These changes can be put into six groups: (1) industrialization and overall economic development, (2) population growth and urbanization, (3) the creation of absolute private property, especially in land, (4) the formation of a working class and with it some form of working class organization, (5) the changing place of religion and the Church(es), and (6) the creation of a constitutional political system and of a centralized state which came to have an increasingly prominent place in the life of its citizens. They were all present in Spain.

Industrialization began early in Spain but soon fell behind that in other countries. The economy never ceased to grow and change but it did so at a slower rate than the economies of countries such as France, Britain or even Italy. The stagnation of the first twenty years of the Franco regime put the country even further behind, but the 'economic miracle' of the 1960s allowed Spain to narrow the gap so that today its level of economic development is more similar to that of its principal competitors than at any time since 1800.

Demographic change in Spain has followed the broader European pattern: falling death rates, falling birth rates, sustained population growth, although with its own chronology. Today its principal demographic indicators are virtually indistinguishable from those of its west European neighbors. Spaniards were central to the emigration which was such a common European experience, except for France, in the nineteenth century, although emigration was an important factor in Spanish life longer than anywhere else in western Europe, except for Italy and Portugal.

By 1856 the fragmented form of land ownership which was characteristic of the Ancien Regime was, with a couple of exceptions, eliminated and was replaced by absolute ownership. The nobility became landowners like any others, stripped of the protection of entail, and some found that they could not survive without that safety net. Others found the new atmosphere quite congenial. The Church and the municipalities were stripped of their lands which were sold to new owners, although the structure of landholding changed little. Many peasants were disadvantaged by these changes and they resisted. Some, mostly in regions of independent smallholders, did so under the Carlist banner of reaction. Others, mostly in regions of large estates, did so under the banner of revolution. The tensions in the rural world were defused only after the Civil War, when emigration, industrialization and the rise of a consumer society led most of the discontented to abandon the countryside altogether rather than try to change it.

Industrialization created a working class, although before the Civil War it was relatively small and concentrated in a few parts of the country: Catalonia, Asturias, the Basque Country and Madrid. Working class organization came more slowly, perhaps, and came in a different way from elsewhere. Nonetheless, it did share some central features – a large Marxist Socialist party with an associated union federation and a more overtly revolutionary alternative, although in Spain it was anarchosyndicalist not Communist.

As has been the case everywhere, organized religion, which in Spain means the Catholic Church, has had to find ways of dealing with changing political and social circumstances. In the nineteenth and early twentieth centuries the Spanish Church was perhaps slower than most in finding ways to do so and more inclined to straight resistance. Spain produced little of the popular Catholicism of the sort described for Germany by Jonathan Sperber,[2] no real *ralliement* as in France and nothing even approaching the Partito Popolare in Italy. The Civil War and the two subsequent decades showed just how late in the day the Church clung to its desire to dominate Spanish society and to its willingness to use the state to do so. Only since the 1960s has the Church come to accept democracy and social pluralism, although on questions such as education and abortion it has continued to fight hard to try to dictate terms.

If the Church could pretend to such a central social role for as long as it did this was in part due to the weakness of the Spanish state. Nineteenth-century liberals built a centralized state structure using the ambitions of eighteenth-century reformers and imported French models, but this liberal state was unable to attract the loyalty of many people. It was strong on the maintenance of law and order and weak on the provision of public services. And, as John Davis has observed of Italy, a violent or forceful state is not the same as a strong state.[3] The Spanish liberal state was also unable, and seemingly unwilling, to develop its own set of symbols, a secular nationalism to supplant, or even supplement, the country's alleged religious identity. Ironically, it was the Franco regime which extended the sphere of activity of the Spanish state, balancing its law and order functions with a social welfare role and bringing it more, and more benevolently, into the everyday lives of ordinary Spaniards.

This book has given a much more optimistic reading than is usual of Spain's modern history, but such a reading is fully justified. This is not to say, of course, that the Spanish past has not been difficult or to deny that contemporary Spain is a country with pressing problems. However, as with the problems of the past, the problems of the present are ones that Spain shares with many other European nations: inflation, government debt, unemployment – especially among young people – outmoded heavy industries, terrorism and pollution are among the first that come to mind. In the 1980s many Spaniards, and certainly Spanish governments, have gambled heavily on a 'European' solution, counting on Spain's membership of the European Economic Community to help overcome their problems. And within the EEC Spain has been one of the most vocal proponents of greater integration. Throughout the modern period Spain has been fully European. Has it now become the most European of all?[4]

Notes

Introduction

1   E. P. Thompson, 'The peculiarities of the English', in R. Miliband and J. Saville (eds), *The Socialist Register* (London, 1985); D. Blackbourn and G. Eley, *The Peculiarities of German History* (Oxford, 1984).
2   P. Vilar, *Spain: A Brief History* (Oxford, 1967), pp. 67, 69.
3   M. Tuñón de Lara, *Estudios de Historia contemporánea* (Barcelona, 1977), p. 98; *Historia y Realidad del Poder* (Madrid, 1967), p. 83.
4   Tuñón de Lara, *Estudios*, pp. 102–9.
5   R. Herr, 'Spain', in D. Spring, ed. *European Landed Elites in the Nineteenth Century* (Baltimore, 1977), pp. 108–10; 'El significado de la desamortización', Moneda y Crédito 131, 1974 p. 85.
6   D. Ringrose, 'Ciudad, país y revolución burguesa', in *Madrid en la sociedad*, vol. 1, pp. 319–23.
7   Blackbourn and Eley, *The Peculiarities*.
8   ibid., pp. 54–5, 59, 81, 86–7, 144.
9   ibid., pp. 170, 230.
10 W. Reddy, *Money and Liberty in Modern Europe* (Cambridge, 1987), p. 5.
11 A. García Sanz, 'Introductión', in A. Garcia Sanz and R. Garrabou, *Historia agraria de la España contemporánea* (Barcelona, 1985), p. 14.
12 B. Clavero et al., *Estudios de la revolución burguesa en España* (Madrid, 1979), pp. 41–3.
13 There were two brief periods, 1812–14 and 1820–3, during which Spain was governed under the Constitution of Cadiz before constitutional government was definitively established in 1833. For the next ninety years, until the beginning of the dictatorship of Primo de Rivera in September 1923, there was always some form of representative government, generally with the very narrow property-based franchise typical of nineteenth-century liberalism. France enjoyed representative government from 1830 on, but one might question the twenty years of the Second Empire.
14 P. Preston, *The Coming of the Spanish Civil War* (London, 1983), p. 25.

A Century of Dynamism

1   *Selections from the Letters of Robert Southey*, (New York, 1977), vol. 1, p. 23.

An Evolving Economy

1   L. Prados de la Escosura, *De Imperio a Nación. Crecimiento y Atraso Económico en España, 1780–1930* (Madrid, 1988), pp. 20, 241.

2   N. Sánchez Albornoz, *España Hace un Siglo: Una Economía Dual* (Madrid, 1977), p. 23.

3   Prados de la Escosura, *De Imperio*, p. 30.

4   J. Nadal, 'Spain, 1830–1914', in C. Cipolla (ed.), *Fontana Economic History of Europe*, (London, 1973), vol. 4, pt 2, p. 617.

5   J. Fontana, 'Colapso y transformación del comercio exterior español entre 1792 y 1827', in *Moneda y Credito*, 1970.

6   G. Anes, 'La agricultura española desde comienzos del siglo XIX hasta 1868: algunos problemas', in *Ensayos sobre la Economía Española a Mediados del Siglo XIX* (Madrid, 1970), p. 257.

7   F. Heran, 'Tierra y parentesco en el campo sevillano. La revolución agricola del siglo XIX' in R. Garrabou and J. Sanz (eds), *Historia Agraria de la España Contemporánea: Expansión y Crisis* (Barcelona, 1985), p. 473.

8   N. Sánchez Albornoz, 'Castilla en el siglo XIX: una involución económica', in *Revista de Occidente*, October 1982, pp. 37, 40.

9   D. Ringrose, *Madrid and the Spanish Economy, 1560–1850* (Berkeley, 1983), p. 310.

10   ibid., p. 327.

11   T. Kaplan, *Anarchists of Andalucia, 1868–1903* (Princeton, 1977), p. 47.

12   R. Garrabou and J. Sanz, 'Introducción', in Garrabou and Sanz (eds), *Historia Agraria*, p. 186.

13   Prados de la Escosura, *De Imperio*, pp. 132–5.

14   Nadal, 'Spain', p. 614.

15   Prados de la Escosura, *De Imperio*, pp. 170–5.

16   D. Ringrose, *Transportation and Stagnation, 1750–1850* (Durham, 1970), pp. xxiv, 133, 141.

17   J. Nadal, 'Spain, 1830–1914', in C. Copolla (ed.), *Fontana Economic History, Europe*, vol. 4, pt 4 (London, 1973), p. 597; L. Jenks, *The Migration of British Capital before 1875* (London, 1963), pp. 174–5.

18   M.T. Costa, *Financión Exterior del Capitalismo Español en el Siglo XIX* (Barcelona, 1983), p. 162.

19   Cited in R. Cameron, *France and the Economic Development of Europe* (Princeton, 1961), p. 212.

20   G. Tortella, 'An interpretation of economic stagnation in nineteenth century Spain', in *Historia Iberica*, 1973, p. 131.

21   Garcia, Sanz and Garrabou, 'Introducción', p. 55.

22   C. Harvey, *The Río Tinto Company, 1873–1954* (Penzance, 1981), pp. 117–23, 314.

23   Prados de la Escosura, *De Imperio*, p. 197.

24   González Portilla, *La Formación de la Sociedad Capitalista en el País Vasco, 1876–1913* (San Sebastián, 1981), vol. 1, p. 46.

25   S. Ben–Ami, *Fascism From Above. The Dictatorship of Primo de Rivera in Spain* (Oxford, 1983), pp. 240–1.

26   See my article, 'Oil companies and governments: the nationalization of the petroleum industry in Spain, 1927-1930', in *Journal of Contemporary History*, October 1980.

27 Fontana and Nadal, 'Spain', p. 474.
28 Ben-Ami, *Fascism From Above*, p. 313.
29 ibid., p. 280.

Men, Women and Children

1 J. Rodríguez Osuna, *Población y Territorio en España* (Madrid, 1985), p. 26.
2 V. Pérez Moreda, *La Crisis de la Mortalidad en la España Interior* (Madrid, 1980), p. 117.
3 ibid., p. 128.
4 J. Sánchez Jiménez, 'La población, el campo y las ciudades', in *Historia de España*, vol. 37 (Madrid, 1984), p. 189.
5 Pérez Moreda, *La Crisis*, pp. 146–67, 420–2.
6 J. Nadal, *La Población Española* (Barcelona, 1976), p. 203.
7 ibid., p. 204.
8 V. Cabezas de Herrera y Fernández, 'El cumplimiento de los preceptos religiosos en Madrid (1885–1932)', in *Hispania*, 1985, pp. 114–16.
9 Cited in J. Diez Nicolás and J.M. de Miguel, *El Control de la Natalidad en España* (Barcelona, 1981), p. 31.
10 M. Livi Bacci, 'Fertility and nuptiality changes in Spain from the late eighteenth century to the early twentieth century', in *Population Studies*, 1968, pp. 222–4.
11 ibid., pp. 214–22.
12 G. Scanlon, *La Polémica Feminista en la España Contemporánea, (1868–1974)* (Madrid, 1976), p. 123.
13 Archivo Diocesano de Ciudad Rodrigo, Legajo 47, Expediente 2632.
14 S. Tartilán, *Páginas para la Educación Popular* (Madrid, 1877), p. 250.
15 G. McDonogh, 'Good Families: a social history of power in industrial Barcelona', PhD. thesis, Johns Hopkins University, 1981, pp. 110–58, 517–25.
16 G. González Arranz, *Memorias del Alcalde de Roa, 1788–1840* (Madrid, 1935), pp. 24–6, 62, 69–70, 93.
17 J. Castro y Serrano, *Cartas Trascendentales* (Madrid, 1862), pp. 207–8.
18 P. Laslett, 'Family and household as work group and kin areas in traditional Europe compared', in R. Wall, J. Robin and P. Laslett (eds), *Family Forms in Historic Europe* (Cambridge, 1983), p. 529.
19 R. Behar, *Santa María del Monte* (Princeton, 1986), p. 105.
20 W.A. Douglass, 'The Basque stem family household: myth or reality?', in *Journal of Family History*, no. 13, 1988, pp. 75–89.
21 D. Rehr, 'Household and family on the Castilian Meseta. The Province of Cuenca, 1750–1970', in *Journal of Family History*, no. 13, 1988, pp. 59–74.
22 J.A. Martínez Carrión, 'Peasant household formation and the organization of rural labor in the valley of the Segura during the nineteenth century', in ibid., pp. 91–109.
23 Scanlon, *Polémica*, pp. 18–20.
24 Tartilán, *Páginas*, pp. 9–10, 190–2, 233.
25 P. Mérimée, *Viajes a España* (Madrid, 1988), p. 255.
26 M. Izard, *Industrialización y Obrerismo* (Barcelona, 1973), p. 74.
27 R. M. Capel Martínez, *El trabajo y la educación de la mujer en España 1900–1930* (Madrid, 1986), pp. 169–70.

28　P. Ratcliffe, 'Carmen revisited: the cigarette makers of Gijón, 1890–1930' (unpublished paper), pp. 1–9.

29　ibid., 150–9; C. Morange, 'De manola a obrera', in *Estudios de Historia Social*, nos. 12–13, 1980, pp. 307–21; S. Vallejo Fernandez, 'Las cigarreras de la Fábrica Nacional de Tabacos de Madrid', in *Madrid en la sociedad del Siglo XIX*, vol.2, pp. 135–50.

30　Capel Martínez, *Trabajo y la educación*, p. 194.

31　G. Nielfa Cristobal, 'Las dependientas de comercio: un ejemplo peculiar de trabajo "feminino" en Madrid', in *La mujer en la historia de España* (Madrid, 1986), pp. 159–76

32　Scanlon, *La Polémica*, p. 74.

33　Capel Martínez, *El Trabajo y la Educación de la Mujer en España, 1900–1930* (Madrid, 1986), pp. 424–8.

34　*El Adelanto*, June 5, 1890.

35　P. Baroja, *El Arbol de la Ciencia* (Madrid, 1978), pp. 213, 219.

36　Capel Martínez, *El trabajo y la educación*, pp. 271–5; Scanlon, *La Polémica*, p. 111.

37　S. Fernández Arlaud, 'La emigración española a America durante el reinado de Isabel II', in *Estudios sobre la España liberal, 1808–1848* (Madrid, 1973), p. 427.

38　M.X. Rodríguez Galdo, *Crisis Agrarias y Crecimiento Económico en Galicia en el Siglo XIX* (La Coruña, 1981), pp. 81–97.

39　Nadal, *La Población*, pp. 184–96.

40　ibid., pp. 185–6.

41　ibid., 209–14.

42　B. Lozano, 'The Andalucia–Hawaii–California Migration', in *Comparative Studies in Society and History*, April 1981.

43　Cited in Rodríguez Osuna, *Población*, p. 97.

44　D. Ringrose, *Madrid and the Spanish Economy, 1560–1850* (Berkeley, 1983), pp. 34–57.

45　J. P. Fusi, *Política Obrera en El País Vasco* (Madrid, 1979), pp. 33.

46　ibid., pp. 43–7.

47　S. Juliá, *Madrid, 1931–1934. De la Fiesta Popular a la Lucha de Clases* (Madrid, 1984), p. 56.

48　*El Socialista*, October 11, 1923.

49　A. Shubert, *The Road to Revolution in Spain* (Urbana–Champaign, 1987), p. 77. For a similar situation in the Vizcayan mines see Fusi, *Política Obrera*, pp. 33–8.

50　Cited in C. Diez de Baldeón, 'Barrios obreros en el Madrid del siglo XIX', in *Madrid en la Sociedad del Siglo XIX* (Madrid, 1986), p. 122.

51　A. de Llano, *Hogar y Patria* (Oviedo, 1906), p. 12.

52　Diez de Baldeón, 'Barrios obreros'.

53　Shubert, *The Road*, pp. 82–5.

54　D. Velez, 'Late nineteenth-century Spanish progressivism. Arturo Soria's linear city', *Journal of Urban History*, February 1983, pp. 133–4.

55　P. Caraso Soto, *Pauperismo y Revolución Burguesa (Burgos, 1750–1900)* (Valladolid, 1987), p. 639.

56　J. Townsend, *A Journey Through Spain*, (London, 1797), vol. 2, pp. 8–9.

57　Sociedad Matritense de los Amigos del País, *Memorias sobre la Extinción de la Mendicidad* (Madrid, 1850), pp. 128–9; R. Mesonero Romanos, *Escenas Matritenses* (Madrid, 1967), vol. 2, pp. 205–6; E. Canal y Migolla, *Trabajos municipales*,

(Seville, nd), p. ix; Canal y Migolla, *La Mendicidad en Sevilla* (Seville, 1900), pp. 9–10; *Memoria de la Real Asociación de Beneficencia Domiciliaria* (Madrid, 1864), p. 7.

58 C. Arenal, *La Beneficencia, la Filantropía y la Caridad* (Madrid, 1861), p. 163.

59 *Reglamento de la Real Asociación de Beneficencia-Cocina Económica de Oviedo* (Oviedo, 1904).

60 C. Arenal, *El Visitador del Pobre* (Madrid, 1863), pp. 92–3, 116–19, 205–6; Arenal, *El Pauperismo* (Madrid, 1897), vol. 1, pp. 238-9, 306–19.

61 Arenal, *Cartas a un Señor* (Madrid, 1880), p. 72.

62 *Reglamento Provisional del Asilo de Mendicidad de San Bernardino* (Madrid, 1836).

63 *Reglamento de la Real Asociación de Beneficencia-Cocina.*

64 F. Lannon, *Privilege, Persecution and Prophecy. The Catholic Church in Spain, 1875–1975* (Oxford, 1987), p. 63

65 A. Balbín de Unquera, *Reseña histórica y Teórica de la Beneficencia* (Madrid, 1862), pp. 226–7; Sociedad Matritense, *Memorias*, pp. 99–108.

66 Arenal, *Beneficencia*, pp. 213–23.

67 Mesonero Romanos, *Nuevo Manual de Madrid* (Madrid, 1967), p. 436; Real Asociación de Beneficencia Domiciliaria, *Memoria* (Madrid, 1864).

68 Sociedad Matritense, *Memorias*, pp. 15, 77.

69 Arenal, *Cartas*, pp. 9–10, 27–8, 439–40.

The Land

The Creation of Private Property

1 S. Moxó, *La Disolución del Antiguo Régimen en España* (Madrid, 1965), p. 58

2 Cited in ibid., p. 106.

Landowners

1 E. Malefakis, *Agrarian Reform and Peasant Revolution in Spain* (New Haven, 1980), p. 71.

2 See below pages 92–3

3 J. Millán Chivite, 'El final del más poderoso señorío andaluz: el ducado de Medinasidonia', in *Actas del III Coloquio de Historia de Andalucía. Historia Contemporánea* (Cordoba, 1985), vol. 1, pp. 77–90.

4 I. Atienza Hernández and R. Mata Olmo. 'La quiebra de la Casa de Osuna', in *Moneda y Crédito*, 1986, pp. 73, 76.

5 Atienza Hernández, *Aristocracia, Poder y Riqueza en la España Moderna: La Casa de Osuna Siglos XV-XIX* (Madrid, 1987), p. 374.

6 J.A. Martínez Andaluz, 'Préstamo privado y élites en el Madrid isabelino', in *Madrid en la Sociedad del Siglo XIX* (Madrid, 1986), vol. 1, p. 500. On the Marquis of Alcañíces see J.A. Carmona Pidal, 'Aproximación a un noble madrileño', in ibid., pp. 505–13.

7 A. Bahamonde, 'Crisis de la nobleza de cuna y consolidación burguesa (1840–1880) in ibid., pp. 325–74.

8 G. Cortázar, *Alfonso XIII: Hombre de Negocios* (Madrid, 1986).

9 R. de Mesonero Romanos, *Obras*, vol. 1 (Madrid, 1967), pp. 119–23.

10   M. Tuñón de Lara, *Estudios sobre el Siglo XIX Español* (Madrid, 1971), p. 196.

11   G. Cortázar, 'La saga de los Figueroa. Una familia de elite de la Restauración'. Paper presented at the annual meeting of the Society for Spanish and Portuguese Historical Studies, April 1988. I want to thank Professor Cortázar for allowing me to cite his paper.

12   J. Becarud, 'La nobleza Española desde Alfonso XII hasta 1931', in *Les Elites Espagnole a L'Epoque Contemporaine* (Pau, 1983), pp. 67–8.

13   ibid., pp. 67–76.

14   F. Fernández Córdova, *Mis Intimas Memorias* (Madrid, 1965), vol. 2, pp. 147–9.

15   ibid., pp. 147–8.

16   J.M. Jover, *Política, Diplomacia y Humanismo Popular* (Madrid, 1976), pp. 306–8.

17   Malefakis, *Agrarian Reform*, pp. 73–6.

18   F. Heran, *Tierra y Parentesco en el Campo Sevillano* (Madrid, 1980), p. 205.

19   G. Rueda, *La Desamortización de Mendizábal y Espartero en España* (Madrid, 1986), p. 159.

20   Rueda, *La Desamortización de Mendizábal y Espartero*, p. 40.

21   M. Artola, *Antiguo Régimen y Revolución Liberal* (Barcelona, 1978), p. 66.

22   G. Rueda, *La Desamortización de Mendizábal en Valladolid* (Valladolid, 1980), pp. 244–7.

23   J. Cruz Villalón, *Propiedad y Uso de la Tierra en la Baja Andalucía* (Madrid, 1980), pp. 106, 220.

24   J. Merino Navarro, *Notas sobre la desamortización en Extremadura* (Madrid, 1976), p. 77.

25   J. Fontana, 'La desamortización de Mendizábal y sus antecedentes', in *Historia agraria*, vol. 1, p. 233.

26   Heran, *Tierra y Parentesco*, p. 133.

27   ibid., pp. 134–5.

28   Rueda, *Valladolid*, pp. 256–303.

29   Ortega Canadel, *La Desamortización de Mendizábal y Madoz en Soria*, (Soria, 1982), p. 107.

30   Rueda, *La Desamortización de Mendizábal y Espartero*, pp. 172–4

31   ibid. p. 62.

32   R. Villares, *La Propiedad de la Tierra en Galicia, 1500–1936* (Madrid, 1982), pp. 155–6.

33   Rueda, *La Desamortización de Mendizábal y Espartero*, pp. 175–6.

34   R. Herr, 'El significado de la desamortización en España', *Moneda y Credito*, pp. 1974, p. 80.

35   Fontana, 'La desamortización', p. 244.

36   J. Vicens Vives, *Economic History of Spain* (Princeton, 1969), pp. 638–9.

37   J. Nadal, 'Spain, 1830–1914', in C. Cipolla (ed.), *The Fontana Economic History of Europe*, vol. 4, pt 2 (London, 1973), pp. 566–7.

38   Fontana, 'La desamortización', pp. 236–7.

39   R. Garrabou and J. Sanz (eds), *Historia Agraria de la España Contemporánea*, (Barcelona, 1985), vol. 2 pp. 186–7.

Rural Social Relations

1   E. Malefakis, *Agrarian Reform and Peasant Revolution in Spain* (New Haven, 1980), pp. 83–5.

2   A. M. Bernal, *La Lucha por la Tierra en la Crisis del Antiguo Regimen* (Madrid, 1979), pp. 362–3.

3   Cruz Villalón, *Propiedad y uso de la Tierra en la Baja Andalucía* (Madrid, 1980), pp. 278–85.

4   Malefakis, *Agrarian Reform*, pp. 90–1.

5   R. Robledo Hernández, 'Los arrendamientos castellanos antes y después de la crisis de fines del siglo XIX', in Garrabou and Sanz (eds), *Historia agrária*, vol. 2, p. 378.

6   Bernal, *La Lucha*, p. 367; Malefakis, *Agrarian Reform*, pp. 88–9.

7   F. Heran, *Tierra y Parentesco en el Campo Sevillano* (Madrid, 1980), pp. 165–6.

8   J. Mintz, *The Anarchists of Casas Viejas*, (Chicago, 1982), p. 35.

9   ibid., p. 57.

10 Bernal, *La Lucha*, pp. 392–3; Malefakis, *Agrarian Reform*, p. 111.

11 Bernal, *La Lucha*, pp. 407–5.

12 Mintz, *The Anarchists*, p. 48.

13 Reddy, *Money and Liberty in Modern Europe* (Cambridge, 1987), pp. 64–73.

14 Bernal, *La Lucha*, p. 400.

15 E. Camacho Rueda, *Propiedad y explotación agrarias en el Aljarife Sevillano* (Seville, 1984), pp. 111–14, 127–33.

16 Bernal, *La Lucha*, pp. 289–90.

17 Heran, *Tierra y parentesco*, p. 169. See also Bernal, *La Lucha*, pp. 272–3.

18 Bernal, *La Lucha*, p. 273.

19 ibid., pp. 297–300.

20 A. Balcells, *El Problema Agraria en Cataluña. La Cuestión Rabassaire* (Madrid, 1980), p. 73.

21 Bernal, 'La llamada crisis finisecular', in J. L. García Delgado (ed.), *La España de la Restauración* (Madrid, 1985), pp. 238–9.

22 Cited in J.J. Castillo, *Propietarios muy Pobres* (Madrid, 1979), p. 17.

23 Cited in ibid., p. 230.

24 F. Simón Segura, 'Aspectos del nivel de vida del campesinado español', *Hacienda Pública Española*, 1976, p. 234.

25 ibid., p. 242.

Social Conflict

1   J. Torras, *Liberalismo y Rebeldía Campesina, 1820–1823* (Barcelona, 1976), pp. 30–1.

2   García Sanz, *Desarrollo y Crisis del Antiguo Régimen en Castilla la Vieja, 1500–1814* (Madrid, 1977), pp. 449–51

3   E. Badosa i Coll, 'Procés d'una resisténcia pagesa. El poble de Navarcles contra el monestir de Sant Benet de Bagés, 1711–1835', in *Primer Colloqui d'Historia Agraria* (Valencia, 1983), p. 423.

4   J.M. Torras i Ribe, *Evolució Social i Economica d'una Familia Catalana de l'Antic Règim: Els Padro d'Igualada* (Barcelona, 1976), pp. 77–91.

5   R. Villares, *La Propiedad de la Tierra en Galicia, 1500–1936* (Madrid, 1982), p. 136.

6   M. Ardit Lucas, *Revolución Liberal y Revuelta Campesina, 1793–1840* (Madrid, 1977), pp. 115–18.

7   Cited in ibid., p. 47.

8   Cited in ibid., p. 225.

9   Cited in ibid., p. 253.

10   ibid., p. 282.

11   ibid., p. 300.

12   Torras, *Liberalismo*, pp. 107, 116.

13   P. Pascual i Domenech, 'Carlisme i societat rural: la Guerra del Set Anys a la Conca d'Odena', *Recerques*, 10, 1980, pp. 51–91.

14   V. Benítez Fernández, *Carlismo y Rebeldía Campesina. Un estudio sobre la conflictividad social en Cantabria durante la crisis final del Antiguo Régimen* (Madrid, 1988).

15   J. Coverdale, *The Basque Phase of Spain's First Carlist War* (Princeton, 1984), pp. 9, 257, 263.

16   Beltza, *Del Carlismo al Nacionalismo Burgués* (San Sebastian, 1978), pp. 12–14; Cited in Coverdale, *Basque Phase*, p. 257, fn. 4.

17   A. M. Bernal, *La Lucha por la Tierra en la Crisis del Antiguo Régimen* (Madrid, 1979), pp. 443–6

18   I. Moreno Navarro, *Propiedad, Clases Sociales y Hermandades en la Baja Andalucía* (Madrid, 1972), pp. 185–6.

19   Bernal, *La Lucha*, pp. 442, 450; R. Pérez del Alamo, *Apuntes Sobre Dos Revoluciones Andaluzas* (Madrid, 1971).

20   Bernal, *La Lucha*, p. 452.

21   Pérez Yruela, *La Conflictividad en la provincia de Córdoba, 1931–1936* (Madrid, 1974), p. 59.

22   E. Hobsbawm, *Primitive Rebels* (London, 1959), pp. 90–2.

23   R. Carr, *Spain, 1808–1975* (Oxford, 1982), pp. 443–5.

24   V. Pérez Díaz, *Pueblo y Clases Sociales en el Campo Español* (Madrid, 1974), pp. 7–35; Pérez Yruela, *Conflictividad Campesina*, pp. 64–7.

25   This case was brought to my attention by my wife, who is from Saelices and whose grandfather was one of the defendants in the case. I want to thank her brother, Agustín Palacios, and Salustiano de Paz, of the Faculty of Law of the University of Salamanca, for providing me with the text of the Supreme Court decision. All quotations are from that text which is in *Colección Legislativa* (Madrid, 1930), pp. 1007–24.

26   E. Malefakis, *Agrarian Reform and Peasant Revolution in Spain* (New Haven, 1980), p. 235.

27   G. Collier, *Socialists of Rural Andalucia* (Stanford, 1987), pp. 89–108.

28   P. Preston, 'The Agrarian War in the South', in P. Preston (ed.) *Revolution and War in Spain* (London, 1984), p. 175.

29   Cited in A. Balcells, *El Problema Agraria en Cataluña. La Cuestión Rabassaire* (Madrid, 1980), p. 174.

30   Pérez Yruela, *Conflictividad*, p. 206, fn 8

Cities and Towns

Elites and White Collars

1   G. W. McDonogh, 'Good Families: a social history of power in industrial Barcelona', PhD thesis, Johns Hopkins University, 1981, p. 3.

2 ibid., pp. 488–9.
3 F. Erice, *La Burguesía Industrial Asturiana*, (Gijón, 1980), pp. 109–40.
4 McDonogh, 'Good Families', p. 301.
5 ibid., p. 346.
6 Cited in ibid., p. 409.
7 R. Carr, *Spain 1808–1975* (Oxford, 1982), p. 283.
8 F. Fernández Bastarreche, *El Ejército español en el Siglo XIX* (Madrid, 1978), p. 121.
9 D. Headrick, *Ejército y Política en España, 1866–1898* (Madrid, 1981) pp. 58–62.
10 T. Hughes, *Revelations of Spain in 1845* (London, 1845), p. 267; Cited in Carr, *Spain*, p. 231.
11 S. Payne, *Politics and the Military in Modern Spain*, (Stanford, 1967), pp. 126–7.
12 J.M. Jover, *Política, Diplomacia y Humanismo Popular en la España del Siglo XIX* (Madrid, 1976), pp. 236–40.
13 Cited in ibid., pp. 241–2.
14 Carr, *Spain*, p. 287.
15 A. Flores, *Ayer, Hoy y Mañana*, (Madrid, 1863), vol. 4, pp. 275–8.
16 A. Bahamonde Magro and J. Toro Mérida, *Burguesía, Especulación y Cuestión Social en el Madrid del Siglo XIX* (Madrid, 1978), pp. 202–3; M.T. Pérez Picazo, *Oligarquía Urbana y Campesinado en Murcia, 1872–1902* (Murcia, 1979), pp. 143–50.
17 M. Bald i Lacomba, *Profesores y estudiantes en la España romántica: la Universidad de Valencia, 1786–1843* (Valencia, 1984), 82; M. Peset y J.L. Peset, *La Universidad española (Siglos XVIII y XIX)*, (Madrid, 1974), 528.
18 G. Borrow, *The Bible in Spain* (London, 1985), pp. 110–11.
19 D. Ringrose, *Imperio y peninsula* (Madrid, 1987), pp. 161–2.
20 A. Burdick, 'The Madrid writer in Spanish society, 1833–43', PhD Thesis, University of California at San Diego, 1983.
21 Flores, *Ayer*, vol. 4, p. 11.
22 Carr, *Spain*, p. 167.
23 Flores, *Ayer*, vol. 4, pp. 7–8.
24 Romanones, Count, *Notas de una vida* (Madrid, nd), vol. 1, p. 125.
25 *Los Españoles Pintados por sí mismos* (Madrid, 1851), pp. 44–7.

Working Class Formation

1 P. Molas Ribalta, *Los Gremios Barceloneses del Siglo XVIII* (Madrid, 1970), pp. 186–96.
2 ibid., p. 44; Molas Ribalta, *Economía y Societat al Segle XVIII* Barcelona, 1975), p. 16; A.M. Bernal, A. Collantes and A. Garcia Bacquero, 'Sevilla de los gremios a la industrialización', *Estudios de Historia Social*, 5–6, 1978, pp. 269–70.
3 ibid., p. 16.
4 V.M. Santos Isern, *Cara y Cruz de la Sedería Valenciana*, (Valencia, 1981), pp. 118–19.
5 G. Sheridan, 'Household and craft in an industrializing economy: the case of the silk weavers of Lyons' in J. Merriman (ed.), *Consciousness and Class Experience in Nineteenth Century Europe*, pp. 107–28.
6 R. Aminzade, 'Reinterpreting capitalist industrialization: a study of nineteenth century France', *Social History*, October 1984, pp. 330–1.
7 M. Izard, *El Segle XIX. Burgesos i Proletaris*, (Barcelona, 1978), pp. 64–5.

8   W. Lazonick, 'Industrial relations and technical change: the case of the self-acting mule', *Cambridge Journal of Economics*, 1979, pp. 231–62.

9   P. Gabriel, 'La població obrera catalana. Una població industrial?', *Estudios de Historia Social*, 32–3, 1985, pp. 191-260.

10 See below, pp. 184–9.

11 I. Terrades Saborit, *La Colonia Industrial com a Particularisme Historic: L'Ametlla de Merola* (Barcelona, 1979), pp. 40–3.

12 ibid., pp. 157, 164.

13 J.C. Ullman, *The Tragic Week* (Cambridge, 1968). See below, pp. 300.

14 G. Meaker, *The Revolutionary Left in Spain* (Stanford, 1974).

15 W. Bernecker, *Colectividades y Revolución Social* (Barcelona, 1982).

16 S. Hickey, *Workers in Imperial Germany: The Miners of the Ruhr* (Oxford, 1985); C. Kerr and A. Siegel, 'The inter-industry propensity to strike: an international comparison', in A. Kornhauser (ed.), *Roots of Industrial Conflict* (New York, 1954), pp. 189–212.

17 Dirección General de Minas, Montes y Agricultura, *Informe Relativo al Estado Económico de las Minas de España y la Situación de los Obreros*, (Madrid, 1911).

18 Civil Governor to Minister of the Interior, July 4, 1923, Gobernación, Legajo 58A, Expediente 16, Archivo Histórico Nacional; *Avance* (Oviedo), September 22, 1933.

19 R. Alvarez Buylla, *Observaciones Prácticas Sobre la Minería Carbonera de Asturias*, (Oviedo, 1861)

20 Fondos del Sindicato Minero Asturiano, Fundación Francisco Largo Caballero, Madrid.

21 A Pestaña, *Trayectoría Sindicalista* (Madrid, 1974), pp. 142–3.

22 See above, chapter 2.

23 D. Ibarruri, *They Shall Not Pass* (New York, 1966), pp. 19–20.

24 J.P. Fusi, *El País Vasco: Pluralismo y Nacionalidad* (Madrid, 1984), pp. 43–6.

25 L. Castells, *Modernización y Dinámica Política en la Sociedad Guipuzcoana de la Restauración, 1876–1915* (Madrid, 1987).

26 S. Juliá, *Madrid, 1931–1934: De la Fiesta Popular a la Lucha de Clases*, (Madrid, 1984), p. 71.

27 ibid., pp. 78–80.

28 ibid., pp. 172–90, 258–63.

29 I. Katznelson and A. Zolberg, *Working Class Formation* (Princeton, 1986), p. 14.

30 V. Lidtke, *The Alternative Culture. Socialist Labor in Imperial Germany* (New York, 1985).

31 D. Geary, *European Labour Protest, 1848–1939* (London, 1981), p. 103.

32 E. Shorter and C. Tilly, *Strikes in France, 1830–1968* (London, 1974).

Working Class Experience

1   For discussions of the advantages and disadvantages of working class autobiography as a source see: D. Vincent, *Bread, Knowledge and Freedom* (London, 1981); J. Burnet, *Useful Toil* (London, 1971); A. Kelly, *The German Worker*, (Berkeley, Calif., 1987); M.J. Maynes, 'Gender and class in working women's autobiographies', in R.E. Joires and M.J. Maynes, (eds.), *German Women in the 18th and 19th Centuries* (Bloomington, 1986).

2   F. Largo Caballero, *Mis Recuerdos*, (Mexico, 1954), p. 30.

3   M. Vigil, 'Recuerdos de un octogenario', *Estudios de Historia Social*, vols 18–19, 1981; pp. 327, 250.
4   A. Pestaña, 'Lo que aprendí en la vida, in A. Elorza (ed.), *Trayectoria Sindicalista* (Madrid, 1976), pp. 99, 104, 152.
5   Largo Caballero, *Mis Recuerdos*, p. 32.
6   Pestaña,'Lo que aprendí', pp. 143–4.
7   Vigil, 'Recuerdos', pp. 323–4; Ibarruri, *They Shall Not Pass* (New York, 1966), p. 62.
8   Pestaña, 'Lo que aprendí', p. 98.
9   Largo Caballero, *Mis Recuerdos*, pp. 37–8.
10 D. Ibarruri, *They Shall Not*, pp. 49–50.
11 Vigil, 'Recuerdos', p. 321.
12 Pestaña, 'Lo que aprendí', pp. 81–2, 140, 143.
13 Ibarruri, *They Shall Not*, pp. 44–5.
14 Pestaña, 'Lo que aprendí', pp. 85–7
15 L. Carro, 'Escritos autobiográficos', *Estudios de Historia Social*, vol. 32–3, 1985, p. 339; Largo Caballero, *Mis Recuerdos*, pp. 28-32; Pestaña, 'Lo que aprendí', pp. 84–90.
16 Vigil, 'Recuerdos', p. 321.
17 Ibarruri, *They Shall Not*, p. 53.
18 Largo Caballero, *Mis Recuerdos*, p. 28; Pestaña, 'Lo que aprendí', pp. 80–1.
19 Carro, 'Escritos', p. 339.
20 Ibarruri, *They Shall Not*, pp. 65–6, 80.
21 ibid., pp. 65–6, 80.
22 Pestaña, 'Lo que aprendí', p. 86.
23 Ibarruri, *They Shall Not*, pp. 76, 108.
24 ibid., pp. 59–60.
25 ibid., pp. 61–2, 73, 84. Emphasis added.
26 ibid., pp. 62–3.
27 Carro, 'Escritos', p. 340.
28 Pestaña, 'Lo que aprendí', p. 80.
29 Vigil, 'Recuerdos', p. 319.
30 Ibarruri, *They Shall Not*, pp. 48, 61.
31 Carro, 'Escritos', p. 339.
32 Largo Caballero, *Mis recuerdos*, pp. 35–6.
33 Pestaña, 'Lo que aprendí', pp. 146–8.
34 Vigil, 'Recuerdos', pp. 323–8.

Identities

The Church, Religion and Belief

1   W.J. Callahan, *Church, Society and Politics in Spain, 1750-1874*, (Cambridge, 1984), p. 45
2   ibid, p. 49.
3   Spain. Congreso de los Diputados. *Diario de las Sesiones*, April 6, 1837.
4   J. Longares Alonso, *Política y Religión en Barcelona, 1833-1843* (Madrid, 1976), p. 287.

5   E. Sainz Repa, 'La religiosidad en la Rioja durante el siglo XIX', in *Berceo*, 1972, pp. 178–80.

6   J. Saez Marín, *Datos sobre la Iglesia Española Contemporánea, 1768–1868* (Madrid, 1975), p. 258.

7   F. Lannon, *Privilege, Persecution and Prophecy. The Catholic Church in Spain, 1875–1975* (Oxford, 1987), pp. 70–1

8   R. Sarabia, *España, es Católica?* (Madrid, 1939), pp. 129–32.

9   C. Martí, *L'Esglesia de Barcelona, 1850–1857*, (Barcelona, 1985) vol. 2, p. 485; J. Romero Maura, *La Rosa de Fuego* (Barcelona, 1975), p. 525.

10   J. Cuenca Toribio, *Aproximación a la Historia de la Iglesia Contemporánea en España* (Madrid, 1978), p. 292.

11   Martí, *Esglesia*, vol. 1, pp. 47–8.

12   Callahan, *Church*, p. 115. See pp. 158–9.

13   Martí, *Esglesia*, vol. 1, pp. 48–9.

14   Callahan, *Church*, p. 210.

15   M. Revuelta González, 'Clero viejo y clero nuevo en el siglo XIX', in *Estudios históricos sobre la Iglesia española contemporanea* (Madrid, 1979), p. 163.

16   Martí, *Esglesia*, vol. 1, p. 127.

17   Callahan, *Church*, p. 233; Sainz Repa, 'Religiosidad', pp. 176–7.

18   Lannon, *Privilege*, p. 93.

19   J. Cuenca Toribio, *Sociedad y Clero en la España del Siglo XIX* (Córdoba, 1980), pp. 329–30.

20   Revuelta González, 'Clero Viejo', p. 176.

21   García de Cortázar, 'La Iglesia Española de la Restauración: definición de objectivos y prácticas religiosas', in *Letras de Deusto*, July–December, 1978, p. 20.

22   Cited in. P.R. Santidrián, *El Padre Sarabia Escribe su Historia* (Madrid, 1963), pp. 31–2; Sarabia, *España*, p. 169.

23   J. Ordóñez Márquez, *La Apostasia de las Masas* (Madrid, 1968), pp. 218–21.

24   A. Borras i Feliu, 'La librería religiosa de Barcelona', in *Traditió, Krisis, Renovation* (Marburg, 1976), pp. 380–2.

25   L. Higuerela, *Clero de Toledo, 1820–1823* (Madrid, 1979), p. 78.

26   Callahan, *Church*, pp. 194–5.

27   Lannon, *Privilege*, p. 131.

28   F. García de Cortázar, 'La Iglesia Española', p. 10.

29   J.A. Portero, *Púlpito e Ideología en la España del Siglo XIX* (Zaragoza, 1978).

30   ibid., p. 231.

31   Lannon, 'Basque challenge', pp. 31–5. Martí describes a similar situation in the Barcelona seminary in the 1850s. *Esglesia*, vol. 1, pp. 33–44.

32   Lannon, 'The socio-political role of the Spanish church: a case study', *Journal of Contemporary History*, April 1979, pp. 204–8.

33   Martí, *Esglesia*, vol. 1, p. 222.

34   Callahan, *Church*, p. 229.

35   Lannon, *Privilege*, p. 160.

36   Cited in D. Benavides, *El Fracaso del Catolicismo Español* (Madrid, 1970), p. 85.

37   M. Arboleya, *El Caso de Asturias* (Barcelona, 1918), pp. 41, 63.

38   Benavides, *Fracaso*, p. 57.

39   Ordóñez Márquez, *Apostasia*, p. 217.

40   Callahan, *Church*, p. 244.

41   M. Saez de Ocariz, 'El cumplimiento pascual en la Ciudad de Logroño a lo largo

del siglo XIX', *Berceo*, 1965, pp. 275–82; Lisón Tolosana, *Belmonte de los Caballeros* (Oxford, 1966), pp. 284–5.

42 F. Peiró, *El Problema Religioso-Social de España* (Madrid, 1936), p. 13.

43 García de Cortázar, 'Iglesia', p. 32; Moreno Navarro, *Propiedad, Clases Sociales y Hermandades en la Baja Andalucia*, p. 295.

44 J. Mintz, *The Anarchists of Casas Viejas* (Chicago, 1982), pp. 68–70.

45 Ordóñez Márquez, *Apostasia*, p. 87, fn. 31.

46 W. Christian, *Person and God in a Spanish Valley* (New York, 1972), p. 180–1.

47 M. Blinkhorn, 'War on two fronts: politics and society in Navarre, 1931–1936', in P. Preston, (ed.), *Revolution and War* (London, 1984), pp. 64–5.

48 Martí, *Esglesia*, vol. 1, pp. 41, 61.

49 J. Massot i Muntaner, *Esglesia i Societat a la Mallorca del Segle XX*, (Barcelona, 1977), pp. 311–21.

50 Callahan, *Church*, pp. 233–5.

51 Christian, *Person*, pp. 88–93.

52 Mintz, *Anarchists*, pp. 64–6.

53 Martí, *Esglesia*, vol. 1, pp. 196–7; B. Bennassar, *Los Españoles* (Barcelona, 1978), pp. 94–6.

54 Mintz, *Anarchists*, pp. 361–3.

55 J. Caro Baroja, *Introducción a una Historia Contemporánea del Anticlericalismo Español* (Madrid, 1980); B. Hortelano, *Memorias de Benito Hortelano* (Madrid, 1936), p. 99.

56 Callahan, *Church*, p. 134.

57 J. Ullman, *The Tragic Week* (Cambridge, 1968), p. 227.

The Limits of the State

1 C. Tilly, *Big Structures; Large Processes; Huge Comparisons* (New York, 1984), p. 10.

2 Cited in R. Carr, *Spain, 1808–1975* (Oxford, 1982), p. 62.

3 ibid., p. 61.

4 D. López Garrido, *La Guardia Civil y los orígenes del Estado centralista* (Barcelona, 1982), p. 37.

5 E. García de Enterria, *La Administración Española* (Madrid, 1961), p. 96.

6 María Cruz Mina Apat, *Fueros y Revolución Liberal en Navarra* (Madrid, 1981), p. 221.

7 N. Sales, *Sobre Esclavos, Reclutas y Mercaderes de Quintos* (Barcelona, 1974), p. 214.

8 Cited in M.T. Pérez Picazo, *Oligarquía Urbana y Campesinado en Murcia, 1872–1902* (Murcia, 1979), p. 296.

9 Sales, *Sobre esclavos*, p. 221.

10 D. Headrick, *Ejército y política en España, 1866–1898* (Madrid, 1981), p. 103.

11 J.C. Ullman, *The Tragic Week* (Cambridge, 1968), pp. 135–6.

12 M. Ballbé, *Orden Publico y Militarismo en la España Constitucional* (Madrid, 1983), p. 21.

13 ibid., p. 22; J. Lleixà, *Cien años de militarismo en España*, (Barcelona, 1986), p. 13.

14 Ballbé, *Orden público*, p. 40.

15 Cited in ibid., p. 112.

16   ibid., p. 210.

17   C. Boyd, *Praetorian Politics in Liberal Spain* (Chapel Hill, 1979), p. 64.

18   Cited in Ballbé, *Orden público*, p. 279.

19   J.S. Pérez Garzón, *Milicia Naciónal y Revolución Burguesa. El Prototipo Madrileño, 1808–1874* (Madrid, 1978), p. 107.

20   ibid., p. 520.

21   López Garrido, *Guardia Civil*, p. 89.

22   Cited in ibid., pp. 189–90. Emphasis added.

23   ibid., p. 102.

24   ibid., pp. 166–6.

25   Cited in ibid., p. 164.

26   Lleixá, *Cien años*, p. 69.

27   E. Weber, *Peasants into Frenchmen* (Stanford, 1976), pp. 70–72, 334.

28   A. Balcells, *Historia Contemporánea de Cataluña* (Barcelona, 1983), p. 171.

29   Weber, *Peasants*, p. 89.

30   G. McDonogh, 'Good families. a social history of power in industrial Barcelona', PhD thesis, Johns Hopkins University, 1982, pp. 359–75.

31   J. Coroleu e Inglada, *Memorias de un menestral de Barcelona, 1792–1854* (Barcelona, 1946), pp. 219, 269–70, 295; C. Roure, *Recuerdos de mi larga vida*, (Barcelona, 1925), vol. 2, p. 9.

32   J. Benet and C. Martí, *Barcelona a Mitjan Segle XIX* (Barcelona, 1976), p. 171.

33   C. Tilly, *Big Structures; Large Processes; Huge Comparisons* (New York, 1989), pp. 9–11.

34   J. Tusell, *Oligarquía y caciquismo en Andalucia, 1890–1923* (Barcelona, 1976), p. 31.

35   ibid., p. 42.

36   J. Romero Maura, 'El caciquismo: tentativa de conceptualización' in *Revista de Occidente*, 127 1973, p. 39.

37   F. de León y Castillo, *Mis tiempos* (Madrid, 1921), pp. 45–6.

38   Varela Ortega, *Los amigos políticos* (Madrid, 1979), p. 417.

39   Romero Maura, 'El Caciquismo', pp. 33–4.

40   Tusell, *Oligarquía*, p. 75.

41   E. Azcoaga, 'Las misiones pedagógicas', *Revista de Occidente*, November 1981, pp. 226–7.

42   G. Collier, *Socialists of Rural Andalusia* (Stanford, 1987), pp. 89–108.

43   M. Pérez Yruela, *La Conflictividad*, pp. 201–6.

Communities

1   J. Blum, 'The internal structure and polity of the European village community from the 15th to the 19th century', *Journal of Modern History*, 1971, p. 542.

2   R. Behar, *Santa María del Monte* (Princeton, 1986), p. 137

3   ibid., pp. 156–7.

4   ibid., p. 230.

5   ibid., pp. 257–8.

6   ibid., p. 167.

7   ibid., p. 164.

8   I. Moreno Navarro, *Propiedad, Clases Sociales y Hermandades En la Baja Andalucía* (Madrid, 1972), p. 298.

9   F. Lannon, *Privilege: Persecution and Prophecy. The Catholic Church in Spain, 1875–1975* (Oxford, 1987), p. 27.
10 S. Freeman, 'Faith and fashion in religion: notes on the observation of observance', *Peasant Studies* (Spring, 1978), p. 114.
11 *Revista Minera*, 1883, p. 388.
12 Cited in Ardit Lucas, *Revolución Liberal y Revuelta Campesina, 1793–1840* (Madrid, 1977), p. 47
13 See E.P. Thompson, 'The moral economy of the English crowd in the 18th century', *Past and Present*, 1971, pp. 76–136.
14 Oviedo, 34005, 3282-7, 1854, Gobernación, Archivo General de la Administración, Alcalá de Henares.
15 P. Hanson, 'The Vie Chere Riots of 1911: traditional protests in modern garb', *Journal of Social History*, 1988, pp. 463–82.
16 M.L. Arriero, 'Los motines de subsistencias en España, 1895-1905', *Estudios de Historia Social*, 30, 1984, p. 216.
17 C. Serrano, 'Guerra y crisis social. Los motines de mayo del 98', *Estudios sobre la historia de España* (Madrid, 1981), vol. 1, p. 444.
18 Asunto relativo a los sucesos conocidos con el nombre de SANJUANA', Archivo Municipal de Mieres; *Eco de Mieres*, June 27, 1897; *El Carbayón*, June 23, 1897; *Aurora Social*, June 27, 1897.
19 Serrano, 'Guerra y crisis social', p. 444.
20 T. Kaplan, 'Female consciousness and collective action: Barcelona, 1910–1918', *Signs*, Spring 1982, pp. 545, 561.
21 P. Ratcliffe, 'Carmen revisited: the cigarette makers of Gijón, 1890–1930', (Unpublished paper), pp. 10–18. I want to thank Ms. Ratcliffe for allowing me to cite this paper.
22 V. Turner, *From Ritual to Theatre* (New York, 1982), p. 32.
23 A. Moreno Garbayo, Catálogo de los documentos referentes a Diversiones Públicas (Madrid, 1958), p. 245.
24 Cited in G.W. McDonogh, 'Good Families: a social history of power in industrial Barcelona', PhD thesis, Johns Hopkins University, 1981, pp. 603–4.
25 Cited in C. Ariza, *Los jardines de Madrid en el Siglo XIX* (Madrid, 1988), p. 248.
26 S.T. Wallis, *Glimpses of Spain* (New York, 1842), p. 185.
27 H.B. Segal, *Turn of the Century Cabaret* (New York, 1987), pp. xiv-xv.
28 ibid., pp. 86–112.
29 D. Shaw, *Fútbol y franquismo* (Madrid, 1987), p. 22.
30 *Aurora Social*, May 25, 1926, February 11, 1927.
31 Jiménez to Rubiera, August 1, 1922, Archivo de la Hullera Española, Ujo, 12/5.
32 Archivo Municipal de la Villa, Madrid, 2–412–7.
33 Archivo Municipal, Alcalà de Henares, pp. 678–91.
34 *Adelante* (Salamanca), May 5, 1861.
35 AMV, 4–28–13.
36 P. Mérimée, *Viajes a España* (Madrid, 1988) p. 45.
37 S. Bensusan, *Home Life in Spain* (London, 1910), p. 143; A. Fernández de los Ríos, *Guía de Madrid* (Madrid, 1876), p. 597.
38 Costa to Montaves, June 19, 1909, AHE, 55/2.
39 *Revista Minera*, 1883, p. 388.

40   Montaves to Parent, March 28, 1891, AHE 2/5; *Boletín Oficial de Minería y Metalurgia*, March 1918, p. 33.
41   M. Vigil, *Los mineros asturianos* (Oviedo, 1900), p. 27.
42   E.J. Hobsbawm and T. Ranger, eds., *The Invention of Tradition* (Cambridge, 1983).
43   J. Hay, *Castilian Days* (Boston, 1903), p. 117.
44   This section is based on documents in the archive of the Congress of Deputies in Madrid.
45   L. Teste, *Viaje por España* (Valencia, 1959), p. 184.
46   Hay, *Castilian Days*, p. 120; E. Tamarit, *Memoria histórica del día 2 de mayo de 1808 en Madrid* (Madrid, 1852), p. 53.
47   G. Di Febo, *La Santa de la Raza*, (Madrid, 1988); Lannon, *Privilege*, p. 132.
48   P. Sahlins, 'The nation in the village: state building and communal struggles in the Catalan borderlands during the 18th and 19th centuries', *Journal of Modern History*, June 1988, pp. 237, 261
49   ibid., p. 252.

The Franco Regime and After

A Belated Miracle

1   S. Lieberman, *The Contemporary Spanish Economy* (London, 1982), pp. 296–7.

Men, Women and Children

1   J. Nadal, *La Población Española* (Barcelona, 1976), p. 233.
2   A. Arbel, *La Mortalidad de la Infancia en España, 1901–1950* (Madrid, 1962), pp. 192–3.
3   J. Diez Nicolás and J.M. de Miguel, *Control de la Natalidad en España* (Barcelona, 1981), pp. 31, 33–4.
4   A. de Miguel, *La Pirámide Social Española*, (Madrid, 1977), pp. 34–9.
5   Diez Nicolás, *Control*, pp. 205–28.
6   ibid., p. 241.
7   ibid., p. 271.
8   *Ms*, October 1972, p. 12.
9   Cited in C. Martín Gaite, *Usos Amorosos de la Postguerra Española*, (Barcelona, 1987), p. 91.
10   ibid., pp. 184, 204
11   ibid., p. 203.
12   M. Telo, 'La evolución de los derechos de la mujer en España', in C. Borreguero *et al.*, *La mujer española: de la Tradición a la Modernidad (1960–1980)* (Madrid, 1986), p. 89.
13   SESM, 'El movimiento feminista en España', in ibid., p. 29.
14   Collier, *Socialists*, 165–85
15   J. Caro Baroja, 'La despoblación de los campos', in *Revista de Occidente*, July 1966, p. 31; *El País*, September 17, 1984.
16   S. Brandes, *Migration, Kinship and Community* (New York, 1975), pp. 40–6.

17   S.T. Freeman, *Neighbors* (Chicago, 1970), pp. 134–49.
18   D. Gilmore, *The People of the Plain* (New York, 1980), pp. 35–7.
19   D. Greenwood, *Unrewarding Wealth* (Cambridge, 1976), pp. 50–1.
20   A. Linares Sánchez, 'Problemas urbanísticos de Madrid', in *La Concentración urbana en España* (Madrid, 1969), pp. 209–10, 224.
21   S. Balfour, *Dictatorship, Workers and the City* (Oxford, 1989), pp. 49–50

The Land

1   J. Martínez Alier, *Laborers and Landowners in Southern Spain* (Totawa, 1971), p. 320.
2   E. Sevilla Guzmán, *La Evolución del Campesinado en España* (Barcelona, 1979), pp. 141–2.
3   Cited in ibid., p. 78 In translation the phrase loses the play on the word 'exploitation': the family farm (*explotación*) has a double meaning. A family works, 'exploits' the land by 'exploiting' itself.
4   Naredo, *La Evolución de la agricultura en España* (Barcelona, 1971), p. 78.
5   P. Preston, 'The agrarian war in the south', in Preston, (ed.), *Revolution and War in Spain* (London, 1984), p. 160.
6   Collier, *Socialists of Rural Andalucia* (Stanford, 1987), p. 168.
7   Cited in C. Barciela, 'Introducción, in R. Garrabou and C. Barciela, *Historia agraria de la España contemporánea*, vol. 3, (Barcelona, 1987), p. 404.
8   Martínez Alier, *Laborers*, pp. 243, 260.
9   ibid., pp. 265–9.
10   D. Gilmore, *The People of the Plain* (New York, 1980), pp. 36–7.
11   Martínez Alier, *Laborers*, pp. 77–8.
12   Gilmore, *People*, p. 93.
13   Gilmore, *People*, p. 84.
14   Martínez Alier, *Laborers*, p. 140.
15   Gilmore, *People*, pp. 94–5.
16   M. Mauss, *The Gift* (London, 1970), p. 72.
17   J. Pitt-Rivers, *People of the Sierra* (Chicago, 1971), pp. 140–1.
18   Martínez Alier, *Laborers*, pp. 220–38.
19   ibid., pp. 174–8, 317.

Cities and Towns

1   J. Foweraker, 'The role of labour organizations in the transition to democracy in Spain' in R. Clark and M. Haltzel (eds), *Spain in the 1980s* (Cambridge, 1987), p. 107.
2   J.F. Tezanos, *Estructura de Clases y Conflictos de Poder en la España Postfranquista*, (Madrid, 1978), p. 213.

The Church, Religion and Belief

1   *Joint Letter of the Spanish Bishops to the Bishops of the Whole World* (London, 1937), pp. 15, 28–9.
2   N. Cooper, 'The Church: from Crusade to Christianity', in P. Preston, (ed.), *Spain in Crisis* (Hassocks, 1976), pp. 61–73.

3 ibid., p. 73.
4 ibid., p. 79.
5 J.A. Tello, *Ideología y Política. La Iglesia Católica Española, 1936–1959*, (Zaragoza, 1984), p. 129.
6 Cited in J.M. Martín Patino, 'La Iglesia en la sociedad española', in *España: Un Presente para el Futuro* (Madrid, 1984), vol. 1, pp. 180–1.
7 S. Payne, *Spanish Catholicism* (Madison, 1984), p. 202.
8 R. Duocastella, *Analisis Sociológico del Catolicismo Español* (Barcelona, 1967), p. 16.
9 A.L. Orensanz, *La Religiosidad Popular Española* (Madrid, 1974), pp. 9–10, 17. In the Carlist stronghold of Navarre, there was 'an official, Church sponsored war on so-called political and sexual pornography in print and on film' during the Civil War. M. Blinkhorn, *Carlism and Crisis in Spain, 1931–1939* (Cambridge, 1975), p. 275.
10 Cited in Cooper, 'The Church', in P. Preston, *Spain in Crisis* (Hassocks, 1976) p. 52.
11 J. Linz and J. Cazorla, 'Religiosidad y estructura social en Andalucía: la práctica religiosa', in *Anales de Sociología*.
12 D. Gilmore, *The People of the Plain* (New York, 1980), pp. 144–7, 153–4.
13 S.T. Freeman, *Neighbors* (Chicago, 1970), p. 97.
14 S. Brandes, *Migration, Kinship and Community* (New York, 1975), pp. 162–74; J. Moreno Navarro, *Propiedad, Clases Sociales y Hermandades en la Baja Andalucia* (Madrid, 1972), p. 161; S.T. Freeman, 'Faith and fashion in religion: notes on the observation of observance', *Peasant Studies* Spring 1978, pp. 115–16; W. Christian, *Local Religion in Sixteenth Century Spain* (Princeton, 1981), pp. 206–8.
15 F. Lannon, *Privilege, Persecution and Prophecy. The Catholic Church in Spain 1875–1975* (Oxford, 1987), pp. 230–1.
16 Payne, *Spanish*, p. 208; W. Ebenstein, *Church and State in Franco Spain* (Princeton, 1960), p. 27.
17 Cited in Fundación FOESSA, *Informe*, p. 728. This experience was identical to that of the CNCA in Andalucia after the *trienio bolchevique*.
18 Lannon, *Privilege*, p. 232.
19 Payne, *Spanish*, p. 210; Fundación FOESSA, *Informe*, p. 598.
20 Lannon, *Privilege*, p. 226.
21 Jesús Ynfante described the Opus as a 'holy mafia'. Cited in Hermet, *Les Catholiques dans l'Espagne Franquiste* (Paris, 1980), p. 245.

The Extension of the State

1 Preston, *The Triumph of Democracy in Spain* (London, 1986), pp. 32–3.
2 M. Ballbé, *Orden Público y Militarismo en la España Constitucional* (Madrid, 1983) p. 400.
3 ibid., p. 412
4 D. López Garrido, *El Aparato Policial en España* (Barcelona, 1987), p. 14.
5 E.D. Solans, 'El Comportamiento diferencial del sector público español' in *España: un Presente para el Futuro* (Madrid, 1984) vol. 2, p. 306.
6 S. Balfour, *Workers, the Dictatorship and the City* (Oxford, 1989), p. 248.
7 M. Puelles Benítez, *Educación e ideología en la España contemporánea* (Barcelona, 1980), pp. 365–6.

8   J.M. Maravall, *La Reforma de la Enseñanza* (Barcelona, 1984), p. 27.
9   J.M. de Azaola, 'El Hecho vasco' in *España: un presente*, vol. 1, p. 262.
10 J.González Anleo, 'El sistema educativo español: tensiones y futuro' in ibid., vol. I, p. 320.
11 ibid., p. 165.

The Consumer Society

1   M. Delibes, *Castilla, lo Castellano y los Castellanos* (Barcelona, 1979), p. 260.
2   R. Barrett, *Benabarre* (New York, 1974), p. 51.
3   D. Greenwood, *Unrewarding Wealth* (Cambridge, 1976), p. 28; W.A. Douglass, 'Serving girl and sheepherder: emigration and continuity in a Basque village', in J. Aceves and W.A. Douglass (eds.), *The Changing Face of Rural Spain* (New York, 1976), pp. 53–7; W. Christian, *Person and God in a Spanish Valley* (New York, 1972), pp. 40–1.
4   S.T. Freeman, *Neighbors* (Chicago, 1970), pp. 173, 133.
5   Collier, *Socialists of Rural Andalusia* (Stanford, 1987), p. 200.
6   Christian, *Person*, p. 42; E.C. Hansen, *Rural Catalonia under the Franco Regime* (Cambridge, 1977), p. 20.
7   C. Lisón Tolosana, *Belmonte de los Caballeros* (Oxford, 1966), p. 195.
8   Barrett, *Benabarre*, p. 101.
9   Lisón Tolosana, *Belmonte*, p. 194.
10 S. Brandes, *Migration, Kinship and Community* (New York, 1975), pp. 162–74, 184–94.
11 Freeman, *Neighbors*, p. 185.
12 J.W. Fernández and R.L. Fernández, 'Under one roof: household formation and cultural ideals in an Asturian mountain village', in *Journal of Family History*, vol. 13, 1988, pp. 123–42.

Conclusion

1   See, for example, R. Roehl, 'French industrialization: a reconsideration', in *Explorations in Economic History*, 1976, pp. 233–81.
2   J. Sperber, *Popular Catholicism in Nineteenth Century Germany* (Princeton, 1984).
3   J. Davis, *Conflict and Control: Law and Order in Nineteenth Century Italy*, (London, 1988), p. 5.
4   After these lines were written, an opinion poll conducted in November 1989 by *The Independent* and *El País* revealed that Spaniards were the strongest supporters of the EEC.

Bibliography

Aceves, J. and Douglass, W.A. (eds), The Changing Face of Rural Spain (New York, 1976).

Duocastello, R., Analisis Sociológico de Catolicismo Español (Barcelona, 1967).

Ardit Lucas, M., Revolución Liberal y Revuelta Campesina, 1793-1840 (Madrid, 1977).

Atienza Hernández, I., Aristocracia, Poder y Riqueza en la España Moderna: La Casa de Osuna, Siglos XV–XIX (Madrid, 1987).

Balcells, A., El Problema Agraria en Cataluña. La Cuestión Rabassaire (Madrid, 1980).

Balfour, S., Workers, the Dictatorship and the City (Oxford, 1989).

Ballbé, M, Orden Público y Militarismo en la España Constitucional (Madrid, 1983).

Barrett, R., Benabarre (New York, 1974).

Benítez Fernández, V., Carlismo y Rebeldía Campesina (Madrid, 1988).

Bernal, A.M., La Lucha por la Tierra en la Crisis del Antiguo Régimen (Madrid, 1979).

Bernecker, W., Colectividades y Revolución Social (Barcelona, 1982).

Borreguero, C., Catero, E., de la Gándera, C., and Salas, M. La Mujer Española: De la Tradición a la Modernidad, (1960–1980) (Madrid, 1986).

Brandes, S., Migration, Kinship and Community (New York, 1975).

Callahan, W.J., Church, Society and Politics in Spain, 1750–1874 (Cambridge, 1984).

Capel Martínez, R.M., El Trabajo y la Educación de la Mujer en España, 1900–1930 (Madrid, 1986).

Carr, R. and Fusi, J.P., Spain: Dictatorship to Democracy (Oxford, 1979).

Castillo, J.J., Propietarios muy Pequeños (Madrid, 1979).

Christian, W., Person and God in a Spanish Valley (New York, 1972).

Diez Nicolás, J., and de Miguel, J.M., El Control de la Natalidad en España (Barcelona, 1981).

DiFebo, G., La Santa de la Raza (Madrid, 1988).

España: Un Presente para un Futuro (Madrid, 1984).

Fernández Bastarreche, F., El Ejército Español en el Siglo XIX (Madrid, 1978).

Fontana, J. and Nadal, J., 'Spain, 1914–1970' in C. Cipolla (ed.), Fontana Economic History of Europe, vol. 6, pt 2 (London, 1976).

Freeman, S.T., Neighbors (Chicago, 1970).

Freeman, S.T., 'Faith and fashion in religion: notes on the observation of observance', Peasant Studies Spring 1978.

Fundación FOESSA, Informe Sociológico sobre el cambio social en España, 1975–1983 (Madrid, 1983).

Fusi, J.P., El País Vasco: Pluralismo y Nacionalidad (Madrid, 1984).

Fusi, J.P., Política Obrera en el País Vasco (Madrid, 1979).

Gabriel, P., 'La població obrera catalana. Una població industrial?', Estudios de Historia Social, pp. 32–3, 1985.

García Sanz, A.., and Garrabou, R. (eds), Historia Agraria de la España Contemporánea vol. 1, (Barcelona, 1985).

Gilmore, D., The People of the Plain (New York, 1980).

Greenwood, D., Unrewarding Wealth (Cambridge, 1976).

Hansen, E.C., Rural Catalonia under the Franco Regime (Cambridge, 1977).

Headrick, D., Ejército y Política en España, 1866–1898 (Madrid, 1981).

Heran, F., Tierra y Parentesco en el Campo Sevillano (Madrid, 1980).

Herr, R., 'Hacia el derrumbe del Antiguo Régimen: crisis feudal y desamortización bajo Carlos IV', in Moneda y Crédito, 1971.

Herr, R., 'El Significado de la desamortización en España', Moneda y Crédito, 131, 1974.

Higuerela, L., El Clero de Toledo, 1820–1823 (Madrid, 1979).

Hobsbawm, E.J., Primitive Rebels (London, 1959).

Izard, M., Industrialización y Obrerismo (Barcelona, 1973).

Journal of Family History, no. 13, 1988. Special issue on Spain and Portugal.

Juliá, S., Madrid, 1931–1934. De la Fiesta Popular a la Lucha de Clases (Madrid, 1984).

Kaplan, T., 'Female consciousness and collective action, Barcelona, 1910–1918', Signs, Spring 1982.

Lannon, F., Privilege, Persecution and Prophecy. The Catholic Church in Spain, 1875–1975 (Oxford, 1987).

Lieberman, S., The Contemporary Spanish Economy (London, 1982).

Lisón Tolosana, C., Belmonte de los Caballeros (Oxford, 1966).

Livi Bacci, 'Fertility and nuptiality changes in Spain from the late eighteenth century to the early twentieth century', in Population Studies, 1968.

Longares Alonso, J., Política y Religión en Barcelona, 1833–1843 (Madrid, 1976).

López Garrido, D., El Aparato Policial en España (Barcelona, 1987).

López Garrido, D., La Guardia Civil y los Orígenes del Estado Centralista (Barcelona, 1982).

McDonogh, G.W., 'Good Families: a social history of power in industrial Barcelona', PhD thesis, Johns Hopkins University, 1981.

Madrid en la Sociedad del Siglo XIX (Madrid, 1986).

Malefakis, E., Agrarian Reform and Peasant Revolution in Spain (New Haven, 1980).

Martín Gaite, C., Usos Amorosos de la Postguerra Española (Barcelona, 1987).

Martínez Alier, J., Laborers and Landowners in Southern Spain (Totawa, 1971).

Massot i Muntaner, J., Esglesia i Societat a la Mallorca del Segle XX (Barcelona, 1977).

Mintz, J. The Anarchists of Casas Viejas (Chicago, 1982).

Molas Ribalta, P., Los Gremios Barceloneses del Siglo XVIII (Madrid, 1970).

Monant Deusa, I., El Declive del Señorío (Valencia, 1984).

Monant Deusa, I., Economía y Sociedad en un Señorío del País Valenciano: El Ducado de Gandía (Gandía, 1978).

Moxó, S., La Disolución del Antiguo Régimen en España (Madrid, 1965).

La Mujer en la Historia de España (Madrid, 1986).

Pérez Moreda, V., 'La Modernización Demográfica, 1800–1930', in N. Sánchez Albornoz (ed.), *La Modernización Económica en España* (Madrid, 1985).

Pérez Moreda, V., *La Crisis de la Mortalidad en la España Interior* (Madrid, 1980).

Pérez Yruela, M., *La Conflictividad en la Provincia de Córdoba, 1931–1936* (Madrid, 1979).

Portero, J.A., *Púlpito e Ideología en la España del Siglo XIX* (Zaragoza, 1978).

Prados de la Escosura, L., *De Imperio a Nación. Crecimiento y Atraso Económico en España, 1780–1930* (Madrid, 1988).

Preston, P., 'The agrarian war in the south', in P. Preston (ed.), *Revolution and War in Spain* (London, 1984).

Revista de Occidente no. 127, 1973. Special issue on *caciquismo*.

Ringrose, D., *Madrid and the Spanish Economy, 1560–1850* (Berkeley, 1983).

Ringrose, D., *Imperio y Península* (Madrid, 1987).

Rodríguez Osuna, J., *Población y Territorio en España* (Madrid, 1985).

Rueda, G., *La Desamortización de Mendizábal en Valladolid* (Valladolid, 1980).

Rueda, G., *La Desamortización de Mendizábal y Espartero en España* (Madrid, 1986).

Ruíz Giménez, J. (ed.), *Iglesia, Estado y Sociedad en España 1930–1982* (Barcelona, 1984).

Sales, N., *Sobre Esclavos, Reclutas y Mercaderes de Quintas* (Barcelona, 1974).

Santos Isern, V., *Cara y Cruz de la Sedería Valenciana* (Valencia, 1981).

Scanlon, G., *La Polémica Feminista en la España Contemporánea, 1868–1974* (Madrid, 1976).

Sevilla Guzmán, E., *La Evolución del Campesinado en España* (Barcelona, 1979).

Shubert, A., *The Road to Revolution in Spain* (Urbana–Champaign, 1987).

Tello, J.A., *Ideología y Política. La Iglesia Católica Española, 1936–1959* (Zaragoza, 1984).

Terrades Saborit, I., *La Colonia Industrial com a Particularisme Històric: L'Ametlla de Merola* (Barcelona, 1979).

Tezanos, J.F., *Estructura de Clases y Conflictos de Poder en la España Postfranquista* (Madrid, 1978).

Torras, J., *Liberalismo y Rebeldía Campesina, 1820–1823* (Barcelona, 1976).

Ullman, J.C., *The Tragic Week* (Cambridge, 1968).

Vicens Vives, J., *An Economic History of Spain* (Princeton, 1969).

Villares, R., *La Propiedad de la Tierra en Galicia, 1500–1936* (Madrid, 1982).

Chronology

December 1807	French invasion of Spain
May 2, 1808	Popular rising against the French in Madrid
September 24, 1810	Cortes of Cádiz meets
March 19, 1812	Constitution of Cádiz proclaimed
March 24, 1814	Ferdinand VII returns to Spain
May 4, 1814	Constitution of Cádiz revoked
January 1, 1820	Riego's revolt begins the Revolution of 1820
March 7, 1820	Ferdinand VII restores the Constitution of Cádiz
April 7, 1823	French army invades Spain
October 1, 1823	Ferdinand VII revokes all legislation of the Liberal triennium
September 1827	Revolt of the Malcontents in Catalonia
October 10, 1830	Birth of Isabella II
September 29, 1833	Death of Fernando VII
October 1833	Beginning of Carlist revolt
February 19, 1836	Mendizábal's first disentailment law
June 28, 1837	Constitution of 1837 proclaimed
July 29, 1837	Mendizábal's second disentailment law
August 31, 1839	Treaty of Vergara ends Carlist War
May 9, 1841	Espartero named Regent
October 26, 1841	Suppression of Basque *fueros*
July 30, 1843	Espartero goes into exile after military revolt
March 1844	Guardia Civil created
May 24, 1845	Constitution of 1845 proclaimed
March 16, 1851	Concordat with the Church
June 28, 1854	Revolution of 1854 begins
November 8, 1854	Constituent Cortes opens
May 1, 1855	Madoz's disentailment law
September 18, 1868	Revolution of 1868 begins
September 30, 1868	Isabella II leaves Spain
June 1869	Constitution of 1869 proclaimed
February 1873	Creation of the First Republic
December 29, 1874	Alfonso XII proclaimed king
June 30, 1876	Constitution of 1876 proclaimed
1879	Foundation of Socialist Party
1882	Foundation of General Workers' Union (UGT)
April–December 1898	Spanish–American War
1906	Law of Jurisdictions

July 26, 1909	Tragic Week begins
1910	Foundation of National Labor Confederation (CNT)
August 1917	General strike
September 13, 1923	Primo de Rivera's military coup
January 28, 1930	Primo de Rivera resigns
April 14, 1931	Second Republic declared
October 4, 1934	Asturian revolution begins
February 1936	Popular Front election victory
July 18, 1936	Military rising begins the Spanish Civil War
April 1, 1939	Franco proclaims the end of the war
August 27, 1953	Concordat with the Church
July 22, 1959	Stabilization Plan
November 20, 1975	Franco dies
November 22, 1975	Juan Carlos crowned
June 1977	First democratic elections
December 1978	Constitution proclaimed
March 1979	Second democratic elections
February 23, 1981	Attempted military coup
October 1982	Socialists win elections and form government
January 1986	Spain joins the European Economic Community
June 1986	Socialists win second majority
October, 1989	Socialists win third majority

Index